To Mary,

On her

29th April 1971

Pa

STORIES OF THE BALLETS

STORIES
OF THE BALLETS

GLADYS   DAVIDSON

WERNER LAURIE
LONDON

SBN 370 00320 9
© Gladys Davidson 1958
Printed in Great Britain for
T. Werner Laurie Ltd
9 Bow Street, London, wc2
by Lowe & Brydone (Printers) Ltd, London

First Published 1949
Eighth Impression 1968

For my Niece

HELEN

in whose company I have enjoyed

many of these wonderful

Ballets.

PREFACE

THE TITLE of this book describes it exactly. It is simply a book of romantic stories, derived from some of the most famous Ballets which have been produced since the beginning of the nineteenth century to the present day. No attempt has been made to provide anything in the nature of critical analyses of the choreography of the ballets selected, or of the world-renowned performers in them ; and it is emphasised that the stories are written in accordance with the author's own impressions.

It is felt that, whereas there are already many excellent books on the market dealing with the ever-increasingly popular Art of Ballet from the critical angle, and also from the historical side, there yet seems to be a possible need for a book treating this fascinating subject solely from the story point of view.

It is hoped, therefore, that the present work may, to some extent, help to satisfy this need.

From the immense number of ballets that have been produced during the past one hundred and ten years alone—and this exquisite art dates back to the beginnings of human history—it has been extremely difficult to make an adequately representative selection for a book of the present necessarily somewhat restricted size. In addition, however, to the inclusion of those popularly known as the " Classical Ballets "—*Giselle* (Coralli) ; *Coppélia* and *Sylvia* (Mérante) ; *The Nutcracker* (Ivanov) ; *La Bayadère, The Sleeping Princess*, and *The Swan Lake* (Petipa)—as many as possible of the ballet stories of the following famous modern choreographers have been selected :—Fokine, Nijinsky, Massine, Pavlova, Genée, Balanchine, Ninette de Valois, Frederick Ashton, Robert Helpmann, Antony Tudor, Roland Petit, Kurt Jooss, Mona Inglesby, Andrée Howard, Walter Gore, Michael Kidd, Agnès de Mille, Simon Semenoff and Susan Salaman.

There are, necessarily, many omissions. It should be remembered that many very beautiful ballets do not lend themselves readily to a short-story form. Also, identical subjects have sometimes been dealt with by different choreographers.

The stories appear in the book in the alphabetical order of the various choreographers concerned ; and a full alphabetical index is given at the end, together with a Table showing the source of the " book," the composer of the music, the choreographer, the scenery and costume designers and the first production of each ballet herewith told in short-story form.

G.D.

LIST OF CONTENTS

CONTENTS

CONTENTS

AUTHOR'S ACKNOWLEDGMENTS

I wish to express my sincere thanks to the following Ballet Companies for their kind permission to include the stories of their various ballets in this book, and also for the generous assistance they have given me regarding synopses, programmes, dates of first performances, etc. :—

THE SADLER'S WELLS BALLET

Through Mr. David Webster, General Administrator, Royal Opera House, Covent Garden, London ,W.C.2.

SADLER'S WELLS OPERA-BALLET

Through Mr. George Chamberlain, General Manager, Old Vic & Sadler's Wells Theatre, Rosebery Avenue, London, E.C.1.

BALLET RAMBERT

Through Madame Marie Rambert, Directing The Ballet Rambert, The Mercury Theatre, Ladbroke Road, London, W.11.

INTERNATIONAL BALLET

Through Mr. E. G. Derrington, for the Directors of International Ballet, Irving House, Irving Street, Leicester Square, London, W.C.2.

THE BALLET THEATRE INC.

Through Mr. Peter Lawrence, Executive Manager, Ballet Theatre, 25 West 45th Street, New York 19, U.S.A.

BALLET DES CHAMPS-ELYSEES

>Through Madame Iréne Lidova, General Secretary of the Ballet des Champs-Elysées, Paris ; and Jean Robin, Administrateur of the Company.

BALLETS JOOSS

>Through Mr. Kurt Jooss, Dance Theatre, Dartington Hall, Totnes, Devon.

My thanks are likewise due to M. Leonide Massine, Mr. Robert Helpmann, Mr. Frederick Ashton, Mr. Kurt Jooss, Miss Ninette de Valois, Madame Iréne Lidova and Miss Mona Inglesby for their personal permission and interest ; also to the various other choreographers concerned, with whom I have not been able to establish direct contact. I also wish to acknowledge my gratitude to Mr. Sacheverell Sitwell for permitting me to include the story of his original *libretto* to *The Triumph of Neptune* ; to Miss Dorothy Shepherd, M.A., B.Litt., for much helpful research on my behalf ; and to Mr. Cyril Beaumont, whose many excellent books on the Ballet have been of great assistance to me.

The photographs illustrating the ballets produced by INTERNATIONAL BALLET—with the exception of the coloured frontispiece—have been personally presented to the author for reproduction in this book by that Company, whose generosity in this respect is herewith acknowledged with much appreciation.

G.D.

STORIES OF THE BALLETS

APPARITIONS

In a large and rather gloomy room of a splendid old Gothic mansion, a romantic young Poet of the Byronic period sat alone, late at night, endeavouring to write a poem which should express his idealistic conception of the beauty and meaning of Love. He knew and felt acutely what he desired to say, but he could not express his meaning in words in the particular poetic form he had chosen.

It may have been that the atmosphere of the room itself was not entirely in sympathy with one who wished to write on such a theme. Although that part of the room where the young Poet sat had been given the conventional appearance of a library or study, with bookshelves near at hand, the light from the one oil-lamp on the worker's table scarcely penetrated into the dark recesses beyond ; the long, narrow, uncurtained windows were of a somewhat ecclesiastical design, and there was a mysterious and almost sinister atmosphere about the apartment.

How could one write of Love amid such gloomy, unsympathetic surroundings ? The young Poet, how-ever, longed to set his half-formed but deeply-felt longings and ideas into perfect sonnet form—but the beauty of living words to clothe the stark framework of the poem still eluded him.

Then, as he turned his troubled gaze towards the gloomy depths beyond his own dimly-lit corner, he beheld a strange sight. The three long, church-like windows suddenly became illuminated by a pale unearthly light, revealing plainly a visionary figure enclosed within the framework of each.

One of the figures took the form of a soldier, a Hussar in full-dress uniform ; another was a monk, with cold and sternly forbidding features ; and the third was that of a beautiful young woman wearing a rich ball-dress. The latter smiled so sweetly and alluringly upon the young Poet that he instantly fell in love with her ; and she seemed, for the moment, to reveal to him the meaning of the emotions he had been unable to express in words in the poem he had for so long a time been attempting to write.

Only for a brief moment, however ; the dim visionary figures quickly vanished, and the now distracted writer still could not put his thoughts upon paper. The face of the beautiful young woman in the ball-dress seemed pictured on his heart for ever ; and he could think of nothing else.

Hopelessly flinging his work aside, he poured out and swallowed a sleeping draught ; and thus drugged into semi-consciousness, he fell into a troubled dream, in which his recent vision became a living reality.

* * * * *

The young Poet now found himself taking part in a brilliant ballroom scene, in which many happy couples were dancing. He, himself, however, was partnerless ; so was another guest — the handsome Hussar, whose soldierly form he had beheld framed in the illuminated window of his library.

Then, presently, to his joy, he saw that the same beautiful young woman whose picture he had also so recently seen window-framed, had now entered the ballroom and was dancing alone, her every movement full of grace and allurement. Drawn as by a magnet, he glided to her side ; and next moment, during a gay change of partners during a certain dance *mêlée*, she slid into his arms. He was filled with ecstasy as he floated about the room with his beloved one thus held closely to his heart.

But, to his grief, he soon realised that, though her body moved in perfect unison and rhythm with his own, her thoughts were not with him ; and, following the direction of her love-lit eyes, he saw, with a pang of jealousy, that they had met those of the handsome Hussar, who held them with an equal passion. Surely, these two were lovers, and he, the unhappy Poet, had no real share in their joy. Even as he realised the hopelessness of his own desires, another change of partners took her away from him — into the eagerly waiting arms of his rival.

And so it went on until, presently, the ball came to an end, and all the guests departed. The beautiful woman of his vision floated away still in the embrace of her soldier lover ; and the disappointed young Poet, sad at heart, was left alone with his dreams.

* * * * *

The Poet's troubled vision now took on a more sinister tone. He could hear the chiming of bells ; and he found himself standing in a lonely place, with snow on the ground, not far from a church belfry. As he listened to these rather doleful chimes it seemed to him that the Spirits of the Belfry descended to the ground, where they took on the form of ethereal maidens. They danced lightly about him, in wide bell-shaped garments, with flowing bell-like sleeves ; and soon they formed a circle with the Poet in the centre held as an unwilling captive.

Just as he was wondering how he could escape from these whirling and ever-chiming Bell-Maidens, a solemn funeral procession was seen to be approaching ; and at the sight of this mournful company the Belfry Spirits quickly departed and, next moment, the bells were once more heard chiming forth a sad funeral dirge from their proper habitation.

As the funeral procession drew near, the Poet saw, with a shudder, that it was headed by the strange Monk whom he had seen framed in his library window and whose cadaverous features now seemed even more sinister than before.

Feeling strangely drawn — again as though by a magnet — towards the draped bier being carried in the midst of the procession, the young Poet somewhat fearfully lifted the rich shroud that covered it ; and there, to his horror, he beheld the now waxen dead features of his beloved Woman in the Ball-dress, whom he had so recently held in his arms.

The sinister Monk, with cruel elation, roughly pushed him aside ; and the stricken Poet staggered to the snow-covered ground beyond, where he knelt humbly for a moment in prayer, his heart bowed down with grief.

The funeral procession moved on ; and the Poet was again left alone.

* * * * *

Yet another strange vision passed before the Poet's drug-bemused senses.

This scene took place in a brilliantly-lighted cave, and was a more horrible one for him. The same ball-room guests were present ; but now they were all dressed in scarlet and seemed to be indulging in an unholy orgy with devils and witches. The Poet, against his will, found himself compelled to join in these heathenish rites.

Then he received a terrible shock. The beautiful and beloved lady of his first vision, the Woman in the

Ball-dress, entered the cave and began to join in the unholy revels being held ; and when she presently turned her face to look upon him, she revealed to the Poet's horrified gaze the most hideous and even bestial features he had ever beheld. As he retreated from her side in terrified disgust and tried to escape, she gave chase to him, until he fell to the ground exhausted. Then, suddenly, her distorted features once more resumed their former exquisite beauty.

* * * * *

When the Poet finally awakened from his drugged slumber and remembered his strange and disturbing dreams, it seemed to him that he was being haunted by a picture of his own past and future life.

Feeling in his present bemused state that he might, possibly, overcome his lower self if only he could have the aid of the lady of his vision, the beautiful Woman in the Ball-dress, he ran to the window where he had first beheld her and looked forth. But she was not there ; and believing now that she could be merely a figment of his own distorted imagination and that she would thus never come to his aid, he was filled with utter despair and, drawing forth a dagger, stabbed himself.

And now came another strange procession. From one of the shadowy corners of the room, there softly glided the dream-like figure of the beautiful Woman in the Ball-dress, followed by her attendants and friends— the latter now all draped in long mourning garments. This sombrely-clad company gently lifted up the dead body of the Poet and held it high above their heads ; and, as they slowly bore away his limp corpse, the Woman in the Ball-dress, more beautiful than ever, glided beside them in deep distress and sympathy, with her hands held before her face as though to shut out the sad spectacle.

LE BAISER DE LA FEE
(*The Fairy's Kiss*)

In the midst of a terrific tempest, a lovely young woman, carrying a baby boy in her arms, struggled along a lonely country-side, vainly trying to reach the happy village where she had been born. Who she was, or why she found herself in such distress, without shelter, abandoned and burdened, none can say. Wearied and weakened by journeying through the storm, pursued by evil spirits who taunted her and impeded her movements, and overwhelmed by the ever-increasing raging elements, she staggered along until she could struggle no longer.

Then, with no strength left, the unfortunate traveller sank to the ground, utterly exhausted, sighed softly once or twice, and died there where she had fallen.

The spirits that had mocked her now departed in triumph. The young baby in the dead woman's arms, however, was no weakling; and he cried aloud lustily, eager to live. What was more, his cries were heard by a passing fairy; and, feeling pity for the lonely orphan, this lovely being — who hailed from the Eternal Dwellings — bestowed upon him a mysterious kiss which should seal him to her will for evermore and bring him happiness.

The fairy then vanished; and when the storm had abated somewhat, a group of villagers came by that way and discovered the dead mother and the still living baby. Full of sympathy, some reverently carried away the body of the dead woman, while the remainder followed with the now quite lively infant; and on reaching the village, they placed the latter in the care of an honest, kindly couple, who gladly received him into their humble home and brought him up as their own child.

* * * * *

Years passed by and the foundling boy grew up into a handsome young man, the pride of his foster-parents and the most popular youth in the village. He had such a happy disposition that everybody loved him ; and, unlike his village companions, he seemed to be gifted with every human grace, almost as though he belonged to another world. But he was so charming and pleasant to everyone that no jealousy or envy was felt against him. Nor did his friends ever guess that his unusual charms and graces were due to the fact that a lovely fairy had kissed him in his infancy.

In the course of time, this always happy young man became betrothed to the prettiest girl in the village ; and on the evening before their marriage was to be celebrated, a festival of singing and dancing was held on the village green.

The bridegroom-elect danced with his pretty *fiancée* and their mutual friends many times ; and the greatest rejoicings took place. Later on, as dusk began to fall, the village youths and maidens all danced away to their own homes ; but their favoured companion decided to remain on the green alone for a short while longer.

The happy youth wandered a little aside, thinking blissfully of his wedding which was to take place within the next few hours. His fair betrothed was already in the hands of her attendant maidens who were to robe her in her wedding garments ; and, presently, he himself would join her as her chosen bridegroom.

As he strolled along, thus wrapped up in his thoughts of delight, he was presently joined by the same fairy who had kissed him as a baby. This time, however, she was disguised as a gypsy ; and he had no idea of her true identity, nor that she had ever seen him before.

The pretended gypsy took him by the hand and told him his fortune, speaking to him of the beauty of Love, and declaring that perfect happiness now awaited him.

The young man, believing that she spoke of his coming marriage, became full of excitement and eagerly entreated her to take him to his bride, who would now be awaiting him. With many mysterious gestures, the fairy-gypsy led the way ; and the young man joyfully followed in her footsteps.

*   *   *   *   *

On arriving in the bridal chamber, the young man found his pretty *fiancée* surrounded by her girl friends, all busily preparing her for the marriage ceremony. Forgetful of his gypsy companion — who had immediately vanished on reaching the room — he seized the somewhat startled bride and entreated her to dance with him — which she quite willingly did, even though such a proceeding seemed to her a little strange and unconventional at that particular moment.

After a joyous dance and a passionate embrace, the bride ran tremulously out of the room to join her bridesmaids, who were about to dress her in her bridal gown and veil.

As the young man waited alone for a moment, full of impatience, the fairy entered the room, enveloped in a close bridal veil ; and imagining that this charming but mysterious figure was his beloved bride at last, the eager bridegroom clasped her lovingly in his arms, and once more declared his passion for her.

Then the fairy flung off her veil, revealing herself to him in all her elfin loveliness and grace ; but the young man drew back in dismay, as he realised his mistake. Though enthralled by her radiant beauty, he tried to escape from her allurements ; but the fairy's supernatural charm was so great that he found himself compelled to submit to her magic power.

So the exquisite fairy visitant who had laid her irresistible charm upon him in babyhood, now bore him away with her to the Eternal Dwellings in Fairyland ; and here, she once more sealed him with her mysterious kiss and so preserved for him the happiest moment of his life—for ever unaltered.

CUPID AND PSYCHE

A CERTAIN King of Ancient Greece had three lovely daughters, the youngest of whom was the fairest of them all. So lovely, indeed, was Psyche, that she was regarded by many as even more beautiful than Venus herself, the Goddess of Beauty ; and she was often carried in triumph around her native city by her admirers — who were ready, even, to worship her.

Such extravagant admiration of a mere mortal maiden angered Venus and made her jealous ; and she commanded her mischievous young son, Cupid, to visit the audacious princess who dared to rival a goddess and, by shooting one of his fatal arrows into her heart, to inspire her with love for some terrible monster and so to bring disgrace upon her.

Always ready for an adventure, the golden-winged young Cupid rendered himself invisible and flew off instantly to obey the command of his exquisite mother. When, however, he arrived in the royal palace gardens and beheld the fair mortal maid he had come to wound, he was himself so entranced by her wonderful beauty that he instantly fell hopelessly in love with her.

Caring naught for his mother's displeasure, Cupid snatched up the lovely royal maiden and wafted her away with him, far over the mountain-tops, until he reached his own domain, where he set her down in a secret Bower of Delight. He built for her a fairy-like palace, almost buried in roses and other sweet-scented flowers ; and here Psyche lived in blissful happiness for a while. In the daytime she played and danced with the Zephyrs — dainty, airy-fairy sylphs brought thither by Cupid to attend to her every need ; and, in company with them, she roamed about the flowery garden, decking herself gaily with roses and flitting hither and thither after the myriads of rainbow-tinted butterflies that danced in the glowing sunshine.

Then, when darkness fell, she was visited every night by Cupid, whose love she quickly returned — although he still remained invisible to her and with his identity unknown. He explained to her that only thus could their love-dream last ; and he warned her that she must not seek to look upon his face or to discover what sort of a being he might be, or great trouble would fall upon them both. And Psyche was so happy with her unknown, unseen lover that, for a long time, she was willing to observe the conditions laid upon her.

Then, one day, she was seized by an insistent nostalgia to behold her beloved sisters once more ; and she besought Cupid so earnestly to satisfy her longing that, at last, he agreed—though somewhat reluctantly.

Next morning, therefore, her sister princesses appeared also in the garden, having been wafted thither by the Zephyr attendants ; and Psyche was delighted to see them again, and spent a happy day with them. The two elder princesses, however, though they admired the magnificent palace that had been built for her, soon became jealous of her good fortune and ecstatic happiness ; and, seeking to poison the mind of their beautiful sister against her unknown invisible lover, they spitefully suggested that he was probably some horrible monster who did not dare to reveal hinself to her lest his ugliness should chase away her love for him. He might then, even, devour her.

Though Psyche indignantly repudiated such a hateful suggestion, the poisonous idea remained in her mind after the Zephyrs had wafted her envious sisters back

11

to their own palace home ; and when darkness once more brought the still invisible Cupid to her side, she longed more than ever to behold his face. Indeed, so strong did her desire become that, later on, when Cupid had fallen asleep, she could no longer refrain from indulging her curiosity and so quelling the horrid fear that now beset her.

Taking up a small lamp, she lighted it, and, shading it with her hand, crept softly to the side of her sleeping lover ; and, after a further moment's hesitation, she swiftly drew back the curtain behind which he slept and gazed down upon him fearfully.

Her fear, however, quickly vanished when, instead of a monster, she beheld the entrancing features of the God of Love ; and she was so filled with ecstatic joy upon beholding his radiant beauty that, in her excitement, she let fall a drop of warm oil from the lamp upon his shoulder and awakened him.

Instantly, Cupid sprang to his feet ; and realising what had happened, he sorrowfully reproached her and declared that he must now leave her for ever. Then, spreading his golden wings, he rose up into the air and vanished from sight ; and Psyche, remorseful and heart-broken, sank back upon the empty couch, weeping bitterly because her rosy dreams had thus come to an end.

* * * * *

But Psyche did not despair ; and, presently, she set forth to wander through the world in search of her lost lover. After wandering about for many months, she at length came, unawares, to the Temple of Venus. The Goddess of Beauty was still angry with her mortal rival ; and when the latter now arrived at the Temple, a weary and sorrowful wanderer, she took her in, but began to treat her very harshly as a punishment for having unwittingly caused the youthful Cupid to disobey his mother's command.

A time of severe trial had now to be endured by the unhappy Psyche ; for Venus kept the poor wanderer in close attendance upon her own whims as a slave, and laid upon her the hardest and most trying of menial tasks. These the drooping maiden could never have accomplished had she not discovered, to her amazement and joy, her lost lover, Cupid. For here, in her Temple, Venus had kept her erring son a captive ; and since he had already forgotten his own brief anger against the lovely Psyche, and because he still tenderly loved her it was not long ere the gentle God of Love revealed himself once more to his mother's suffering victim. He would gladly have helped her against the harsh treatment of Venus, had not the latter prevented him from doing so.

At last, so severe were the persecutions of her harsh task-mistress that the wretched maiden, despairing of ever regaining her liberty, determined to put an end to her life ; and, one day, she rushed away madly from the Temple to the top of a high precipice, intending to cast herself into the depths of the raging sea below.

It happened, however, that at that moment Pan, the God of Shepherds and Flocks, was passing by ; and he was just in time to seize the frantic maiden and to prevent the terrible catastrophe.

Pan, having been told her sad story, called upon the Gods of Olympus to intervene — which they willingly did. Minerva, Ceres, Apollo and Diana, all pleaded in their turn with the angry Venus to have pity upon the beautiful maiden and her lover ; and, finally, Jupiter and Juno added their entreaties and used their mighty powers of persuasion likewise.

At last, the obdurate Goddess relented ; and when

she now realised how steadfast the love of Cupid and Psyche had been during the latter's ordeal, her heart melted and she had sympathy for their sufferings. Having conquered her own jealousy, she no longer offered opposition to her radiant son's wooing of the lovely mortal maid but became reconciled to the devoted pair's happiness.

So Cupid and Psyche were re-united ; and, at their wedding, all the gods and goddesses came to the festival. Apollo sang sweet songs to his lyre, and Pan played gaily upon his reed pipes ; and Zephyrs, Nymphs and Fauns danced to the sweet and lovely tunes made by these famous inventors of musical instruments. To complete their bliss, and as a mark of his especial favour towards them, Jupiter crowned Psyche with immortality ; and thus, these beautiful and faithful lovers were united to one another for ever.

THE FAIRY QUEEN

A CERTAIN leafy grove in the heart of the woodlands near Athens was so exquisite a sylvan scene that it had become a favourite haunt of the fairies. Here, one late summer evening, came Titania, the Fairy Queen herself — an exquisitely dainty little lady, gorgeously garbed in fairy fashion, full of grace, and every inch a Queen.

Titania was attended by a group of light-hearted, colourful fairy folk, who entertained her with their charming songs and dances while she reclined upon a green and flowery bank and played with a pretty little Indian boy. The latter was her latest treasured possession ; and he was the innocent cause of a sad quarrel between her and her royal husband, Oberon, the Fairy King.

Oberon not only envied his Queen the possession of this new human toy — whom he desired to enrol among his own personal courtiers — but was likewise jealous of the loving favour she lavished upon him. So the royal pair had parted in anger, and for several nights past had held their revels separately in different parts of the woods. This evening, however, they were fated to meet again.

While Titania played games with her little Indian boy, one of her attendant elves strayed away into another glade and enjoyed a stolen chat with Puck, one of Oberon's most impish followers. Puck — or Robin Goodfellow, as he was sometimes called — was the jolliest and most mischievous little fairy fellow in the magic wood ; he was also the fleetest of foot and could cover the ground in half no time. It was his job to keep his royal master merry and to make him smile ; and he had always succeeded in his task — until now. He told his elfin companion that Oberon at present was too angry and upset by the quarrel with his Queen even to smile. He added ·that Oberon was even then approaching ; and he skipped away to attend on him.

Titania had just crowned and garlanded with flowers her dusky-skinned pet, when Oberon and his fairy courtiers entered the glade ; and she quickly drew the boy closer to her side and stood apart with her own attendants, refusing to be gracious to her fairy lord.

Again the quarrel broke forth, both parties pouring recriminations upon each other. At first, however, Oberon made a bid for peace, declaring plaintively that all he desired was to have her little Indian boy to be trained as his own page ; but Titania replied firmly : " The fairy land·buys not the child of me ! " She added that the boy's mother had been a votaress of her order and had died in giving him birth, being merely a mortal ; and for the sake of her votaress — whom she had dearly loved — she intended to keep the child by her side, and would not part with him.

Learning from Oberon that he and his courtiers intended to remain in the woods until a certain festival had taken place — the wedding of Theseus, Duke of Athens, to Hippolyta, Queen of the Amazons — Titania declared that she and her attendants likewise intended to remain there until the revels were over, but that they would keep at a distance from him.

Once more the jealous Oberon entreated : " Give me that boy, and I will go with thee ! " But Titania teasingly cried : " Not for thy Fairy Kingdom ! Fairies, away ! "

And off she flitted, holding the flower-garlanded

boy by the hand and followed by her fairy retinue.

Oberon, though still angry and disappointed, did not despair of securing his wish or of regaining the loving favour of his Queen ; and he quickly thought out an amusing little plot whereby, by bringing ridicule upon her, he hoped to gain his ends.

Calling Puck to his side, he bade him seek out in a far-distant place a certain flower and to bring it to him " ere the leviathan can swim a league "; and the lively elf replied, as he vanished with a skip and a bound : " I'll put a girdle round about the earth in forty minutes ! "

The juice of this magic flower, squeezed upon the eyes of Titania while she slept, would cause her to fall in love with the first object she looked upon on awaking — and Oberon meant to take care that this object should be a comical one ; and in that lovelorn state he would keep her until she had given up her Indian boy to him. Then, with the juice of another magic herb, he would transfer her love once more to him, her rightful lord.

While Oberon thus arranged his little plot as he wandered away, the Birds of the Woodlands indulged in a revel of their own before retiring to rest. The God of the Birds appeared in the glade and, at his call, his feathered subjects came fluttering and dancing around him. Spreading their dainty wings out wide like ballet-skirts, they went through all the movements of a wonderful dance, while he sang a sweet song to them as an accompaniment.

As the birds and their god flew away once more, Titania and her retinue now returned to this same spot ; and while their Queen again reclined on a mossy flower-spangled bank, still fondling her Indian boy, her fairy attendants indulged in a dancing revel before her. The feathered dancers returned presently, and joined also in the fairies' graceful movements ; then, as the twilight deepened, the birds fluttered away once more, and the revels came to an end.

As silvery moonbeams began to appear among the shadows, Titania now lay back on her mossy bank and softly sank into a deep slumber ; and her fairy attendants and the little Indian boy arranged themselves about her in groups and fell asleep likewise.

Then came Night and her attendants, Mystery, Secrecy and Sleep — each with a song to sing, while their duskily-robed companions danced and glided in and out among the trees, with soft and soothing movements.

When all these denizens of the darkness had noiselessly disappeared, Oberon, now wrapped closely in his magnificent cloak, drew near to the flowery bank whereon his lovely Queen lay sleeping. In his hand he held the magic flower which Puck had found and brought to him ; and, bending over Titania, he softly pressed a few drops of its juice over her closed eyelids. Then, stepping back as silently as he had come, he floated away into the darkness of the woods beyond.

* * * * *

Scarcely had Oberon departed, than a group of Athenian clownish yokels came into the moonlit glade to rehearse there, unobserved, a play they were to perform at the forthcoming festival in honour of the wedding of Theseus and Hippolyta to take place a few days hence. The play dealt with the classic story of Pyramus and Thisbe and was being produced by one of their number, Peter Quince, a carpenter. His co-actors were Bottom, a weaver ; Snug, a joiner ; Flute, a bellows-mender ; Snout, a tinker ; and Starveling, a tailor. All these rustic, would-be actors were somewhat nervously diffident of the task before them — with the exception of Nick Bottom, the weaver, who had a considerably good opinion of himself and was eager to play any or all of the parts. He had, however, to content himself with the main character of Pyramus, allotted to him by Peter Quince because of his bucolic good looks ; but he did not fail to offer illustrative advice to all the others.

While this comic rehearsal was taking place, the mischievous Puck slipped into the midst of the rustic players ; and, being invisible, he stayed to listen and to watch their antics — soon discovering a means of using one of the yokels in the carrying out of his royal master's little plan regarding the Fairy Queen.

So busily occupied were the rustic players that they had not even noticed the group of sleeping fairies not far away ; and presently, when Bottom, as Pyramus, had to slip behind a bush to await his cue for re-entry, the nimble, invisible Puck followed him in a trice and, by means of his magic, set an ass's head upon his homespun shoulders.

Consequently, when his cue was spoken and Pyramus appeared from behind the bush, he caused a great sensation among his friends. Terrified at the sight of this strange monster — a man with an ass's head — and imagining that their fellow-actor had been suddenly bewitched, all the yokels shrieked and fled away as fast as their legs would carry them.

But Bottom, thinking the others had but played a trick upon him, sturdily remained ; and, singing a gay little song to reassure himself, he strolled towards the flowery bank whereon lay the sleeping Fairy Queen and her attendants.

As the transformed yokel gazed, with open-mouthed amazement at the wonderful sight before him, Titania awakened ; and when her eyes rested upon Bottom, decorated with his ass's head, she instantly fell in love with him — as the result of Oberon's flower charm. Calling the comical-looking fellow to her side, she poured forth sweet words of love upon him, declaring him to be beautiful, fondling his ass's ears, and stroking his long furry snout with her dainty hands ; and she commanded her fairy attendants to bow down before him and hail him as her beloved one, and to fetch him rare fruits and honey to feed upon.

The astounded Bottom did not puzzle himself for long ; finding it very pleasant to be admired and made love to by so exquisite a lady, he decided to make the most of his good fortune and to enjoy the favours lavished upon him. So the disguised rustic weaver danced and sang to his heart's content ; and although his every movement was comical and his appearance ridiculous in the extreme, Titania vowed that he was full of grace and beauty, and, deserting her Indian boy, draped garlands of flowers about the shoulders and over the ass's head of her beloved monster.

When she was tired of fondling and walking about with the transformed Bottom, Titania made him recline beside her on the flower-spangled bank, while a Masque of Love was performed for their amusement at her request. A nymph and her lover enacted a sweet romance before them ; the fairies danced a more intricate dance than before ; and even a group of brown savages in tall feathered head-dresses, rushed in to perform a marvellous war-dance.

When Bottom showed some alarm at the sight of these fearsome savages, Titania soothed him reassuringly with gentle caresses ; and when this dance was over, he was entertained by a still more elaborate performance. The Ruler of the Spirits appeared and sang sweetly ; and as she sang, two lovely Spirits of the Air flew down the glade like blue-winged swallows and floated hither and thither in a dance that was truly the poetry of motion.

This charming interlude ended with the coming of the first signs of rosy dawn ; then, on Bottom declaring himself to be drowsy, Titania drew him down beside her on her mossy couch — and there they both fell asleep, while their fairy entertainers drew aside and likewise rested.

All this time, Oberon had watched the scene from a short distance away ; and having secured the little Indian boy for himself while Titania was engaged with her foolish love-making, he now had pity for the ludicrous obsession of his beautiful Queen and longed for her love to be restored to himself alone. Therefore, he drew near to the flower-starred bank once more and squeezed the juice of the antidote herb he had secured over the eyelids of his sleeping spouse.

Titania soon awakened and opened her eyes, and, beholding Oberon standing beside her, all her former love for him was instantly restored, and a happy reconciliation took place. And when the now normal Fairy Queen looked upon the comical clown, crowned with an ass's head, she soon turned from him with loathing and all her recent infatuation for this strange monster vanished as though it had been a distorted dream.

But Oberon had good reason to be grateful to Bottom — who had certainly played this particular part well, whatever he might do with the part of Pyramus later on ; and he bade Puck to release him from his ass's head and to restore to him his own honest yokel features once more.

When this had been done, the rosy dawn deepened and brightened ; and presently, the Sun-God, Phoebus, appeared in a blaze of glory, crowned with dazzling rays of sunlight and seated upon his golden chariot-throne. At the same time, Hymen also appeared to bless the reunited royal Fairy couple ; and a gorgeous revel took place in celebration of this happy event. The Gods and Goddesses of the Seasons appeared, in turn — Spring, Summer, Autumn and Winter ; and a brilliant Masque of singing and dancing was performed by them and their graceful attendants. After this there followed yet another dazzling transformation scene — and this time a Masque in a charming Chinese setting was performed.

When this interlude had ended, the whole company of revellers arranged themselves into a colourful living picture, revealing the Sun-God, Phoebus, in their midst, sitting within his glittering golden chariot, with Hymen and the Fairy Royalties at his feet ; and all the elfin attendants and other immortals and symbolic folk grouped themselves on either side.

Thus the confused memories of a Midsummer Night's tricksy Dreams and Fantasies faded away into the awakening joys of an equally fantastic Midsummer Day.

NOCTURNE

ON a late evening in Paris, during the opening years of the twentieth century, a middle-aged, aristocratic gentleman wearing a long black cloak over his perfect evening dress clothes, stood on the heights of Montmartre, looking over a stone balustrade towards the distant lights of the great city. The balustrade he leaned upon bordered the outer courtyard of a splendid mansion, whence came the sounds of gay music and the rising and falling murmur of a revel taking place within. A passage at either end of the courtyard led into the streets of Montmartre; and imposing stone columns flanked the entrance to the mansion.

For a short time the cloaked gentleman stood with his back to the mansion, his arms slightly raised, gazing across at the Gay City beyond — a lonely Stranger, who appeared to have no companions but was content to be merely a Spectator of any scene that might be enacted under his sympathetic gaze. For, although but a looker-on, a lone member of the audience at a play — comedy or tragedy — he was one who would have sympathy for any of the players in any drama who needed it.

This was plainly manifest presently, when some of the revellers from the mansion behind him came dancing out through the open door, laughing gaily as they emerged into the shadowy courtyard. The cloaked gentleman slipped silently aside and stood apart near an alcove — an unseen Spectator looking on at a new little slice of Life, not yet knowing whether this would prove to be comedy or tragedy.

At first it appeared to be comedy. The richly-dressed dancing couples were all lively and happy-go-lucky folk, enjoying the revel that had been prepared for them. The ladies of the party were young and beautiful ; and they all wore the elegant and elaborate long flowing evening gowns of Edwardian days. Their partners were likewise young and carefree, and were garbed, as was the hidden Spectator, in exquisitely-cut evening clothes.

The leader of the little group was an extremely handsome young man, who wore an expensive-looking gardenia in his coat ; but his good-looking features were slightly marred by the first signs of early dissipation. He was, however, of a fascinating personality, and was obviously the most popular male guest present. All the girls around showed their appreciation of his good looks by casting soft admiring glances upon him as they whirled past in the dance.

Though obviously aware of this flattering attention, the young man himself had eyes and thoughts for his own partner only — the most beautiful girl in the company, whose richly extravagant dress and sparkling jewels had already plainly revealed to him the pleasant fact that she had considerable wealth and social assets in addition to her great beauty.

The Rich Girl herself seemed equally captivated by the handsome young man, and was already inclined to favour him as a suitor for her hand. Nevertheless, feeling that a little coquetry might help to bring matters to the climax she desired, she willingly enough accepted the invitations of two other young men who presently approached her and allowed them to dance her back to the ballroom ; and, as the other guests had likewise danced away, her deserted partner was left alone for a few moments.

And now it was that the Spectator in the background began to see that this little comedy might presently take on a more dramatic character.

From one of the passages leading to and from the streets of Montmartre, there came a sweet and gentle-looking Flower-Girl, carrying a basket of violets upon her slender arm. She was poorly but neatly dressed in a simple grey frock; and she had a delicate and wistful beauty that was appealing in the extreme. Approaching the young man reveller, she respectfully offered her flowers to him; and as she looked up into his handsome face, she trembled slightly — for here was the Fairy Prince of her maiden dreams, and she loved him from that first glance, as the hidden Spectator plainly saw.

The young man hastily picked out one of the sweet-scented bunches of violets from the basket, kissed it with passionate fervour, and flung it away in the wake of his temporarily lost partner. Then, presently realising that the Flower-Girl was young and very pretty, he seized her suddenly around the waist and easily made her dance with him to the strains of the gay music which could be plainly heard floating forth into the soft night air through the open door of the mansion.

The simple Flower-Girl, already in love with him, was only too happy at finding herself whirling across the courtyard in his arms; and she trembled at his every touch and movement. Her intense joy, however, lasted for a few moments only. Then a fresh group of revellers in fancy dress and wearing masks danced out from the shadows and began to chase the pair. Finally the masqueraders laughingly snatched up the Flower-Girl and ran off with her down one of the passages; and the young man was again left alone.

But not for long. The Rich Girl joined him once

more; and as the happy pair again danced together joyfully, the other dancing couples likewise returned, and the revel once more approached its height.

As one of the dance tunes ended, the Rich Girl's partner held her in his arms in a loving embrace for a short ecstatic spell; and at that same moment the Flower-Girl — having escaped from the masked revellers — re-entered the courtyard and was filled with woe at the sight. As her head drooped in distress, however, the maskers returned and snatched her away again to take part, now unwillingly, in their own gay frolics.

And as the Rich Girl still felt like teasing her handsome lover and so allowed herself again to be claimed by other partners, the young man once more found himself alone. However, he also was presently enticed away by two other flirtatious young women.

A minute or two later, the Flower-Girl, having again given the slip to her rowdy captors, came back to the courtyard to look for the handsome young man who had so enthralled her; but, finding him absent and realising the hopelessness of her poor little romance, she sank weeping to the ground.

The hidden Spectator, still watching the scene with interest, now beheld the climax of the little drama.

All the revellers returned; and when the Flower-Girl, on approaching the popular young man she now loved, was carelessly pushed aside by him, the Masqueraders were indignant at his slighting and almost rough treatment of their pretty little *protegée*. Consequently, they closed around the young man and demanded that he should now declare definitely which should be his choice — the Flower-Girl or the Rich Girl.

Without a moment's hesitation, the philandering young man announced that the Rich Girl was his final choice ; and as he took the latter in his arms and danced away with her, the unhappy Flower-Girl sank half-fainting to the ground, utterly heart-broken.

The maskers had no choice but to abide by this decision ; and, with glances of pity and sympathy at their recent playmate, they likewise danced back into the passage when the other revellers retired into the mansion.

And now the watching Man in the Cloak came forth from the shadows and, compassionately raising up the Flower-Girl, endeavoured to comfort her. For a few moments he seemed to succeed somewhat in calming the wild paroxysms of sobbing that shook the slender form of the prostrate girl ; and then his soothing efforts were dashed once more.

The Rich Girl and her lover passed in front of the doorway for a brief moment, their arms still entwined lovingly ; and, catching sight of them and realising more painfully still the fact of her lost happiness, the Flower-Girl fell back again, unconscious.

And thus our story ends. Having watched yet another of Life's sad little dramas unfold itself before his sympathetic gaze, the Spectator once more stood beside the stone balustrade with his back to the mansion and looked out towards the distant lights of the great city of Paris, marvelling at its beauty and its gaiety ; and he heaved a sigh of compassion as he remembered also its many aching hearts — to which yet another had now been added.

THE QUEST

A STORM was brewing in the dark forest where dwelt the wicked Magician, Archimago; vivid flashes of lightning flickered ever and anon revealing the density of the vegetation and the gnarled trunks and twisted serpentine branches of its ancient trees. It looked an evil place, and the gathering storm made it seem even more so. Surely this terrifying forest was the abode of Black Magic, and was haunted by one who consorted with evil spirits and would use his unholy powers to drive forth Goodness if he could?

This was indeed the case. Down one of the lonely forest glades came the fearsome Magician, Archimago, in person, his form illumined by the lightning. Not that he looked fearsome just then; for he had taken on the form and garments of a harmless old man, whose long flowing black robes and sober bearing suggested that he might be some learned scholar, or humble hermit.

But, as he moved slowly along, he was hatching a plot in his evil heart. He knew that in the adjoining glade nearby, there walked wearily the noble Christian Knight, St. George, who had made himself the protector of the fair and pure maiden, Una, whom he had discovered, lost and alone, in the forest, and who now walked beside him, even more wearily still.

Although this gentle pair walking hand in hand, symbolised Goodness and Purity, the wicked Magician planned not only to separate them, but also to induce them to forswear their Faith and Virtue. Hearing his intended victims approaching nearer, he called to his aid two evil spirits, a male and a female, bidding them await his commands in the background, together with two other gruesome bat-like creatures, who had hovered about him from time to time as he came along the glade.

He was, therefore, alone for the moment as St. George and the beautiful Lady Una came into sight.

St. George was a truly splendid youth of regal bearing; and he wore pure white garments over his armour. The brilliant scarlet symbol of a Red Cross Knight was blazoned upon his surcoat ; and a helmet was upon his head, while a flashing sword was belted around his middle. His fair companion was clad entirely in white.

Assuming a most sympathetic and benevolent air, the wily old Magician approached the weary pair and invited them to rest for a while in his humble hermitage nearby. The travellers gladly accepted this timely invitation, and thankfully entered the so-called hermitage.

After drinking some wine offered to them by this seemingly kind old man, they both sank back into a deep slumber — for the wine had been heavily drugged.

And now the wicked Archimago was free to carry out his vile plot. By means of his sorceries, he first of all caused the subservient female spirit to take on the form of Fair Una and to visit St. George in his drugged dream, enticing him therein to dance with her and to hold her in a loving embrace. Then, in a second vision, he showed him this evil spirit, still in the form of Una, lying in the arms of the male spirit — who had now assumed the human shape of a stranger gallant.

So vivid was this dream, that St. George believed it to be an actual occurrence ; and, full of disappointment and grief that the lovely Una was thus faithless, he departed from the hermitage forthwith, and sadly continued his journey alone. When the real Una, therefore, presently awakened, she found that her protector Knight had vanished ; and, full of grief, she set forth in haste to seek him.

The old Magician, delighted at the success of his first plan, now continued his sorceries. With the aid of his evil spirits and bat attendants, he himself took on the form and appearance of St. George and, thus equipped, gleefully set forth to carry on a series of deeds of deception.

* * * * *

In another part of the forest stood the rich and splendid Palace of Pride ; and, a short distance away, a wild and rocky space had to be passed in order to reach it.

Here a couple of Saracen Knights, by name Sansloy, or Lawless, and Faithless, stood waiting to attack any Christian Knights who might happen to pass by. Instead of their hoped-for enemies, however, a lovely Witch-Maiden, in whom dwelt the Spirit of Falsehood and whose name was Duessa, came by, accompanied by another Saracen Knight known as Sansjoy, or Joyless.

Two of the heathen Knights, Lawless and Joyless, now went on their way, leaving Faithless to champion Duessa should an enemy appear on the scene. Scarcely had they departed, than St. George, the noble Christian Knight, was seen approaching, somewhat slowly and listlessly — for he was still sad at heart because of the supposed defection of the fair maiden, Una.

However, St. George quickly regained his alertness at the sight of the heathen Saracen Knight ; for it was an important part of his constant Quest for Holiness and Goodness to attack and conquer the enemies of Christendom. Consequently, he dashed forward and challenged the heathen Knight to mortal combat. The duel was short but sharp ; and, in a few moments, St. George had laid his enemy dead at his feet.

Then the crafty Duessa, eager to secure a new Champion and to use him for her own dubious ends, declared to St. George that the Saracen Knight had captured her by force ; and, handing him the shield of Faithless, she now begged her former lover's slayer to become her protector. Deceived by her wily witcheries and believing her indeed to be another of the hapless maidens in distress it was his knightly duty to aid, St. George agreed to become her Champion. As they then went on their way towards the Palace of Pride—where Duessa suggested they might rest for a while—the Witch Maiden continued her pretence of helpless innocence, hoping, thereby, to secure the splendid Knight more firmly within her toils.

As the ill-assorted pair vanished from sight, Fair Una, again weary after her frantic search for her lost protector, arrived, sad and hopeless, at this same spot ; here, sinking exhausted to the ground, she fell asleep. She was quickly followed by Archimago and his attendant bats — the wicked Magician now in the form of St. George, which, by means of his magic, he had temporarily assumed on departing from his forest abode.

The bat-like creatures hovered about the sleeping form of Una for a moment or two, and then vanished at the command of their master, whom they left guarding his desired prey. When the fair maiden awoke, therefore, and beheld, as she imagined, her beloved protector Knight once more standing beside her, she was filled with great joy. Acting his part perfectly, the wicked Magician now invited his willing companion to attend him to a pleasant place of shelter — in reality, however, he led her to the infamous Palace of Pride.

* * * * *

Meanwhile, a gorgeous but wild orgy of licentious revelry was taking place in the Palace of Queen Pride. The scene was a brilliant one, since the Queen's vicious courtiers and ladies-in-waiting were all garbed richly and sparkled with priceless jewels ; and unrestrained feasting and dancing was being indulged in.

All the Vices were welcome at the Court of Queen Pride ; and the Seven Deadly sins came as honoured guests. The latter, when they danced, expressed their own particular characters in every horrible movement ; and hilarious applause greeted the appearance of each —Sloth, Gluttony, Wrath, Lechery, Avarice, Envy. The last of the Deadly Sins was Pride herself ; and when the haughty Queen, gorgeously robed and crowned with gems, entered the Hall of Revelry — handsome, disdainful, vain, and puffed-up with her own importance — she was pleased with the burst of cheering that greeted her.

Queen Pride's own dance was a slow and stately one ; and she held in her hand a glittering mirror, in which she gazed admiringly at herself with almost every step she took.

As the dance of Pride came to an end, a sudden disturbance was heard ; and a group of newcomers entered the Hall of Revelry. These were the Witch Maiden, Duessa, and her new Champion, St. George. The latter was still sufficiently in the toils of the Sorceress to remain at her side, and even to dance with her, despite his repugnance at finding himself in such licentious company.

The Saracen Knight, Joyless, had followed Duessa and her Champion into the Hall ; and beholding the shield of his fellow Knight, Faithless, in the possession of St. George and realising that the latter must have slain the former, he challenged him to mortal combat.

St. George was again the conqueror ; but having observed, before striking the last fatal blow, that Duessa was furtively inciting her former lover to slay her new Champion, he now realised that she was false and treacherous. As she fell in despair upon the dead body of Faithless, he spurned her and turned from her with scorn.

Then the Queen, Pride, desiring the handsome conquering Knight as her own lover, again offered him the shield of Faithless together with that of Joyless, and invited him to become her champion, since he no longer cared to act as protector to Duessa. But St. George spurned her likewise ; and, holding up his sword aloft, he forced her and her vile companions into the background, where they remained helpless and cowed under the holy symbol of the Cross.

St. George, after first engaging in a short Vigil of Prayer, now made his way from the Palace of Pride, and soon came once more to the rocky pass where he had met the treacherous Witch Maiden, Duessa.

Just before the noble, victorious Knight appeared again at that fateful spot, his false impersonator, the wicked Magician, Archimago, arrived there, still pretending to act as the Champion of the maid Una, who accompanied him. It happened that the Saracen Knight, Lawless, was likewise at that same spot, whither he had come to perform certain rites in honour of his dead brother Knights. Seeing, as he supposed, the all-conquering St. George himself approaching in company with the beautiful maiden, Una, he rushed forward in wrath and furiously challenged him. So quick was his onslaught that the disguised Magician was slain before he had time to make use of his magic arts in order to save himself.

Una was filled with woe on thus seeing her Champion slain before her eyes — still believing him to be her noble Christian Knight ; but she was quickly unde-ceived and relieved when Lawless lifted the visor of his vanquished foe and revealed the crafty features and hoary locks of the wicked Magician.

As Lawless likewise gazed in amazement at his fallen antagonist, the bat attendants of the sorcerer came flitting up to mourn their dead master ; and Una drew back in horror. Then Lawless, noting her beauty and realising her helplessness, seized her in his arms, intending to carry her off as his captive. At that moment, however, the true St. George arrived upon the scene, who, instantly challenging Lawless, quickly vanquished him.

Overjoyed at thus meeting once more, the lovers remained for a short time wrapped in perfect happiness and contentment ; and then, hand-in-hand, they wandered forth together again.

* * * * *

Guided by the sound of chiming bells, Una and St. George came at last to a shining river, upon the banks of which rose the spire-crowned House of Holiness. Here they were received joyfully by Faith, Hope and Charity, all clad in radiant robes and attended by other holy women. After resting and refreshing themselves, the wayfarers were next clad in new garments — Una in long, shimmering, softly-flowing robes, and St. George again in the garb of a Red Cross Knight.

Then, after this happy ceremony of welcome, there came the ceremony of farewell and of arming the noble Christian Knight, who knew he must continue to work for the Master whose holy symbol he bore on his breast

—the splendid task of bringing Goodness and Light into every dark place, and of driving forth Evil from the face of the earth.

Fair Una herself bound on her true Knight's sword, and handed him his helmet and shield ; and, thus equipped, St. George bade farewell to his beloved one —whom he now left in the care of the Holy Women who had blessed them both — and resolutely set forth once more upon his never-ending Quest.

THE LADY OF SHALOTT

On a little green island in the middle of the softly-moving river that flowed past Camelot — the stately Castle of King Arthur and his noble Knights of the Round Table — stood the abode of the lovely Lady of Shalott. It was enclosed within four grey walls, surmounted by four grey towers; and all around it was a deep bed of many kinds of flowers, while beyond these, in the river, bloomed fairy-like water-lilies.

From the banks of the river on one side spread wide meadows and smiling cornfields; on the other side wound a long white road, following the line of the river likewise past Camelot.

By the margin of the willow-bordered river, barges sometimes trailed through the water, drawn by horses plodding along on the banks above; and small skiffs with silken sails often skimmed over the rippling wavelets down to Camelot.

Nobody in the barges or in the skiffs ever saw the Lady of Shalott waving her white hand to them from her narrow casements; but the reapers sometimes heard the sound of a sweet song floating across to them as they piled up their sheaves at sunset. Then they would whisper in awe-struck tones: " 'Tis the Lady of Shalott ! "

Was she a fairy lady ? Who knows ? Certain it was that she spent all her days, and many of her nights, weaving a magic web with gay colours; and now and again she would stop her weaving to gaze into a long wide mirror that stood at her side. In this mirror she could see reflected all that passed in the river and on its banks beyond; and the scenes she saw she would weave into her magic web. Sometimes she saw an abbot go by on his ambling sturdy cob ; or a curly-haired shepherd boy, a royal page in crimson and gold, a group of red-cloaked market-girls — even at times, Knights riding past, in varying numbers.

At sight of the latter, the Lady of Shalott would sigh ; for she had no true Knight of her own. Then she would put the sad thought from her mind and return to her weaving more industriously than before.

The reason for this was her fear lest she might be tempted to let her longing eyes follow the cavalcade of Knights until it turned into the gates of Camelot ; and to gaze upon Camelot had been forbidden to her. A spell to this effect had been laid upon her by a Magician ; and should she dare to raise her eyes and behold the towers of Camelot, a curse would fall upon her then and there, and she would surely die. And she did not wish to die.

So she had placed her mirror near her open window, so that it reflected to her all who passed by on the river, the road, and the meadows beyond — but never a glimpse of Camelot could it show ; and when these living pictures had moved out of her mirror's range, she followed their movements no longer.

* * * * *

Then, one day, the lovely Lady of Shalott felt restless, and was no longer contented with her restricted life. Up to the present, nothing had been reflected in her mirror that had disturbed her unduly ; but today was, somehow, different.

True, as she gazed into its bluish depths, she saw many of the same simple sights she had seen before. There again were the rustic reapers at work in the golden cornfields ; but as they looked no different from usual, she soon returned to the weaving of her magic web. Other country folk likewise passed by from time to time ; but she scarcely raised her beautiful eyes from her work to glance upon them.

And then, a new scene was revealed to her in the depths of the mirror ; and she felt strangely disturbed. A pair of young lovers, lately wed, came strolling by, their arms around each other's necks ; and presently they stood still for a few moments and embraced one another passionately.

The heart of the Lady of Shalott fluttered and beat more quickly as she gazed upon this picture of happy love ; and she sighed more deeply than ever as she returned to her work — also she began to pull her threads unevenly.

For quite a long time she refused to look up from the weaving of her magic web ; and then, when next she gazed into the depths of her mirror, her heart seemed to stand still.

Riding along the road came the most splendid Knight she had ever beheld :

"All in the blue unclouded weather,
Thick jewelled shone the saddle leather,
The helmet and the helmet feather
Burned like one burning flame together,
    As he rode down to Camelot.
His broad clear brow in sunlight glow'd ;
On burnished hooves his war-horse trode ;
From underneath his helmet flow'd
His coal-black curls as on he rode,
    As he rode down to Camelot :
From the bank and from the river,
He flashed into the crystal mirror,
'Tirra-lirra,' by the river
    Sang Sir Lancelot."

Yes, it was Sir Lancelot, the most glorious of all the Knights of the Round Table ; and at the sight of that noble figure, a burning love for him now consumed the whole being of the fair Lady of Shalott.

All recollection of her restricted life left her ; and as the dazzling Knight passed out of the mirror's range, she rushed to the open window to gaze once more upon him as he rode down to Camelot, crying aloud frantically : " I am sick of pale shadows ! "

But, alas ! Though she indeed once more thus beheld for a moment the noble Knight for whom she had so suddenly conceived a consuming love, she had also turned her eyes towards the towers of Camelot — forbidden to her gaze — and the fore-ordained curse instantly fell upon her :

> "Out flew the web and floated wide ;
> The mirror cracked from side to side :
> ' The Curse is come upon me ! ' cried
> The Lady of Shalott."

* * * * *

Down by the riverside wandered the unhappy victim of the curse, rushing hither and thither in the madness of despair, knowing that joy could never be hers and that the doom of an early death was already upon her. All too soon her movements grew slower and weaker ; and at last she sank dying on a grassy flower-strewn mound.

As she drew her last breath, some of the reapers, and the pair of newly-wedded lovers drew near to gaze upon her with awe and pity ; and presently, Sir Lancelot himself was likewise drawn thither, as though by some inner chord of sympathy.

But though the noble Knight reverently murmured a prayer that her soul might rest in peace, he never knew that it was love for him that had brought to her doom the fair Lady of Shalott.

> "He said : 'She has a lovely face,
> God in His mercy lend her grace ! ' "

LES SIRENES
(*The Sirens*)

ON a certain bright summer's day in the year 1904, at a fashionable Riviera pleasure-resort, the following most amusing interlude took place.

To begin with, all was peaceful and quiet — so peaceful and quiet, indeed, that a couple of lovely Mermaids had come out on to the rocks to comb out their long flowing hair as they sang softly to one another. Their only audience was a pair of newly-mated Seagulls who nodded, and bowed, and made love to one another as they stepped daintily about on their scarlet feet in and out among the rocks — darting hither and thither, preening their snowy plumage, and picking up any tit-bits they could spy.

Both Mermaids and Seagulls, however, were not left long in their happy solitude ; and, presently, they were all scared away by the sudden arrival of a party of very lively children, accompanied by their nannies. The latter primly seated themselves on the steps of the bathing-vans, while their young charges played about with balls and hoops, and even indulged in jolly games of leap-frog.

As signs of movement and bustle began to be observed in a nearby refreshment pavilion, the nannies, realising that this heralded the approach of important grown-up visitors, prudently decided to move on a little further ; and, gathering their exuberant flocks together, they hurried away.

Scarcely had they departed than a large party of fashionable folk invaded the scene. They were headed by the Countess Kitty, a smart Society hostess ; and all were dressed in the very latest Edwardian style of the day. The ladies wore long, voluminous flowered gowns of silk, chiffon and tulle ; their small waists were swathed in broad, tight belts ; and they all wore the enormous, flower-laden hats of the period and carried frilly parasols. The gentlemen likewise sported the latest exaggerated tailoring of that decade, mostly carried out in cream or light-coloured flannels, topped with brightly-coloured and striped "blazers" and straw "boaters"; and they were further adorned with the then fashionable facial ornaments of long heavy moustaches.

All these gay and smartly-dressed people were chattering and relating the latest bits of gossip to one another as they moved about ; and many of the ladies were also indulging in flirtatious competition for the favours of the gentlemen of the party — especially with a certain Captain Bay Vavaseur, who appeared to be one of the popular "eligibles" present. They even enjoyed a dance on the sands to the strains of the not too far distant promenade band. The Seagulls — who had quickly returned to their rock once more — looked on at this scene with astonished curiosity ; and they seemed much amused at the antics and ways of human beings.

Into the midst of this lively scene there soon came a most disturbing element. This was caused by the arrival of one of the new "horseless carriages," honking, puffing and blowing its awkward passage into the centre of the plage — an unusual and thrilling sight entirely on its own account. When, however, assisted by an ultra-smart chauffeur, there stepped down from this rare type of vehicle, a female figure, completely enveloped in a voluminous dust-coat and full motor-veil, excitement reached its height — for very few ladies had ever been seen in these modern mechanical contraptions.

Then, when this adventurous lady removed her cloak and veil with a fine flourish, dismay and strong disapproval were clearly revealed in the faces of the fashionable dames present, while signs of secret admiration and delighted anticipation showed instantly in the eyes of their cavaliers.

For this exciting newcomer was none other than the famous La Bolero, the most beautiful and exquisite dancer of the day. She was also notorious for her temperamental and flirtatious ways ; and her romantic reputation was well-known to all the ladies present. She was dressed entirely in black, but her frock was of a very daring and frivolous design ; and she wore a large bunch of blood-red roses at her breast, and carried another single rose coquettishly at the corner of her mouth, Carmen fashion.

It was soon evident that the sudden intrusion of such a disturbing, not to say distracting, element would cause many flutterings in this fashionable Edwardian dove-cote. Though Countess Kitty and her well-established lady friends tried to ignore the famous dancer, their attendant swains did not follow their example, but even deserted them for the lovely and coquettish newcomer, who was soon surrounded by them as a Queen by her Court. Her male admirers invited her to dance for them, and with them ; and then led her to a seat outside the pavilion-restaurant, and hovered about her like bees around a honey-pot. Consequently, while La Bolero flirted and laughed with all the more desirable males present, the fashionable ladies of the party had to content themselves with swains of lesser charm ; but gaiety still reigned supreme.

Then, again, there came an even more thrilling interruption, in the form of a rich and important Oriental potentate who, seeking relaxation from cares of State, had decided that this same Riviera pleasure resort would provide him with amusement and excitement. It certainly did.

This Eastern potentate was King Hihat of Agpar ; and he now arrived in a luxurious palanquin borne by slaves, and accompanied by a bevy of gorgeously garbed male and female attendants — the latter probably privileged members of his harem. All the attendants wore the most dazzling oriental garb ; but King Hihat himself, as he emerged from the palanquin, was seen to be dressed in a somewhat exaggeratedly formal European style. He wore a suit of palest grey, with a long-skirted frock-coat, in the lapel of which had been placed a bright crimson flower. With this Western garb, however, he wore a very tall crimson fez ; and this, together with his coal-black hair and beard, and his flashing black eyes, proclaimed him as an undoubted Oriental. He waved his attendants and menials aside with an imperious gesture.

The Countess Kitty, delighted at the prospect of including an Eastern potentate in her holiday party, immediately went forward and greeted the newcomer with a deep respectful curtsey ; and she then led him around her circle of amazed and excited guests — being very careful to avoid the seats near the resplendent pavilion, where La Bolero sat with her admirers, fanning herself with an enormous fan and fluttering and arranging about her shoulders a gorgeous crimson Spanish shawl.

But La Bolero was not to be ignored. At once realising the importance of the new arrival, she deserted her less dazzling admirers and moved forward with slow languorous steps, inviting eyes, and coquettish smile, from the opposite side, meeting her intended victim half-way.

King Hihat was instantly bowled over by the glamorous beauty and enticing coquetry of the lovely dancer ; and very soon he left the disgusted ladies of the Smart Set to sit and flirt with the triumphant La Bolero at the latter's table outside the Pavilion.

It was at this moment that yet a third important visitor arrived — and by a most unusual mode of transport. He alighted from a balloon in the midst of the company on the beach ; and he greeted the astonished visitors with brilliant smiles and graceful wavings of his hands. This new arrival was Adelino Canberra, of the Adelaide Opera House, a world-famous tenor of fascinating personality, who quickly had the deserted ladies of the party buzzing happily around him.

Like the Oriental visitor, the handsome tenor was dressed in the height of the exaggerated fashion of the Western world — wearing very long trousers and a tight-fitting frock-coat of the palest shade of fawn ; and he swept from his elegantly arranged hair a soft, wide and somewhat shapeless hat of the same pale tint.

No sooner did the fickle La Bolero — who seemed possessed by the very spirit of flirtatious mischief — catch sight of the fascinating newcomer, than she left her Oriental captive and rushed forward almost into the opening arms of the gladly-welcoming tenor — and it was plain to see that these two were not meeting for the first time, but had probably even been lovers in the past. As though partners of old, they almost instantly began to dance together in a most sensuous manner. After a while, however, they reluctantly drew apart once more.

Then, La Bolero began to entertain her various

44

other admirers by dancing for them a glamorous solo Spanish dance — a dance so excitingly and passionately Spanish as to out-Spanish any dance that had ever come out of Spain. Her continual coquettish glances were mainly cast in the direction of the handsome tenor ; and, seeing this, King Hihat decided to make use of a bribe in order to recapture the smiles and company of the alluring dancer.

On clapping his hands, a slave came forward, whom he dismissed with a message ; and, next moment, another attendant appeared, bearing in his hands a rich crimson velvet cushion, upon which lay a magnificent diamond necklace.

Taking this glittering ornament from the cushion, the King clasped it around the neck of La Bolero who, delighted with this priceless gift, now smiled graciously upon the donor and allowed him to lead her away into the Pavilion.

As the other guests had now departed to change into bathing attire, the deserted tenor was thus left alone — save for the company of the two sympathetic Seagulls, who now left their rock and began to flap their wings and to dance about him as though offering their comfort. The disappointed tenor, however, now began to sing, in exaggerated style and with his best operatic lover's fervour, a romantic serenade at the base of the Pavilion steps.

Presently the singer was rewarded by the reappearance of the fickle La Bolero who, taking advantage of her Oriental admirer's desire for a short siesta, had gladly enough left his side on hearing the tender love-song being sung outside, knowing only too well that it was intended for her own ears. She had now changed into one of her most charming and alluring ballet-dresses ; and in this abbreviated frilly confection of orange and yellow tulle, she presented a dazzling vision indeed.

Full of joy, the tenor and the dancer resumed their interrupted flirtation ; and then they danced together again with glamorous movements and the utmost abandon. Indeed, so enraptured were they with each other's company, and so passionate did their dancing movements become, that the diamond necklace around the neck of La Bolero became unclasped and fell on to the sandy beach unheeded by her. The glittering bauble, however, was quickly observed by the male Seagull, who promptly snatched it up and flew off with it to his perch on the rocks.

When their dance came to an end, La Bolero and the tenor each retired to a bathing-van to change into bathing garb ; for water-sports and revels were about to be held.

From all sides, the smart guests of Countess Kitty now appeared, dressed for their frolics in the sea. Their costumes were all of the prim-and-proper early Edwardian type. The ladies wore long knickerbockers fastened well below the knees and with full-skirted tunics over them. They also wore hats, stockings and shoes ; and though their costumes were in light and bright colours, they were certainly of the kind approved by Mrs. Grundy. The men were likewise well-clad in long tunic tops over knee-length trousers ; and their costumes were patterned in vivid broad stripes of scarlet and white, blue and yellow, green and pink, and so on.

For a long while this motley group of rainbow-costumed holiday folk disported themselves in the shallow waves, bobbing about hand-in-hand, only the more adventurous males attempting to dive or swim ; and presently they were joined by La Bolero — whose own costume, however, was a much daintier and slightly more abbreviated version of those of the other ladies — who gazed at her in scornful askance, in consequence.

The dancer was quickly followed and partnered once more by the tenor — who now wore a bathing-costume of black and white, more elegantly styled than those of the men already taking part in the water-sports ; and the pair were soon engaged in another decidedly flirtatious encounter.

King Hihat, having finished his siesta, now strolled out to join the bathing company — or, rather, to watch their amusing antics, since he himself was stil clad in his immaculate morning attire ; but his attention was soon diverted. Suddenly observing his new innamorata again flirting with the handsome tenor and, apparently, totally indifferent to his own claims upon her favour, he became furiously angry. Rushing up to the beautiful dancer, he seized her violently by the arm ; then, noticing that she no longer wore the glittering necklace he had given her, he asked where it was and demanded to have it returned to him.

La Bolero, though shocked and disappointed at the loss of her valuable necklace, declared that she knew nothing of its disappearance or present whereabouts ; but the King, more angry than ever at the obvious bestowal of her favours elsewhere, refused to believe her, and called up the *gens-d'armes* to arrest her.

A wild scene of confusion followed ; but the dancer, assisted by her various admirers — in particular by the gay Captain Bay Vavaseur, who laid about him lustily with his fists — and by making lavish use of her glamorous charm, managed to free herself from all who would restrain her. Then she made a dash for her horseless carriage, which had luckily just been brought up by her smart and most discerning chauffeur ; and, springing inside, she was driven away in triumph, to the tootling and honking of the horn as the strange vehicle was set in motion.

What was more, La Bolero did not depart alone, but was accompanied by her hefty champion, the Captain, who had eagerly jumped in beside her ; and both the tenor and the Oriental potentate were thus left behind, disconsolate.

Countess Kitty and her party, however, were glad to be rid of such a disturbing element in their midst ; and their bathing revels having now come to an end, they all trooped away. The tenor and King Hihat were the last to take their departure. They both felt decidedly flat and disgruntled.

But there was a charming little sequel to this amusing interlude.

When the sea-shore was finally deserted, the two lovely Mermaids reappeared on the rocks once more, to enjoy peace and quietness after the welcome departure of the noisy humans who had driven them away ; and soon they began to sing a sweet song as they combed out their long flowing locks of waving hair.

Then it was that the Seagulls flew back again to step daintily to and fro upon the sandy beach, and to nod, and bow, and dance together ; and the very first thing the proud Seagull lord did was to adorn his pretty chosen mate with the glittering diamond necklace he had so eagerly picked up for her. The lady Seagull was delighted with it !

THE WANDERER

A MAN, past middle-age, but not yet very old, took a walk one day. Though dressed in suitable clothes for walking some considerable distance, he seemed to have no special interest in the actual physical journey he was making ; nor did it appear to matter when he would reach his journey's end. Even the direction he took was obviously of no great consequence, for he paid little attention to the roads he traversed, or to the objects he passed.

This wanderer's mind was entirely occupied by the thoughts that obsessed him — for, whether of his own free will, or against it, he was reviewing and reliving the various phases of his life, so far as it had already gone. In other words, as he wandered along, he was taking, subconsciously, a journey into his own past. He would stop every now and again and press his hands over his eyes, as though to shut out all physical objects around him ; and thus he conjured up visions of his earlier life and wandered again through the many scenes that had built up the simple drama of his history.

So we will call him the Wanderer, and try to visualise some of the pictures that flashed into his mind and to wander with him backwards through the Gates of Experience.

* * * * *

The first pictures seen by the Wanderer were those of his early youth, when he had not a care in the world. He and his youthful companions were full of physical strength and beauty ; and they were free to laugh, and to dance, and to enjoy all the good things of early life that came their way. They shared in each other's freedom and joys, finding the world a very happy and wonderful place ; and they rejoiced in their own irresponsibility and light-heartedness.

But care-free youth, with its lightsome pleasures, could not continue with the coming of full man's estate ; and now thoughts of the ambitions, aspirations and responsibilities of early Manhood began to flash and dance back into the Wanderer's mind like a kaleidoscope turning a thousand facets to be caught and seen for a few seconds only. He and his friends seemed to be for ever straining to reach some desirable goal, to be chasing and seeking to lay hold upon an elusive but enthralling figure.

This elusive figure, in the Wanderer's subconscious mind, took the form of a lovely woman clad in dazzling garments, who shone and sparkled, now close, now far — the glamorous form of the Success they longed for.

Sometimes this dazzling figure of Success would allow herself to be seized by one young man, held by him for a brief spell, and then tossed to another, and yet another ; and always she held out towards them rich gifts which might be theirs if they cared to reach and get them. But, more often than not, she skilfully eluded their eager grasp ; and some of them tired of the game and sought her no more, while others could not resist continuing the chase.

Sometimes the pursuit of Success was interrupted by the counter-attractions of light and worthless pleasures. Giddy young girls would appear from time to time and drag the young men away from the goals they had set themselves to reach, luring them aside to indulge in frivolous and even degrading dissipations.

The Wanderer was one of those who were thus

tempted and fell ; and, for a while, he was filled with despair. Then, for the first time in his life, he was visited by the lovely figure of Compassion, who brought consolation to him and helped him to go forward on his way once more.

The Wanderer next looked back upon the most beautiful scene of his young Manhood. He saw himself as a happy lover ; and he relived the joy of holding his beloved one in his arms and of walking with her in a world of Enchantment. Never, before nor since, had he known such perfect and intense happiness — the unbelievable happiness of sweet and innocent Love.

After this wonderful period of magical joy, the Wanderer looked back upon some black clouds that had darkened his life at various times. He could not escape the troubles and woes of life — Disease, Suffering, Misfortunes of many kinds, Disappointments and similar other ills that beset the wayfarer ; but again Compassion came to sympathise with him and, in the end, his character gained strength from the ills that had beset him.

* * * * *

As all these kaleidoscopic pictured scenes — now melting away and anon taking shape once more — gradually ceased to whirl through his subconscious mind, the Wanderer felt himself in an exalted mood ; for he realised that out of Trial, and even Chaos, there had come to him a certain sense of more restful and deeper values to accompany him for the remainder of his life.

THE WISE VIRGINS

THIS story of an Eastern Wedding, told as a parable in the New Testament, has come down to us through the centuries with simple forcefulness ; and it still presents before our modern eyes a vivid and beautiful picture.

In this particular version the symbolism seems to be even more strongly emphasised. The Bridegroom appears as a Heavenly Being, He and His Bride being attended by Angels and Cherubs ; and their abode and wedding garments are rich and magnificent.

Imagine, then, the ante-chamber or courtyard of a wealthy personage's dwelling-house in ancient Jerusalem where an important marriage was being celebrated. High walls bounded it ; and in the centre of one of the walls forming part of the mansion itself was a flight of marble steps, at the top of which was a closed door made of solid gold. Beautifully sculptured figures of long-winged Angels and child-like Cherubs flanked the door on either side ; and other carved stone decorations of dignified design, and pedestal vases of growing flowers, were to be seen at occasional intervals.

It was late evening, and darkness had already begun to set in beyond this quiet courtyard where a soft, subdued light from a single lamp now shone forth. The pale glow from the lamp irradiated the ethereal forms of a group of dainty Cherubs dancing happily from side to side. When the Cherubs had arrived, or how they came upon the scene, no one could say ; but there they were, dancing and fluttering hither and thither as they joyously awaited the coming of the bridal party due to appear with the arrival of night in accordance with Eastern custom.

In most countries of the world, the ceremony of marriage is attended with all the rejoicings of a great Festival. Sometimes the Festival takes the form of feasting, dancing and gaieties of many kinds ; at other times it consists mainly of religious services with choral chanting, solemn temple or church ceremonies, and dignified and symbolic feastings ; and, frequently, these two forms of celebration are combined, a grand or a simple religious ceremonial first being held to consecrate and bless the bride and bridegroom in their new united lives, this being followed by merry feastings and lively entertainments to suit the characters and worldly means of their relatives and friends.

Whatever form the wedding festivities may take, however, much careful preparation is always necessary beforehand, if the great event is to be celebrated successfully. Every person connected with the festival —the bridal pair and their relatives, their attendants, those who serve them, and even the invited guests— has his or her appointed part to play and is expected to make preparation accordingly, to see that nothing essential is forgotten, and to be in readiness to behave in a manner befitting a professed friend of the principals and their families. Foolish forgetfulness on some careless person's part may affect the beauty of the whole ceremony, or, at least, mar his or her own particular part therein, and so cause trouble and distress. A vivid example of such foolish irresponsibility is revealed in the famous Bible parable-story of the Ten Virgins now being re-told.

The preparations for this particular wedding had long since been completed — or, at least, so it was believed by most of those concerned — all being now in readiness for the great event ; and quietness reigned within and without during the present short waiting period.

The dancing Cherubs held the scene alone for the moment ; but, presently, they knew that the time had come for them to end their dance of joy and they withdrew to the marble steps leading up to the golden door. Here they took up positions on either side, as though to provide a guard of honour for those about to enter therein.

At this same moment, the Bride's wedding party entered the courtyard ; and life and colour came with it.

First came five fair Virgins, young girl friends of the Bride. They were simply and somewhat plainly garbed in unobtrusive garments, as though regardless of their own attractions and desirous only of forming a quiet feminine background in support of their beloved friend, the Bride ; and each carried in her hand a lamp already burning brightly and providing a steady glow of light on all around. Their lamps were well-filled with oil, in readiness for all emergencies : so we will call them the Wise Virgins.

The Virgin attendants moved forward slowly and rhythmically, and were closely followed by the Bride, led by her father and mother. The Bride was a young innocent maiden, sweet and kind, and pure in heart ; and she was very beautiful. At first, as she entered, her beauty could not be fully realised, since she was closely veiled from head to foot ; but her slow movements were full of grace and gave promise of physical perfection.

The parents of this lovely Bride were handsomely dressed ; for they were important and wealthy Eastern folk and accustomed to oriental splendour. So they wore long heavy silken robes of rich colourings, trimmed with fur and fringes, and were adorned with fine jewels ; and a high turban added to the natural dignity of the male parent.

Following on in a somewhat less orderly manner came the remainder of the Bride's retinue — five more fair maidens who, however, showed by their over-gay attire and careless movements that they were far from being as serious-minded as their leading companions and took their present office in a much more light-hearted and care-free manner. They looked like a group of tropical, rainbow-tinted birds ; and their light diaphanous robes of many colours, coupled with their giddy and slightly voluptuous movements, gave them a more frivolous aspect than seemed entirely consistent with the obvious solemnity of the other participants. They likewise carried lighted lamps ; but they swung these about in a careless manner, as though the oil in them was already low : so we will call them the Foolish Virgins. They provided an entire contrast to their more sedate and serious companions ; and one could readily imagine them to be careless and, perhaps, even lazy, thinking only of their own pleasures.

This, then, was the Bride's procession, which had thus arrived in the early hours of darkness, to be in readiness for reception and greeting by the Bridegroom and his retinue — this also being an Eastern custom.

As the time of the Bridegroom's reception of them was not yet, an hour was spent in ceremonial dances to show the happiness of the Bride and her friends. The Bride's veil was lovingly unwound ; and the young maiden now stood revealed in all her matchless beauty, set off by her simple, but rich, robes of pure virginal white. As she danced before her parents and friends, in answer to their request, her graceful actions were equally simple and quietly modest ; but a subdued air of deep happiness and expectant joy seemed to radiate from her with every movement.

When the Bride's quiet festive dance came to an end, her leading attendants, the five Wise Virgins, likewise went through a stately ceremonial measure, their flowing draperies moving softly and gracefully with every step they took. They seemed to realise that the occasion was a solemn one, and that even their festive dancing should be conducted in a quiet and dignified manner.

Not so the five Foolish Virgins. On the contrary, when their turn came to dance, they soon betrayed their more frivolous and careless natures by quick and lively movements, exposing their limbs almost wantonly and flinging themselves about in a much wilder and more abandoned manner than was quite seemly compared with the quietly restrained attitude of the former dancers.

But even these giddy young maidens grew tired of their airy-fairy frolicsome movements at last; and then, as the Bridegroom and his friends were still not expected to appear yet awhile, it was decided that the Bride's party should rest and even sleep for a short time in the courtyard. The lovely Bride was tenderly made to lie down beside her parents, whose larger bodies and more voluminous draperies provided protection for her slender form; and the five Wise Virgins also grouped themselves about her, after they had first knelt to pray for a few moments. Nor did the latter neglect to extinguish their lamps during this short resting time so that there should still be plenty of oil left in them to burn brightly once more when the Bridegroom should appear.

But the five Foolish Virgins just flung themselves down carelessly on completion of their dance and did

not even trouble to extinguish their lamps or to make
sure that plenty of oil was left in them for re-lighting ;
and they were soon fast asleep, while their lamps, one
by one, burned for a short time longer and then flickered
and went out.

All the rest of the party likewise slept quietly and
in calm repose ; and, for a while, complete darkness
reigned, save for the glistening white wings of the
Cherubs on the steps.

While she slept, the Bride enjoyed a wonderful
dream. She dreamt that she was surrounded by a
group of Angels from Heaven, who awakened her and
led her forward to meet other Angels who had in their
midst her own beloved Bridegroom — a dazzling young
man wearing upon his head a crown of light which
sparkled and shone like the sun in splendour. The
radiant youth smiled upon her with a lover's greeting ;
and then he was led away again by his attendant
Angels, while the fair dreamer likewise felt herself
wafted back into a happy oblivion.

A few moments later the Bride and her immediate
companions were awakened by the joyful cry : " The
Bridegroom cometh ! Go ye forth to meet Him ! "

The five Wise Virgins were instantly on their feet,
lighting their well-filled lamps once more, and arranging
their scarcely-disturbed draperies ; and in a few
moments they were ready.

But the Foolish Virgins were soon in a great fluster
and turmoil. Four only of them awakened at first,
stretching their limbs and yawning lazily ; then, seeing
that their better prepared companions were already
about to move forward, they hastily took up their
lamps to light them. Then, to their dismay, they
discovered that the oil had all burned away — the
result of their own carelessness in having brought an

insufficient supply, and also in not having extinguished their lamps before settling down to rest and thus not conserving the little they had brought.

Now full of distress, they begged their more provident companions to help them out with a little oil from the latters' well-filled lamps ; but this the Wise Virgins were unable to do, lest they should not have enough for their own needs. All they could do was to advise their careless young friends to go forth and seek to buy some oil in the town. This suggestion the distracted young women decided to follow ; and after vainly trying to awaken their still sleeping companion — who was the leader of their own little group — they rushed off in mad haste to buy or to borrow some fuel for their lamps.

Presently, the chief attendant awakened at last and was not only alarmed by the disappearance of her foolish young friends, but likewise horrified because her own lamp could not be lighted. Applying in vain for assistance from the now ready and waiting Wise Virgins, and receiving similar advice from them, she likewise ran off to the town to buy oil.

Meanwhile the fair young Bride had been gently awakened by her parents, who smoothed and arranged the folds of her pure white robe ; and she and her immediate attendants, the five Wise Virgins, now stood waiting in eager suspense at the foot of the steps leading up to the Golden Door, where the Cherubs still stood, one on each step. Almost immediately after, the golden door opened wide, to the accompaniment of a burst of glorious music, and the Bridegroom's procession issued forth from within its brilliantly lighted portals.

A group of dazzling Angels came first, gliding down the steps and ranging themselves about the attendant Virgins ; and following them came the long-expected

Bridegroom, a radiant, heavenly figure clad in glittering wedding garments.

As the Bride and her parents humbly knelt before him, the Bridegroom eagerly moved towards his beloved one and, graciously raising her from her knees, clasped her lovingly in his arms ; and the Angels likewise raised up the attendant Virgins in a soaring attitude. After these few moments of perfect joy, tinged almost with awe, the Cherubs brought forth and placed upon the Bride's shoulders a floating white cloak, symbolic of their lord's acceptance of her purity. They also laid a lily in her hand, and presented the Bridegroom with a sceptre of shining gold.

The Bridegroom, having thus received his Bride with all honour and gracious dignity, the final wedding procession was formed, headed by the Angels, five of whom partnered the five Wise Virgins and led them in through the open door. The happy Bride and Bridegroom, hand in hand and escorted by Cherubs, were the last to pass in through the glittering portals — a radiantly beautiful pair, symbolic of Purity and the Perfect Love that passeth all understanding.

As the golden door closed behind them, the parents of the Bride moved sadly away, the mother weeping because this beautiful young daughter had now left the home of her youth, yet glad for her to seek the fuller life of a happy marriage ; the father likewise feeling the sense of loss, but tenderly drawing his own life-partner into the comfort of his loving arms.

*   *   *   *   *

No sooner had the courtyard become empty than the five Foolish Virgin attendants came hurrying back, feeling very pleased with themselves once more, as they now held aloft their hastily re-filled lamps. When, however, their brilliant lights revealed the unhappy fact that the bridal procession had already entered in through the golden door and that they were now too late to rejoin their companion attendants in the final celebrations, they were greatly surprised and overwhelmed with distress. They knocked impatiently upon the door, eagerly expecting to be admitted at once — for they had long looked forward to taking part in these happy rejoicings.

But, although the golden door was indeed opened in answer to their loud clamourings, they were refused admittance by the Cherubs, who now mounted guard within.

As the sad and disappointed Foolish Virgins were waved down the steps by the Cherubs, they turned to gaze once more upon the joyous scene they would have shared also, but for their own slothful and foolish conduct. They beheld the gloriously radiant Bridegroom in the act of crowning his pure and lovely Bride ; and they also saw that each of the virtuous and more duty-loving Wise Virgins had now become admitted to the heavenly companionship of an Angel.

Sorrowfully realising how great was their own loss, the Foolish Virgins now humbly bowed their heads and knelt in deep contrition before the glorious Beings into whose joy they were not yet permitted to enter.

THE GODS GO A-BEGGING

THIS story seems to have issued forth as a Living Picture straight from a canvas by Watteau, to which elegant and sophisticated period it belongs.

A Picnic Revel, or *Fête Champêtre* was being held one fine summer day in an open forest glade near the country estate of a certain French nobleman, during the brilliant reign of Louis XIV — so flatteringly spoken of by his courtiers as the Sun-God King.

Just before the high-born guests appeared upon the scene a charmingly pretty and vivacious serving-maid busily prepared the *al fresco* meal to be partaken of amidst this happily-chosen sylvan scene. She was assisted by other less important maids, and also by half-a-dozen negro lackeys — the latter dressed in the rich livery-garb of the period, with the addition of pierrot ruffles around their necks, above which their ebony grinning faces, vivid scarlet lips and woolly heads appeared in startling contrast.

The negro lackeys seemed somewhat in awe of the lovely serving-maid, though delighted to obey the behests of so fascinating a maiden — who had about her an air of dignified authority, despite her merry gestures and light dancing movements. She flitted gaily here and there, giving directions to the other maids and lackeys — who all hovered about her like worker-bees around their Queen.

Soon all was set in readiness ; and almost immediately afterwards, the noble host arrived upon the scene, followed by musicians, and attended by his guests, who were all lords and ladies of high degree. The aristocratic host and his guests were magnificently dressed in silks and satins in the highly decorative and formal fashion of the day ; and their courtly sophistication was thrown into strong relief by their Arcadian surroundings.

Not that these pleasure-loving lords and ladies were too high and mighty to enjoy themselves in such a rustic scene. They were only too glad to relax for a while from the stiffness of their usual formal lives ; and the young lords did not hesitate to flirt with the gay little maids who waited upon them. They were particularly attracted by the charming looks of the chief serving-maid, whose beauty and grace not only delighted but astonished them — they declared they had never before beheld so beautiful and graceful a maiden.

As soon as the musicians began to play, the guests sought their partners and went through a performance of the usual formal dances then in vogue — gavottes, minuets, musettes and so on ; but the serving folk indulged in much more lively movements in the background, dancing hornpipes and other quick-step frolics of a similar kind. These so intrigued some of the high-born guests that they likewise could not resist joining in this humbler type of terpsichorean fun.

The lovely chief serving-maid was quickly claimed by two of the more susceptible young lords, who were amazed to find her also capable of partnering them in their own more formal Court dances with an unusual grace. They were, however, so audacious in their flirtatious antics — being obviously completely enthralled by her beauty and fascination — that the serving-maid became somewhat alarmed by their persistent attentions.

She was greatly relieved, therefore, when presently

a simple Shepherd wandered into the glade and found himself in the midst of this *al fresco* entertainment ; for here was a youth of her own standing, with whom she would feel more akin.

The newly-arrived shepherd, however, was so extremely handsome, and was likewise possessed of such far more natural grace and dignity than any of the sophisticated nobles present, that the fine lady guests were charmed by his appearance. Despite the fact, therefore, that the newcomer instantly cast looks of unmistakable admiration upon the pretty serving-maid and seemed far more interested in her than in her betters, the richly-dressed lady guests quickly surrounded him and claimed him, one after the other, as a dancing partner, flirting and coquetting openly with him.

This annoyed the young lords considerably ; and presently, they pushed aside the simple shepherd, and again danced formally with their Court lady friends.

Then, wishing to explore the neighbouring forest paths — and, possibly, to indulge in more secret flirtations — the guests gradually strolled away in couples ; and the shepherd now found himself alone with the humble serving folk. The latter immediately began to amuse themselves in the absence of their noble master and his guests. The black-faced lackeys gave an exhibition of their own barbaric native dances, executing high acrobatic leaps and indulging in many comical antics — to the laughing delight of the under maids.

After this, they all sat back to watch the young shepherd dance an exquisitely graceful measure with the beautiful chief serving-maid. It was soon evident that these two exquisite dancers were already deeply in love ; for, as their dance proceeded, they could not refrain from revealing the fact by their loving gestures.

As the graceful dance drew to an end, these undoubted love gestures became more apparent still ; and it was at that particular moment that the noble guests returned from their forest stroll — and stood aghast and offended by the charming spectacle before them.

The ladies of the party were annoyed because the handsome young shepherd they had so condescendingly patronised a short time ago should show such undoubted preference for a mere serving-maid — of whose exquisite beauty and natural charm they were certainly jealous ; and the noble lords were likewise furious on thus realising that the pretty maiden of humble degree they had honoured with their admiration and favour obviously preferred a lowly shepherd to themselves.

An angry scene quickly followed, all the highly-born company surrounding the pair of humble lovers and ordering them to leave the glade immediately.

The haughty nobles even decided to go further still and personally to chastise the handsome shepherd who had dared to steal their prize ; but just as they were about to belabour him, a sudden transformation scene took place before their astonished eyes.

A momentary darkness descended upon the glade ; then, in the midst of the gloom, there shone forth the light and airy form of Mercury, the wing-footed Messenger of the Gods, indicating with his caduceus two other radiant beings who, as the sunlight appeared once more, were seen to be none other than two Divine Visitants from Olympus, who had thus indulged in a summer's day frolic on the earth below.

As the now awe-struck company fell to their knees in adoration and craved pardon for their rough behaviour, the two Divinities graciously granted their request. Then they moved with regal dignity towards two marble pedestals in the background, which they mounted with graceful ease and stood there as living statues, while Mercury took up a position between them.

And thus the *fête champêtre* came to an end, with all the guests, after kneeling for a few moments in humble homage, rising and performing a joyful dance of honour before the Divinities from Olympus, who had deigned to honour an earthly revel with their dazzling presence.

THE TRIUMPH OF NEPTUNE

THERE is nothing real, or sensible, or stable, or even the least bit likely about this story — far from it. It is, in fact, fantastic and extravagant in the extreme ; and it does not attempt to make sense. Why should it ? Is our present-day, muddled-up world real, or sensible, or stable ? It certainly is not. Then, let us get away from it for a brief spell.

To begin with, let us set forth jauntily upon an anything-but-real adventure, similar to those related in boys' fanciful adventure tales of Victorian times. Then let us pass through the kaleidoscopic scenes of a first-class popular pantomime of those prim-and-proper crinolined and stove-pipe-hatted days — complete with Enchanted Frozen Woods, Cloudland Revels, Davy Jones' Lockers, Ogres' Castles, Fairy Realms, Harlequinades and magical Transformation Scenes.

For these few irresponsible moments, we will forget the drab present and take a peep backwards into those thrillingly unreal, but fearful and wonderful, Penny-Plain and Twopence-Coloured days of the Victorian Toy-Theatres.

Come, then, to the Land-of-Make-Believe !

* * * * *

London Bridge, in early Victorian times, was one of the liveliest spots in the City ; and on the day when this story opens, it was even livelier than usual.

The reason for this unusual liveliness was that a Magic Telescope had been set up in the middle of the Bridge ; and a huge crowd of happy-go-lucky folk had quickly gathered around, eager to look through it.

Nobody could say how, when, or why this valuable scientific instrument had been placed in that particular position, nor to whom it belonged ; and nobody cared. There it was ; and a very wonderful Telescope it proved to be.

When one looked through its magic lenses, one could actually see straight into the hitherto unknown world of Fairyland ; and this was certainly very exciting — so exciting, indeed, that two of the telescope-peepers decided that they would go forth at once and explore the newly-revealed dazzling realms.

These two bold adventurers were W. Brown, a "scoop"-hunting Journalist, and a Sailor rejoicing in the name of Tom Tug ; and it was not long before they found patrons eager to help them in carrying out their thrilling scheme. The editors and pro-prietors of two rival newspapers in Fleet Street were only too eager to be supplied with early news from the reporter and his companion, and so were willing enough to finance them ; a special vessel was chartered ; and all the necessary arrangements were made for them to set forth without delay upon their adventurous voyage of discovery.

The Magic Telescope had revealed the astounding fact that such a place as Fairyland did, indeed, exist outside the gay covers of nursery-books ; and it was up to the self-appointed adventurers to find it and to come back with a story such as Fleet Street had never had the luck to tackle before.

Consequently, all their jolly plans were fixed up in half no time ; and as soon as the ship was ready to sail, the two adventurers said goodbye to their friends and relatives, and set forth.

All Fleet Street turned out to give Brown, the Journalist, a good send-off ; and all kinds of festivities were held in his honour. Hornpipes were danced in the streets ; and all the well-wishers were as jolly as sand-boys.

Tom Tug, the Sailor, found it hard to part with his mother and his very pretty and attractive young wife ; but, being a cheery fellow, he was not downcast for long. Nevertheless, he received rather a bad shock as, with his fellow adventurer, he was about to step into the coach that was to take them down to the seaport where their ship awaited them. A gaily-dressed, dandified young fellow came up to the sailor's pretty wife and began to pay her compliments and even to flirt outrageously with her ; and poor Tom was further upset to note that the saucy young chit seemed somewhat pleased with her new admirer. For the moment, he wished he could turn back and drive off the cheeky fellow ; but the coach was already moving, and he now had no time to think of anything but the adventure in hand. All he could do was to wave his Jack Tar hat once more, as the coach rattled away with tootling horn and to the wild cheers of the crowd.

When they reached the port, they boarded the ship at once ; and the great adventure began.

* * * * *

Up in the clouds above, the Daughters of the Air danced about in a mad frolic amidst their billowy misty regions ; and perhaps it was because of their whirling Cloudland revels that a terrible storm arose and that the adventurers' boat was unable to withstand its onslaught.

For some time the Captain and his crew struggled against the tempestuous winds and the wildly-tossing mountainous waves ; but at last they could struggle no longer and the ship broke up and became a total wreck. Do you remember the shipwreck scene in the pantomime of Sindbad the Sailor or that of Robinson Crusoe ? Well, this particular shipwreck presented exactly the same sort of a spectacle. There was thunder and lightning, and a mighty upheaval ; and the ship fell to pieces neatly, just as though stage carpenters were at work below and in the background.

Everybody on board the ship was lost — except our two adventurers, who managed to keep themselves afloat on a piece of wreckage and thus to reach a rock, to which they clung in desperation.

And now began the really fantastic part of their adventure. While they were still clinging to the rock, with the wild waves dashing up high around them, who should appear before them but Amphitrite, the lovely Goddess of the Sea, who arose from amidst the swirling waters and rescued them in a trice. The two exhausted mortals were not only amazed but delighted to be saved by the Queen of the Seas ; and Amphitrite conducted them at once to the royal palace at the bottom of the Ocean and introduced them to her lord and master, Neptune, King of the Seas. Yes ; there was Neptune, complete with crown and trident and attended by his Tritons, looking simply marvellous as he sat upon his throne, surrounded by his fish-tailed subjects.

Here, in the rainbow-tinted Realms of the Sea, the two adventurers were made very welcome ; and they certainly found it thrilling to be received so graciously by Neptune in his gorgeous palace of coral and pearl, and to be entertained by Mermaids and Sea Princesses. They soon accustomed themselves to their new element — how, they never bothered to enquire !— and Tom Tug, the Sailor would have liked to remain there for ever, since he was greatly attracted by the charms of the Sea-King's most beautiful daughter, who also was attracted by him. He soon became very popular, because — well, just because everybody always loves a sailor, you know !

But Brown, the Journalist, still had a nose as keen as ever for news ; and he would not let his companion forget his contract or the main job in hand — namely, the exploration of Fairyland. So, as soon as they had recovered from the shock of the shipwreck and had rested for a while, the two adventurers left the watery regions of Neptune and Amphitrite, and set forth upon their travels once more.

* * * * *

Meanwhile, all Fleet Street was agog for news of the two bold explorers sent forth to discover and report upon the new region of Fairyland revealed by means of the Magic Telescope ; and when the weeks went by and still no news came as to their whereabouts, the editors of the rival newspapers concerned became more and more anxious.

Then, when it became evident that Brown and his companion had been shipwrecked, there was much consternation and speculation as to their fate. Special edition after special edition was issued, and newsboy urchins dashed forth with bundles of newspapers hot from the press under their arms ; and there was great activity amongst the newsvendors.

Though nothing was heard of the bold and reckless adventurers, it was still hoped that they might have been rescued from the wreck and that they would turn up again eventually ; and with this faint hope, Fleet Street had to be content.

* * * * *

As we have seen, the Explorers had, indeed, been rescued from the shipwreck ; and they now continued upon their wonderful journey.

Their short sojourn in the rainbow-tinted under-sea realms of Neptune had been their first introduction to Fairyland ; and as they issued forth from this watery world, they found themselves in other parts of the Fairy world.

One of their loveliest experiences was when they entered an Enchanted Frozen Wood ; for here they beheld a Fairy Revel by Moonlight. They had never before imagined any scene more beautiful than this magical Frozen Wood, with its trees hung with glittering icicles and its snowy glades sparkling with frost. It was like a world of diamonds scintillating in the silvery moonlight.

Here they saw a complete ballet danced by Snow Fairies — a much more intricate ballet than any they had ever seen danced in the pantomimes at home. As for the Fairy Queen and her special attendants, they were quite unbelievably intriguing in their brilliant performances. Finally, their breath was almost taken away, when a group of Fairies floated gracefully about the glade in the regular formation of a Flying Ballet ; and the two mortal spectators gazed with awe upon this truly amazing scene.

Then, again, they were wafted away to fresh fields and pastures new ; and here, misfortune fell upon them.

* * * * *

It was about the time when the explorers were watching the marvellous Flying Ballet in the Enchanted Frozen Wood that Tom Tug, the Sailor, had an uneasy feeling that all was not going well with his home interests on earth. He knew only too well from the incident he had witnessed just as he boarded the coach for the seaport that his pretty young wife was flirtatious and frivolous ; and his anxiety about her conduct during his absence increased as his adventure proceeded. He now determined to find out exactly what was happening; and by the mere fact that he was in the magic Land of the Fairies, he was able to separate his spirit from his body and to send the former back to his home on Earth to conduct an investigation for· him. This investigation easily proved that his anxiety was well grounded.

When the Sailor's Spirit Form had reached his home village and was lurking in the background, his pretty young wife was seen to be enjoying herself very much indeed with the giddy and gay Dandy who had obviously approached her many times again; and the pair soon began to dance a lively polka together just outside the young woman's house. Thinking themselves unobserved, they danced with great abandonment, engaging in many flirtatious actions; and when, at last, they grew tired, they retired into the house to rest and to continue their love-making there. It was already dusk; and the lower room into which the lovers had entered was well-lighted behind the blind drawn across the window.

If, however, they imagined their actions were now hidden from sight, they were mistaken; for, presently, their reflections began to show vividly upon the drawn blind like a shadow-pantomime. To the dismay and indignation of the Sailor's Spirit Form, a shadow picture of his wife held in a close embrace by the Dandy was plainly revealed upon this unthought-of screen; and many times the pair were seen to be kissing and cuddling one another with obvious delight.

Furious at this sight, the Spirit of Tom Tug hurried towards the window — against which another and sinister shadow was now cast. The new shadow revealed a menacing giant hand, with a fearsome-looking knife held within its grasp, as though ready to strike.

This ominous shadow was observed by a couple of village policemen, who both rushed up to apprehend the would-be murderer. But, to their horror, instead of the hefty mortal they had expected to grasp, their clutching hands went clean through the shadowy form, since there was nothing tangible for them to seize ; and as they fell back, gasping and quaking with fright, the Spirit Form of Tom Tug vanished from sight and returned into the substantial and handsome form of the Sailor adventurer in the magic Land of the Fairies.

*   *   *   *   *

When the two explorers came away from the exquisite Enchanted Frozen Wood, they found themselves up against one of the more gruesome sides of Fairyland. In the dim distant past they had read in their vividly-pictured nursery-books about Ogres — those terrible Giants with horrible out-size heads, gnashing teeth, and glaring eyes ; and now they were about to meet them face to face.

They would like to have omitted this part of their adventure, but knew they could not do so. They had been sent out to explore Fairyland, and not only its fair side but its dark places, also ; and since Ogres were still to be found there, Brown, the conscientious reporter, realised only too well that his newspaper supporters would expect to receive his personal report upon these obnoxious spoil-sports.

So the reluctant Tom Tug was seized by his determined companion ; and the pair began this perilous and most alarming part of their adventure. First of all, they had to pass through an Evil Grotto, in which a number of these hideous Ogres were mounting guard and lying in wait for them ; and they likewise had to pass through the Castle of the King of the Ogres which lay beyond.

The bold explorers met with great opposition ; but, having taken the precaution to arm themselves with axes, they were able to hack their way through the monsters in the Evil Grotto. Then they passed on to the great Castle, where still more Ogres attacked them, led by the terrible King of the Ogres himself.

And, now, disaster fell upon the leader of the expedition. Sad to relate, he was captured and overpowered by the Ogre King, who commanded his horrible henchmen to saw the intruder in half. So that was the end of Brown, the Journalist ; and he never experienced the honour and glory of bringing home to his newspapers the really good "scoop" he had hoped to secure. It was a grim and gruesome end for the poor fellow ; and he must have been born under an unlucky star. But not so Tom Tug, the Sailor. He, of course, had the Luck of the Navy, and so managed to make his escape from this tight corner ; and then he hurried back to the Sea Kingdom of Neptune, as fast as he could go. He never wished to see an Ogre again.

* * * * *

Just about the time when poor Brown, the Journalist, was being sawn in half by the Ogres, the Magic Telescope on London Bridge came to grief.

The newspaper editors were becoming more and more depressed because of the non-return from Fairyland of their adventurous representatives ; but they were, of course, quite helpless in the matter.

The Magic Telescope on London Bridge, however, was still bringing in a large revenue to those in charge of it ; and crowds of people continued to throng the Bridge and to enjoy taking occasional peeps into Fairyland.

Then, one day, there came on to the Bridge a drunken Negro, rejoicing in the name of Snowball, who likewise insisted on peeping into the Telescope. The attendants in charge, however, tried to prevent him from approaching the valuable instrument because of his uncertain movements; and for a short time, the Negro — who was a fine-looking fellow, and splendidly dressed — amused himself and the onlookers by performing a marvellous dance, the like of which had never before been seen on London Bridge.

When his dance came to an end, however, the ebony-skinned Snowball again began to lurch and stagger towards the famous instrument, demanding to be allowed to peep within its depths; and in the struggle that ensued, the Magic Telescope was knocked over and smashed.

Thus, because of the foolish actions of a drunken Negro, all contact with Fairyland was broken off; and nobody was ever again able to catch a glimpse of that wonderful place.

All the people on London Bridge were wild about this mishap; and the newspaper folk were the wildest of all.

* * * * *

And what about our friend, Tom Tug, the Sailor? As soon as he reached the watery abode of Neptune and Amphitrite after his horrible adventure with the Ogres, he felt happy once more.

What was more, all the Sea Folk were very pleased to see him again — especially Neptune himself, who desired him as a son-in-law, knowing that his fairest daughter had fallen in love with this handsome and jolly mortal. Therefore, he now offered the Sailor immortality as a Fairy Prince if he would remain and marry the lovely Princess.

And Tom Tug was so thoroughly disgruntled by the unfaithfulness of his giddy young wife, that he never wished to see the latter again ; and, consequently, he gladly accepted thc Sea-King's offer — to the great joy and triumph of Neptune, who had taken a real fancy to the jolly young man and would have been considerably annoyed had the latter decided to return to his home-land.

So Tom Tug, the Sailor, was instantly transformed into a charming Fairy Prince, complete with the traditional brief but sparkling nether garments, flowing cloak and gracefully plumed hat ; and he then received the beautiful Sea Princess as his bride.

In celebration of the happy young pair's nuptials, a grand Festival took place. There were Transformation Scenes, and Harlequinades, and all kinds of unexpected and wonderful spectacles. Indeed, so truly gorgeous were these Revels that they can be described only as another Triumph of Neptune !

GISELLE

In the quaint little villages snuggling amidst the romantic forest and mountain regions of the Rhineland, many strange, mystic legends of fairies and ghostly visitants were once firmly believed in by the simple peasants who dwelt therein. Even at the beginning of the nineteenth century, these country folk carefully kept away from any lonely spots said to be haunted by such uncanny beings — especially so after darkness had fallen.

One of the most curious of these strange legends concerned that of the Wilis who were said to reveal themselves in many a forest glade from midnight until four o'clock in the morning. The Wilis were believed to be the ghostly sylph-like spirits of young maidens who had been deserted or deceived by their lovers and had died of grief before their wedding bells had chimed — and, in particular, of girls who had had a great love of dancing in their former lives. The Wilis spent most of their hours as sylphs in dancing together in a maze of wonderful formations, their ethereal figures in filmy draperies weaving endless patterns as they floated over the flower-starred emerald grass.

But, lovely though they were to look at, the Wilis kept up a dangerous grudge against all the male mortals they came in contact with. If any young man happened to be out alone in the forest late at night and was unlucky enough to fall in with a group of Wilis dancing as sylphs in the moonlight, he was never seen alive again. The dancing phantoms would quickly surround him and compel him to join in their giddy whirling movements until he became too exhausted to recover and, at last, fell to the ground, dead.

Consequently, at the time when this story opens, in the early part of the nineteenth century, it was no wonder that most of the young men in one of these pretty little Rhineland villages were still unwilling to find themselves out after midnight in forest glades said to be haunted by the Wilis. Even the girls were often warned by their parents to be careful to avoid such danger spots — especially if they happened to be unusually fond of dancing. It was believed in this village that girls with a passion for dancing were more likely to become Wilis, should they die young and brokenhearted, than those who did not care whether they danced or not.

One of the girls most frequently warned about this was a fair young maiden named Giselle, who, besides being the best dancer, was also the prettiest girl in the village.

So beautiful, indeed, was this young peasant maiden, Giselle, that she already had two sweethearts. One of these was Hilarion, a forest-ranger or game-keeper, who had loved her deeply for a long time and was hoping to become betrothed to her in due course. Of late, however, he had felt that Giselle was no longer interested in him, as was formerly the case, and that he had a rival.

This was the truth. The beautiful Giselle had recently attracted the attention and admiration of Albrecht, the handsome young Duke of Silesia, whose Castle overlooked the village; and he soon fell desperately in love with her. But there were difficulties in the way of his romance. In the first place, he was already betrothed to the proud Princess Bathilde of Courland, whom he was expected to marry at some not too distant date. Secondly, he was aware that his high social position would not permit of his marriage with a peasant maid. Nevertheless, he had conceived so deep a passion for the beautiful Giselle that he was determined to see her as frequently as possible ; and he hoped thus to win her love.

Suspecting that the simple village beauty might be unwilling to meet him as the powerful Duke of that district, and also wishing to keep his sweet romance a secret for the time being, he devised a plan of action with the help of his favourite attendant, a young squire named Wilfred. He made use of an empty cottage which stood opposite the rustic home of Giselle and her mother, Berthe. Here he would arrive secretly and discard his fine clothes as a young lord ; and then he would issue forth from the cottage dressed in the simple garb of a peasant. Thus disguised, he made the acquaintance of Giselle, to whom he introduced himself as Loys, a rustic youth.

So charming was the newcomer that Giselle all too quickly fell in love with him ; and she believed the handsome Loys to be indeed a peasant such as Hilarion and her other village friends.

The lovers met many times, and their ecstatic happiness increased with every meeting. Giselle danced now more than ever before, and was overjoyed on discovering that her beloved Loys was likewise a splendid dancer. He was infinitely more graceful than any of the village youths who had formerly been her partners.

But Hilarion, the game-keeper, was far from happy. He became furiously jealous whenever he saw Giselle in the company of the stranger, Loys. He also nursed dark suspicions of the latter, not knowing whence he came nor why he had appeared so unexpectedly in the village. Full of mistrust, he determined to keep a close watch upon this hated newcomer who had so quickly stolen away from him the heart of the village belle. He believed him to be a masquerader.

Another person likewise uneasy in his mind was the squire attendant, Wilfred, who felt that the young Duke's secret romance could not long remain hidden and that it might end disastrously.

One morning, therefore, the anxious Wilfred endeavoured to persuade Albrecht to abandon his dangerous deception ; but the latter refused to listen to his wise counsel and angrily ordered him to return to the Castle and attend to certain urgent matters there. And Wilfred perforce had to obey ; but he departed with a heavy heart, full of foreboding.

Then Albrecht waited for Giselle to come forth from her cottage home ; and when the fair maiden presently appeared, the happy lovers talked and danced together, full of ecstasy.

Meanwhile, Hilarion, who had been lurking in the background and watching them, could restrain himself no longer ; and, full of jealous envy at the sight of the happy lovers, he now rushed forth and boldly denounced the stranger Loys as an unknown adventurer not to be trusted. Then he entreated his former sweetheart to have nothing to do with the newcomer, but to accept his own deep and long-standing love instead.

But Giselle had already given her heart to the handsome stranger and had eyes for no one else ; and when Hilarion presently began roughly to upbraid her in his own jealous disappointment, the pretended Loys attacked him instantly and soon drove him back to the forest paths. The disguised Duke then returned to his beloved one, and the lovers were joyful together once more.

Presently, the happy pair were joined by a lively group of village lads and maidens carrying baskets of grapes — for it was the vintage season ; and the whole party, quickly realising how matters stood between the newcomer and their own lovely Queen of the Village, rejoiced with them, dancing and singing in the most hilarious manner.

Presently, Berthe, the somewhat severe mother of Giselle, disturbed by the noise, came forth from her cottage to see what was afoot and to chide the young people for their over-exuberance. Like Hilarion, she did not approve of the handsome stranger who had so recently and unaccountably appeared in their midst ; and she now commanded Giselle to return to her home and to her neglected work. She scolded her roundly for thus wasting her time — even declaring warningly that the young girl might presently be transformed into a Wili, if she continued to dance so frequently and extravagantly.

The merry party thus broke up and departed ; and Albrecht, satisfied that his disguise as Loys the peasant was still a safe one, wandered off into the woodlands, hoping to see his beloved Giselle again later on.

Very soon afterwards, the sound of hunting-horns was heard ; and presently a formal hunting-party arrived upon the scene, headed by the Prince of Courland and his daughter, the Princess Bathilde. Among the party was the Duke's squire, Wilfred, who appeared anxious and troubled because his young master had not returned to the Castle in time to receive these important visitors and to join in their sport.

To conceal his anxiety somewhat, Wilfred arranged for some light refreshment to be brought out from Berthe's cottage for the enjoyment of the Princess and her royal father. This was set out upon a rustic table ; and the high-born visitors condescendingly sat down to refresh themselves.

When Giselle presently appeared, curtseying shyly, the great lady talked to her with pleasant interest — totally unaware that the somewhat awed maiden was her rival in the affections of the young Duke, her betrothed ; and presently, she graciously slipped her own jewelled necklace around the neck of the pretty peasant girl, to the latter's great delight.

The aristocratic guests now accepted Berthe's respectful invitation to rest a short time in her humble abode ; and when they had retired into the cottage and the huntsman had strolled off into the forest, Giselle returned alone to look for her beloved Loys. She soon saw him approaching eagerly towards her ; and the reunited lovers once more danced with the youthful peasants, who had likewise returned.

But tragedy was already in their midst. The jealous and suspicious Hilarion had, meanwhile, found an opportunity for making his way, unobserved, into the stranger youth's cottage ; and he now rushed forth therefrom in a furious rage, and stopped the dancing. He then flung down before Giselle and her lover the latter's rich garments as a Duke, together with his bejewelled sword, declaring that he had found these suspicious objects in the cottage of the stranger, proving that the latter was no peasant but a nobleman of high degree. Next, he blew a loud blast upon a hunting-horn, which quickly brought back the strolling huntsmen, and likewise caused the Prince of Courland and his daughter to come forth from the cottage in haste.

Thus the young Duke's masquerade came to end, since he was instantly recognised by the amazed Bathilde and all the royal party as her betrothed, despite the peasant garb he was wearing; and an angry scene followed.

But soon anger changed to dismay. The beautiful Giselle was so overcome by grief and shame as she realised her deception by the young Duke and now learned also that the Princess Bathilde was, in truth, his betrothed future wife, that she snatched the jewelled chain from her neck and flung it away as she sank to the ground in a paroxysm of sobs.

Then, before the now remorseful Albrecht could reach her side, she sprang up once more and began to fling herself about and to dash hither and thither in a dance of such utter madness that the alarmed company quickly realised that the terrible shock she had received had disturbed the balance of her mind and that she had, indeed, lost her reason. As though living in the recent past, she enacted some of the scenes of her tragic deception — to the frantic grief of Albrecht, who vainly implored her forgiveness and endeavoured to calm her. But the distraught girl broke away from his restraining arms almost in horror; and snatching up his sword she plunged the point of it into her breast.

Then, with her last remaining strength, she continued her wild dance. Nobody could stop her uncontrolled but beautifully rhythmic movements; and all the sympathetic spectators could do was to gaze upon the distracted girl in awe-struck horror — in particular, her once severe but now unhappy mother, Berthe, who wrung her hands in the deepest distress, but was powerless to prevent the sad fate she had only so recently predicted for her beautiful and beloved daughter.

Then came the tragic climax. Even as the horror-struck company gazed upon the madly-whirling girl, Giselle suddenly stopped and wavered uncertainly for a moment or two ; then, uttering a soft sigh, she fell back, dead, into the arms of her weeping mother.

* * * * *

A short time after this sad tragedy, another hunting-party was in progress one moonlit night ; and the huntsmen, led by the game-keeper, Hilarion, were so eager about their sport that they lingered in the forest much later than usual and lost their way.

Presently, they all trooped into a deep mysterious glade, at one side of which stood a newly-made grave on a little mound in a sheltered spot. A small cross had been placed at the head of the grave ; and upon this holy symbol appeared the one word, *"Giselle."*

The huntsmen, however, did not notice the newly-made grave of the unhappy Giselle ; but feeling that this was a somewhat eerie spot into which they had wandered, they began to shiver slightly. Their uneasiness increased presently when Hilarion informed them that this part of the forest was believed to be haunted by those strange unearthly beings, the Wilis — those dangerously transformed maidens who had been unlucky in love and had died before their wedding-days had dawned, and who were doomed by a magic enchantment to lure mortal young men to a last fatal dance with them.

The huntsmen were now thoroughly alarmed, for midnight was fast approaching, the hour when the Wilis were due to appear ; and, in haste, they hurried away, followed by Hilarion, all hoping to escape in time.

Scarcely had the young men departed than the chimes of midnight sounded faintly from the distant village ; and instantly, the haunted glade became filled with the floating ethereal sylph-like forms of the Wilis, gliding in noiselessly from every side like will-o'-the-wisps. They were led by Myrta, Queen of the

Wilis, who bade them follow her to the newly-made grave of the beautiful Giselle, their new companion, whom she now proceeded to call forth, waving her magic wand as she did so.

Almost immediately, the ghostly form of Giselle appeared in their midst — an airy-fairy sprite now clad in misty, filmy draperies and having small white wings between her shoulders. She was already a Wili ; and she felt light as air as she joined her newly-found sister-Wilis in their wonderful dances. They were all fated to dance continuously until four o'clock, when they would vanish once more until midnight came again.

As the Wilis presently danced away down the glade, the young Duke Albrecht came into it from the other side, attended by his faithful squire, Wilfred. He was now very contrite and sorrowful, for he had truly loved the gentle Giselle, and was full of sincere remorse for having been the cause of her tragic end. Having learned that her simple grave was in this forest glade, he had now come to lay a wreath of lilies at the foot of the little white cross. He had also lost his way, and so had arrived thus late in the glade.

Wilfred, knowing that his beloved master was in danger in this haunted spot now that midnight had chimed, begged him to leave the glade quickly ; but Albrecht refused to do so. Instead, he commanded Wilfred to return to the Castle immediately, and to leave him alone with his dead beloved one ; and the young squire had no choice but to obey.

When Wilfred had reluctantly departed, the unhappy Duke moved forward and laid his wreath of lilies upon the little white cross at the head of Giselle's grave ; and he remained standing there for a short time, his head bowed with grief. Then, looking up, he suddenly beheld his beloved one, more beautiful than ever in her Wili form ; and he was instantly full of joy once more.

The glade was now filled with the sylph-like figures of her companion Wilis, all dancing and holding high revels ; but Albrecht had eyes for none but his lovely Giselle, whom he chased hither and thither — for she kept teasingly vanishing and then appearing again. At last, however, she took pity upon him and allowed him to join her in a wonderful fairy-like dance — having first made sure that her sylph companions had danced away to the other end of the glade and that she was alone with her former lover.

The other Wilis, indeed, were fully occupied. They had found and surrounded the young game-keeper, Hilarion, who, over-venturesome, had returned to the glade alone to look for the grave of Giselle ; and, seizing him in triumph as their lawful prize, they compelled him to dance with them until he fell, dying from exhaustion. Then they tossed him laughingly into a dark pool nearby — it being their dreadful fate and duty as Wilis thus to lure young men to their doom.

Presently, they returned with their Queen to deal with the other mortal youth they already knew to be in their haunted glade.

Seeing them coming, and knowing their terrible intention, Giselle frantically bade Albrecht cling to the little cross on her grave, this being a symbol of Sanctuary, while she herself stood over him and tried to save him from destruction.

The Queen of the Wilis now became furious, since her magic wand had no power over one who clung to the cross ; but she still had power over each and all of her subject Wilis. Therefore, she sternly bade the trembling Giselle to lure the Duke away from the cross by means of her own unearthly beauty and exquisite dancing.

Unable to disobey this absolute command of her Queen, since she was herself now an avenging Wili, the unhappy sprite was thus compelled to lure her mortal lover away from the cross to his doom by revealing to him the irresistible grace of her movements in sylph form. Her agonised pleas for mercy having been scornfully rejected, and under the cold stony glances of the implacable Myrta, she found herself forced to dance in a most seductive and exciting manner which the young Duke was powerless to resist ; and, all too soon, he joined her, even with eagerness.

Never before had such marvellous dancing been seen in the haunted glade as that of Giselle and Albrecht ; and the revel became madder than ever as the other Wilis surrounded the whirling pair and enticed them on to faster and wilder movements.

This exciting and most enthralling dance continued for a very long time ; but at last Albrecht began to falter and realised that his waning strength was ebbing fast. And still the unhappy Giselle was compelled by renewed commands of the vengeful Wili Queen, Myrta, to continue her alluring movements, ever faster and more furious, even though she knew her beloved one was gradually failing and that his mortal strength was already almost exhausted. Then, at last, she saw that the first pale flicker of early dawn was beginning to enter the haunted glade ; and the chimes of four o'clock were now faintly heard striking from the distant village church clock. Would the sinister design of the Wili Queen now be frustrated ?

Instantly, with the coming of dawn, the power of the Wilis left them, and they had to return to their graves until the following midnight.

Gradually, the haunted glade was deserted ; and as the Wilis, still dancing, vanished from sight, Albrecht fell to the ground. Giselle longed to remain with him and help him to recover ; but she found herself powerless to do so, since she was now a Wili and must return to her grave. Compelled against her will, and powerless to resist the magic spell, she moved, slowly and reluctantly, away from her lover's side.

The prostrate Albrecht made a last despairing effort to keep her with him. He even managed to struggle painfully to his feet once more and follow her ; then, sorrowfully realising that they could not fight against the magic of the Wilis, he resigned himself to their sad parting.

As the lovely sylph form of Giselle vanished from sight behind the little white cross on her grave— around which sweet-scented flowers were already blossoming — her exhausted mortal lover again fell prostrate to the ground above.

NOTE :—*When the ballet, "Giselle," was first performed in Paris, at the Théâtre de l'Académie Royale du Musique, 28th June, 1841, the final scene was given exactly in accordance with the original "book" by MM. de Saint-George, Théophile Gautier and Jean Coralli (choreographer). In this original version, Albrecht was shown as reconciled to the Princess Bathilde, who appeared on the scene just as Giselle was about to vanish into her grave. The latter had seen the Princess coming and indicated to her despairing lover that it was her wish he should return to his betrothed — which he did, staggering towards Bathilde with his hands outstretched entreating forgiveness, and then falling back exhausted into the arms of the attendants as the curtain descended.*

In modern versions, however, Bathilde does not appear

again ; and Albrecht either actually falls dead as Giselle vanishes from sight, or he becomes unconscious from sheer exhaustion—or he falls, shaken with sobs, as the curtain descends.

The final scene, as related in the story above, is one of the more usual present-day versions.

LE CARNAVAL
(*The Carnival*)

THIS is a Fantasy — or, perhaps, it is a Romantic Dream ? Is it real, or just a pretty Picture come to life ? Who cares ? It charms everybody ; and nobody can fail to fall under its irresistible spell.

The setting of this airy-fairy, irresponsible spell-binder is an ante-room in a Hall of Carnival in Victorian times. Quaint little striped sofas are to be seen against the walls — sofas that seem almost too small to hold a crinolined lady *and* her gay cavalier. But perhaps the flirtatious dames of this seemingly prim-and-proper period were expected to sit on the knees of their escorts in this particular Hall of Pleasure ?

Bright lights are shining everywhere ; and silken curtains shut out the soft fresh air of the Spring night. Gay, romantic, and soft sentimental music is being played by an orchestra not far away ; just the kind of music designed for care-free youth in its irresponsible quest of Love.

The scene is set ; and anything may happen. Let us, then, slip behind the curtain, from which we may peep forth unobserved, and see what *does* happen. Perhaps we ought not to do so ; but this is Carnival time and Cupid's hour, when Mrs. Grundy is forgotten for the moment ; so, let us put on rose-coloured spectacles and see what that giddy fellow, Eros, is up to.

Ah ! Here comes a group of dancing Carnival revellers, each with a partner, but interchangeable one with another. The girls are dressed in swaying flirta-tious crinolines and do not hesitate to reveal beneath their tempestuous petticoats the daintiest of long lace-edged pantalettes ; and they wear the most ravishing poke-bonnets above their prim little black masks. Their swains wear such tight fitting trousers below their neatly-waisted pale-coloured coats that the wonder is they can dance so freely and gracefully ; and it also seems miraculous that their tall stove-pipe hats manage to stick so jauntily on their well-curled and pomaded heads, despite their lively movements.

Scarcely have they danced a dozen times round the room than these gay cavaliers whisk their crinolined ladies away in a flash ; and in comes Pierrot, alone, and looking extremely woe-begone in these gay surroundings. He has all the appearance of one disappointed in love ; and that is the case. The love-lorn fellow flaps his much-too-long wide white sleeves about disconsolately, and seems almost in the last depths of despair. Deserted by his fascinating, beautiful and much too popular Columbine, what does the Carnival now hold for him ? Just nothing. So poor Pierrot curls himself up behind a sofa and, falling asleep, forgets his woes for the moment.

While Pierrot sleeps, in comes Florestan, a gay, impetuous fellow, out to flirt with all the pretty girls he meets. As the crinolined ladies and their smart partners come dancing back through the ante-room, he snatches at each hooped skirt that passes by ; but their swains whisk them all away once more.

Two super-flirtatious maidens, wearing much shorter and more frivolous skirts, now appear on the scene ; and one of these, Estrella, seems more than willing to dance away with the *débonnaire* Florestan.

The other tricksy lady, Chiarina, now sets out to charm a newcomer. This is Eusebius, a dreamy poet, who meanders in, seemingly unaware of his surroundings and deep in the writing of a poem. Whether or not the latter is a sonnet to his lady's eyebrows, matters not, for he is not allowed to finish it. Chiarina lures him from his task by offering him a red rose as an invitation to a dance — or to her arms! She soon deserts him, however, and offers her red roses to other swains — in particular, to that most brilliant and lively of all the Carnival dancers, Harlequin.

What a dazzling, desirable fellow is this spangled Adonis! But he is not for Chiarina. He has eyes and arms for no one but the Beauty of the Ball, that Queen of Smiles and Pirouettes, Columbine. Fickle, and having already deserted her devoted Pierrot, the lovely Columbine cannot resist the quite irresistible Harlequin. Despite the fact that she flirts outrageously with Florestan whenever the latter appears on the scene, and even with the dreamy, up-in-the-clouds Eusebius, it is not long ere she succumbs to the superior attractions of the spangled, diamond-deviced King of the Revels, and dances off with him.

Meanwhile, during a quiet interval, Pierrot has awakened from his little nap, as woe-begone as ever. Then, suddenly, he becomes alert for a moment. From his hiding-place behind the sofa, he espies the daintiest little fairy-like person flitting across the ante-room. It is Papillon, a real Butterfly-Lady, who charms him instantly by her airy-fairy dancing. She scarcely seems to touch the floor at all, but is more like a fluffy bit of thistle-down floating before his wondering gaze.

Entranced by this exquisite vision, Pierrot decides to think no more about his fickle Columbine and sets off in pursuit of the Butterfly Maiden. But, alas, poor Pierrot! Papillon, light as air, entices him with her shining wings so that he chases her hither and thither with eager steps; and then, just as he imagines he has captured her — having gone through all the school-boy actions of flinging his sugar-loaf hat over her — she slips from his grasp and vanishes. When he triumphantly lifts his hat, there is nothing beneath it, after all : and Papillon has flitted away, laughing—with Pantalon, a somewhat conceited old fellow, who has been lurking around waiting for just such an opportunity of securing a charming partner. So the unlucky Pierrot is more woe-begone than ever.

But the Carnival fun now waxes faster and more furious with every moment that passes, as all the revellers return to the ante-room. The crinolined ladies and their cavaliers skim about in the maddest of mad frolics ; Florestan and Estrella, Chiarina and Eusebius, Harlequin and Columbine, and Papillon and Pantalon, all perform the most marvellous dances. The fun goes to the head of the latter, so that he tries to snatch the prettiest girls from the arms of their lovers — but without success, since he is not so spry as he used to be.

Some of the merry revellers set upon the dreamy Eusebius and mischievously tear up the poem he has been attempting to write and make him dance instead ; and all is laughter, kisses and frolicsome fun. Even when the Philistines now appear upon the scene — in the shape of an elderly pair of real Victorian Spoil-Sports, very prim and proper, who express themselves as shocked at such goings-on — they could not stop this high-speed frolic ; and presently, they, too, find themselves whirled away into the vortex, willy-nilly.

Finally, the hilarious crowd dance joyfully round and about the most unjoyful Pierrot, who now seeks among them for a partner — but in vain, though he appeals to each pretty maiden in turn. Again, alas, poor Pierrot ! Nobody wants such a woe-begone fellow at Carnival time ; and as he flops to the ground and spreads out his grotesquely long sleeves in front of him, drooping his head disconsolately, our little stolen peep at this giddy scene must come to an end.

So, with the sound of happy Carnival music and laughter in our ears, and with our eyes still dazzled by the bewildering kaleidoscopic paint-box colours that have passed before them, we will ring down the curtain.

CLEOPATRA
(*Cléopâtre*)

THIS is the story of a single Night of Love in the life of Cleopatra, Queen of Egypt — the fatally beautiful, but terrible, Serpent of the Nile — whom to look upon and to love was, for many, to live and to die.

An Enchantress ? Without doubt ; but one who used only the magic of Beauty, Passion and Power. Cruel, ruthless, relentless ? Yes ; but her countless lovers cared naught for such sinister qualities if only they might gaze upon her matchless beauty and consume themselves in the fiery furnace of her passion for a few ecstatic moments. . . . even when, serpent-like, she struck, they were ready and willing enough to accept the agony of her fangs, after experiencing the supreme joy of having charmed her to their short-lived pleasure.

Here, then, is the story of one such charmer, who fell a willing victim to the Serpent of the Nile.

* * * * *

It was evening in an oasis near the edge of the Egyptian Desert ; and behind the pillars of a certain temple, the pale green Nile could be seen winding like some sinister serpent in the distance. The last rays of the blazing sun had already dipped beyond the rolling sea of hot sand ; and the quickly approaching twilight caused long dark shadows to lengthen and deepen about the Temple.

From the depths of these shadows there stepped forth a graceful young priestess, the Princess Ta-Hor, to look for her lover, Amoun — a handsome young chief, who arrived almost simultaneously and clasped her in his arms.

Ta-Hor had been promised to Amoun by the High Priest of the Temple, and they were to be wedded in due course. They loved one another dearly, and met thus every evening after the young girl's temple service had ended for the day. This evening the young chief carried a bow and arrows, for he had been hunting ; but all thoughts of the pleasures of the chase were now forgotten in the joy of meeting his beloved one.

Yet, as they now clung together, a slight tremor, a shiver of apprehension, passed over the lovers — unaccountably, it seemed to them, since nothing untoward could happen to mar their happiness when their union was to be blessed by the High Priest himself.

Nevertheless, a strange feeling of approaching danger was plainly felt by both — rather like the instinctive, indefinable warning experienced by some sensitive folk at the unseen approach of a cobra.

Then, quite suddenly, there came the trampling, tinkling noise of an approaching cavalcade ; and the lovers drew back hastily as the High Priest now appeared and announced that the Queen was about to honour him with her presence within the Temple precincts for a few hours — whither she had casually decreed to come and be entertained by her vast retinue in the cool of the late evening.

Cleopatra, whose dazzling beauty entranced every male she looked upon ! Ta-Hor knew now what the strange shivery apprehensions she had just felt meant ; and she implored her lover to withdraw with her and to remain unobserved lest the Enchantress Queen should cast her fatal glance upon him.

But Amoun laughed at her fears, and declared himself impervious to the charms of any other woman than

his own well-beloved Ta-Hor ; and though he withdrew with her somewhat into the shadows, he would
not depart altogether — for he was curious to behold
the far-famed Queen, whom he had not yet seen.
Ta-Hor, however, was still fearful, and rightly so ;
for the instinctive warning felt by those happy lovers
as of the unseen approach of a cobra was one to have
heeded instantly. The Serpent of the Nile would soon
be in their midst !

The royal procession quickly arrived upon the scene.
Soldiers, slaves, dancers, musicians, all crowded round
about the Temple ; and in the open columned entrance
the curtained litter of the Queen was placed.

As the musicians began to play soft sensuous airs,
the slaves drew back the curtains of the litter, and
carefully unswathed the mummy-like wrappings that
enveloped their royal mistress and had protected her
loveliness from the sandy dust of her short Desert
journey. Veil after veil of rainbow-tinted gauze was
gently untwined from her graceful sinuous form ; and
at last, she stood revealed in all her dazzling beauty,
clad only in a single garment of light semi-transparent
golden gauze, but laden with jewels and crowned with
the royal insignia of the hooded cobra.

What fatal beauty was here ! Bronze-red hair that
glowed in the lights that now blazed forth from the
Temple precincts ; skin like old ivory or mellowed
parchment ; almond eyes as black as night, now languorous and sultry, now flashing and brilliant ; long
sinuous limbs ; slender hands and feet ; a body voluptuous in its perfect curves and contours — a beauty
so intense that it thrilled and almost hurt the beholder
to gaze upon it.

It certainly thrilled and physically hurt one of the
hidden observers amidst the shadows ; and as Cleopatra

now sank back among the silken cushions of the couch that had been prepared for her, Amoun, the young chieftain, betrothed of Ta-Hor the gentle priestess, stepped forward a few steps with an instinctive cry as though struck by an arrow — an arrow, indeed, for the arrow of Love had entered his heart on thus first beholding the dazzling Queen of Egypt, whose fatal enchantment had already fallen upon him

The now distracted and terrified Ta-Hor tried to drag him back into the shadows ; but the Queen had seen him and had noted the look of awed admiration in his eyes. She had also observed the young girl who clung to him ; and she smiled in contempt. She was already bored by this early night festival in the Desert, almost before it had properly begun ; but now her boredom passed — for here was a new lover she might take did she care to do so.

She gave the signal for a dancing revel to begin ; and surrounded by her favourite slaves, and with one specially-devoted well-armed negro at her feet, she watched the first part of the festival which had been arranged for her delight by the Temple servers. This was a graceful but serious dance-procession ; and it was led by the now unhappy Ta-Hor herself, whose duty thus separated her from her lover's side. She could still see him in the shadows ; and, to her dismay, she noted that his ardent gaze was constantly directed towards the lovely Queen.

Once or twice, the anxious maiden managed to move towards her preoccupied lover during the progress of her sacred dance and to whisper an imploring entreaty for him to remember their avowed love ; and again she tried to induce him to withdraw into the shadows. But her efforts were in vain ; for Amoun was already in thrall to, and transfixed by, the Serpent of the Nile.

Suddenly an arrow whizzed through the air, and fell within a few inches of the royal couch. It had been shot from the bow of Amoun ; and it had attached to it a small piece of papyrus upon which the infatuated youth had hastily written a declaration of his burning love for the beautiful Queen.

The sacred dance was stopped, and a wave of horror swept through the throng of attendants. Who was the bold stranger who thus dared to insult their royal mistress — or was the villain making an attempt on her precious life ?

Amoun was soon discovered by the furiously angry slaves ; but when brought face to face with Cleopatra, he showed no fear or compunction for the enormity of his deed, but continued to gaze steadfastly at her with the glowing eyes of an impatient lover. Even when the Queen — though secretly glad at the thought of a new lover and already feeling passion for the handsome youth — sternly announced that to love her meant death, he boldly declared that he would willingly welcome death could he but be permitted to love her.

Cleopatra, knowing that her own sudden passion would be short-lived, then fixed her cobra-like gaze upon him with a cruel intensity and declared that he might enjoy her kisses and caresses during this present festival hour, after which he must be prepared to die. No stranger could be permitted to live after receiving the kisses of Cleopatra.

Amoun eagerly accepted this terrible condition, despite the entreaties of the despairing Ta-Hor, who had again managed to reach his side. Even when, fear lending her courage, she flung herself on her knees before the Queen and entreated her to spare Amoun, her request was scornfully refused and she was driven away once more and forbidden to return.

The revel was now resumed ; and Amoun sat on the royal couch beside Cleopatra — her accepted lover of the moment. Intoxicated by her beauty and her passionate kisses — which he returned with an ever-increasing passion — the infatuated young chief gave himself up blindly to the joy of this ecstatic hour.

The Temple dancers having retired, other dancers took their place ; and Cleopatra's own Egyptian Palace performers and Greek slaves now provided a marvellous display, which almost became an orgy, for the further entertainment of their royal mistress and her lover.

But, all too soon, the festival hour passed away ; and, with it, passed the short-lived passion of the love-sated Queen for her doomed favourite of an evening's revel.

The High Priest of the Temple now appeared with a cup of poison in his hand, which he handed to Cleopatra who, no longer the gracious bestower of sweet love favours but once more the cruel Serpent of the Nile, contemptuously presented it to her lover of an hour.

Amoun, though he had possibly forgotten during that one glamorous hour what the end of it must be, met his doom bravely ; and proudly drawing himself up, he drank the poisoned draught and fell writhing at the feet of the beautiful but callous Queen.

Cleopatra gazed down coldly upon her willing victim until he had drawn his last agonizing breath ; and then she gave the signal for departure. The lovely Queen was swathed once more in her many shimmering veils ; and then she was borne away in her curtained litter, followed by her brilliant but now somewhat subdued and silent retinue. The revel was over ; and the Serpent of the Nile had claimed another victim.

The High Priest came forward slowly and laid a black cloth over the dead crumpled form of Amoun ; and then he sadly retired within the now darkened Temple.

But who is this cloaked form now issuing forth from the shadows ? It is Ta-Hor, full of grief and seeking her lost lover. She soon drew near to the sable-draped corpse and, lifting the cloth, uttered a cry of woe as she beheld the contorted body of her beloved one. Tenderly she kissed his stiff lips ; and then, beating her breast, and with another wailing cry, she fell unconscious by his side.

DAPHNIS AND CHLOE

In an exquisite green and flowery grove, sacred to the god Pan and his Nymphs, there came one day a group of youths and maidens carrying baskets of fruits, flowers and other offerings for the rustic deity, whose altar they served.

Having deposited their offerings before the altar and made their reverent obeisances to the invisible God of Shepherds, the young people began to dance a solemn ritual measure, as befitted the occasion. Very soon, however, they abandoned solemnity and broke forth into a much livelier dance.

Among the throng of young people were a shepherd named Daphnis and a fair and gentle shepherdess named Chloe. These two had been lovers since childhood and could scarcely bear to be parted ; and they were both more beautiful and spiritual than any of their companions.

Presently, they came away from the other dancers ; and then, hand-in-hand, they bowed again in reverent awe before the altar of Pan. As they turned aside once more, the handsome Daphnis was playfully seized by some of the girl dancers and enticed by them to join in the dance — which had now become more like a revel.

This unexpected diversion of her lover was disappointing and disturbing to Chloe, and she felt a slight twinge of jealousy for the first time in her young life ; but, determined to show a pretended indifference to the incident, she allowed herself to be drawn into the opposite group of young men dancers, who received her with delighted eagerness. This was especially the case with one of their number, a boorish herdsman named Darkon, who had already conceived a rough passion for the lovely Chloe and longed to possess her.

Now, seeing his coveted prize unattended by her true lover, and considering her, in consequence, an easy prey, Darkon began to press his unwelcome attentions upon the fair shepherdess and even attempted to snatch a kiss from her — to her utter dismay. This little incident, however, had been noted by Daphnis, who instantly left the girl dancers who had enticed him away and hastened to protect his beloved one from her unwelcome admirer.

A quarrel now ensued between the shepherd and the herdsman ; and the young people suggested merrily that the rivals should compete in a dance contest for a kiss from the gentle shepherdess. When, however, the boorish Darkon began his performance, his dancing movements were so heavy, clumsy and roughly uncouth that all the company laughed at him in mocking amusement ; and he had, perforce, to retire from the contest in high dudgeon and deep humiliation. So the prize fell to the handsome Daphnis, who was a very graceful dancer ; and when he claimed his reward, Chloe gladly responded, her temporary twinge of jealousy now forgotten.

After this, the young people danced away out of the grove — all but Daphnis, who lingered behind for a short time longer and, consequently, met with a strange experience.

A beautiful and sophisticated young woman temptress, Lisinion, entered the sacred glade and endeavoured to draw the handsome shepherd from his allegiance to the gentle Chloe during the latter's absence. Languorous and full of glamour she danced before the young man with enticingly sensuous movements, casting aside her veils and seeking to inflame his youthful passions by revealing to him her hidden charms. Daphnis, however, refused to be thus seduced by her voluptuous movements and over-eager enticements ; and the unscrupulous Lisinion was compelled to leave her intended victim in angry defeat.

But trouble was yet to befall the virtuous shepherd and his fair shepherdess. Suddenly, there came the alarming sounds of a great tumult from the seashore beyond the glade. Pirates had landed and were already chasing and seeking to capture the women folk in that district. Knowing at once what this tumult meant, Daphnis rushed away to seek and rescue his beloved Chloe.

Scarcely had the anxious shepherd vanished from sight than Chloe herself ran into the sacred grove, closely pursued by the brigands, who quickly seized her and carried her off to their ship in triumph.

Next moment, the distracted Daphnis dashed back into the grove hot on the trail of the pirates and the rescue of his beloved one. But he was too late. To his horror, all he found was the fair Chloe's scarf, which had fallen to the ground as she was carried away ; and snatching this precious object to his heart, he railed in anger against the gods for bringing this terrible woe upon him — and then fell to the ground, senseless.

The gods, however, did not intend to desert one who had always served them well. Suddenly, a mysterious light began to glow from the altar ; and then, the Sacred Nymphs descended therefrom. They first of all danced a formal ritual measure, with utmost grace ; and, finally, on behalf of the unconscious Daphnis, they invoked the aid of Pan himself, who graciously promised to set this evil matter right.

* * * * *

Meanwhile, the abducted Chloe, held captive in the Pirates' stronghold, was overcome with fear and grief. On being carried off the robbers' ship, she was set down in the midst of her lawless captors' camp on the shores of a wild and lonely part of the coast, closely hemmed in by high rocky cliffs. Here she was compelled to await the will of the Pirate Chief regarding her fate, and to be a spectator of the riotous revels that took place immediately a landing had been effected.

Having disposed of their booty in various places, the brigands began to feast upon the food and wine they had stolen ; and a most hilarious dancing entertainment followed, which quickly developed into a drunken orgy and ended in savage quarrels and violence.

The gentle shepherdess drew back into the shadows, filled with horror at the alarming spectacle before her and hoping that her own presence would not be remembered until a more propitious moment. This, however, was a vain hope. The Pirate Chief still retained some control over his drink-maddened crew ; and soon recollecting the lovely maiden he had captured, he caused her — unwilling, struggling and terrified — to be dragged before him. He smiled upon her amorously and indicated that he intended to hold her as his slave and paramour ; and when the helpless captive fell upon her knees and begged for pity, he laughed derisively and, lurching towards her, snatched her into his arms.

Despite the unhappy Chloe's pleas for mercy, and her wildly-uttered cries to the gods for help, he was about to stagger away with her to his tent, when a strange apprehension fell upon all the riotous company. A mysterious Presence was felt, and as darkness began to fall upon the scene, the Shadow of Pan, the God of

Shepherds and Shepherdesses, was seen, plainly silhouetted upon the face of the cliffs.

With now trembling hands, the Pirate Chief let slip from his grasp the still feebly struggling form of his intended victim ; and, with shrieks of abject terror, he and his villainous companions fled to seek safety as best they could.

Thus, the great god Pan came to the rescue of his beautiful worshipper ; and Chloe fell upon her knees and uttered prayers of thanksgiving in awe and gratitude.

*   *   *   *   *

While these exciting events were taking place in the Pirates' stronghold, the young shepherd Daphnis still remained in an unconscious, trance-like state beside the altar of Pan, whence the sacred Nymphs had so recently descended.

When, at last, he awakened to consciousness and remembered what had happened, he was still heartbroken because of the loss of his beloved Chloe ; and, leaping to his feet, he was about to rush forth madly once more in search of her when, to his amazement and joy, she came tripping lightly into the sacred grove. Next moment, the lovers were clasped in each other's arms, filled with happiness at their wonderful reunion ; and then they danced together in an ecstasy of delight.

While they were still dancing, their youthful friends reappeared to welcome them back ; and with them came an old shepherd named Lammon, who declared that Pan must have intervened on Chloe's behalf in memory of his own adventure with the lovely nymph, Syrinx.

Whether this latter supposition was actually the case, or whether the kindly god had appeared on the scene in the Pirates' Camp in answer to the shepherdess's own distressful prayers, mattered not ; but, to please their friends, Daphnis and Chloe proceeded to enact the well-known old story of the pursuit of the beautiful nymph Syrinx by the amorous god and of her transformation into a bunch of reeds — from which Pan had then made his famous musical instrument, the Pandæan Pipes.

After this, the lovers next made their solemn betrothal vows before the altar of their guardian deity ; and then all the young people performed a gay festival dance in honour of this happy occasion.

And who can doubt but that the merry Pipes of Pan were heard in the sacred grove, mingling with the lighthearted laughter of the youthful dancers, at the betrothal of Daphnis and Chloe ?

L'EPREUVE D'AMOUR
(*The Test of Love*)

THIS is a real fairy-tale, with its scene set in China ; so, look out for dragons and gentle lovers of the Willow-Pattern-Plate variety.

Amidst a rainbow-tinted and impossibly-flowery garden scene — which seemed to have been translated straight from a Chinese screen or fan — and with a couple of porcelain-like pagodas rising on either side of him, a richly-dressed Mandarin appeared one day.

His appearance had been noted by a group of chattering grey monkeys playing among the creeper-hung trees and flowering bushes ; and because they knew him well as the lord and master of the neighbouring mansion, they became more noisy than before and even began to dance around him in a circle with comical loping movements.

But the Mandarin was busy with his own thoughts and could not be bothered with the chattering monkeys. So he testily drove them away with his fan ; and then he sat down on a flowery bank and tried to collect his thoughts once more. This, however, he found an impossible thing to do ; for a lovely butterfly now came fluttering around him, teasing and distracting him with the glistening beauty of its blue and purple iridescent wings, ever and anon settling upon his gorgeous robe, or coquettishly bestowing upon his yellow cheek a delicate butterfly-kiss. Driven nearly frantic by this mischievous insect — though strangely fascinated, too— the Mandarin hastily wandered off to cogitate in another part of his estate

No sooner had the Mandarin moved away than a

handsome Chinese youth came from behind the bushes, where he had been hiding and waiting for the great lord to depart ; for he was in love with the Mandarin's daughter, with whom he had an assignation in that same spot. He could meet the lovely maiden only in secret, because he was poor and the Mandarin preferred to consider a more wealthy suitor for the hand of his daughter. Nevertheless, the latter loved her impecunious sweetheart with an equal love ; and the pair often met, despite the difficulties in their path.

Presently, the pretty Chung-Yang came tripping to the rendezvous, anxiously peering this way and that ; and, next moment, the lovers were clasped in each other's arms.

But their bliss was short-lived on this occasion ; for the Mandarin returned unexpectedly and made an angry scene. He announced that he had already planned a splendid marriage for his daughter with the Ambassador of a rich foreign potentate, and that he expected this more desirable suitor to arrive at any moment ; and he forced the unluckily poor lover to depart from the garden, and forbade him to join in the forthcoming festivities in honour of the rich guest. He likewise commanded his lovely daughter to array herself in her finest attire and to join her attendant maidens in readiness to dance and sing before the expected visitors.

Scarcely were all the festive preparations completed than the wealthy Ambassador arrived, attended by two smartly-garbed *aides-de-camp* and a splendid retinue of pages and coolies carrying coffers full of treasures, jewels and fine gifts of all kinds. The Ambassador himself, dressed very magnificently, was haughty, vain and pompous ; and he seemed to expect awed admiration from everybody.

The ambitious Mandarin received his exalted visitor with the utmost satisfaction ; and he was even more delighted still on beholding the vast treasures he had brought. This was exactly the proper kind of suitor he desired ; and when the Ambassador had distributed some of the gifts so lavishly displayed to all, the Mandarin commanded his daughter and her attendant maidens to dance before their splendid guest — and his satisfaction was deeper still when he observed how greatly the latter admired the beautiful Chung-Yang.

At first the fair maiden was unhappy at the loveless prospect that lay before her ; but when her own true lover suddenly showed himself for a moment from a hiding-place nearby and indicated by signs that he was planning to rescue her from her unwanted suitor, she smiled again, believing that all would be well, after all.

When the Ambassador had also shown off his own dancing capabilities before the admiring company, he was led by his obsequious host to a pavilion that had now been erected for him to rest within. A second pavilion had also been set up alongside for the accommodation of the two smart *aides-de-camp ;* and having seen his guests thus comfortably installed for their siesta hour, the Mandarin himself retired with his own attendants — but he bade his daughter to remain nearby, in case her future bridegroom should desire her to entertain him with her charming company.

Chung-Yang was full of dismay at this alarming command of her already chuckling father ; and she fell on her knees and prayed for protection.

Presently, and almost simultaneously, the Ambassador and his two *aides-de-camp* emerged from their tents ; but the latter were instantly driven back angrily by their over-lord. Then the latter drew near to the now terrified Chung-Yang, and began to make love to her; and he was about to carry off the half-swooning maiden to his tent when there came a sudden and most alarming interruption.

A fearsome dragon of monstrous size came rolling and writhing out from the bushes in dreadful curving arches, making hideous loud noises like approaching thunder; and, at the sight of this terrible creature, the Ambassador quickly released his struggling victim and fled, pell-mell, to hide in his tent-pavilion; his example being hastily followed by his equally-terrified *aides* — who had again issued forth to spy upon their lord.

Full of thankfulness for her release, Chung-Yang herself had no fear of the strange though truly hideous monster, whose timely arrival had saved her from the clutches of the amorous foreigners; and she even began to caress the scaly creature's most alarming-looking head. Then, to her amazement, the top of the dragon's head was suddenly lifted, as though it had been the lid of a box; and there stepped forth from it her own true lover, who clasped her in his arms with the utmost joy. The monster that had so scared the would-be ravishers was nothing but a pasteboard affair contrived by this bright-witted youth, who, though poor, was brave and clever.

The resourceful young man, however, knew only too well that he must use his keen wits still further if he was to save his beloved one from a loveless marriage and prove himself a more worthy suitor in the eyes of her ambitious and mercenary father; so, after they had rejoiced together for a short time, he sent Chung-Yang back to the safety of her own apartments, while he planned another clever plot.

With the help of some of his own young men friends, all disguised as brigands and wearing masks, he broke down the tents of the foreigners, and drove off the Ambassador and the *aides-de-camp* ; and then the plotters removed all the money and caskets of treasures placed therein and hid their booty in a safe place.

The consequence was that the Mandarin now refused to consider the suit of the Ambassador, since the latter was no longer a wealthy man ; and he was even inclined to permit his daughter to marry her poor suitor.

Then when the latter, having gained his heart's desire, very honestly restored the temporarily stolen treasure to the Ambassador, the mercenary Mandarin went back on his word and once more declared that his daughter should still become the bride of the splendid foreigner, since the latter had regained his riches.

But the Ambassador would no longer agree to this, being deeply offended because his treasures were so obviously preferred to himself by his greedy host ; and, in high dudgeon, he gathered his retinue together and marched away.

The lovers once more rushed rapturously into each other's arms ; and the disappointed Mandarin, realising that the rich suitor was lost to him for ever, now gave his consent to the wedding of his daughter with her poor but faithful lover, whose devotion and love had been proved beyond the shadow of a doubt by the brave deeds he had performed on her behalf.

So the marriage of the long-suffering true lovers was celebrated at once amidst great rejoicing ; and everybody was happy — except the disappointed Mandarin. Full of self-pity, because his ambitious schemes to secure a wealthy son-in-law had thus come to naught by his own over-greediness, he left the gay wedding scene and flung himself down on a flowery bank in the garden to ponder upon his well-deserved woes.

But he was not allowed even to ponder in peace. A

group of chattering monkeys quickly returned to mock at him, so that he shook his fists at them angrily and drove them away.

Even then his ponderings were not left undisturbed. Next moment the same lovely blue and purple butterfly which had teased him but a few hours ago, also came back and seemed to taunt him with her fascinating allurements, fluttering around him, resting upon his gorgeous garments, and even saucily bestowing upon his yellow cheek a delicate butterfly-kiss — until, at last, he flung his fan at her in a rage, when she fluttered away, full of lighthearted joyousness.

Thus the Mandarin was left alone, his head in his hands and looking and feeling extremely glum — an unhappy state of mind he richly deserved.

THE FIRE-BIRD
(*L'Oiseau de Feu*)

ONE glorious moonlit summer night in mediæval times the young Prince Ivan of Russia found himself alone, separated from his retinue, and lost in an enchanted forest. However, he was an adventurous youth, brave and fearless ; and as he wandered about happily, seeking to disentangle his way through the clustering bushes, thickets and groves of tall trees, he hoped to meet with some remarkable adventure. His wish was granted.

Issuing forth at last into an open glade, he suddenly beheld a beautiful tree, which gleamed and glistened in the silvery moonlight as though illuminated from within. Its branches were laden with golden apples, which likewise glowed as though with a hidden inner radiance,.

As the young Prince gazed with amazement and delight upon this magic tree, he saw a gorgeous bird fluttering about it, seeking to pluck its tempting fruit. Though this lovely bird — a female — glowed with ever-changing iridescent rainbow colours, her main plumage was of a dazzling flame-orange tint like fire.

Entranced by the glowing beauty of the Fire-Bird, the Prince tried to shoot at her with the cross-bow he carried ; but his would-be feathered victim was too quick for him, and flew away. However, she quickly returned; and then, as she attempted to seek shelter in the magic tree, the royal huntsman succeeded in capturing her in his arms, not wishing to hurt her. But the Fire-Bird fluttered and struggled pitifully in his grasp ;

and she begged so eagerly to be released — promising, in return, to give him one of her gleaming feathers, declaring that the latter would help him in some moment of danger — that her captor presently agreed to her request.

As soon as she was free, the Fire-Bird plucked forth one of the flame-like feathers from her gleaming plumage and gave this to the Prince ; and then, after promising to return instantly at his call should he ever be in danger, she spread her dazzling wings and flew away joyously to join her mate.

By this time the early dawn began to appear ; and, presently, the lost Prince was surprised to find himself standing quite close to the gates of an ancient castle of gloomy and forbidding aspect.

Nevertheless, wishing for further adventures, the royal youth, on hearing the sound of approaching footsteps, did not move away but stepped aside to see what might happen next. As he stood there, hesitant, upon the threshold, the gate was opened, and there issued forth before his wondering gaze a group of maidens, escorting another maiden of exquisite beauty, whose graceful dignity, rich attire and many jewels, proclaimed her to be of a higher rank.

The group of maidens at once made their way to the magic tree and began to shake some of the golden apples from its heavily-laden branches, chasing the fruit as it rolled away and playing a lively game with these glittering balls, tossing them high up into the air as they skipped about in a merry dance.

When, however, the young Prince stepped forward from the shadows, they crowded around him at once in surprised admiration and joy. Nevertheless, though delighted to see the handsome youth, they entreated him to depart without delay, declaring him to be in great danger ; and the lovely leader of the group explained that the gloomy castle upon the threshold of which he stood was the abode of the terrible Ogre-Enchanter, Kostchei, who captured and imprisoned all intruders upon his domain and frequently turned them into stone by the touch of his magic green fingers.

But the young Prince had no desire to run away from this certain peril ; for he had already fallen in love with the beautiful royal maiden before him ; and observing that the latter could not resist returning his tender glances, he determined to remain and try to release her and her companions. Therefore, he begged the maidens to continue their charming games and dances, and to permit him to take part in them ; and, during the lively evolutions that followed, he managed to exchange his first kisses of love with their graceful leader.

All too soon, however, these early morning revels came to an end ; and suddenly hearing a sinister tramping of heavy feet drawing near, to the accompaniment of many discordant sounds, the group of maidens, terrified because these sounds heralded the approach of the Ogre, hurriedly returned through the gates by which they had issued forth and vanished from sight.

A sudden darkness then descended upon the scene ; and after groping about frantically for the gate, the young Prince managed to find it and pushed it open boldly.

Instantly there came flashes of blazing light, which brilliantly illuminated the forest and castle gardens ; and a vast stream of the Ogre's slaves and satellites — hobgoblins and evil spirits, driving before them oriental slaves, blackamoors and even cowed knights in armour — poured forth through the gates and flung themselves upon the unfortunate intruder. They did not dare to harm him, however, but merely held him captive until the arrival of their lord and master.

While the black slaves played wild and hideous music upon their gongs, drums and other barbaric instruments, this strange and motley crowd continued to pour forth through the gates. They were followed at length by the lovely Princess and her fair maidens ; and finally there appeared the all-powerful Kostchei himself. At sight of the terrible Ogre-Enchanter, all his satellites prostrated themselves before him in the homage of fear.

Upon beholding the intruder who had dared to invade his domain, the Ogre sprang furiously towards him, spreading out the fatal green fingers that would transform him into stone ; but the brave young Prince, though aware of his imminent danger, did not lose his wits. Before his slave captors could rise from their terrified homage prostration to seize him once more, he plucked forth from his tunic the gleaming feather given him by the Fire-Bird ; and, holding it up aloft, he was glad to see that its magic power caused the fearsome Ogre to fall back in dismay.

The Prince then called upon the Fire-Bird to come to his aid, as promised ; and instantly his exquisite feathered friend reappeared in answer to his cry and flew about him like a flash of flaming fire. At her command the entire ghastly group of satellite attendants, together with their terrible master, began to perform the maddest of mad dances ; and thus magic answered magic. But the beautiful royal maiden who loved the young Prince stood aside with her companions to watch what would be the result of this strange orgy.

When the dancers at last fell to the ground, utterly exhausted, the Fire-Bird soothed them with a dreamy lullaby and gentle movements into a deep slumber — with the exception of the Ogre, who, though too sleepy to move, could still follow her actions with alarm, since her magical powers exceeded his own.

The Fire-Bird now bade the Prince to bring forth a mysterious box from a tree-root nearby, which had served as its hiding-place for many years ; and this casket, on being opened, was seen to contain a huge egg, which its royal holder was next commanded to throw to the ground and break, since it contained the soul of the wicked Enchanter.

Well pleased on hearing this and only too eager to destroy its evil contents, Prince Ivan held the monster egg high up above his head and then dashed it triumphantly to the ground. Instantly, there came a tremendous explosion, followed by lightning flashes and crashing thunder ; and, finally, a smoky darkness blotted out the scene.

Presently, the dark cloud rolled away, and brilliant sunshine took its place ; and it was now seen that the fearsome Kostchei and his evil satellite attendants had all disappeared for ever.

Then, as the young Prince now stepped forward boldly to claim as his bride the beautiful royal maiden he had released, all the stone statues within the castle came to life once more, disenchanted on the destruction of the evil Magician-Ogre into whose toils they had fallen ; and a long train of richly dressed lords, ladies and knights, courtiers, pages and other released captives came joyfully forth through the gates and bowed down gratefully before their royal rescuer, eager to serve him to the end of their days. Other pages and knights now appeared bearing magnificent mantles and royal regalia for the Prince and his lovely bride ; and great rejoicings were held.

And now, having thus redeemed her promise, the dazzling Fire-Bird spread her glittering iridescent wings, and flew away like a flash of fire ; and she was full of joy as she hastened to rejoin her own well-beloved mate, knowing that she had left behind real happiness and peace.

LE PAVILLON D'ARMIDE
(*Armida's Pavilion*)

As the young Vicomte de Beaugency rode through a terrific thunder-storm late one night, on a visit to his *fiancée*, he little dreamt that he was about to become the victim of sorcery. True, he might already be regarded as a victim of Magic — the Magic of Love ; but Sorcery was a different matter and belonged to mediæval times and not to the sober early nineteenth century ; but the events that now befell him were to prove otherwise.

The storm developed rapidly ; and the young traveller having no desire for a further soaking, drew rein at the first mansion he came to — the *Château* of a certain Marquis, who received him with the courtesy of the old *régime* and invited him to spend the night in a pavilion annexe in his grounds.

The storm-bound traveller gratefully accepted the invitation, though he thought it somewhat too eagerly given ; also it seemed strange that he should be asked to sleep in a lonely pavilion instead of in the *château* itself. What was more, his host had a sinister look, though polite and seemingly anxious for his comfort ; but, reluctant to brave the storm and torrential rain again, he was willing enough to accept any kind of shelter.

The Marquis personally escorted his guest to the pavilion, and ordered valets to attend him. He explained that the place was known as the Pavillon d'Armide, because the priceless Gobelins tapestries with which its walls were draped illustrated the classic story of

120

Armida, the famous sorceress Princess of crusading times; then, having seen that the valets had performed their duties, he left the weary guest to his lonely slumbers.

Now, unknown to the latter, this sinister-looking Marquis was a Magician, well versed in the Black Art; and the pavilion into which he had put his unexpected guest was haunted by the phantoms called up by his own enchantments — and he was now only too eagerly about to put his powers to the test once more.

Before stretching himself upon the elegant couch prepared for him, the young Vicomte examined the exquisite Gobelins tapestry that hung upon the wall. As stated by his host, it represented the famous sorceress, Princess Armida, seated amidst her Court and surrounded by admiring courtiers and slaves; and it seemed to him that, as he gazed upon it, a strange glow emanated from the needlework picture and that the lovely enchantress smiled upon him — the same magnetic smile that had caused the admirers of her day to fall beneath the spell of her passionate charm.

Strange to say, centuries later, at the instigation of the sorcerer Marquis, another lover was unwillingly coming within the power of that compelling and enigmatic smile; but, though already enthralled, the young Vicomte struggled as best he could against the irresistible spell. Flinging himself upon the bed and endeavouring to fill his mind with sweet images of his own beloved *fiancée*, he fell, at last, into a fitful, uneasy slumber.

* * * * *

At the hour of midnight, strange things began to happen in the pavilion occupied by the storm-bound traveller. To begin with, two carved statues of Time and Love, which stood as supporters to a giant clock in front of the tapestry, came to life and stepped down from their pedestals, Time reversing his hour-glass, and Love driving him away somewhat against his will.

When Time had vanished, another surprising thing happened. All the Hours likewise came to life and tripped forth from their prison-home in the clock-case like a company of little elves, all dancing about the room in a merry frolic and finally tripping away in the wake of their lord and master, Time, until lost in the storm outside.

No sooner had this charming Dance of the Hours ended than the tapestry glowed with a brilliant light, all its subject figures came to life, and the entire needle-work picture gradually melted and merged into the actual Court of the beautiful Enchantress, Princess Armida. Sweet and seductive music filled the air ; and this, with the sound of laughter and tripping feet, awakened the fitfully-sleeping Vicomte, who sprang to his feet in utter astonishment.

What a brilliant scene from classical times now met his wondering gaze ! The beautiful Princess in her jewelled robes, her dazzling Courtiers and attendant ladies ; her slaves, musicians and dancers ; all were there.

One place only was vacant — the seat of honour beside the throne of the Enchantress, once occupied by her lover, Rinaldo, the all-conquering crusader ; but, in a flash, the young Vicomte himself was magic-ally translated to fill the place of that favoured lord and next moment found himself in the clinging arms of the latter's beautiful mistress. All memories of his own beloved *fiancée* faded away ; and, bewitched by the loveliness and charm of the Enchantress, he gave himself up to the pleasures of this wonderful interlude

Armida now clapped her hands, and slave attendants came and danced before her and her newly-translated lover. One of the male slaves was a superb dancer, and enthralled all who watched his exquisite movements. The lovely Enchantress herself danced ; and with soft allurements, she drew her new lover to her inviting arms, so that the young Vicomte, to his amazement, found himself performing elegant movements such as he had never before dreamed of.

Buffoons and tumblers next took the floor, and amused the company with their comical and intricate antics. Feasting upon delicious foods unknown to the Vicomte, and served on golden dishes, followed presently ; and the richest of wines added to the exhilaration of the company. Lovely ladies flirted with soldiers returned from the wars ; and over all flowed the soft music of enchantment.

Excited by the spells and allurements of the beautiful Enchantress-Princess, a deep passion for her already burned in the breast of the translated Vicomte ; and when, presently, there appeared at the festival King Hydraot, her guardian relative — who was none other than the sorcerer-Marquis likewise translated back to the past by his own arts — he willingly accepted the latter's blessing of their betrothal.

Madly in love with the dazzling Princess, no other outside thoughts intruded upon his spellbound state ; and when the Sorceress bound her richly-embroidered scarf over his shoulders as a further token of her love-power over him, he made no attempt to disentangle himself from its clinging folds.

At the command of the Sorcerer-King, a *Bacchanale* took place as a finale, which quickly developed into an orgy.

Bacchantes, crowned with grapes and vine leaves,

danced wildly around the God of Wine himself, who had now entered, attended by Satyrs and Fauns ; and this Festival of Love and Wine grew madder and more unrestrained with every moment that passed. The Princess and her spellbound lover joined the giddy throng, intoxicated by their own passion ; and both were caught up in the dizzy vortex of the *Bacchanale*.

Then, at last, dawn began to break ; and the enchantments ended. First, the merry little Elfin Hours tripped in once more, and settled into their places in the clock-case ; and Time and Love likewise re-entered and again took up their motionless positions as carven supporters of the giant Clock. All the revellers vanished, and the picture of Armida and her brilliant Court once more became an exquisite curtain of Gobelins tapestry, from which the warm glow slowly faded away. The seductive music was heard no longer ; and the storm-bound traveller was once more seen to be lying on his elegant couch-bed, wrapped in a fitful, restless sleep.

* * * * *

Early next morning the young Vicomte was awakened by the rays of the sun shining in upon him — the tempest of the previous night having long since passed away. Birds were singing and shepherds and shepherdesses passed by the windows of the pavilion, leading their flocks to the pasture grounds.

As the Vicomte hastily arose from his couch, his host, the Marquis, entered the Pavilion, cynically smiling to himself as at the recollection of some secret pleasure ; and his guest shivered with apprehension as he now plainly recognised in him the Sorcerer-King of his recent heathen revels.

He hastily arranged his disordered garments, as though about to leave immediately, being only too eager to depart ; but his sardonic host triumphantly led him to the large Clock, where, across the hands of the sculptured figure of Time, lay the embroidered scarf which Armida had wound about his shoulders during the revel.

Scarcely daring to look, the Vicomte at last raised his eyes fearfully to the tapestry that draped the wall — and saw, to his horror, that the silken trifle was no longer to be seen in the needlework picture. What had passed last night, then, had been no phantom vision, but a living reality. He had been the victim of sorcery ; and as he snatched up the gage of unlawful love, he felt that the spell of the Enchantress would be upon him for ever.

Overcome by this terrible thought, and with a loud cry of woe, the young Vicomte fell back, lifeless, at the feet of the sinister Marquis, who chuckled with unholy joy at the success of his wizardry.

PETROUCHKA

DURING the year 1830, when the mighty Czars were still ruling in Russia, a lively Fair was being held in the famous Admiralty Square of St. Petersburg. It was an afternoon in late winter on the last day of the Butter Week Carnival, just before the serious period of Lenten fasting began. Thick snow still lay on the ground, and the pale wintry sun was already beginning to set.

The jolly throngs of holiday-makers, however, were oblivious of the frosty cold that would presently descend upon them ; and the revelry waxed ever faster and more furious as the daylight faded and the bright flaring lights of the many stalls and booths blazed forth. Gay, popular tunes were played by itinerant musicians for the intricate country dances in which peasants and townsfolk alike took part ; and when they were not dancing and singing or riding on the roundabouts, the merry-makers visited the gingerbread and sweetmeat stalls, or bought the ribbons, beads, and fancy goods that were being offered for sale on every side. There were gipsies present to tell fortunes ; and there were acrobats, tumblers and even dancing bears to amuse all who cared to watch their comical antics.

Prosperous merchants with their wives in rich velvets and long fur coats mingled with the gaily-clad peasants ; and happy groups of children romped about and played games, looking like so many big powder-puffs in their short fluffy fur coats and cosy bonnets.

Amidst all this joyous life and movement, there was one theatre booth in the middle of the square which had not yet been opened to the public. This was a gaily-painted Puppet-Show, and everybody was eager to see the dancing-doll performance about to be exhibited.

When, therefore, a couple of youths arrayed in scarlet and gold as drummer-boys, presently came out into the front of the gaily-painted theatre booth and began to bang noisily on their drums, a crowd of eager sight-seers quickly gathered around.

When the drummer-boys had ceased their lively *rat-a-plan*, they retired to the back of the booth; and, immediately after, the curtains of the theatre front were opened and the Puppet-Master appeared. He was a fantastic and rather sinister-looking person, clad in a long flowing cloak and a tall sugar-loaf hat, both decorated with circles, triangles and other mysterious signs and symbols such as those shown on the robes of the ancient Astrologers. In reality he was a Charlatan, but he advertised himself as a Magician; and he did, indeed, dabble in a certain amount of Magic. Sometimes, however, his amateur magic was apt to become somewhat out-of-hand — as we shall presently see. Nevertheless, he was very skilful as a Puppet-Master, and he could make his puppets perform the most astounding antics to entertain an audience.

After this most extraordinary person had announced himself boastfully as the greatest Puppet-Master in the world, who had power even to bring his puppets to life, he played a weird little tune upon a flute; then he drew back the inner curtain of his theatre and showed his puppets to the gaping crowd below. There were three of them, each standing limp and motionless on its own pedestal.

The puppet standing in the middle wore the gay dress of a Ballerina. It consisted of a very short frilly

skirt of stiffened tarletan, with long lace-edged pantalettes showing below ; and a tight little velvet bodice
was neatly fitted above. Her head was crowned with
a fuzzy mop of hair, and she had brightly-painted
cheeks and lips. On one side of this giddy-looking
Ballerina stood Petrouchka, the " Punch" of Russia.
In this present show, however, he was not seen as the
bold comical bully he usually appears to be, but looked
more like a poorly-dressed Pierrot. He had a chalk-
white woe-begone face ; and his clothes were shabby,
consisting of an old cotton coat with very long sleeves,
and widely checked and patched trousers. On the
other side of the dainty Ballerina, however, there
stood a splendid-looking figure known as the Blackamoor, who was dressed magnificently in a glittering
uniform and wore a gaudy Eastern turban around
his black woolly head.

At a wave of their master's magic wand, the three
Puppets suddenly seemed to come to life and began
to dance, each on its own pedestal at first, and then in
an elaborate *ensemble* dance for the three performers.

The audience at first gasped with amazement, and
then clapped their hands with delight ; for they had
never before seen such life-like puppets. And when,
presently, the dolls actually left their pedestals and
tripped down to the front of the stage to dance and act
together like actual human beings, they were more
astonished than ever — and even just a little alarmed.

This Charlatan-Magician of a Puppet-Master seemed
to have put really human movements and attributes
into his puppets, which, while they still had the appearance of mechanical dolls, yet seemed to be as life-like
as anyone in the fair-ground. Did they keep on acting
like human beings when the show was over ? The
wondering audience supposed, however, that the Pup-

pet-Master could control his life-like dummies at will — they certainly hoped so !

But, strange to say, this was just exactly the thing the over-ambitious Charlatan could *not* do. As stated before, his magic did not always work smoothly ; and, today, the puppets seemed to have got out of hand for the time being. Consequently, when the first performance was safely over, he decided to leave them to themselves for an hour or two, hoping they would presently settle down and become normal puppets once more. Accordingly, he shut each one into its own private room behind the theatre front, and hoped for the best.

He was particularly annoyed with Petrouchka, because the latter seemed so miserable. Why couldn't the tiresome puppet be merry and bright like the other two ? As he angrily kicked poor Petrouchka into a safe compartment and slammed the door on him, he began to wish he had never dabbled in magic, after all. He had not expected when he had found himself able to make his dolls so life-like, that they might also develop the feelings and passions of men and women.

But he knew now that this was, indeed, the case. All three were actually behaving as though they were real human beings. They could feel love, and hate, and jealousy ; and they could be miserable or happy.

Petrouchka was certainly the unhappy one ; and tragedy was already awaiting him round the corner.

The reason for Petrouchka's misery was that he had fallen desperately in love with the pretty Ballerina ; but he realised that he was too ugly and ungainly in his movements, and too shabbily dressed, ever to attract her attention. Nevertheless, he longed to see her again, and to tell her how dearly he loved her. Perhaps she might be kind to him after all. But how could he hope to reach her now when the door of his room had been closed by that sinister Puppet-Master ? He had no proper hands, only rough fingerless stumps ; and, in any case, the door had no handle on the inside.

The unhappy puppet began to dash himself against the walls in an attempt to get out of the room. Although it was painted with stars and magic symbols, and even had a picture of the Magician on one side, he did not care whether he damaged it or not ; he kicked and banged at the walls in a frenzied manner, and shrieked aloud as he did so. But his efforts were in vain ; and, presently, he sank to the floor, exhausted.

Then a seemingly miraculous thing happened. The door was suddenly opened from the outside, and in tripped the gay and adorable little Ballerina, dancing daintily on the tips of her toes, curtseying and showing herself off to her admirer — for she liked to be thought beautiful, even though by a shabby, queer-looking puppet such as Petrouchka. She knew, too, that he loved her passionately ; but she did not care two straws for him. She was a born coquette, frivolous and heartless.

Consequently, when Petrouchka, now overjoyed at the mere sight of her, fell on his knees and declared his love, begging her to smile on him, she merely laughed and saucily danced away from him. Then, when he next endeavoured to impress her by exhibiting his really marvellous high jumps and comical twists and turns, she pretended to be alarmed by his antics and ran out of the room, slamming the door once more behind her.

In deeper despair than ever, the unhappy Petrouchka again began to dash himself against the walls and to tear at them in a renewed effort to get out, squeaking aloud as he did so. The walls were not very strong, after all, and at last he managed to find a weak spot and to make a small hole in one of them ; but he was now too much exhausted to do more than try to wriggle a little way through. And there he lay, limp and forlorn, a pathetic figure, waiting for his strength to return.

* * * * *

Meanwhile, in the next compartment, the Blackamoor lay in great luxury on a rich divan, with gorgeous silken cushions piled around him. The walls of his abode were painted in a tropical design ; and a sharply-curved scimitar had been placed in a handy position near the divan.

The Blackamoor, still wearing his magnificent garments, looked rather a fearsome rascal as he lay on his divan, idly playing with a cocoanut, which he tossed high up into the air with glee. Every now and again he would grovel before it in a worshipping attitude as though it were a god. He looked strong and savage.

Just as he was beginning to feel bored with his cocoanut, he also received an unexpected visit from the flirtatious little Ballerina, who came dancing into the room in an even more fascinating manner than when she had exhibited herself to the unhappy Petrouchka. She soon realised that the Blackamoor, though somewhat alarming because of his blackness and savage looks, was likely to be a far more satisfactory admirer than the dismal and shabby puppet next door. How splendidly tall and powerful he was, and how magnificently he was dressed ; and what a richly oriental apartment he lived in ! She did not at first notice the scimitar.

As the charming Ballerina now began to dance her most elaborate and alluring steps to attract him, the Blackamoor was delighted ; for he, likewise, had been deeply in love with her for some time past. What was more, she had already shown signs of admiring him; and he puffed himself out with pride. He, too, was extremely vain. When, presently, he seized her round the waist and invited her to sit on his knee, the Ballerina, though she felt somewhat scared at first, was soon willing to do so. This fine big fellow, she thought, was certainly a lover worth having.

At that moment, however, a loud squeaking and shrieking cry was heard, as some creature came wriggling and tearing its way through a hole in the wall. It was Petrouchka who, now mad with jealousy on beholding his beloved but faithless Ballerina in the arms of the gorgeously-dressed Blackamoor, furiously hurled himself upon his huge and savage rival.

A terrific, but unequal fight followed. The brave little Petrouchka, though weak and, wan as well as passion-torn, stood up to the big bully again and again, eager to prove himself a hero in the eyes of his adored one.

What a forlorn hope was this! The fickle Ballerina was not worthy either of his love or of his fighting prowess. Alarmed at the consequences of her fatal vanity, and fearful for her own safety, she cowered back on the divan as the fight proceeded; and she could only cry out hysterically when the Blackamoor presently seized his scimitar and furiously chased the now terrified and utterly exhausted Petrouchka out of the room to the theatre front and through the curtain into the Square beyond.

* * * * *

Although night had now fallen, the fun of the Carnival Fair was still at its height. The throngs of merry-makers were even bigger and more excited than ever, as they scrambled for a handful of bank-notes which a rich and rather tipsy merchant had just scattered in their midst. A free shower of bank-notes was something to scramble for, indeed! Everybody joined in the hunt, even the owner of the dancing bear.

Then, presently, there came a succession of fearsome shrieks from the Charlatan-Magician's theatre-booth; and, next moment, out rushed the shabby little Petrouchka, closely pursued by the savage Blackamoor, who was furiously brandishing his scimitar on high. These unexpected belligerents were followed by the now terrified Ballerina, who vainly endeavoured to calm the uncontrollable passions she had so carelessly aroused in the breasts of her two lovers.

The scared revellers fell back hurriedly as the tragic trio appeared thus suddenly in their midst; and even as they did so, the Blackamoor brought down his scimitar in a death-blow upon the unfortunate Petrouchka. Then, as his dying victim fell to the ground, the triumphant Blackamoor leaped his way through the half-numbed crowd, and, eagerly followed by the horrified Ballerina, disappeared from sight.

As the quivering Petrouchka breathed his last, the Puppet-Master, who had been hastily summoned, appeared on the scene; and seeing that the revellers were inclined to blame him for the tragedy, he proceeded at once to pacify them. Holding up the now still form of Petrouchka, he showed them that the victim was only a puppet, after all, since sawdust, not blood, was pouring from his gashed body.

The holiday-makers were satisfied and, too tired to worry any more about this last tragic little scene, began to depart for their homes; and soon the fair-ground became empty once more.

Snow began to fall softly as the Charlatan-Magician slowly made his way to the booth entrance, pulling his limp and bedraggled puppet behind him. He did not feel too happy — perhaps he was trying to make up his mind not to dabble in magic any more. If this was the case, his mind was presently made up for him.

Suddenly, as he reached the entrance to the booth, he heard the most unearthly and blood-curdling shrieks, which gradually changed into a triumphantly mocking cry ; and, looking up, he beheld, to his shuddering horror, the pale ghost of the tragic Petrouchka, showering curses upon him from the roof of the booth.

Terrified by this fearsome vision, the Puppet-Master flung down his once suffering doll, and staggered away into the darkness.

SCHEHERAZADE

In the gorgeous harem of Schahriar, King of India and China, one quickly became lost in a sea of rich passionate colour and perfumed air. The King's many beautiful slaves and wives seemed to have stolen all the colours of the rainbow from the skies, and all the intoxicatingly heavy scents of the Orient. Their lovely lissom bodies were scarcely concealed by their voluminous but gauzy draperies and lightly-swathed scarves and veils ; and their chains of jewels sparkled and glistened with their every movement as they reclined on richly gilded divans or sat on tinsel cushions within the many alcoves that were a feature of the room.

But, brilliant and dazzling with colour though the harem was, and despite the murmur of soft, tinkling laughter, there was more than a hint of a sinister note in the actual formation of the vast chamber ; and its perfumed atmosphere was heavily charged with an indefinable sense of coming tragedy. Vast doors of bronze, silver and gold almost panelled one end of the room — leading to what mysterious passages and secret chambers beyond ? And here, no windows let in the free light of day — the splendid softly-lighted hall was but a gilded prison.

At one side of the hall on a mound of piled-up cushions, as though enthroned, sat the great King Schahriar, conversing in low tense tones with his visiting brother, Zeman ; and from the covert glances of suspicion, and even anger, cast upon them by their all-powerful lord, the ladies of the harem gathered that his royal displeasure might be about to fall upon them. A half-suppressed shiver of apprehension passed over some of them — quickly succeeded, however, by renewed smiles and soft laughter, lest such sign of alarm be observed. Could it be that any of their secret misdeeds had become known ?

Their doubts and fears, however, quickly vanished when their lord and master presently announced that he was about to set forth upon a hunting trip ; and, instantly, they all eagerly crowded around him, bringing his equipment, and tumbling over one another in their anxiety to please him as they fastened it upon him. Full of suppressed joy, they thought happily of a day to be spent with their own secret lovers.

All this time, the Chief Wife, Queen Zobeide, loveliest of all that lovely throng, stood slightly apart, half-hidden by an alcove curtain, looking on, slightly contemptuous of the over-anxiety of her, foolish sister-wives to cover their joy and relief at the prospect of their lord's absence for a day. She was a better actress than they ; and the King firmly believed that he was her one and only lover. He revelled in her glorious beauty, she knew ; and he loved her with a passionate intensity never shared by any of the other odalisques. And Zobeide accepted his love with a seemingly equal intensity ; and behind that, surely, he could never imagine that she had room in her heart for another ?

But Schahriar's suspicions of inconstancy in his harem had recently been aroused by his brother, Zeman, now on a visit to him, who had hinted that even the beloved and favoured Queen might also not be beyond doubt ; and with the cruel cunning of an Oriental, he had been persuaded to concoct a plot to discover the truth of what took place in the harem during his absence. His hunting today would be a short event.

As the now suspicious monarch bade farewell to his Queen, he gazed fixedly and even questioningly into her kohl-framed velvet-black eyes ; but Zobeide met the compelling glance unwaveringly, even coldly ; and he departed, still believing that she, at least, was faithful.

When the royal huntsmen had left the magnificent hall, and the sounds of their departure had died away from the courtyard outside, a sigh of deep relief passed over the apparently languishing inhabitants of the harem ; and they languished no longer. Instead, they sprang to their feet and danced gaily around the Chief Eunuch, pretending that they wanted him to dance and play with them.

At first the fat, flabby Eunuch was flattered by their attentions, and let himself be danced about by them until he was too exhausted to frolic any more. But when he discovered, too late, that they had unfastened his belt and stolen his keys from him, he was filled with dismay. He quickly regained them, however ; but the pretty creatures again danced around him, and entreated him to open the bronze panel-doors for them ; and they poured such renewed flattering praises upon him — declaring brazenly that they found him far more charming than their own royal lord and so clever that he could easily hide all their misdoings from the latter — that, at last, he yielded to their demands. As they pointed out, the King was safely away hunting, and their frolics would be over long before he returned. So he opened the heavy panelled doors.

As soon as the doors were opened, there sprang forth a stream of handsome black male slaves, whose glistening limbs were hung with bracelets and chains of gold, and who were splendidly garbed as befitted the household attendants of a great Oriental King.

These dusky youths were the secret lovers of the ladies of the harem ; and, in a moment, each had claimed his own particular partner to join in a dance of delight. Musicians appeared, and a roystering atmosphere immediately settled upon the inhabitants of the harem—from whom all signs of lurking danger had now passed.

The lovely Queen Zobeide still stood apart for a few minutes longer, though she now looked indulgently upon the lively scene ; but, when the last panel-door was opened, her eyes sparkled with eager joy.

With a mighty bound, there now sprang through the opening the handsomest of all the palace slaves — the Queen's own secret lover. He was clad entirely in gold, with a gold scarf wound about his head ; and he was a truly magnificent creature. How different was Zobeide's greeting to this graceful dusky youth from that accorded to her royal lord ! Here was no pretence of love, but love offered freely and as freely accepted.

Zobeide and her lover danced together in an ecstasy of delight ; and, later on, they joined in the revellings of their companions. The revel soon developed into an orgy ; and the dancing became wilder with every moment that passed. The long-pent-up emotions of the captive performers were expressed in every passionate movement ; and the scene took on the unrestrained aspect of a *bacchanale*, in which the dancers became merged in a whirling mass of vivid rainbow colours and writhing limbs.

It was a Dance of Joy — a passionate joy so intense that the performers, free for those glorious moments, felt themselves wafted to the heavens above. But, all too soon, they were brought back to earth ; and the Dance of Joy ended in a Dance of Death.

Suddenly, and without any sound of warning, the

outer doors were burst open ; and the great King Schahriar, attended by his brother, Zeman, and armed royal guards, appeared on the threshold, his eyes flashing and his face flaming with anger at the sight that met his gaze. He had, at the suggestion of his brother, returned from the hunt soon after it had begun — to find his suspicions confirmed, and his harem a wanton one.

As the terrified women and slaves drew back with cries of horror, each seeking in vain for a hiding-place, their terrible doom came upon them. At the stern command of their lord and master, the royal guards drew their flashing scimitars and fell upon the now despairing revellers ; and, in a few moments, the lovely odalisques and their black slave lovers lay dead upon the floor. The Golden Negro was the last to be struck down.

But Zobeide still stood apart, proud and unafraid ; and when Schahriar seized her in his arms and fiercely demanded assurances of her own fidelity, she continued to gaze fearlessly into his blazing eyes.

And Schahriar breathed a sigh of deep relief : so his beautiful and passionately beloved Queen, at least, was faithful to him amidst all her false sister-wives ! He clasped her in his arms, and thrilled with joy as her hands caressed his body and her kisses fell upon his lips.

It was a moment of ecstasy — but a moment only. The royal visitor, Zeman, now kicked over the dead body of the handsome dusky slave, clad in gold and still wearing the jewelled favours of his royal mistress ; and he pointed contemptuously to him as the lover of the Queen. Schahriar loosed the latter from his embrace with a cry of horror and disappointed rage.

Zobeide could no longer deny her guilt ; but she

would not permit herself to be slain as a slave. Before the royal guards could rush upon her with their raised scimitars, she snatched a dagger from one of the nearest of them ; and, proud and fearless to the last, she plunged it into her breast and fell dead at the feet of her deceived and heart-broken royal lord.

THE SPECTRE OF THE ROSE
(*Le Spectre de la Rose*)

CAN a picture speak to you? Imagine, then, a fair young girl's bedroom, on a glorious perfumed night in June. A dainty room, mostly virginal white and soft blues in its decorative scheme; its simple dressing-table, neatly but sparsely furnished, as befitted a presiding deity needing no artificial aids to her natural youthful beauty; its small white bed invitingly open in readiness for the expected occupant.

For the room at present was unoccupied; and its large french windows were wide open to permit the scented air to enter from the garden beyond. Outside there were roses everywhere, climbing around the windows and swarming in clustering masses on the bushes and standards in the adjacent plots.

It was midsummer, and the night sky was of a clear almost ultramarine blue, with silvery moonlight casting a lace-work tracery all around.

The sweet intoxicating scent of roses pervaded the bedroom, almost as though wafted therein by rose-petalled sprites from the very hearts of the blossoms themselves. The short summer night was at the height of its perfumed beauty, with the early dawn not too far away; and the garden was as a jewelled Dream-Garden.

A gentle breeze stirred the dew-spangled roses clustering around the open windows; and, at that same moment, a beautiful young girl entered the bedroom and softly closed the door behind her. She had just returned from her first ball and was dressed entirely

141

in white gauzy draperies, her own sweet and virginal beauty more than compensating for the simplicity of her attire. But she carried in her hand a deep red rose, which, as she pressed it closely to her heart, brought a vivid splash of colour into the picture — the colour of Love.

She had, indeed, glimpsed Love on this evening of her first ball ; and the crimson rose she now held so carefully and tenderly in her hand had been placed there by one whom she knew to be the ideal lover of her girlish dreams.

The young girl softly kissed the rose, and sighed with the satisfying contentment of one who has felt the dawning of life's deepest joy for the first time. How happy she already was ; but how weary, too ! Almost too weary to seek her bed — inviting though its open cool whiteness looked.

No, not yet ! She would enjoy first a sweet waking dream, going over, as in actual vision, each wonderful and lovely moment of the last few hours of enchantment —his whispered words of admiration ; his first lover's kiss, the memory of which still stirred her to the utmost of her being and filled her with ecstasy.

She slipped gladly into an arm-chair as these happy thoughts came crowding into her tired brain ; but scarcely had she sunk into its comfortable depths than, overcome by her physical weariness, she softly fell into a deep slumber, taking her Love Dream with her.

The crimson rose lightly fell from her relaxed hand to the ground beside her. Did it waft a perfumed message as it fell ?

* * * * *

Was that a Spirit form lightly moving in the moonlit garden beyond, among the whispering leaves and the dewy roses ? Did the sleeping girl's awakened soul reach out to the Spirit of the crimson rose love-gage at her feet — that lost Rose-Spirit now wandering in the scented air outside and awaiting the magical transformation only possible in a June summer night's dream? Who knows?

Suddenly the soft breeze stirred more strongly, and upon its airy-fairy crest the Spirit of the Rose leapt into the room through the open window, light as thistle-down — an ethereal being clad in rose-petalled garb, but the beloved image of the young girl's dream!

As though still wafted upon the summer night breeze, the Rose-Spirit danced blithely hither and thither, his joyous movements creating an atmosphere of the sweet abandonment and utter rapture of Love.

Presently, as though a winged creature, he seemed to hover and then actually to alight at the feet of the sleeping form of the young girl; and, bending over her, he kissed her lightly on the lips — a kiss that awakened her soul to the joy of a beloved presence and lured her gladly into his inviting arms, to dance with him as with her lover at the ball just ended.

Is she really awake; or is she dreaming still? The deep arm-chair is certainly empty; and she is as certainly clasped in her Dream-Lover's arms. Together, in enraptured silence, they dance airily about the room, now floating rather than springing high into the air, and now gliding as on the smooth crest of a wave, their dual steps merging as one in the perfect rhythm they had so magically felt at the ball. But that rhythm had been a rapture of the body, whereas this was a rapture of the spirit — intangible, yet the strongly-felt and exquisite enchantment of a brief encounter in Paradise.

Swaying together in each other's arms in the graceful movements of a waltz, and to the strains of most entrancing music — surely breathed into their ears by Elysian musicians in league with the God of Love ?— how the enraptured lovers longed for their Dream Dance to last for ever — to dance thus joyously to- gether through Life, through Death, throughout Eternity ! Here was true Beauty, nay, Truth itself ! The one moment of perfect Joy !

But such ecstasy cannot be held for ever. Dawn was already at hand ; and this brief Rose-Dream must end. The hour of perfect Joy was over.

Trembling with the fervour of his delight, the Rose- Spirit again seemed to hover over the chair as he gently released his beloved one into its depths, his rose-petalled garment fluttering as he bent over her with the soft caressing movements of farewell.

Then, as the first breezes of awakening dawn rose from a gentle rustle almost to a rushing wind, the Spectre of the Rose leapt lightly with it and vanished through the window into the shadowy garden beyond.

* * * * *

The young girl was alone once more, sleeping calmly and sweetly, as though first Love had never awakened her youthful heart, her soft hands drooping limply over her white gauzy gown, the crimson rose still making a vivid splash of colour at her feet.

Slowly the slight chill of early dawn awakened her ; and she opened her eyes in surprise at finding herself still resting in the chair, instead of in her little white bed. But gradually the happy memory of her first ball returned, and a tender smile crossed her face as she thought of her youthful admirer thereat. Then, too, came the memory of her rapturous dream, in which she had been enfolded in the arms of this same lover — transformed into the Rose-Spirit of the crimson blossom he had himself kissed and laid in her hand.

Had she not just glimpsed Paradise with him as they danced in rhythmic movements to the sweet tuneful notes of Elysian musicians ? Then let her dream again.

She gently picked up the crimson rose given to her by her lover of the ball — surely, it was a Rose of Enchantment that had wafted her on to this further ecstasy ? She pressed it closely to her lips once more, and wished upon it — the wish that she might soon be clasped in the arms of her Dream Lover, the Spectre of the Rose, and dance again with him to Paradise.

LES SYLPHIDES
(*The Sylphs*)

On a dazzling moonlit night, a romantic young Poet went to seek solitude and to meditate amidst the ruins of an ancient monastery in an exquisite sylvan glade. Dark yew trees and tall cypresses stood as sentinels beside the crumbling ruins ; and a thick carpet of emerald-green moss, spangled with starry flowers, was spread at the feet of the intruding stranger.

Though he had thought to meditate alone and undisturbed in the silence of this delectable spot, the young Poet's imagination would not permit him to do so. Too many life-stories had been enacted and buried there in bygone days ; and the sylvan glade was full of magical memories brought thither by the dead and gone inhabitants of the monastery. Even those monks of olden times had been young once ; and, before they had shut themselves away from the outside world, they had known the joys of love and romance. The memories of such delights must have remained with them, despite their sombre habits ; for Love is immortal and lingers on in dreams and waking visions.

The young Poet soon began to think of long-parted lovers ; and, in his vivid imagination, he even believed he saw them actually coming to life once more. This, then, was no place for a seeker after solitude, since it soon became peopled with ethereal beings called into existence by his own poetic fancy.

At first, the moonbeams, stealing so softly among the shadows, were moonbeams only ; but, presently, they began to take on the lovely shapes of sylph-like beings gliding hither and thither and dancing together in a joyous reunion. They were moonbeams no longer, but Sylphides, the gentle spirits of departed lovers, many of whom had died for love in years gone by.

As the young man watched these moonbeam maidens, clad in gossamer white, with little silvery wings at their waists, the magical enchantment of the scene became more and more vivid, until he felt himself to be actually a part of it. One of the exquisite sylphides came and leaned softly upon his shoulder, as though he were, indeed, her lover of bygone days ; and as he held her thus in a light embrace, their white-robed companions danced around them, weaving in and out in an ever-changing graceful pattern.

These ethereal beings held their white arms curved above their flower-wreathed heads, or slightly bent them forward as though embracing other spirits hidden from view ; and the moonlight cast a silvery mist over their floating forms from time to time. When, presently, they sank back to rest awhile, they looked like a bank of snow-white flowers. But these white flowers had sweet pale faces, framed in hair as dark as the night ; and their sad dewy eyes shone like stars.

And now the young Poet found himself dancing with the gentle spirit form that had so tenderly clung to him ; and it seemed as though they were floating together in the soft night air, as light as thistledown — spirit lovers wafted hither and thither in an ecstasy of joy. The sweetest music sounded in his ears — the music of one who had known sadness more than joy ; and every note he heard and every movement he made with his ethereal partner was one of beauty and delight.

Presently, his airy-fairy companion drew him aside, and rested lightly upon his shoulder, as before, while the other sylphides arose from their flowery banks and continued their rhythmic movements once more, weaving and inter-weaving like an endless chain of white lilies. Sometimes the chain would seem to dissolve, and two or three of the living flowers would float apart to perform graceful movements by themselves ; and sometimes, the dreamy Poet's own lover-sylph would leave his side and dance alone. Then he would himself float away for a few moments with one of the other moon maidens, or dance alone until his own lovely sylph returned to his arms once more.

And so it went on, like a dancing dream of phantom forms and rhythmic patterns, all bathed in silvery moonlight and moving to the sound of fairy music ; and the romantic young Poet longed to remain for ever with this rapturous vision his vivid imagination had created for him.

But the silvery moonbeams began to fade, for the night was already ending ; and with dawn the lovely phantoms must vanish. It would be sad to see his awakening, wouldn't it ? So, let us leave him now, while he is still enfolded in the magic cloak of his ecstatic fancy.

His spirit lover is again resting her wreathed head lightly upon his shoulder ; and her companion sylphides have grouped themselves gracefully in a half-circle around her, motionless like sleeping flowers. The crumbling moonlit ruins make a mysterious background for this exquisite picture ; and as the thrilling notes of slow soft music steal forth once more to pluck at our heart-strings, we, too, are brought irresistibly into the Land of Enchantment and Romance.

THAMAR

THAMAR, the beautiful, voluptuous, but cruel Queen of Georgia in ancient' barbaric times, lay resting one day in a half slumber upon her luxurious couch in an upper chamber of her castle stronghold. She was surrounded by attendants, slaves and armed guards.

The chamber was a magnificent one, with rich, heavy cloth-of-gold curtains ; and priceless rugs, cushions, and rainbow draperies were scattered lavishly on every side, while bronze and gilded hanging lamps shed a subdued mysterious light over all. The slaves and women attendants were all richly clad ; and the guards wore splendid armour and carried glittering weapons.

The scene was barbaric in the extreme ; and despite the fact that musicians were playing soft subdued music on strange instruments while their mistress rested, there was a sinister suggestion in these scarcely restrained sounds, as though at any moment the music might blare forth into a wild clash of discordant notes — a clamour that would easily drown even human cries of anguish.

Indeed, the whole atmosphere of this luxurious apartment was sinister, with an undercurrent of lurking tragedy. Nor was this strange, for Thamar, though superbly beautiful, was a Queen of evil reputation. In order to feed her insatiable passion for unlawful love, she kept constant watch from this high-turreted chamber in her castle tower upon the hilly passes below and lured to their doom unwary travellers who came wandering by or ventured within hail of her signals. No such travellers who thus came within her castle walls evermore issued forth alive. True, she received them graciously, feasted them lavishly and eagerly accepted their unfailingly proffered love for a few hours ; but when their caresses palled, she ruthlessly slew them with her own hands.

This evening, while she rested from a recent orgy, her slave maidens kept watch from the turret window, while an uneasy gloom deepened upon the faces of the other inhabitants of the luxurious room — for they all had their part to play in every new event or carousal, and woe betide any who failed to give satisfaction !

Suddenly, the watchful slave's vigil was rewarded ; and she lightly touched her already awakening royal mistress on the shoulder. A traveller was approaching. Instantly, the Queen, eager for a new victim, hastened to the open window and waved therefrom a blood-red scarf three times ; then she withdrew it, and a cruel smile of triumph parted her scarlet lips. Her signal of invitation had been acknowledged.

Apathy vanished from the faces of the inmates of the gilded chamber with the bustle of eager preparation ; and the Queen sent forth three of her warriors to bring the expected guest into her presence.

Soon the guards returned with the stranger — a handsome young man of high degree, who entered with eager curiosity to learn what the intriguing scarf signal from the window might mean. He had only too willingly followed the guards into the castle — persuaded that probably some fair maiden in distress awaited his aid within.

He soon understood the truth, however, that no Knight Errant was required here ; but he did not regret answering the scarf signal. The lovely Queen received him graciously ; and as she gazed passionately and compellingly into his eyes, he instantly fell under the spell of her voluptuous beauty and an answering passion held him in thrall.

A table spread with oriental sweetmeats and goblets of rich fiery wine had been placed beside the Queen, who bade him drink and watched him unceasingly over the edge of her own goblet. Nor did the dazzled youth remove his own eager eyes from this unexpected vision of loveliness; and he soon began to offer his royal hostess the caresses of a passionate lover.

But the cunning Thamar, desirous of adding fuel to the fire of his passion by holding him aloof for the moment, clapped her hands; and instantly her slave attendants, male and female, began to dance. At first they moved with languorous steps; but when the music gradually changed to a more sensuously passionate rhythm, a wild note of abandon took possession of them, and their actions developed accordingly.

Then the Queen, with a look of alluring enticement, joined in the dance herself; and, in a flash, the young traveller had reached her side and was moving with her in his close embrace. Thamar's passion now matched his own: and as the music likewise rose to a frenzy of passion, the lips of these so recently-made lovers met and clung in an ecstasy of delight. A moment later, the Queen suddenly slipped from his arms; then, almost with a touch of coquetry as she noted with satisfaction the fever of desire that consumed him, she hastened through a door leading to an inner apartment. But her backward glances still lured him irresistibly; and, with an eager bound, he followed her instantly.

The dances of the revellers left behind now quickly developed into a mad orgy; and the music, though it followed the mood of the dancers for a short time, began to take on a wilder note and to become discordant with the harsh clashing of cymbals, beating of drums and booming and twanging of barbaric instruments, as though leading up to some dreadful climax.

It was. The long-experienced musicians knew exactly what their royal mistress required of them ; and their music inexorably increased in intensity until the last moment of the tragedy was reached.

When the passion-inflamed youth staggered forth from the inner chamber, he was quickly followed by the woman who had so ruthlessly enthralled him ; but it was a changed Thamar who now rejoined him in the bacchanalian dance still in progress. Sated, and already tired of her victim, the beautiful Vampire Queen now revealed only her other ruling passion — the passion of sadistic cruelty. At a signal from her, the guards flung back a heavy panelled door that led direct into open space, beyond which could be seen the glistening angry waters of a mighty river rushing past the cliff-like rocks upon which the castle was built ; and at the same time she drew forth a dagger which had been concealed in her robe.

Both actions were unobserved by the passion-intoxicated youth who still held her in his arms with feverish joy, seeing only the scarlet lips that smiled so enchantingly close to his own — those false but sweet pomegranate lips he was about to taste for the last time. He had forgotten his world of a few hours back, and all it held of adventure for him ; and he was living only in the ecstasy of the present moment's bliss. Little did he dream that the end of that magic moment was at hand.

Presently, the interlocked dancing lovers reached the panel opening ; and suddenly, with a last fierce kiss, Thamar raised her arm and plunged her dagger unerringly into the heart of her victim. She stood for a moment motionless as the dying body of her lover-victim fell backwards through the open space and vanished into the raging torrent below; then, as the panel door was quickly closed once more, she wearily returned to her couch near the window, and calmly composed herself to slumber amongst her silken cushions.

The dancing ceased and the wild music dwindled to a soft murmur; the armed guards stood back against the walls and remained there like ebony statues; the slave attendants arranged themselves in sleepy groups around the couch of their royal mistress; and one wakeful maiden kept watch at the open turret window.

And, thus, the few remaining hours of the night passed by. Then, as the sun began to rise in a splendour of rose and gold, there came a movement from the maiden watcher at the window. Another stranger was approaching. The Vampire Queen awakened and moved eagerly to the turret window; and gracefully she waved forth her blood-red scarf three times — and yet once again her fatal signal of invitation and allurement was answered!

THE DRYAD*

*The Ballet upon which this story is based was made famous by Madame Adeline Genée.

ONCE there lived a fair Dryad, who was the most beautiful of all the Woodland Nymphs. So exquisite was this Nymph that every mortal who beheld her fell under the magic spell of her charming graces.

So entrancing was the Dryad that Aphrodite, the Goddess of Love and Beauty, became extremely jealous of her. How dare a mere Nymph of the Woods charm mortals with her artless beauty — which was, after all, as nothing compared with that of the Goddess of Love and Beauty ! The angry Goddess would permit no rival ; and if this fair Dryad had the temerity to charm so many mortals, she must be taught a lesson.

So the beautiful Dryad was captured by the powerful Aphrodite ; and, as a punishment, she was shut up as a prisoner in an oak tree. Her piteous appeals for mercy so far softened the heart of the jealous Goddess that the latter consented to allow her to come forth from the oak tree once in every ten years, and to remain in the open woodlands for the hours between sunrise and sunset on one summer's day. If, during those few hours of respite she could discover a mortal lover who would remain faithful to her until her next day of freedom ten years hence, then her captivity should end. If, however, this mortal lover should prove unfaithful, then her life within the oak tree must last for ever.

And with this slender proviso the captive Dryad

had to be content ; and the next ten years, therefore, she spent imprisoned within the dark oak tree, looking forward to her one day of liberty.

At last the happy day arrived ; and the released Dryad came forth into the open air once more. From sunrise to sunset, she was free to enjoy the fresh air and the sunshine. How lovely the woodlands were ; and how joyously she skipped about and danced in and out among the trees, listening to the songs of the birds and chasing the butterflies.

Her charm and her beauty were as great as ever ; and when, presently, a handsome young shepherd beheld her gaily dancing towards him, he very promptly fell in love with her. His love was quickly returned by the Dryad ; and the happy pair spent the whole day dancing and singing together, or in wandering hand-in-hand through the woodland glades.

Then, as the hour of sunset drew near and the Dryad knew she must shortly return to her oak-tree prison, she told 'the shepherd of the sad fate awaiting her and entreated him to remain faithful to her during the next ten years, so that she might then regain her lost freedom and live with him for ever afterwards.

The handsome young shepherd swore that he would indeed continue to love her truly with all his heart until she next appeared before him at the trysting-place they had just chosen together ; and, with a last passionate embrace, the lovers separated as the sun set in the rosy West. Then the Dryad sadly departed to her oak-tree prison, where she was compelled to remain for another ten years.

But, this time, the long years passed more quickly, because she knew she was beloved and that her shepherd lover would be there ready to greet her on her next emergence.

After this second decade had passed away, the Dryad again issued forth with joy in her heart ; and she danced away lightly and gaily through the woodlands to the emerald-green mossy glade which was the trysting-place chosen by her lover and herself. Was her handsome shepherd already there, impatiently awaiting her arrival and singing a sweet love-song to greet her as she drew near ? He was not ! Ah, well, he would be coming soon ; and she would dance until he sprang forth from the bushes and clasped her in his loving arms !

But, when her dance of joy came to an end, her lover had still not come to the trysting-place ; and though the beautiful Dryad waited there for him all day long, he still did not come. For, ten years is a long time ; and the handsome shepherd had forgotten his promise to her and had found a new and more easily accessible sweetheart !

Then presently she heard him singing behind some trees ; and her heart gave an esctatic bound, as she eagerly awaited his approach. But when the shepherd at last appeared in sight, he only passed by on his way with a jaunty step, still singing his gay little song. He no longer loved her, and did not mean to keep the tryst !

Heart-broken and full of despair, the unhappy Dryad knew now that she was doomed again to be a captive ; and as the hour of sunset had already come, she was once more drawn into the darkness of her oak-tree prison — there to dream sadly of her faithless lover.

MR. PUNCH

MR. PUNCH was idling as usual and amusing himself in the open space outside his brightly-painted house. He himself was quite as gaily-decorated as the house — indeed, he looked as though his tailor had been very busy and lavish with a paint-box before sending this famous customer's clothes home. One of his trouser legs was scarlet and the other yellow ; and his tunic-top likewise showed rainbow tints of blue, green, yellow, red and white. Even his face and long nose looked as though they had been well daubed with scarlet paint.

He was certainly a very brilliantly-coloured rascal — and rascal was the correct word to apply to Mr. Punch, who was well-known to be unscrupulous, sly, irresponsible and as full of comical tricks as a cartload of monkeys. But he was a jolly rascal, nevertheless ; and he always seemed to be in a mischievous mood, and loved to tease everybody he came in contact with.

Just now he was bent on teasing his long-suffering dog, Toby, who was sitting near the doorstep, watching his rascally master with every sign of loving devotion—also with a little apprehension, since he never knew whether he would be treated well or ill. Despite the fact, however, that he received as many kicks as ha'pence, he adored his unique master and regarded him as a sort of hero — if a somewhat disreputable one. He was a quaint-looking white dog, with mournful eyes ; and he wore a gaily-coloured ruffle around his neck, to match the rainbow tints of Mr. Punch.

It was lucky for Dog Toby that he was on the alert, as usual : for his mischievous master suddenly made up his mind to have a rough-and-tumble with him. He pulled his tail, rolled him over and over, and made him jump and dance about with him on his hind-legs. Then he roughly pushed him aside as suddenly as he had begun the frolic ; and patient Toby returned to his former position, and rested his head on his paws, somewhat breathless after his gymnastic exercises. He was a very philosophical dog.

Punch was soon ready for a little more excitement ; and he quickly got it. His termagant wife, Judy, came flouncing out of the house, carrying her baby in her arms ; and, as usual, she began scolding her rascally husband for his idleness. Judy was a tall, skinny dame, entirely devoid of feminine charm ; and she was dressed in a most fantastic manner, and could boast of as many bright colours in her attire as could her husband.

Punch was quickly annoyed by his wife's scoldings ; but he decided to prove his usefulness by dandling and playing with the baby for awhile. Judy, however, did not see eye to eye with him on this matter ; and she flatly refused to give up her baby into the dangerous charge of such an erratic nurse.

But Punch was determined to have his way ; and he chased his scolding wife hither and thither, and had a great tussle with her for possession of his offspring — the unfortunate infant being nearly torn asunder in the struggle. At last, however, the eager rascal managed to snatch the baby from the hands of Judy — who then flounced back into the house in a state of high dudgeon.

The triumphant Mr. Punch now dandled the baby in his arms for awhile, rocking it jerkily to and fro, and playing with its long nose — which was a replica of his own in miniature ; and at first he seemed to enjoy being a nursemaid. But, presently, the baby became fractious, and its erratic parent quickly lost patience with it and grew wild. He tossed the baby high up into the air and caught it again several times ; then he shook it violently, and spun round and round with it held by the hem of its long gown. Finally, as this rough treatment made the unlucky baby more fractious than ever, he fell into a rage and dashed its head on the ground many times until it ceased to breathe.

For a few moments Punch seemed sobered by the crime he had committed ; and then his exuberant good spirits returned, and he rejoiced at having rid himself of his squalling brat. He picked up the little corpse gingerly, and tossed it callously into the street beyond ; then, returning, he began to dance a merry jig.

His untimely revel was a short one, for the irate Judy soon reappeared, stormily demanding to be given back her baby. Suspecting what had happened from her rascally husband's hang-dog demeanour, she looked out into the street and saw the small body lying on the pavement. Rushing back into the house, she returned instantly with a large rolling-pin, with which she began wildly to belabour Punch ; but she soon received more than she gave. The now thoroughly enraged rogue turned round on her and began to rain heavy blows upon her instead ; and though a truly comical chase and struggle ensued, it ended in another tragedy. The termagant Judy soon fell to the ground in a dead heap — falling in a most ludicrous position, with her two " bloomer "-clad legs sticking straight up in the air.

Punch surveyed his second victim even more gloomily than he had done his first ; then, realising his freedom from a scolding wife, he again began to dance for joy — little dreaming that retribution was likely to fall upon him. But Nemesis was nigh.

It happened that his opposite neighbour, another

rascal of a fellow known as Scaramouche, discovered the dead body of the baby in the street; and, picking it up, he rushed back to confront Punch with the crime — having no doubt as to its author. He was, however, horrified to find another victim lying on the ground; and, drawing out a dagger, he moved around the deliriously gyrating figure, hoping to despatch him suddenly. But the boot was quickly on the other leg. The wily Punch saw him coming, and instantly began to chase the now scared Scaramouche and quickly drove him off.

Mr. Punch now retired into his house for a few moments to recover his breath; and during his absence the officers of the law entered the courtyard and bore off the two dead bodies, intending shortly to return and capture the murderer.

The latter, however, felt no alarm at the moment, having always been able to depend on his own bright wits to get him out of even the worst scrapes; and, presently, he emerged once more from his house in the most hilarious spirits and chuckling heartily at his own cleverness in having rid himself of his troublesome encumbrances.

Just then, his latest sweetheart, Pretty Polly, appeared on the scene; and Punch, delighted at the thought of a flirtation, began to dance about with her, and to fondle her to his heart's content, without fear of awkward consequences from a jealous wife. What was more, Pretty Polly seemed to enjoy his somewhat rough attentions and to reciprocate his obvious pleasure in her company; for Mr. Punch, despite his well-deserved shocking reputation, was a gay, jovial fellow, full of frolicsome fun.

She did not, of course, yet know of his recent bad deeds; and when Punch presently went off for a moment and came back riding on a hobby-horse, she was willing enough to join in the fun once more, and to continue her coquettish flirtation. When, however, by means of some clever trick, the hobby-horse seemed to come to life and to chase them both, she became scared and ran away.

Next moment, Punch, too, was scared when the hobby-horse galloped up and began to kick him ; and he fell to the ground, temporarily knocked out. It happened that a Doctor, dressed in a long black gown, was passing by, and came fussing up to render first-aid ; but when his seemingly dead patient suddenly jumped up and began to dance about once more, very much alive, the leech was likewise scared and quickly hurried away.

At this moment Scaramouche returned and, drawing forth his knife once more, again attempted to catch Punch unawares ; but, as before, the ever-alert rogue saw him coming and this time dealt him a mighty blow that knocked him unconscious.

By this time, the hue and cry after the murderer was in full swing ; and a couple of policemen now came hurrying up to arrest Punch. The latter, however, was ready for them ; and after a rough-and-tumble fight, he knocked them both silly and sent them heavily to the ground beside Scaramouche.

Thinking himself safe at last, Punch now strolled aside to play with his dog for a moment — and he thought it strange when Toby suddenly turned and scampered off, as though he, too, felt scared.

There was a good reason, however, for the dog's unusual action ; for the two policemen and Scaramouche were no longer seemingly dead but had recovered their lost senses once more and were already on their feet, stealthily stalking their prey. Next moment, all three of them sprang vigorously upon the back-turned Punch

— for once off his guard — and triumphantly bore him off on their shoulders to prison.

* * * * *

Mr. Punch felt extremely dismal behind prison bars, awaiting his exit from life as a murderer. Nor did he feel any more cheerful when he was almost immediately visited by Jack Ketch, the famous hangman, complete with black mask and long dangling rope, who grimly bade him prepare for his well-deserved end.

The now thoroughly alarmed captive fell on his knees and begged for mercy ; but the hangman's only reply to his plea was to lead him to the place where the gibbet had been set up. When, however, Jack Ketch fixed the rope in a noose upon the gibbet in readiness for the execution, a sly little plan came into the fertile brain of the wily Punch. He pretended to be ignorant of hanging procedure, and humbly begged Ketch to show him exactly how he should place his head in the noose ; and the foolish hangman, conceitedly pleased to show off how his horrible apparatus worked, willingly enough placed his own head in the noose.

Then, quick as lightning, sly Punch sprang forward and jerked the rope tight with all his might ; and, next moment, Jack Ketch himself was dangling at the top of the gibbet, instead of his captive — and clever Mr. Punch escaped back to his home, dancing and laughing all the way.

* * * * *

Dog Toby was delighted to welcome his master back home once more, safe and sound ; and he and Mr. Punch enjoyed a most hilarious game together.

But, all too soon, the dog again began to shiver with fright ; and he slunk away to hide as there came a sudden loud bang and a vivid flash of lightning, followed by a cloud of sulphurous smoke. This heralded the arrival of the Devil, who had come at last to claim his own.

But, here again, things did not go according to plan. Bold Mr. Punch offered battle to his sinister, trident-brandishing visitor ; and a mad chase took place in and out of the house windows and doors, and round and about the courtyard.

Finding his intended victim thus so elusive and valiantly determined to stand up against him, the surprised infernal visitor tried other tactics. Raising his trident on high, he caused the once familiar forms of the murderer's own victims to appear as gibbering ghosts which surrounded and menaced him — the ghosts of the hangman, Scaramouche and Judy. Even the tiny ghost of the long-nosed baby hovered for a few moments in mid-air, as though temporarily suspended from the heavens above ; and then it was drawn up again.

But, though these ghastly visions did, indeed, scare Mr. Punch very considerably, they did not put him off his present job — that of defying his unwelcome visitor from the nether regions. Again he attacked the latter violently ; and finally succeeding in disarming him of his most unpleasant sharply-stabbing trident, he thus rendered him helpless and finally knocked him out entirely — with the result that the Devil, defeated and rueful, suddenly vanished from sight again amidst thunder, lightning and clouds of sulphur-laden smoke.

Having thus overcome — temporarily, at least — his last dread enemy, Mr. Punch gaily welcomed his returning dog ; and he and Toby danced and kicked up their heels with joy at his escape, turning somersaults, and hugging one another with the utmost abandon.

Has anyone ever heard of a luckier and more undeserving rascal than Mr. Punch ?

THE BIRDS

IN a lovely Chinese garden glade, an amusing little comedy was taking place. The scene itself was so exquisite that it seemed to have come straight from the *crêpe* pages of a Chinese fairy-tale book — or, perhaps, from a dainty porcelain tea-cup without a handle, or even from a fan unfurled by a Princess of the Ming dynasty.

The most unbotanical-looking tall trees and rounded shrubs rose stiffly on all sides ; and upon them hung strange but exotic fruits and flowers of many colours — pink, blue, crimson, rose, yellow, mauve, jade, amber. The mossy carpet of the glade vanished into a dim, misty-blue vista, spangled with flowers ; and soft golden sunlight cast the magic of summer warmth upon the whole scene. It was just one of those charmingly unlikely garden-glades seen in the Fairyland of Dreams ; and it proved exactly the right setting for the quaint little Bird Fantasy now to be told.

A beautiful Dove, as he circled and wheeled about this colourful glade of flowering, fruitful trees, had seen and fallen in love with a wonderful lady Nightingale. True, the Nightingale was by no means a spectacular bird and could boast of no brilliant plumage ; but she was neat and trim, and modest in her demeanour, and her voice was the sweetest and most melodious of all the singing birds. Her thrilling notes, indeed, would have charmed a dragon from its lair ; and they had completely won the heart of the romantic Dove. He flew round about the tall tree where his lady-love poured forth her liquid notes ; but she was too shy and retiring to show herself frequently in answer to her admirer's soft "coo-roo-roo," and would even fly away from him at times. When she did this, the disappointed Dove would become quite melancholy ; and then he would return to the glade and mope a little while.

But the Dove was never allowed to mope for long ; for he was constantly pestered by the unwelcome attentions of an extremely forward barnyard Hen, who had strayed into the glade in search of Romance — oh, yes, Romance spelt with a large capital R ! What was more, she had found it instantly on first beholding the melancholy love-lorn Dove — despite the fact that she soon learned of his passion for the Nightingale.

Though really a very unromantic-looking fowl herself, she felt that she was quite as attractive a bird as that plain little Nightingale clad in russet-brown. So she fluffed out her own mingled plumage and made her small top-knot as bright a red as she could — oh, how she longed for her barnyard lord's fine scarlet comb !— and set herself the task of cutting out her modest rival.

Whenever the Dove appeared in the glade, she followed him about, rolling her bright eyes at him, flapping her wings and striking unusual attitudes of all kinds.

So comical were the Hen's antics that they caused immense amusement to a couple of cheeky Sparrows who often perched on a rustic fence nearby ; and these pert little brownies — the guttersnipe urchins of the feathered world — laughed and chirped immoderately and capered about in derision as they watched her ridiculous attempts at love-making.

The Hen's outrageously eager advances were, however, most unwelcome to the Dove, who simply hated being so blatantly chased by her; and he always tried his best to elude his barnyard admirer. How different were her ludicrous posturings from the graceful, retiring demeanour of the simple Nightingale, he thought; and how truly awful were the loud unmusical cluckings she uttered, compared with the exquisite trilling of his own beloved songster — the Prima Donna of the Woodlands!

Now, strange to say, the Nightingale, too, had an unwanted admirer. This was none other than a Cuckoo — a dashing, high-cock-a-lorum sort of fellow, who was just as greedy and grasping in his love affairs as was his own legitimate mate in her house-hunting and family matters. Having taken a roving fancy to the sweetly-singing Nightingale, he boldly made love to her, conceitedly expecting to make a quick conquest from his cooing rival, since he cared nothing for fair-play.

But the gentle Nightingale would have nothing to do with this unscrupulous sweetheart-snatcher; and, in order to escape from the impudent Don Juan, she began to seek out more frequently the faithful Dove — whom she truly loved, despite her shyness.

The disgruntled Cuckoo found his ardour burning more brightly still because of this rebuff to his vanity; and he now had recourse to cunning. He dressed himself up in the plumage of a dove — or, rather, in some scattered feathers he had found; and in this not too good disguise, he hoped to pass himself off as his gentle rival and thus to deceive the Nightingale into accepting him as her own true lover.

As it happened, the equally disgruntled Hen had concocted a similar plan. She decided to dress herself up as a Nightingale; and in these borrowed plumes, she firmly, but vainly, expected to inspire the love of her adored Dove.

But, alas! Both these foolish deceivers deceived only themselves. When next the Dove appeared in the flowery glade, he was melancholy no longer, having already received many signs from his beloved Nightingale that she was about to accept his affections; and as he fluttered about and danced with his companions, he felt very happy indeed. When, however, the infatuated Hen, looking ridiculous in her inadequate disguise, approached him in a mincing and love-sick manner he was somewhat alarmed, and drew back hastily; for, despite her disguise, he knew only too well that this absurd creature was certainly not his beloved Nightingale.

The same thing happened to the cocksure Cuckoo. When the neat and dainty Nightingale appeared in the glade, he eagerly accosted her, firmly believing that his disguise would cause her to mistake him for her favoured Dove. This, however, was not the case; and the scared Nightingale refused to have anything to do with such an obviously outrageous hoaxer, but fluttered away quickly to the protective care of her own true lover.

The consequence was that the two impostors, finding their deceitful plans a failure, now actually began to deceive themselves. As the comically posturing Hen ambled and strutted towards the disguised Cuckoo, fondly imagining herself the living image of the Nightingale, he was, indeed, deceived for the moment; and in his vanity, believing his present appearance to be precisely the same as that of the handsome Dove he was pretending to be, he opened wide his wings, into which his fellow-deceiver fell happily.

Meanwhile, the two cheeky Sparrow urchins had not been merely idle onlookers at this absurd little comedy; but, being real nosey-parkers, they had been peering and snooping around, trying to find out all they could about this feathered masquerade. When, therefore, the well-pleased Hen had first strutted in, wearing the bunch of brown feathers she had picked up, they had mocked at her patent disguise and made hilarious fun of her ; and, though a little afraid of the sinister Cuckoo, they had likewise cast aspersions upon his equally inadequate fancy-dress.

Now, however, they waxed much bolder ; and, hopping down from their perch on the fence, they flew towards the deceptive couple and began to tear off the masqueraders' borrowed plumes.

Having thus been unmasked by the mischievous Sparrows, there was nothing else for the discomfited Cuckoo to do but to fly back to the woodlands, while the equally discomfited Hen scuttled after him, clucking discordantly as she went ; and both were followed by the scornful jeers of the feathered folk they had so conceitedly hoped to deceive.

Having thus successfully disposed of these disturbing elements in their peaceful garden-glade, the Sparrows and their friends danced for joy ; and the little comedy ended happily with a grand revel of feathered folk in honour of the wedding of the Dove and his beloved Nightingale.

HAMLET

As Hamlet, Prince of Denmark, lay dying of the fatal poisoned-dagger thrust dealt him by his one-time friend, Laertes, he provided a personal example of those strange prophetic words he had himself but recently uttered :

"For in that sleep of death what dreams may come
 When we have shuffled off this mortal coil,
 Must give us pause."

In the few brief moments that remained to him as his dying body was borne on a bier carried by four sable-garbed retainers across the reception-hall of his ancestral palace-home, the unhappy young Prince relived in rapid succession most of the poignantly dramatic events that had led up to his own untimely end. True, owing to his semi-conscious state, these dreadful scenes at times appeared cloudy, incoherent, and far from clear, and some of the incidents and characters in them became strangely mingled with other events and characters. Nevertheless, in that short, slow-moving passage of the sombre procession through the darkened, moon-lit hall, with his limp arms and his head with its now chalk-white face hanging down over one end of the bier, Hamlet's fevered imagination brought back to him in vivid revelation the following pictures of his last black hours :

* * * * *

In the deserted reception hall of the Castle of Elsinore, only a dim red light glowed ; but this was sufficient to reveal its magnificent but unusual decorations — tapestries or statuary depicting a monstrous crowned giant wielding a naked sword, pillars culminating in hands grasping daggers, and other grotesquely sinister designs. At one side of the hall rose a splendid crimson-draped 'stone stairway, with a deep curtained passage alcove nearby ; and another alcove was to be seen on the opposite side, while a further arched opening marked the centre of the hall.

Into the midst of the dimly-glowing red light there came a half-drunken grave-digger, rolling from side to side with an unsteady gait and shouldering a spade as though in readiness for his usual gruesome occupation.

When the grave-digger's somewhat fantastic figure had passed along out of sight, there entered the young Prince Hamlet, clad in mourning garments and deeply wrapt in his unhappy thoughts — for he was still grieving for the sudden and suspicious death of his royal father and was gloomily angered by the in-decently hasty re-marriage of his mother, Queen Ger-trude, with his already hated uncle, Claudius, who had usurped the throne.

These disturbing thoughts were interrupted by the grave-digger, who had now returned, rolling a skull along the floor like a ball — the skull of the former Court Jester, Yorick. Observing the Prince, he offered him the skull ; but when Hamlet turned from it with a shiver, he sat on the floor and tossed it up gleefully, playing with it in a drunken manner. Then, feeling a sudden chill in the air, he staggered off with his sinister play-thing.

This change in the atmosphere had been caused by the appearance of a ghostly figure clad in translucent shining armour and wearing a halo crown upon its head ; and when Hamlet, feeling himself drawn as by an invisible force, turned about, he found himself gazing upon the Spirit form of his late royal father.

He fell upon his knees with awed reverence, while the ghost of the departed King related to him the grim story of his murder at the hands of his over-ambitious brother. Hamlet now learned that the dastardly Claudius had thus contrived this murder that he might not only himself become King but might also marry his brother's beautiful widowed Queen, for whom he had already conceived an unlawful love.

The royal Ghost now sternly commanded his son to avenge his death by bringing justice upon his murderer ; and having thus delivered his compelling message, he vanished from sight, leaving Hamlet in a prostrate attitude upon the floor but now effectually convinced of the truth of his former suspicions and determined to bring retribution upon his regicide uncle.

Scarcely had the ghostly visitant departed than the reception-hall became brilliantly illuminated, as the usurper King and his morally-guilty Queen, with the lords and ladies of their Court, entered from the broad staircase and took up their positions on a dais near the adjoining alcove. Among the courtiers was the King's chief minister, Polonius, the latter's son, Laertes, and his daughter, Ophelia.

Ophelia was a beautiful young maiden who had long loved Hamlet, and whose love had been returned by the Prince without reserve until the tragic death of his father ; and their marriage had likewise at first been desired by Polonius. But the latter was an ambitious man ; and when Claudius usurped the throne, he was no longer eager for his fair daughter to wed with the now less important Prince. He knew, likewise, that the latter had no love for him, Polonius, but was more than suspicious of his possible connivance at the death of the recent King. He was now anxious, therefore, to keep the former lovers apart ; and though his son, Laertes, had also been a friend of the Prince's, he did not hesitate to poison the young man's mind against the latter. Laertes was the more easily influenced in this connection because of the strangeness of Hamlet's recent conduct, which caused the latter frequently to treat the gentle Ophelia with cool indifference or even direct unkindness — for the young Prince was at times inclined to think that the son and daughter of Polonius might be acting in concert with their father against him.

Now observing Hamlet lying on the floor apart from the rest of the company, casting gloomily suspicious looks upon the royal party, Polonius took the King aside and indicated that the young Prince showed signs of madness and that a watch should be kept upon him. He even suggested that it would be wise for the King to withdraw for a while ; but when the latter had done so, he himself remained to watch what Hamlet did.

Laertes was about to take an important journey, but anxiety about his beloved sister's relations with Hamlet caused him to delay his immediate departure in order that he might have a brotherly talk with Ophelia, who was sad because of her lover's neglect and present unaccountable coldness.

Polonius, however, did not desire his son's intrusion at that moment ; and he quickly separated the pair. He then very craftily arranged for Ophelia and Hamlet to be left alone for a short time, hoping that the latter would show further signs of his supposed madness by treating the girl roughly ; and he himself retired to bring back the King also to watch, unseen, what happened and to have his pretended suspicions confirmed regarding the disturbed state of the Prince's mind. If Hamlet could be proved insane, he thought, so much the better for the guilty royal pair he served with the flattering zeal of a sycophant and for the continuance of the usurper's occupation of the throne.

Left alone with her one-time lover, Ophelia gently soothed him with her loving endearments; and, for a few moments, the pair were happily lost in the joy of each other's presence as of yore. Then, Hamlet suddenly caught sight of the King and Polonius lurking in one of the alcoves, obviously spying upon them; and realising that they were hatching some plot against him and wrongly imagining that Ophelia herself must be aware of this plot, he cast off her clinging arms and flung her from his side with such contemptuous violence that she staggered away, weeping with grief because he seemed no longer to love her.

* * * * *

The next few scenes that passed through the fading consciousness of the dying Hamlet became more and more confused.

The first of these was the enactment of the play he had contrived to prove the guilt of the usurper, Claudius. After some gorgeous pageantry and stately Court dances, the actual play began; but, instead of the correct performers, Ophelia was now seen in the part of the Player Queen, while the Ghost of the murdered King took the part of the Player King. After the Player King and Queen had performed their introductory love scene, the latter left the stage, while the former lay down with his sceptre by his side, and pretended to sleep; and then an even more confusing misrepresentation occurred. Hamlet himself was seen to approach the seemingly sleeping King, creeping forward on his hands and knees and accompanied by the usurper, Claudius, likewise crawling on hands and knees; and this most unlikely pair, on reaching the sleeping King, both poured poison in the victim's ear at identically the same moment. Hamlet next turned to embrace Ophelia as the Player Queen, while Claudius seized the sleeping King's sceptre ; and, after this, events happened rapidly amidst further confusion.

The players disappeared, the Courtiers ran hither and thither in alarm, and the tragedy moved inexorably to its climax. The usurper, Claudius, seemed conscious-stricken after seeing his crime thus enacted before all ; and he fell upon his knees, as though praying. Hamlet, observing this, drew his dagger and rushed forward, about to kill him — then, changing his mind, he dashed up the steps of one of the alcoves and stabbed Polonius, who had been there endeavouring to calm the now frightened Queen.

Staggering back, as the dead body of Polonius rolled down the steps, Hamlet again beheld his father's ghost ; and he was about to follow the Spirit when Laertes and Claudius appeared again. He now crouched back once more, awaiting the right moment to slay the murderer. Laertes would have rushed upon Hamlet at once, but was held back by the Queen, who still loved her distraught son, despite her own infamous conduct ; and all these conflicting passions were now held in abeyance by a sad and most pathetic interlude.

The gentle Ophelia entered with flowers in her arms, which she scattered about as she crooned a little song. Heart-broken by Hamlet's unaccountably harsh treatment of her, she had lost her reason and had no recognition for any of her pitying friends. Her dress was torn, and she had hung long garlands of flowers around her neck ; and she moved softly among the company, offering blossoms first to one and then to another.

The Queen could not long bear to look upon the poor mad Ophelia, and soon withdrew, accompanied by her lover, Claudius ; and the deranged Ophelia, after being tenderly kissed by her brother, Laertes, moved away out of sight, with slow and ever-weakening steps.

Another confused vision quickly followed. A funeral procession passed by, slowly and solemnly, accompanied by the King, Laertes and the grave-digger; but though the body on the bier was expected to be that of the unhappy mad Ophelia — who had just drowned herself in her despair — it was seen in Hamlet's own disordered mind as that of his mother, the Queen — who, however, was still alive at that moment.

As the bier was borne away, Laertes would have sprung upon Hamlet then and there, eager to slay him for having been the cause of his fair sister's death; but the King bade him wait awhile, and handed to him a poisoned dagger with which this fell deed might be done more effectively later on.

* * * * *

Finally, there came the last visions of the dying Hamlet.

The King and Queen, desiring some distraction from these tragic events, had commanded the gorgeously garbed lords and ladies of their Court to dance for them. This they did, the dance being almost a *bacchanale*, in which the performers held on high flowing cups of wine. These they offerred to one another and to the onlookers, as they moved rhythmically to the strains of a wildly gay tune; and though the gaiety was somewhat forced, there was a sinister reason for the cups of wine held so gracefully by the dancers.

When the royal party joined the company, better relations seemed temporarily to hold sway among them. The King and Queen were affectionate as usual; and the Queen kissed Hamlet, and seemed anxious about his welfare. But Laertes looked on at this family scene still with black thoughts in his heart ; and he clutched the half-hidden poisoned dagger in his hand grimly on beholding Hamlet.

The King, still seemingly urbane, now seized from one particular dancer a cup of wine into which a deadly poison had been dropped before the performance began ; and, stepping forward, he ·offered this graciously to Hamlet. The Queen, however, observing that her son was about to refuse such a seeming peace-offering and eager to cover his apparent boorishness, snatched at the cup herself, and—unaware that it was poisoned — drank the wine to the last drop, bowing to Hamlet as though toasting him.

The horrified King quickly hastened to her side and helped her to a seat near the alcove, heedless of everyone else. Meanwhile, Hamlet, now ready to carry out the deed of justice enjoined upon him by his ghostly father, bent forward to select a rapier from one of the pages ; and, at that moment, Laertes sprang forward stealthily and stabbed him viciously in the back with the poisoned dagger given him by the King. Instantly, Hamlet swung back, snatched the dagger from his assassin's hand and plunged it into the latter's heart.

As Laertes fell dying to the ground, Hamlet still had strength left to stagger towards the now terrified King and to stab him likewise with his own poisoned dagger. Then, before the Courtiers could recover from the horror of these ghastly occurrences, the Queen now succumbed to the effects of the deadly poison she had so unwittingly swallowed ; and, with a final gasp of agony, she also fell dying to the ground.

Filial love once more filled the heart of the dying Hamlet, and he tried to stagger towards his mother's fallen body ; but, before he could reach her side, his failing attention was distracted by the sudden re-appearance of the grave-digger, who lurched up to him with Yorick's skull still in his hand. Then to the horrified revulsion of all, the grave-digger filled the skull with wine and invited the gasping Prince to drink from this gruesome vessel. On his offer being refused, he drank the wine himself with great gusto.

Hamlet's last moment of consciousness had now come ; and with a final choking cry, he rolled over on to the floor, dead.

* * * * *

The four sable-cloaked retainers carrying the motion-less body of the murdered Hamlet, with his limp arms and head with its ghastly chalk-white face hanging down over the bier, had now crossed the hall and vanished into the darkness beyond ; and the curtain was rung down for ever upon the confused scenes and dreams that had come to this unhappy young Prince's mind during the last few moments of his passing into the quiet sleep of death.

MIRACLE IN THE GORBALS

IT was early evening in the Gorbals dockyard area of Glasgow ; and in one of the drab tenement parts of the district the usual amusements of the inhabitants had already begun after the heavy toil of the day was done. The gaunt grey tenement buildings that rose on either side of the street looked somewhat less drab now that the workers who occupied them began to appear at the windows and doorways. They brought sudden flashes of colour into the dreary scene — a scarlet or green skirt here, a blue or a yellow scarf there ; even the cheap and tawdry finery of girls out to cadge an evening's amusement from their dockyard admirers was a welcome sight for sore eyes. At least, so thought a wretched and ragged beggar who crouched outside a doorway, always on the look-out for some free entertainment, or free food, to come his way.

The girls — most of them factory hands — sauntered about, sometimes arm-in-arm, sometimes singly, making overtures to the freshly-smartened youths intent on finding partners for their evening's amusement. But it was a motley crowd of old and young, dockers and factory workers mainly ; and many of them drifted in and out of the already brightly illuminated public-house on one side of the street, or of the cheap cooked-fish shop labelled " Mac's" on the other. A group of rough boys played with an old motor tyre they had retrieved from a dump nearby ; and they rolled this object across the street with many noisy cries, caring nothing whether they "barged into" anyone or not

Adjoining " Mac's" fish shop, a short flight of steps

ended in a balcony, at one side of which was a door leading to an apartment in which lived a prostitute, who presently came down and stood smoking a cigarette near the fish-shop entrance. She was a handsome girl of a flashy type ; and she wore a very short scarlet frock of cheap quality, but cut in the latest fashion. The other women standing by glanced at her with disdain ; but the girl in scarlet merely returned their looks with an equal scorn. Then, nonchalantly, she set about attracting clients with her usual professional skill.

At this moment there came into the street a good-looking middle-aged man, whose dark, respectable clothes of a semi-clerical and semi-official cut, proclaimed him to be a person of some authority in the district — probably a slum missionary or a Club leader of some kind. He seemed to have a certain amount of influence with the people about him who, for the most part, returned his greetings respectfully enough — with the exception of the prostitute, who took little notice of the look of strong disapproval he cast upon her. She even threw a backward glance of contempt and triumph upon him when, on being accosted by a momentarily affluent young man, she led the latter up the steps to her apartment beyond.

The Official seemed somewhat disturbed by this incident ; for, despite his own obvious respectability, he was undoubtedly attracted by the handsome street-girl. He sauntered about, settled a street fight, lightly cuffed a group of rowdy urchins ; and then, for a time, he remained in the background, watching the kaleidoscopic scene around him.

He was interested in a pair of charming young lovers who now strolled into the street and began to dance happily with one another, so wrapped-up in their own sweet love-dream as to be quite oblivious of those around them. This happy pair brought a sudden beauty into the sordid scene.

When the young girl was presently called indoors by an irate and overworked mother who needed her services, her companion remained in the street, alone ; and presently he was accosted by the prostitute who, having just parted with one client was now on the look-out for another. This time, however, her efforts were frustrated by the Official, who came forward and authoritatively persuaded the hesitant young man to remember his sweetheart and depart from temptation.

Furious at his interference with her trade, the prostitute attacked him at once, calling upon a docker friend to join her ; and, for a few moments, there was a wild uproar. The Official, however, stood his ground, and soon quelled what looked like the beginning of an ugly scene.

Just then a disturbance of a tragic kind took place. A few moments before the lovers had enjoyed their happy meeting a pale and sad-looking young girl, dressed in shabby black, had entered the street somewhat fearfully. She seemed to be in the depths of despair ; but, despite her look of misery, she was sufficiently pretty to attract the attention of a bold-eyed lounger, who approached her with leering glances. But the unhappy girl had been terrified by his eagerly-whispered suggestions and had fled quickly out of the street, leaving her would-be admirer laughing at her dismay. A street urchin, seeing that the girl in black had fled in the direction of the docks, followed her out of curiosity to see what she did. This urchin now rushed back into the street, full of importance as a news-bearer and shouting that the girl in black had just flung herself into the water.

The street crowd was instantly full of excited chatter and surmise as a few lusty young men seized ropes and ran to the dockside ; but when, a few minutes later, they returned with the already dead and dripping body of the unhappy suicide, a sudden hush fell upon all. Fully capable of dealing with a situation of this kind, the Official stepped forward and ordered the bystanders to move back from the body ; and then he placed a scarf over the dead girl's face and murmured a prayer, while the rough crowd, now subdued and silent, stood by quietly with bared heads.

Then it was that a newcomer appeared on the scene, a Stranger whom none had ever seen before — a Man with a beautiful and serene face and with the Light of Heavenly Love shining in his eyes. Slowly moving forward until he stood beside the suicide, the Stranger gazed down upon her with every sign of deep compassion ; then he made the Sign of the Cross over her and quietly bade her arise once more.

As the young girl in black now rose up slowly and stood beside the Stranger, alive and well, the bystanders were filled with awe ; and when she presently began to perform a lively dance to express her joy in this happy resurrection, they gazed upon her with amazement. Her joy, however, was so infectious that, presently, they all began to join in the dance themselves, and ended by lifting both the girl and the Stranger high up into the air.

Meanwhile, the Official gazed upon this joyful scene with bitter jealousy, envious of One obviously greater than himself, whose Divine authority so far exceeded his own. Until this hour, he had himself been the most respected man in that district ; but now his authority had suddenly been usurped by this strange miracle-worker. But was it a true miracle ? He tried to per-

suade himself that it was not, despite the fact tha
the unhappy girl in black who had drowned herself in
despair was once more alive and dancing for joy. He
even endeavoured to point out to the bystanders that
the Stranger was merely a charlatan and that the girl
would probably have recovered without his aid ; but
they were still awe-struck and refused to listen to him.
All the co-operation he was able to secure was to
induce one of the street urchins, by means of a bribe,
to spy upon the movements of the Stranger when the
latter presently strolled away a short distance with
the restored suicide to talk with her and certain other
bystanders eager to listen to him. Quite soon, he found
himself alone.

Knowing himself to be superseded, he now felt completely frustrated ; and when the prostitute appeared
before him a few moments later, he suddenly gave way
to his lower nature and entreated her to receive him
in her apartment. Though at first she scornfully
refused his unexpected request, remembering his former disapproval of her, the girl finally consented, feeling
cynically elated by her conquest of one so highly
respected ; and she led the way up the steps to her
apartment.

Her conquest was short-lived, however. The Official
soon fled from her presence, full of self-contempt for
his own temporary moral weakness ; and he now
began to plan how he might avenge himself upon the
miracle-worker, whose unwelcome advent had thus
caused him to lose control of himself and to lower his
own standards of conduct. Still burning with jealousy
of the newcomer, he determined to get rid of him at
all costs — or, at least, to discredit him with the dock
people.

Consequently, when the Stranger again appeared in

the street with his new friends, he sent him a message by his urchin-spy to the effect that the prostitute had invited him to visit her in her apartment. To the surprise of all, the Stranger accepted this invitation — which, to their simple minds, had but one meaning ; and he immediately walked up the steps that led to the street-walker's room with an eager look upon his tranquil countenance.

No sooner had the door closed upon him than the now triumphant Official declared contemptuously to the puzzled and disappointed onlookers that, as they could plainly see, their precious miracle-worker was no more saintly than they were themselves, but should be despised for such a blatant moral lapse.

The men in the crowd were particularly infuriated, believing now that they had been deceived in the apparently virtuous newcomer ; and they declared themselves ready to attack him on his return to the street. The girl in black, still believing in the saint-liness of her saviour, endeavoured to restrain their anger ; but she was roughly thrust aside into a dark alcove, where the wretched beggar crawled towards her and tried to soothe her. He also believed in the miracle-worker.

In a short time, the Stranger issued forth from the apartment of the prostitute, his face radiant and shining with joy ; for he had spoken sweet words of comfort and encouragement to the poor sinner, and had already persuaded her to renounce her present profession and to live a better life.

But when he stepped into the street, the urchins all spat in his face, and angry murmurs arose around him from the already menacing crowd. Then the prostitute likewise came down into the street ; and it was seen that her face was now irradiated with happiness, as though she had received tidings of great joy.

When the still jealous Official thus realised that the street-walker's conversion — which he had failed to secure himself — had, indeed, been brought about by this Stranger he envied, he was more furiously embittered against him than before ; and he called upon a gang of hooligans who had now joined the crowd to dispose of his hated rival for him, offering them money to do so.

The rough gangsters stealthily surrounded their victim ; and as the Stranger calmly turned to greet them, they set upon him with knives and razor-blades, and stabbed him to death. And the fickle crowd, who but a short hour previously had gazed upon him with awe and gratitude and had regarded him as a Heavenly Visitant or, at least, a holy Saint, raised not a hand in his defence ; they merely hurried away with the Official, being soon followed by the gangster-murderers.

But, as the gentle Stranger fell to the ground, dead, the poor beggar drew near to lift his head and to arrange his limbs with decent care ; and the former prostitute and the girl in black likewise came to help him, with deep sorrow in their hearts. They softly covered his face with the scarf of the unhappy suicide for whom he had performed the miracle ; and then the new friends walked away, hand in hand, to begin a fresh life together.

LA FETE ETRANGE
(*The Strange Festival*)

THE scene of this story is laid in France. An unsophisticated country youth named Julien wandered forth one early winter morning and met with a very strange adventure. He was passing by the grounds of a fine *château*, wondering to whom it belonged, when a beautiful young girl came tripping up to him as though about to greet him joyfully. Then she stopped suddenly, and drew back in confusion ; for she had made a mistake.

For the moment, in the half-light, she had taken the figure of the youth to be that of her own *fiancé*, whom she was expecting to arrive at the gates about that time.

Seeing the country youth standing there, however, she gazed at him for a moment in surprise and a strange unaccountable interest ; then she turned away and hurried back into the *château*, not wishing to meet her *fiancé* in the presence of a stranger.

The boy Julien, however, remained standing, as though he had seen a wonderful vision. Never before had he beheld so beautiful a maiden, nor one of such obviously high degree ; and his youthful heart was suddenly filled with an exquisite joy. So rapt was he, indeed, that he scarcely noticed the arrival of the young nobleman who was the *fiancé* of the beautiful girl he had just seen, and who passed quickly on into the *château*, after a curious glance at him.

As Julien stood there, like one wrapped in a lovely dream, a party of gay young people arrived at the gates ; and from their conversation and fine clothes he gathered that they were about to join in a revel at the *château* in honour of the young *châtelaine's* forthcoming marriage.

As the laughing guests passed into the grounds, Julien suddenly decided to follow them, in the hope of getting another glimpse of the beautiful girl whose image now filled his heart ; and the young people, observing him following them, regarded him as one of themselves and gladly received him into their midst.

*   *   *   *   *

The winter day was so fine and the snowy ground and frosty trees sparkled so brightly in the sunshine that the preliminary wedding revels at the *château* were being held out-of-doors upon a broad and splendid terrace. At one side of the terrace a wide staircase led into the mansion, and upon this the wedding guests sat and rested from time to time as the revels continued.

The gaiety was at its height when the group of young people, of whom Julien was one, appeared upon the scene ; and, to the surprise and joy of the country youth, he found himself given as warm a welcome as any of the other guests by the lovely young *châtelaine* who was so shortly to be wedded.

He was delighted with the scene that met his astonished gaze ; for he had never before seen such exquisite clothes, such wonderful surroundings, and such gracious young people ; and he was so occupied in observing these new wonders, that it never occurred to him that his own appearance was different from theirs. He was a handsome youth, and had a natural grace and an innate charm of manner ; but his clothes were definitely of a country cut and looked strange among the elegant garments on every side of him.

However, he was instantly received as one of themselves by these gay young people ; and he quickly found himself mingling with them in the lively games and dances that had been arranged for the revel. But, though he played Blind-Man's-Buff and joined in all the other games and dances, he had eyes only for the beautiful young *châtelaine* herself ; and he was filled with an ecstasy of joy when she invited him to dance with her.

For a short time longer, as he danced with his radiant partner — already feeling the rapture of early-dawning love within his breast — he revelled in this fairy-like scene, which seemed to him as vivid and real as a glorious dream come true.

Then, a curious change seemed to come over the company ; and, gradually, the light-hearted gaiety became strained, as though a dark shadow had fallen upon the scene. Though Julien still danced on with his lovely partner, he felt that a change had also taken place in her and that her thoughts, now troubled ones, were elsewhere ; and presently, she stopped dancing, and he stood waiting in surprise at her side.

He now noticed that some of the young people who had received him in so comradely a fashion, were looking upon him with curious glances, as though doubtful whether he should be in their midst or not ; and for the first time since he had joined the revel, he realised the difference between himself and these more fortunate folk. But what had caused this sudden change ? Julien was puzzled and could not at first account for it.

Presently, however, he noticed that his fair partner was gazing with distress and questioning apprehension in her eyes at a figure standing at the top of the broad staircase leading from the inside of the *château* ; and then he understood.

The magnificently dressed young nobleman who stood there, looking down upon the revelling company, was the beautiful *châtelaine's fiancé ;* and his face expressed disapproval, not of the invited guests, but of himself only, Julien, the country youth who belonged to a different social sphere and was not of his own elegant world.

Nor was this entirely all. The nobly-born bridegroom-elect, on appearing at the top of the staircase in readiness to join the revel, had noted with surprise and angry jealousy the look of rapture in the eyes of the simple country youth who was so joyously partnering the fair *châtelaine ;* and mistaking the latter's kindly interest in her stranger guest for something deeper, he now believed her to be unfaithful to him.

Instantly realising this terrible misunderstanding on the part of her *fiancé*—whom she passionately loved— the young hostess hastened to his side, eager to explain the unexpected presence of the country youth ; but her proud lover, believing only the seeming evidence of his own eyes revealed to him as he had stood, unnoticed, at the top of the staircase and refusing to be convinced otherwise, now announced that he would leave her and never return again.

Despite the young *châtelaine's* declaration of innocence and her agonised pleadings that he would remain— to which Julien himself and all the company added their entreaties—the haughty, but likewise grief-stricken bridegroom, still believing that he had been deceived by his betrothed, turned away from her and returned to his own home.

The now deeply-distressed Julien, still perplexed and scarcely realising his own implication in this apparently tragic happening, tried to offer comfort to his lovely recent partner ; but his efforts were in vain, and the heart-broken *châtelaine* turned away from him and, entering the *château*, passed out from his life for ever.

The guests likewise sadly departed ; and the country youth was left to wander forth alone once more. The day that had begun as a glorious dream and had brought ecstasy into his heart for the first time, had ended in the sad awakening of disillusionment.

THE FUGITIVE

ONE late summer evening, two young sisters, charmingly dressed in party frocks, were awaiting the arrival of guests in the garden just outside the entrance to their home.

The younger girl, fair and sylph-like, was scarcely yet on the threshold of womanhood; but the elder sister, a beautiful brunette, was several years older and was more sophisticated. The latter wore an elegant gown of conventional type, black, with touches of deep magenta and green; the younger girl was dressed simply in white, with blue ribbons around her waist and binding her bright fair hair.

The two sisters seemed very fond of one another; and they sat together on a garden seat with their arms entwined, talking happily of the party they were about to enjoy.

So engrossed were the sisters in each other's gay conversation that at first they did not notice the presence of an intruder. This was a wild-looking young man, a fugitive from justice, who had rushed blindly into the garden, seeking a hiding-place from the pursuers he had only just managed to elude. He was already completely exhausted, breathless and spent from a long, dangerous, and anxious journey; and he was staggering about in a distracted manner, now falling and anon dragging himself to his feet again with an agonizing effort.

The noise of the stranger's movements brought the sisters quickly to their feet; and they clung to one another in terror when the fugitive, seeing them, pulled out a revolver and feebly pointed it at them, shivering and shaking with an equal fright.

The two young women, however, did not scream or call for help ; and seeing that they seemed to regard him with as much pity as fear, the escaped captive fell upon his knees and entreated their aid, begging them to help him to hide from his pursuers.

At first, the sisters, not knowing what to do, drew back in alarm at such a dangerous suggestion ; then, when the unfortunate young man rolled over to the ground, half-swooning with fatigue and despair, real pity for his desperate plight filled their hearts and they ran to help him to rise and supported him in their arms.

They were both of a romantic temperament, and the young man was handsome and had the aspect of an adventurous hero, despite his dishevelled and torn garments. His utter exhaustion and forlorn helplessness proved him to be at the end of his tether ; and this caused a compassionate pity to surge up within them, so that they were ready enough to throw caution to the winds.

The fugitive, noting the rising and pitying interest in their eyes, now offered his revolver to them as a sign that he trusted them ; but the younger sister eagerly put the weapon back into his pocket as an intimation that they likewise trusted him. Then the two sisters, supporting him carefully on either side, walked him up and down a few paces, trying to help him recover his balance somewhat and to move more normally.

Every now and again, first one sister and then the other would turn aside to ascertain anxiously if anyone was in sight. They explained to the fugitive that they were expecting guests to arrive at any moment ; but they declared they would, nevertheless, hide him temporarily and then return to help him to get away safely when the party was over.

With these assurances, the fugitive became calmer; and for a few moments the three young people forgot their dangerous predicament and seemed to be wandering in a strange new world of unusual and hitherto unknown happiness. For a sudden flame of passion had blazed up in their young hearts in that unexpected experience of romantic adventure; and every moment that followed was a moment of delight.

Both sisters felt curiously drawn to the helpless stranger they had sworn to protect—an ever-growing interest that quickly developed into a deep, passionate love. The fugitive, however, had eyes only for the younger sister, the sweet simplicity of whose early blooming had filled him with enchantment; and he revealed his increasing joy in her presence with many loving movements.

At first the more sophisticated young woman did not realise this obvious preference on the part of the stranger, since she still regarded her sister as almost a child; and, fully confident in her own maturer charms of attraction, she now stepped stealthily into the house through the open doorway to seek a safe hiding-place for the young man she already truly loved.

Left alone in the garden, the fugitive and the young girl instantly rushed into each other's arms with an ecstasy of joy; and, for a few moments, they were utterly lost to the unkind world around them. Then, a beckoning arm from within the doorway recalled them both to the dangerous present, and they slipped noiselessly into the house.

The evening shadows had now fallen, and the rosy glow of a lighted lamp suddenly shone out through the doorway, as though to welcome the expected guests.

Before the latter arrived, however, the fugitive and his protectors rushed out once more, not having dared to venture far into the house, after all. The young man's fears had returned ; but the girls, though eager to get him to a place of safety, were reluctant to part with him.

And now they found themselves in a worse predicament than before ; for the sound of chattering voices heralded the arrival of the approaching guests. There was only just time to push the terrified youth behind a tall screen near the entrance, when the gaily-dressed guests trooped up the garden path in pairs. At the same moment, the host and hostess appeared in the doorway and came out to greet them with gracious smiles and bows.

The first part of the evening's entertainment was to be a formal dance in the garden ; and the host, somewhat surprised at his daughters' curious lack of enthusiasm, peremptorily called upon them to join in the dance at once, which he himself led with one of the many charming ladies present. All the guests joined in with eager pleasure.

The two sisters, however, were too full of anxiety to enjoy the dance, or their partners' company ; and every now and again the younger sister would find an opportunity to stop for a moment beside the screen to whisper an agitated word of encouragement to her hidden lover behind it. The elder sister frowned upon her for this suspicious action, and even hastily dragged her away, fearing lest she should arouse the curiosity of their guests.

At last this introductory dance came to an end ; and the host and hostess led the way into the house, followed by the laughing guests. The two daughters of the house, however, quickly returned to the garden ; and the still terrified fugitive instantly dashed out from behind the screen. The young girl was soon clasped in his arms ; and now it was that the elder sister suddenly realised that the stranger's love was not for her. She immediately became furiously jealous of the fair young sister she had hitherto so dearly loved and had never suspected would ever become her rival ; and, in that one black moment, hatred and a sudden desire for revenge upon the lovers reigned in her heart. Unobserved by the rapt pair, she hastened back into the house ; and, approaching her father, she told him hurriedly the story of the hiding of the fugitive, laying all the blame for this flagrant flouting of the law upon her innocent and over-romantic young sister.

Instantly, all was excitement and concern at the party ; and the guests came trooping out into the garden, led by their perturbed host—who had hastily seized a stick as the first weapon that came to his hand.

Meanwhile, the lovers, while still clasped in each other's arms, became aware of the approaching danger on hearing the sound of excited voices ; and, separating hastily, the young girl wildly thrust the fugitive behind the nearest bushes, bidding him run for his life. Then she stood aside, trembling with apprehension as the party guests came pouring through the doorway.

The father, furious at such an untoward occurrence—which he regarded as an outrage against Society—hastened towards his younger daughter, pouring abuse upon her for her unorthodox conduct ; and he demanded that she should instantly reveal the whereabouts of the escaped captive. When the unhappy girl, though terrified, bravely refused to betray the youth who had so suddenly become precious to her, her father angrily raised his stick and seized her by the arm.

He was about to attempt to beat the truth out of her, when, to the astonishment of all and the dismay of his protectors, the hidden fugitive staggered forth from behind the bushes—whence he had not stirred—willing to give himself up rather than that his protectors should suffer. He quickly realised from the many hostile looks he encountered that all were against him, and that no mercy was to be expected ; but he no longer cared about mercy, for he was already overwrought and utterly exhausted beyond recovery. The sudden excitement of this additional effort being more than his strength could support, he wavered and swayed uncertainly for a moment, and then fell to the ground—dead !

With cries of woe, both the sisters sprang forward, ready to fling themselves upon the body of the unfortunate youth for whom they both had conceived so deep a love ; but they were instantly seized and held back by some of the horrified guests—all of whom now slowly returned to the house at the authoritative command of their host. The latter, his anger gone and now satisfied that the intruder was indeed dead and beyond the reach of the law, declared that nothing more could be done in the matter ; and he added that the festivities should immediately be resumed. The whole party, therefore, trooped back into the house, leaving the fugitive's body in a crumpled heap outside ; but the younger daughter of their host wept bitterly and cast longing looks behind her as she was gently, but firmly, led away.

A few moments later, when all, the company had vanished within, the elder sister managed to creep back, alone ; and hastening to the deserted corpse, she eagerly lifted first one arm and then the other, in the vain hope that life might not, after all, have entirely departed. Already she had sincerely regretted her rash act, which had ended so much more disastrously than she had expected or desired ; and her own love, more maturely deep than that of her younger sister, again surged up passionately in her heart, so that she longed more than ever for it to be returned by the one who had so strangely and suddenly set it alight.

But the lifeless arms of the fallen fugitive still continued to fall back limply as she again tenderly and hopefully raised them ; and, realising that he was indeed lost to her for ever, she uttered a loud cry of remorse and anguish and fell unconscious across his dead body.

THE MERMAID

In the Sea-King's Palace at the bottom of the ocean,
six Mermaid Princesses amused themselves with songs
and games, or swam in and out of the coral-framed
windows. Sometimes they swam towards the shore
and sat on the rocks that rose out of the shallows,
combing their long flowing locks of hair as they sang
to one another; and from these vantage spots they
could see something of the human world and of the
strange beings who dwelt therein.

Usually, however, after thus roaming afar, the
Mermaid wanderers were glad enough to slip back into
the water once more and return to their exquisite
pearl-decorated Palace home—all save the youngest
Princess, who was more thrilled by the strange world
of the land and was never tired of gazing at it from the
sun-bathed or moon-lit rocks she sat upon.

The youngest Mermaid Princess was the most beautiful of all the royal sisters; and her voice was sweeter
than that of any other mermaid in the sea. She was
also more thoughtful and eager to acquire knowledge;
and her gentleness and unselfishness made her the
most beloved member of her family.

One day, when the Mermaid Princesses were playing
happily together at the bottom of the sea, the dark
shadow of a ship passed over them on the water above;
and the youngest sister swam swiftly to the surface,
hoping to catch a glimpse of some more of the human
beings she found so wonderful.

It happened that the ship was a royal barge and that
a handsome young Prince, with sparkling black eyes
and clad in gorgeous clothes, stood in the prow of the

vessel ; and as the eager Mermaid gazed upon this radiant royal youth, she instantly fell deeply in love with him.

A little later on, a terrific storm arose, which caused the royal barge to founder ; and the young Prince was thrown into the sea. Seeing him struggling in the waves, the youngest Mermaid sister was eager to save him from drowning ; and, swimming beneath him and keeping his head above water, she managed to rescue him and to bring him safely ashore, where she tended him lovingly until he regained consciousness. Then, as he began to show signs of recovery, she slipped back into the sea ; and the young Prince, not knowing who had rescued him or how he had been saved from death, was only glad to find that he had fortunately been cast up on the shores of his own country. So he returned to his royal palace with joyful steps.

The Mermaid Princess longed passionately to follow him ; but this she could not do, since her graceful body ended in a fish's tail. She knew that if only she could reach the Prince and win his love and be wedded to him, she would also gain an immortal soul—a divine possession denied to all ordinary mermaids.

Her own love for the wonderful mortal she had rescued grew deeper with every moment that passed ; and at last she determined to visit the terrible, but all-powerful, Sea-Witch, in the hope that the latter might help her to gain her heart's desire.

Late one night, therefore, while her sisters were asleep, she left the royal palace and made her way to the Sea-Witch's abode—a gruesome place beside a roaring whirlpool, in which sea-snakes abounded and which was surrounded by giant polypi ; and here the Sea-Witch sat waiting for her, having learned by magical means of her approach and purpose in coming.

The Witch promised to give the royal visitor a potion that would cause her fish's tail to vanish and to be replaced by a pair of charming little human legs and feet ; but there was a terrible condition attached to this transformation and the price to be paid was extremely heavy. Though her human feet would carry her wherever she wished to go and enable her to dance with the utmost grace, every step she took would give her agonising pain as though treading upon sharp knives ; and the price she must pay for the potion would be the loss of her tongue — and, consequently, of her lovely sweet voice ! Nor would she be able to regain her Mermaid form again ; and if the Prince did not love her sufficiently to make her his wife, she would not secure the immortal soul she craved for. In addition, if the Prince should choose another maiden as his bride, the transformed Mermaid must die on his wedding night and become as foam on the wave-tops.

Though shuddering at the prospect of the suffering she must endure, and despite the risks she must take, the deeply-loving Mermaid bravely declared herself willing to accept these hard conditions and to pay the terrible price demanded. Then the grasping Sea-Witch brewed a horrible potion, which she gave to the royal Mermaid, bidding her swim to the shore of the Prince's land and drink it on arrival ; and afterwards she cut out her tongue in payment.

No longer able to speak or to sing, the Mermaid yet swam courageously to the shores of the young Prince's land ; and there, seated on the Palace steps—which extended to the edge of the sea—she drank the magic potion. Next moment, to her delighted satisfaction, she saw that her fish's tail had vanished, and that, in its place, she now possessed a pair of graceful legs and the daintiest little feet. But the first time she stood upon her wonderful new feet, it was as though she stood upon sharp knives ; and this first pain she had ever felt was so intense that she fainted. But when she next opened her eyes, the handsome young Prince was bending over her with deep admiration in his eyes ; and as he led her into the palace, the joy she felt in his beloved presence was worth every pang she suffered.

The lovely strange maiden so romantically discovered on his palace steps by the young Prince quickly became the most favoured member of his Court. She was dressed in the richest of silken garments, and hung with chains of glittering jewels ; and everybody declared her to be the loveliest maiden ever seen in the land.

The young Prince delighted in her company, but was much distressed on discovering her to be dumb and unable to speak or sing to him. He much enjoyed music, and when his prettiest ladies sang to him, he clapped his hands and smiled upon them. This made the transformed Mermaid very sad, for she would have liked to have enchanted him with her once lovely singing ; and she also longed to tell him that it was she who had rescued him from the shipwreck—a fact he did not know.

However, since she could not charm him with sweet singing, she determined to delight him with her exquisite dancing. She seemed to float like thistledown upon the air when she danced lightly across the palace ballroom ; and though every step she took caused a sharp stabbing pain to pass through her feet, she still danced about softly and with the utmost grace like a butterfly on the wing—and always with the sweetest smile upon her lips.

But though the Prince delighted in her sweet company, and admired her beauty and her graceful dancing, his love for her was more like that of a brotherly protector than of a lover ; and he never thought for a moment of making her his wife—he did not desire a dumb maiden as his royal bride.

So the beautiful stranger maiden became sadder and sadder ; and when one day it was anounced that the Prince was to marry a lovely Princess from another land, she was filled with despair.

That night, when the moon was up, she wandered out on to the shore ; and there she saw her mermaid sisters sitting on the rocks and singing their sweet songs. They greeted her with joy and said how much they had grieved when she had left them, and how they wished she had never chosen to take on the form of a mortal. Then they told her they knew she would never now secure the immortal soul for which she craved, since her human lover was about to wed another maiden ; and they knew also that she must die on his marriage night and become as foam on the wave-tops. They added, however, that they, her loving sisters, had all cut off their long waving hair and given it to the greedy Sea-Witch as the price of saving her from death. They then handed her a knife given them by the Witch, with instructions that she should plunge it into the heart of the Prince as he lay sleeping on his wedding-night—thus, the spell would be broken, her mortal legs would vanish, her fish's tail would reappear, and she could rejoin them in the sea and continue to live as a Mermaid once more.

Their despairing young sister took the knife ; but she could not bring herself to the point of using it.

On the Prince's wedding-day, all was merriment ; and the revels were kept up until late at night, when the royal bride and bridegroom went on board a gaily-decorated barge for a honeymoon trip. The transformed

Mermaid went with them among other attendants ; and when everybody had retired to rest, she took the knife given her by her sisters and crept towards the curtained recess where the happy newly-wedded pair lay sleeping in each other's arms. She bent over her beloved one and gazed at him tenderly for the last time. Then she flung away the Sea-Witch's knife and, running to the side of the barge, sprang overboard into the rippling waves below.

The five Princess Mermaids waited for many hours for their beloved sister to reappear in their midst once more in her mermaid form ; but they waited in vain. When dawn came, they saw nothing but foam on the wave-tops ; and sadly they realised that now they would never see her again.

TWELFTH NIGHT

HERE we have a story of cross-purposes in love that ended happily, after many vicissitudes.

Orsino, the handsome young Duke of Illyria, had conceived a deep passion for the fair Lady Olivia—who would, however, not consider his suit. The excuse she gave was that she was still mourning for her brother, who had recently died. Nevertheless, the beautiful Olivia did not seem to be duly unhappy because of this latter sad event ; for she frequently jested with the various members of her household and appeared to enjoy life well.

The fact was that the youthful heart of Olivia had not yet been touched by love ; and, consequently, she was merely bored by the amorous addresses of the love-sick Duke. Orsino, however, would not give up hope ; and he spent his days in sentimental languishment, sending messenger after messenger with poetic addresses to his lady-love, and turning constantly to music for consolation.

It was at this time that there landed on the shores of Illyria a sweet and charming young girl, named Viola, whose life had been saved when the ship in which she was travelling was wrecked. In this ship-wreck, her beloved twin-brother had been lost ; and she believed him to be drowned. Lonely and unprotected, she decided to enter the service of Duke Orsino as a page-attendant ; and she begged the ship's captain—who had brought her ashore in safety—to find her suitable garments and to introduce her, thus garbed, into the great lord's household. This he did.

Duke Orsino was delighted with his new page—

introduced to him as Cesario—and constantly had the supposed youth in attendance, making a confident of him and showing him every sign of affection—with the result that the disguised Viola quickly fell in love with him. It was, therefore, quite agonising for her when Orsino presently sent her to plead his cause once more with the beautiful Olivia. However, desirous only of pleasing the man she loved, as well as served, she set forth on her unwanted mission.

Before the so-called page arrived at the mansion of Olivia, the latter's kinsman who lived with her, a ne'er-do-well Knight named Sir Toby Belch—fat, lazy, and jolly—had been complaining of his cousin's overlong mourning for her brother. His complaints were addressed to Maria, Olivia's gentlewoman-attendant.

Maria, a bright and lively young woman, though herself equally fond of merriment, instead of listening to his quite unnecessary complaints, roundly scolded him for his late hours, his drinking habits, and the roystering company he kept. Even as she spoke, Sir Toby's latest idle companion, a foolish chicken-hearted Knight, Sir Andrew Aguecheek, joined the pair — a fop who soon added fuel to the fire of her indignation by his many flowery compliments to herself and his stupid remarks and actions.

Then the steward of the household, Malvolio, appeared on the scene, and likewise expressed his disapproval of the two lazy, bibulous knights. Malvolio was a vain and pompous fellow, and was constantly the butt of these household hangers on who found great delight in holding him up to ridicule. Now, however, on learning that a messenger from the Duke Orsino waited at the door, Malvolio stalked off with exaggerated dignity to interview the new page and bring him into the presence of his mistress.

The Lady Olivia had been enjoying a lively conversation and some merry back-chat with Feste, the witty Jester attached to her household ; and, at first, she refused to give audience to the Duke's messenger. Then, on learning that the latter was extremely importunate and refused to depart without seeing her, she dismissed the Clown, called Maria to attend her, and ordered the page to be brought into her presence.

When the disguised Viola appeared, Olivia was at once deeply attracted to her ; and before the end of the former's eloquent pleading of the Duke's suit—which she again declined to consider—she had fallen in love with the charming new page. This latter fact—which was soon quite apparent—caused amusement as well as dismay to the latter ; and she was greatly relieved when the interview came to an end, even though she had to return to her already beloved master with news of the failure of her mission.

The love-sick Orsino now became even more languishing and sad ; and he turned more eagerly than before to his sympathetic page—who, though suffering the pangs of her own unrequited love, was yet glad that he should find her pity a comfort to him.

Meanwhile, the amusing feud in Olivia's household between her ne'er-do-well kinsman, Sir Toby Belch, and the pompous steward, Malvolio, was growing apace; and it presently came to a climax.

Late one night, Sir Toby, his foolish friend, Sir Andrew Aguecheek, and the witty Clown, held a great carousal in an upper room, where they had been drinking much wine, cracking jokes, and cutting capers to their hearts' content. The noise became so great that, presently, the lively Maria ran in, bidding them to be quieter, lest the Steward should hear them and make complaint to his mistress.

The revellers, however, ignored her warning ; but, being delighted to see the gay and pretty Maria and knowing well enough that she loved jollity as well as they did themselves, they persuaded her to remain and keep them company. The fun now became more uproarious than before ; and, in a short time, Maria was gaily dancing on the table for the amusement of the jolly roysterers.

Then it was that the door was suddenly flung open, and Malvolio entered, wearing a long gown and a night-cap and carrying a lighted candle ; and, trembling with indignation, the pompous Steward began roundly to scold the revellers for making so much noise and behaving in such an unseemly manner. For answer, however, they merely laughed at him ; and the Clown and Maria made fun of his night garb, and imitated his pompous actions in a very comical manner.

In a rage at their contempt of his authority, Malvolio departed, declaring that he would report their rowdy conduct to his mistress and bring them all into disfavour with her.

Knowing that the Steward would undoubtedly carry out his threat and that their merry activities might, in consequence, be somewhat curtailed, the revellers now determined to play a trick upon him in revenge ; and they hatched an amusing plot forthwith.

Next day, they dropped a perfumed letter in the path of the self-important official ; and then they hid themselves behind some bushes to see what happened.

Malvolio picked up the letter, which purported to come from the Lady Olivia and in which she declared that she loved him ; and, the letter added, she desired above all things to see his elegant limbs clad in yellow stockings and cross-gartered.

The vain and gullible Malvolio was completely

deceived by this letter ; and, overjoyed to learn from
it that his beautiful mistress loved and admired him,
he hurried away at once to carry out her supposed desire
regarding his nether limbs—to the huge and hilarious
delight of the four hidden conspirators.

A little later on, as Olivia and Maria were walking
in the garden, Malvolio appeared before them, wearing
bright yellow stockings, cross-gartered most elaborately ;
and with mincing steps and exaggerated actions, he
proceeded to address his mistress as though paying
welcome love-addresses to her. When Olivia showed
astonishment and displeasure at such impertinent
behaviour on the part of one in her employ, Malvolio
began to utter quotations from the letter he believed
she had written to him, striking ludicrous attitudes and
falling on his knees as he indicated that his heart was
hers and that he joyfully returned the love she had
offered to him.

By this time, Olivia was alarmed as well as angry ; and
thinking that her usually sedate and pompous steward
had suddenly gone mad, she called some of her lackeys
and ordered them to lock him up in a cellar—hoping
that would cool his ardour somewhat. And there the
unlucky Malvolio had to remain and endure the gibes
of the plotters, until the truth of the whole matter
regarding the perfumed letter became known, when he
was released once more—a wiser and a sadder man.

Meanwhile, the tangled love affairs of the Duke and
Lady Olivia also moved to a climax. It happened that
Sebastian, the young twin-brother of Viola, had not, after
all, been drowned during the shipwreck but had been
likewise rescued by a friend—with whom he had remained for some time, full of woe because he believed his fair
sister had been lost. Later on, he arrived in Illyria,
little dreaming that his beloved Viola was also there, in

disguise ; and here, as he moved about the streets, a whole chapter of misapprehensions occurred.

Meeting the friends and attendants of both Duke Orsino and the Lady Olivia, Sebastian was mistaken by them for the young page they knew as Cesario—whom he so closely resembled ; and many awkward scenes occurred, before the brother and sister actually met.

Finally, however, these mistaken identities were discovered ; and then a joyful reunion took place between the long-separated twin brother and sister. After this, the Lady Olivia was not long in transferring her infatuation for the former page to the handsome Sebastian, who gladly responded to her love ; and when Viola had doffed her disguise as a male and appeared before the Duke as a beautiful young girl who could no longer hide her secret passion for him, Orsino likewise now eagerly reciprocated it.

So, with all their difficulties and cross-purposes thus smoothed away, these happy lovers and their friends all rejoiced together ; and we may be sure that Sir Toby and his roystering friends took their full share in the ensuing wedding revels.

AMORAS

IN a certain chapel near Windsor, during the fifteenth century, a strange and sinister scene took place one day. It depicted yet once again the everlasting struggle between Good and Evil.

A dissipated young Knight, named Amoras, though not wholly bad, was fast heading towards a downward course of evil. Despite the fact that he loved his fair and virtuous young wife, he had been persuaded to sell her to the Devil, in order to gain more money with which to gamble and so to continue his life of dissipation.

His unhappy wife was as good and patient as she was fair ; and when her evil-living husband bade her set forth with him upon a journey—at the end of which he intended to hand her over to the Devil in return for the large sum of money the latter had promised to give him—she meekly and even willingly obeyed him, believing that a good wife should obey her husband in all things.

Nevertheless, she was horrified when she learned presently what was the object of this present journey she was taking with her lord—whom she still loved, despite his wicked ways ; but she continued to put her trust in the Heavenly protection that had kept her safe until now, and she never ceased to pray for guidance.

As this strange pair of travellers went on their way, they came to a chapel by the roadside ; and the lady entreated her now gloomy lord to permit her to enter the sacred building, and to offer more prayers therein for them both. At first, Amoras impatiently refused her request, being anxious to complete the journey as quickly as possible ; for he was already beginning to regret his terrible bargain, though still eager to receive the promised reward, and he feared lest his resolve should be weakened by delay.

His wife, however, was so pathetically insistent that she should be allowed to pray for awhile in this quiet little wayside chapel, that he had not the heart to refuse her last earthly request ; so he gave her the permission she desired, but bade her hasten with her devotions and rejoin him quickly.

Then, as he walked on alone for a few steps, intending to return shortly, he beheld the Devil approaching the chapel ; and, conscience-stricken, he was filled with despair, believing that he would now never look upon the features of his fair wife again. It was already too late for him to withdraw from his fearful bargain, as he might have been inclined to do had the Evil One not been in such a hurry to claim his prize.

But divine help was at hand. The unhappy lady, on entering the chapel, knelt in prayer and again made supplications to the Virgin that her erring husband might be turned from his evil ways ; and she prayed also that she herself might be preserved from the awful fate that threatened her. Then, suddenly overcome with weariness, she fell asleep beside the statue of the Virgin to whom she had prayed.

Her prayers were heard by the Virgin, who now stepped down from her pedestal and temporarily assumed the form of the sleeping lady. When, therefore, the Evil One presently entered the chapel with a jaunty air and beheld, as he supposed, his beautiful victim standing there, ready for him to take, he was amazed at the transformation scene that instantly took place. The Virgin once more resumed her heavenly form, and sternly bade him depart ; and this sudden appearance of One so much more powerful than himself so alarmed Old Nick that he turned tail and fled in terror from the Chapel—and he was never again seen in that part of the country.

When Amoras beheld the Devil fleeing from the Chapel, he was filled with joy, knowing that he was now freed from the wicked bargain he had made and had so quickly regretted; and when he presently entered the Chapel, his beloved wife awakened and came forward happily to greet him.

The Statue of the Virgin was once more standing upon its pedestal; but the lovely features of the Holy Mother smiled down sweetly and graciously upon the now truly repentant Knight and the fair lady to whom he was again united and whose constant prayers had saved him from a terrible sin.

EVERYMAN

WHEN the High Father of Heaven sent Death to bid Everyman prepare to go with him upon his last dread journey, from which he would never return, and to give an account of his life at the end of it, a scene of panic and dismay took place.

Everyman was a prosperous and happy man, well-beloved by his friends and acquaintances; and he was still living a life of pleasure, which he had no desire to renounce. What was more, he was not ready with a clear reckoning of his life's deeds, good and bad, which would certainly be required of him. He was, indeed, totally unprepared for such a sudden summons into the presence of his Maker; and he entreated his unexpected visitor to give him a little more time to make the necessary preparations before leaving the world he loved so well.

Could not his journey be put off until another day? He even offered Death a thousand pounds if his summons could be deferred. Why had he not been warned of the coming of his unwelcome guest? Then he would have had all his affairs put in order and his reckoning ready. Surely a little longer time might be spared to him? How could he possibly be ready at a moment's notice?

To all these eager questions, Death replied inexorably that Everyman's hour had come to leave his life on earth, and that he must now prepare to go with him through the Valley of Shadows.

Then, when Everyman, sore distressed, realised that his departure from his present world was inevitable, and that no delay was to be granted to him, he begged

that he might be allowed some companionship upon
his last journey. He cried out in fear :

" Shall I have no company from this world
     terrestrial

     Of mine acquaintance that way me to lead ? "

Death replied :

" Yea, if any be so hardy,

     That would go with thee and bear thee company."

He added :

" And now, out of thy sight I will me hie ;

     See thou make thee ready shortly ;

     For thou mayst say this is the day

     That no man living may 'scape away."

So Everyman, though still dismayed, set forth to
seek companionship upon his last journey, while Death
hovered in the background.

The first person he approached was Fellowship,
represented by the gay boon companions who had shared
with him all the many pleasures of his life. But a long
journey through the gloomy Valley of the Shadow of
Death was not to the liking of his jolly companions of
old ; and they one and all refused to go with him.
Even though they had loved him well in the past and
would still have gladly joined him in pleasurable pursuits, they had no desire to go with him upon a gloomy
journey from which there was no return. They still
loved their own bright world too well ; and they shuddered at the mere thought of Death.

Distressed by the defection of Fellowship, Everyman
next sought out his Kinsmen, feeling that those of his
own blood could surely be trusted to help him in this
dire necessity. He found them taking part in the
festivities being held in a certain gay street ; and his
heart felt sadder still as he looked upon this merry-
making which he would no longer enjoy. Nevertheless,

he hopefully invited his kinsfolk to join him in the journey he had so suddenly been called upon to make, saying to each in turn : " Kinsman, wilt thou go with me ? "

When, however, they knew the nature of the journey he suggested to them, they fell back from him in horror, and, refusing his request, had many excuses to make. One had a wife, and could not leave ; another declared he had a cramp in his toe and could not walk ; and so on.

Full of disappointment that neither friends nor relatives would join him on his last journey, Everyman suddenly bethought him of his Worldly Goods. " I have loved Riches all my life," he thought.

But when Riches—in the form of a gay young man— knew what was desired of him, he cried : " May I follow no man in such voyages ! " ; and he departed quickly on his way.

Even though a lovely Temptress joined the anxious companion-seeker for awhile and tried to drag him back into the paths of Pleasure once more, on hearing his request she soon refused to remain with him, preferring more lively friends.

Now completely disillusioned, Everyman cried out aloud :

" All forsake me in the ending !
Of whom shall I now counsel take ?
I think that I shall never speed
Till I go to my Good Deeds."

But, alas, his Good Deeds lay cold on the ground, so weak that she could scarcely stir. Nevertheless, though he had neglected her in the past, she was kind and was still willing to help him ; and she called upon Knowledge to come forth and aid him in the making of his reckoning. So, at the bidding of his Good Deeds,

Knowledge, a splendidly-garbed personage, appeared at his side, and said :

"Everyman, I will go with thee and be thy guide,
In thy most need to go by thy side."

Everyman, now full of gratitude, placed himself in the care of Knowledge ; and, under his wise guidance, he made the final preparations for his journey. Knowledge persuaded him to repent of all his wrong-doings in the past ; and then he led him to Confession, who gave him penances, a scourge, and a garment of sorrow.

Then, to his joy, Everyman, having scourged himself and donned his garment of sorrow, found that his repentance and penances had restored power to the weak limbs of his Good Deeds, and that she was now strong enough to rise and walk by his side. She appeared as a beautiful woman clothed in pure white ; and she brought comfort and encouragement to him declaring his good works to all.

As the happy trio moved on their way—with Death still hovering in the background, but ever drawing nearer—they met with other splendid personages now willing to join them. These newcomers were Discretion, Strength, Beauty, and Everyman's own Five Wits.

Knowledge next proposed that Everyman should now visit a Priest and receive his Last Sacrament— which he very gladly did. He now felt happy and safe with his splendid companions walking with him on his way and conversing with him as he grew weaker and weaker ; and he hoped they would never leave him, but would be his companions to the end.

But, to his regret, though he was no longer dismayed by the fact, even these wonderful companions left him at last.

The first to bid him farewell was Beauty, who departed as they approached the cave-like tomb which was to be the last resting-place of Everyman. It was seen that Death was already there, standing at the top of a flight of steps that led within the gloomy portals; and Beauty, with a look of horror, turned away quickly and vanished from sight.

The next to go was Strength, who seemed to regret having come thus far, and Everyman said sadly :

"He that trusteth in his Strength,
She him deceiveth at the length."

After this, Everyman was scarcely surprised when Discretion, and his Five Wits likewise deserted him, as soon as they set eyes on Death ; but he was again filled with joy when his Good Deeds said :

"Everyman, I will bide with thee,
I will not forsake thee indeed,
Thou shalt find me a good friend at need."

Finally, Knowledge, having brought him safely thus far, now stood aside ; and only Good Deeds remained till the end.

But Everyman, now too weak to move another step, no longer feared to enter the Vale of Shadows ; for he was repentant, and had his reckoning ready.

Down the steps that led to the tomb came the dread Summoner, bearing in his outstretched hands a flowing black and purple cloak ; and as Everyman drew his last breath, Death embraced him and, gently wrapping the sable garment around him, bore him away to the Light that lay beyond the Grave.

"He that hath his account whole and sound,
High in Heaven he shall be crowned."

THE MASQUE OF COMUS

In the bright star-spangled Court of Jove amidst the clouds, the Immortals played their graceful games, dancing hither and thither, as light and airy as the rosy-tipped and violet clouds themselves. Cupid and Psyche tripped together in a dainty winged measure; Venus and Adonis entwined their arms lovingly as they moved from one bright spot to another; and Iris, the lovely Rainbow Messenger of the Gods—an office she shared with Mercury—was close at hand to wait upon the behests of one and all. Many other deities were present, too, on this occasion; and the scene was a brilliant one, indeed.

At the right hand of Jove stood his Attendant Sprite, whose duty it was to be watchful and to look down upon the Earth below and report what he saw there to his enthroned Master. Presently, his watchfulness was rewarded; and he now related to Jove a sad little scene he had just espied.

It was night-time on Earth; and in the midst of a dark sinister forest, a young and lovely mortal Lady had become separated from her two Cavalier brothers, with whom she was taking a journey; and she was now lost and alone in the Enchanted Forest of Comus, the Sorcerer.

In pity for this lost lady's dangerous plight, Jove commanded his Attendant Sprite to descend to earth immediately, and go to her assistance. In order that the Sprite should be able to carry out his mission without let or hindrance and be the better equipped to overcome the forces of Evil around him, Jove also commanded

Iris to spin for him a magic jacket which should render him invisible when necessary ; and he also directed the Sprite to assume the guise of a mortal shepherd to be known as Thyrsis.

Instantly obedient to the powerful divinity's command, Iris and her handmaidens began to spin the magic jacket ; and in a short time it was ready. Then the Attendant Sprite descended to earth ; and garbed in his magic jacket, he became invisible as he entered the Enchanted Forest.

* * * * *

Meanwhile, the lost Lady was still sitting on a mossy stone in the forest, where her two brothers had left her. These young people had lost their way and had become benighted on a journey they were taking. They were about to join their parents, Lord and Lady Bridgwater, who had just taken up residence at Ludlow Castle, the Earl having recently been appointed as President of Wales during that year, 1634.

As night descended upon them, the two brothers were full of concern for the comfort and safety of their fair young sister. The latter was already weary ; and the dense forest in which they had become lost was certainly no safe place for her at night. Though they did not then know that a Sorcerer lived therein, the perils from robbers and from exposure were sufficient to alarm them. They decided, therefore, that they must at least seek some safe lodging for their charge ; and having noticed a twinkling light in the distance and thinking this might be issuing from some shepherd's hut, they set off to find the latter and seek hospitality, after bidding their sister to go no further but to await their return in that spot.

At first, the Lady was willing enough to rest upon the stony seat in the place where her brothers had left her ;

but, after awhile, when the young Cavaliers did not return, she began to grow too alarmed to remain where she was, and determined to seek them. In haste, she set forth once again, only to become more dazed than ever by the encircling labyrinth of gloomy trees around her. Then, suddenly, she heard in the distance the footsteps and voices of an approaching party of revellers ; and though they sounded a wild and noisy throng, she hoped they might be able to assist her. Therefore, with some instinctive doubt and trepidation, she began to make her way towards them.

Well might the lost maiden have an instinctive feeling of doubt as she slowly drew near the approaching revellers ; for the newcomers were none other than the evil Sorcerer, Comus, Lord of these gloomy forest depths, attended by his rout of wild companions.

Now, Comus, though to all outward appearance a handsome but dissolute young man, a reckless and unrestrained libertine, was not an ordinary mortal. He was, in fact, a son of Bacchus, the God of Wine ; and his mother was the wicked Siren, Circe. Like his licentious sire, he loved to engage in drinking orgies and wild carousals ; and from his unscrupulous mother, he had inherited a gift for sorcery and the arts of Black Magic. However, whereas it was the delight of Circe to transform her lovers into swine that grovelled and guzzled at her feet, her evil son, Comus, preferred his boon companions to retain their own human bodies, but, by means of his spells, crowned them with the heads only of all kinds of beasts. By this means, he had gathered around him a large company of gay young men and women, who wore splendid costumes on their human bodies and joined him willingly enough in his orgies of dancing and feasting, but who were yet monsters, since they all wore the heads of wild beasts—wolves, foxes, bears, lions, and horned creatures of many kinds. Comus himself wore no beast's head, but his handsome face was sinister to look upon, since it revealed plainly his evil mind.

In the midst of this Enchanted Forest, Comus had his Palace and Hall of Magic and Iniquity, where he and his monster companions held continual orgies and indulged in their evil and licentious pleasures. Every now and again, however, they issued forth in noisy hordes to hold revels in certain glades and groves, where they took part in unholy abhorrent rites and heathenish sacrifices, in which the Sorcerer himself was the High Priest and administered the terrible Black Magic ritual.

It was when now returning from one of these sacrificial orgies that Comus became aware of the presence in his domain of the lost mortal Lady ; and on presently observing her approaching down a tangled glade, he commanded his rout of monsters to return to his Palace and leave him alone to deal with the fair wanderer.

Always subservient to their evil lord's commands, the drunken mob withdrew to the nearby Palace ; and Comus, composing his sinister features somewhat and assuming the dignified politeness of a well-born Cavalier of the period, approached his hoped-for victim.

The unhappy lost maiden was much relieved to find that the main party of drunken revellers had moved on, and that only one of their number remained ; and hope arose within her. In answer to the seemingly sympathetic and respectful enquiries of Comus, she explained her present predicament to him.

Ravished by the Lady's exquisite beauty, and instantly conceiving a violent passion for her, Comus determined to secure her as another member of his licentious company ; but, observing her innocence and wishing to gain her confidence, he was careful not to reveal his true character to her at first. With pretended solicitude, therefore, he offered himself as her temporary protector, begging her to return with him to his forest abode to await the expected return of her brothers, who would certainly seek her there—adding that it was not safe for her to remain alone another moment in the forest, in which lurked so many hidden dangers.

So full of fears was the unhappy Lady by this time that she allowed herself to be persuaded by this handsome and plausible stranger to place herself in his temporary care ; and Comus triumphantly took her by the arm and led her away to his Enchanted Palace.

* * * * *

All this time, Jove's Attendant Sprite had not been idle in carrying out his mission. Having rendered himself invisible by means of his magic jacket, he had seen and heard all that had passed in the forest during the absence of the two brother Cavaliers. Now hearing the approach of the latter, he discarded his jacket of invisibility and took on the humble form of a mortal shepherd. Introducing himself to them by the name of Thyrsis, he offered to help them in their trouble.

The two brothers, on the approach of Thyrsis, had drawn their swords, thinking he might be a robber ; but quickly realising that he was but a humble shepherd they gladly accepted his aid. They were horrified on learning that their beloved and helpless sister had fallen into the hands of the evil Sorcerer ; and they were youthfully eager to storm the abode of Comus at once. Thyrsis, however, warned them that they must exercise caution in dealing with one versed in the Black Arts, and he instructed them, on entering the Palace, first to secure the magic wand of Comus, when the latter would thus become powerless.

The disguised Attendant Sprite then led the furious and anxious brothers through devious but safer paths to the abode of the wicked Sorcerer.

* * * * *

Meanwhile, Comus had brought his lovely captive into the great hall of his forest Palace of Iniquity. Here he seated her on a throne between two long banqueting-tables laden with rich food and wines ; and he compelled her to look on whilst his horrible rout of monsters feasted and drank like the gluttons they were, or made licentious love on the couches set around the tables.

It was an orgy such as no virtuous maiden should ever have looked upon. All the feasters, male and female, were dressed in the most gorgeous gowns or suits of the latest extravagant fashion ; and they were likewise hung about with chains of flashing jewels. The wearers of these dazzling costumes were all crowned with the heads of beasts ; and the whole grotesque scene was horrible and fantastic in the extreme. Many of the monster guests were already too drunk to sit at the table, and, instead, rolled on the floor, closely wrapped in each others' arms ; some made open love as they lolled in their chairs ; and others still sat guzzling at the table.

The cruelly deceived Lady would gladly have fled away again as soon as she had been led to her throne-like chair ; but, to her horror, she found that she could no longer move her limbs, which had been paralysed instantly by the magic spells of the Sorcerer—who, however, left her the use of her senses and her power of speech, so that her perceptions and feelings were still acute.

Having quickly realised that this fair maiden's purity and love of chastity would have to be overcome before he could win her willingly to his licentious desires—and he preferred a willing victim, if possible—Comus had hoped that, by accustoming her eyes to the degrading scenes around her, he would wear down her resistance and induce her to think that Vice was more amusing than Virtue. To this end, therefore, he caused his vile creatures to dance before her, and to engage in still more boisterous revels; and he also danced before her himself, with increasingly alluring movements.

At the side of the throne there stood a beautiful female attendant, named Cotytto, who had been permitted to retain her own lovely features, instead of taking on those of an animal, and whose special duty seemed to be to help Comus with his spells and enchantments.

Cotytto was the most voluptuous and exquisite dancer of the whole company; and when she presently summoned to her side the Spirit of Wine, the pair danced together with such grace and allurement that all the feasters were filled with delight. But not so the fair captive Lady, who looked on at this performance coldly and unmoved.

Comus now bade Cotytto bring forth a golden cup containing the magic draught that should cause the intended victim to become as the monster humans around her, and thus compel her to his own sensual desires; but the Lady calmly refused to drink. Again, Cotytto brought forth another cup of the same magical compound, but this time craftily pretending that it was pure wine; and again the Lady refused to drink.

Then Comus endeavoured to break down her resistance by becoming tender and even respectful in the offer of his love; and he kissed her gently and entreated her to abandon her scruples and to enjoy the pleasures in store for her.

But again, and yet again, the spell-bound Lady refused to have anything to do with the evil delights offered to her, or to drink the fatal potion that would transform her into a beast. It was a mighty struggle between Virtue and Vice ; and realising that he would never gain his evil ends by persuasion, or secure her love willingly, Comus was now about to resort to force when there came a sudden interruption.

The two Cavalier brothers of the desired victim burst into the banqueting-hall, followed by Thyrsis ; and rushing upon the throne-chair whereon sat their beloved sister, they were just in time to dash the golden cup from the hand of Comus, who was about to compel her to swallow its fatal contents.

Instantly, the wicked Sorcerer made his escape from these sturdy defenders of virtue, with their disguised shepherd assistant—whose divine power he sensed ; and he was followed by his rout of monsters, eager to avoid the blows rained upon them as they vanished.

As the two brothers now joyfully ran to clasp their rescued sister in their arms, they were horrified to find that she was unable to move because of her paralysed limbs ; and Thyrsis upbraided them for having forgotten his instructions to seize the magic wand of Comus, with which they could have broken the spell. But when the young Cavaliers wrung their hands in distress at their forgetfulness, Thyrsis declared that their sister might yet be saved ; and, producing a simple herb he was possessed of, he invoked the aid of Sabrina, the Spirit of the River Severn, which flowed through that part of the country.

In answer to his call, the lovely River Goddess appeared, followed by her attendant River Nymphs, all garbed in flowing gauzy draperies and water-weeds ; and as these graceful beings danced lightly and airily about her, Sabrina waved her wand over the spell-bound Lady, and gently broke the spell.

The captive maiden, her limbs free once more, ran down from her hated throne-chair, and was joyfully clasped in her brothers' arms. Then, after receiving the grateful thanks of the now happy trio, Sabrina and her nymphs returned to their river haunts ; and the young travellers set forth once more upon the last stage of their journey home, accompanied by their temporary protector, Thyrsis.

* * * * *

In the home of the Earl and Countess of Bridgwater, at Ludlow Castle, great festivities were being held to welcome the new Lord of the Manor and Governor of Wales. All the villagers had been invited to take part in a joyous day-time revel in the vast grounds of the Castle.

A flower-decked arbour and dais had been erected in one part of the beautiful gardens ; and a loyal welcome was given to the noble host and hostess when the latter arrived and seated themselves upon the richly-draped chairs set there for them. With them came a number of other lords and ladies to watch the revels, which then began immediately. The villagers performed their favourite gay country dances, including the most popular one of all, known as " the Widdy-Widdy - Way," which was full of fun and aroused much laughter among the guests. The lords and ladies likewise danced some of the graceful measures which were then the fashion in Court circles ; and the rustics gazed open - mouthed at these elegant steps and figures so strange to them.

Just as the revels were at their height, there came a joyful interruption. The once lost Lady and her two Cavalier brothers were seen to be entering through the gateway of the garden ; and the three young people at once ran forward to greet their noble parents, and to receive the latter's fond embraces. It was a happy reunion, and all were thankful for their safe arrival at last ; and gratitude was expressed to their seeming shepherd companion.

Then the revels continued once more—this time more joyfully than before, since all the performers wished to show by their merry laughter and gay dances their real delight at this joyful reunion.

And now it was time for Thyrsis, the Shepherd, to bid farewell to the three young people he had protected from such a great danger ; and then, resuming his dazzling form as an Attendant Sprite, he ascended once more to the glorious realms of the great god, Jove, there to report upon his mission so well fulfilled.

PLANETOMANIA

A YOUNG scientist, whom we will call Adam, sat alone in his laboratory one day. He was feeling rather pleased with himself, for the long and interesting experiments he had been making during recent years showed signs at last of maturing into something tangible.

He was endeavouring to get into touch with the planet, Venus ; and certain vibrations he had felt by means of the original and complicated instruments he had contrived seemed to him to prove that he had nearly, if not quite, established contact with that most intriguing, far-distant sphere—at present a practically closed region to all mortals save himself alone. For he had been careful to keep his experiments entirely a secret, and had not revealed his intentions and approaching success to anyone—not even to his own pretty and gay young wife, Mathilde, nor to the pert maid who helped with the domestic " chores." The latter, incidentally, strongly disapproved of his untidy laboratory, which she was seldom permitted even to surface dust, and never to disturb. She just longed to give it " a good turn-out."

Yes, Adam was well-pleased with the results so far achieved of his vast experiments ; and he rubbed his hands with glee as he reflected that he might soon be able to intercept some sort of a long-distance message—perhaps, a kind of planetary trunk-call !

As he now " twiddled the knobs " of his instruments, he listened for a response.

He was not, however, quite prepared for what actually happened at that same moment. In a brilliant flash of dazzling light, there suddenly appeared before him the ravishing living form of the beautiful Goddess Venus herself, sweetly smiling upon him and greeting him with every sign of more than friendly pleasure ! He certainly had not expected such a stupendous success as this—nor quite such an embarrassing one !

The latter fact was amply and quickly proved. Within a few moments of the sudden arrival of Venus, there came a knock at the laboratory door ; and, without waiting for a reply, in bounced Charlotte, the plain snub-nosed maid of the household, complete with broom and duster, and drastically determined to do some long overdue " cleaning-up," or, at least, as she announced, " to take the thick off."

However, on beholding her master in the act of greeting a gloriously beautiful female—and one most scantily and curiously clad in floating and almost transparent draperies !—she was so amazed that she almost fainted at the sight. Then, gathering together her dropped domestic implements, she turned and marched out, with her snub nose in the air and in high dudgeon, to her own domain.

Adam, realising how awkward the consequences of his too successful experiments might prove to be, hastily did some quick thinking ; and then he went through a formula he luckily remembered, which caused the radiant Venus to disappear to her own planet once more.

He was only just in time ; and, next moment, his pretty and lively wife, Mathilde, ran into the room to announce the arrival of visitors. Adam had, willy-nilly, to help entertain the guests ; but as soon as they had departed, he once more returned to his laboratory and eagerly continued his now most exciting experiments.

To his joy, he again succeeded in causing Venus to materialise and to ravish him with the divine grace of her movements as she now danced before him ; but his joy was short-lived. The lively Mathilde suddenly entered the room, followed by her still shocked and offended maid—who, doubtless, had already informed her of her usually shy and retiring student-husband s outrageous " goings-on."

Despite Adam's frantic explanations regarding his successful contacts with his lovely visitor's planet, Mathilde entirely disapproved of this most distracting result. She emphatically resented the intrusion of any kind of a goddess as a member of her most respectable household—especially such a disturbing element as the lovely Venus. Was not the latter well known to be a designing minx who had flirted with such attractive males as Mars and Adonis instead of keeping house for her own plain hard-working spouse, Vulcan, who, though doubtless a somewhat dull, grimy, and cantankerous fellow, was, nevertheless, the right sort of person to keep such a roving beauty in order ?

Determined that this unwelcome celestial visitant should not secure an additional string to her already well-stretched bow in the person of Adam—a simple soul, foolish Planetomaniac though he was—she firmly commanded her husband to get rid of the dazzling goddess at once.

The distracted Adam, worried to death by this domes tic complication, hastily " twiddled the knobs " and worked the levers of his instrument in every likely and unlikely position and combination ; but, in his acute anxiety to end the present embarrassing situation, he unfortunately mixed up the formula he had previously worked out—with the devastating result that the three women present—the lovely goddess, Mathilde, and

Charlotte—vanished. They had been instantly transported to the planet, Venus ; and the puzzled Adam was left alone in his laboratory, still frantically " twiddling the knobs."

* * * * *

On the planet Venus, all the brightness and joy had temporarily departed with the absence of the lovely, presiding Goddess ; and everybody shivered with cold in the pale bluish-green light.

The exquisite youth, Adonis, stood motionless and disconsolate, waiting for the return of Venus, whose latest lover he was ; and the symbolic Swallow-Guardian of the planet, likewise waited silently and motionless, with sadly-drooping wings, in the distance, watching for the first signs of the reappearance of the lovely Goddess, who had departed so suddenly and unwillingly to the dull Earth.

Presently, however, the accustomed golden light and warmth gradually returned ; and all the inhabitants of the planet rejoiced as the radiant Goddess, Venus, once more appeared in their midst, borne upon the light and airy shoulders of Zephyrs. They danced around her with the utmost joy ; but soon their attention was diverted when it was seen that she was quickly followed by two strangers—the mortals, Mathilde and Charlotte, around whom they crowded with the greatest curiosity.

Leaving her subjects to gaze upon the strangers in their midst, Venus quickly sought the eagerly-welcoming and graceful youth, Adonis, with whom she danced joyously for awhile ; and the happy lovers were about to wander off together and forget all but the bliss of their reunion, when a violent commotion in the elements occurred, and the planet rocked and vibrated unpleasantly.

This disturbance heralded the arrival of Vulcan, the

God of Metals and Fire and the lawful spouse of Venus. Full of anger at the sight of his flirtatious wife in the arms of her latest admirer, Vulcan commanded his handmaidens to fling a net over the lovers, within the meshes of which they had to remain entangled until someone took the trouble to release them.

Most of the company laughed at and made fun of the lovers' undignified plight ; but Charlotte, the domestic maid from Earth, took pity upon the distressed pair, and released them—though she still regarded Venus as an undoubted " hussy," she could not help admiring the handsome youth, Adonis.

The latter, however, on being released from the net, began to be struck with the good looks of the other stranger mortal, Mathilde, evidently finding her lively charms a refreshing change from the perfect classical beauty of Venus ; but the latter was displeased on observing this fact. Not in the least grateful for the kindness of one of the visiting mortals, she now announced that they must both dance before her company of celestial courtiers, in order that the latter might decide whether or not they possessed the necessary qualifications to remain as inhabitants of her planet.

Mathilde was the first to be put on trial ; and her natural grace and vivacious prettiness charmed everybody—especially the susceptible Adonis—a fact that pleased the lively mortal far more than it did the already somewhat jealous Venus. The latter, however, though somewhat against her will, was obliged to declare that Mathilde had passed the test and might remain upon the planet.

The plain and prudish domestic, on the contrary, was declared by one and all to be " a Fright," and was ordered to be cast out at once and to be returned to the dull Earth. So, poor Charlotte, who would have liked to remain in this bright spot—which reminded her of " the Pictures " at home—was ruthlessly pushed aside and tossed back to Earth on a rising wind as a tremendous vibration now shook the planet.

* * * * *

The vibration which had just shaken the planet Venus had been caused by the distracted scientist, Adam, working at high pressure in his laboratory on Earth, in a frantic effort to effect the return of his vanished wife. The latter had become far more desirable in his eyes since her fatal disappearance ; but he did not care two straws whether he ever set eyes on Charlotte again.

He had pulled all the levers in his machine in every possible combination he could think of, without the desired result, having completely forgotten the correct formula. At last, however, he gave one final mighty wrench before giving up altogether ; and, lo and behold ! this combination and formula worked.

There was suddenly a strange sound as of someone rushing through space, followed by a nearby flurry of wind-blown skirts and petticoats ; and Adam turned excitedly to gaze down upon the unharmed figure and crumpled heap of feminine garments now lying at his feet.

But no pretty and lively Mathilde lay there. Instead, it was the broom-and-duster-loving, plain and prudish Charlotte, still indignant and disapproving, who had flopped so heavily at his feet ; and two pairs of astonished eyes now gazed upon one another with the deep gloom of disappointment.

* * * * *

There is a Moral attached to this story. It is not wise to be too clever by half ; and over-daring excursions into the Uncharted Seas of the Unknown are apt to have disconcerting results !

THE NUTCRACKER

(*Casse Noisette*)

IN the splendid mansion of an important high official in a quaint old German town, towards the end of the eighteenth century, all the lights were blazing forth from the uncurtained windows and open door. A Christmas Party was being held within, and the guests were arriving in gay chattering groups—many of them children and young people accompanied by their elders. There was snow on the ground and sparkling frost on the trees ; but the arriving guests were oblivious of the cold weather, for they were well-wrapped in fur coats and cloaks and it did not take them long to step from their sleighs or coaches over the carpeted entrance and into the brilliant warm hall beyond.

In the vast drawing-room, children and adults alike were gaily dressed for the Party—the girls in long white muslin frocks with tiny frills at the hem and coloured sashes around their waists, and the boys in velvet suits with lace collars and cuffs. The adult guests were likewise gracefully attired in the festive fashion of the days of Napoleon ; and everybody was dancing or playing games. An enormous Christmas-tree stood in one corner, brilliantly illuminated with coloured lights.

There was great excitement presently when one of the male guests entered the room with an armful of parcels wrapped in coloured papers and tied with ribbons ; and he soon had all the children dancing around him, eager for the various gifts he had brought for them. Shrieks of delight quickly followed as the parcels were eagerly unwrapped by the lucky recipients—a doll for one, a drum for another, a furry animal for someone else, and so on. The hostess's young daughter, Clara, was overjoyed on being presented with a handsome Nutcracker.

Clara was so pleased with her elegant Nutcracker that she carried it about with her all the evening ; and she was much distressed when, just as the children were trooping into the dining-room beyond for supper, her brother tried to snatch it from her. Young Franz had wanted that Nutcracker for himself and was disappointed when it had been given to Clara ; and he had been lying in wait for a chance to get it from her. But Clara clung fast to her precious gift ; and a battle-royal ensued. The youthful protagonists, however, were soon parted by their mother and sent to join their guests in the supper-room—but not before Franz had succeeded in snatching the Nutcracker from his protesting sister and had flung it on to a deep-seated chair at the other end of the room.

For the remainder of the evening, Clara did not think any more about her lost gift ; and when the Party came to an end she was glad enough to be put to bed by her old nurse at a considerably later hour than usual. She did not, however, at first feel inclined to sleep ; and for a long time she lay awake, still excited and restless. Even when, at length, she managed to fall into a troubled sleep, she was suddenly awakened again by the clock striking midnight.

Clara sat up in bed and counted the chimes. Yes, it was midnight, a time when she was usually fast asleep. And how strange she felt—was something going to happen to her ? She felt curiously grown-up—nearly as old as one of those lovely Princesses she had read about in her beloved fairy-tale books !

Then it was that, princess or no princess, Clara suddenly remembered about her lost Nutcracker—that most charming gift she had received at the Party and which her brother Franz had snatched away from her just before going in to supper. Where had the tiresome boy thrown it ? Ah, she recollected now seeing it fall on to the seat of the big velvet chair at the other end of the drawing-room. How careless of her not to have retrieved it later on ! Perhaps, however, it was still there ? She must go downstairs and rescue it before Franz found it again next morning.

Quick as thought, Clara sprang out of bed, hastily put on her slippers, and groped her way down the broad staircase into the now darkened drawing-room. Everybody in the house had retired to bed by this time ; but, though darkness and silence reigned, Clara, curiously enough, did not feel afraid. The dying fire still threw a faint flicker of light everywhere.

And there, to her joy, on one of the big velvet chairs, lay her precious Nutcracker, safe and sound ! But, surely, it was larger than when she last saw it ? Perhaps, however, the firelight made it look larger. Everything looked bigger—even she, Clara !

Then, a really terrifying thing happened ! From various corners of the room an entire regiment of MICE came scurrying out, all dressed in full battle array and led by one of their number wearing a crown and a royal-purple coat, who was obviously the Mouse King ! What was more, these war-like mice were monsters of their kind and quite as big as Clara herself !

With a wild shriek of horror, Clara jumped on to the big velvet chair and crouched down beside her newly-found Nutcracker, with her trembling legs well tucked up under her nightgown—though, strange to say, this latter garment no longer seemed to be a nightgown but a long silken frock. Another remarkable circumstance —and a very comforting one, too—was that the Nutcracker beside her seemed to be coming to life and gradually taking on the form of a handsome youth.

Then, click-clack, came a sound from a box of toy-soldiers—left by brother Franz on a footstool ; and, next moment, all its contents came tumbling out, helter-skelter—and lo and behold ! a whole regiment of live soldiers stood up boldly in a line, ready to do battle against the King of the Mice and his four-legged warriors with long tails !

" Allow me to defend you, fair Princess ! " cried the Nutcracker youth, now all-alive-O and full of pluck ; and, leaping to the floor from the chair, he dashed forward and placed himself at the head of the now living and moving toy-soldiers.

" ' Fair Princess,' he said ! " murmured the delighted Clara to herself : " Then, I really *am* grown-up ! How wonderful to be a Princess ! "

A great battle now took place on the drawing-room floor. The two opposing armies of warriors advanced and retired for a short time, making stray passes at one another with their toy-like and rather useless-looking weapons ; and then they began to fight in grim earnest. It was a terrible sight to watch ; for the hideous King of the Mice looked most ferocious, since his crown was set around with sharp spikes like teeth. His subjects likewise bristled with teeth and sharp claws ; and it was all the toy soldiers could do to keep them at bay.

When things began to look rather desperate for the boldly-struggling Nutcracker leader, Clara bravely jumped down from her safe perch in the chair and ran to his side to encourage and help him all she could—scared though she was when the giant mice rubbed against her legs and scampered over her feet. They made her shiver with fright.

This last piece of impudence, however, was more than Clara could stand ; and, snatching off her slipper, she hurled it with all her might at the hateful King of the Mice. Luckily, her aim was good, and the slipper hit him well and truly on the nose !

This broke the spell ; and the battle ended as suddenly as it had begun, with a great victory for the toy-soldiers and their splendid leader. What was more, as a reward for their united bravery, the Nutcracker youth was instantly transformed into a handsome and splendidly-arrayed young Prince ; and, at the same time, Clara discovered that she was, indeed, a beautiful Fairy Princess in dazzling garments, such as she had always longed to be.

Immediately, this charmingly transformed pair fell in love with one another ; and, after some happy talking and dancing together, the Nutcracker Prince invited his fair Princess to take a journey with him to the sparkling Kingdom of Sweets. As Clara only too willingly agreed to this delightful plan, they set forth at once.

Magic was certainly in the air ; for, in a moment or two, the Nutcracker Prince and his lovely companion found themselves outside the house—quite regardless of closed windows and bolted doors !—and floating about in a snowstorm. The snow-flakes were now seen to be Snow Fairies, who fluttered and danced about them, inviting them to join in their whirling frolics ; and it was all like a joyous wintry Carnival.

Presently, however, the happy pair left the Snow Fairies far behind, and found themselves sailing gently in a little boat on a rosy and silvery sea. They were gradually approaching a dazzling island in the distance, which appeared to be emerging like a jewelled mound from the sea and which they knew to be the Magic

Kingdom of Sweets. Fairy dolphins began to frolic around them ; and the softest of zephyrs wafted their light skiff forward without any effort on their part.

As they drew near to the shores of this dazzling Island of Enchantment, they had to pass through a cave guarded by strange and rather terrifying creatures, which alarmed Clara considerably, so that she clung to her brave Prince for safety.

But the cave presently melted away before their wondering eyes—it was probably only made of sugar, after all !—and the lovers now found themselves in a beautiful garden in the magical Land of Sweets. Trees and flowers of scintillating sweets and sugar-candy glistened on every side ; and an equally sparkling Palace of Sugar could be seen nearby.

No sooner had the Nutcracker Prince and his charming Princess appeared in this magical garden than they were most graciously welcomed by an exquisite little sylph-like person who introduced herself to them as the Sugar-Plum Fairy. She then announced in a very sweet voice—she couldn't help being sweet !—that, in honour of these royal new arrivals, a grand Festival of Dances would be held at once.

First of all, the dainty Sugar-Plum Fairy and her sylph attendants danced several marvellous dances themselves ; then, with a wave of her wand, the fairy hostess brought before her admiring guests many brilliant dancers from various parts of the world. These visiting artists performed the most amazing dances, one after the other—Turkish, Spanish, Arab, Chinese, Russian, and so on. Then the Nutcracker Prince and his .Princess were invited to dance together ; and the Sugar-Plum Fairy and her special partners danced again. It was, indeed, a dazzling Dance Festival.

However, like all good things, it came to an end at

last—and the *finale* was even more amazing still. It was, in fact, like the Transformation Scene in an old-fashioned Pantomime. All these happily dancing beings were gradually transformed into a vast swarm of equally happy Bees, all buzzing and fluttering with their gauzy wings around an immense Bee-Hive—which, to judge by their eager clustering about it, was probably full of celestial golden Honey.

And there, perforce, we must leave them ; for that is the end of the story.

THE BIG CITY

IT was evening in the Big City ; and the usual crowds were to be seen in the streets, jostling one another good-humouredly as they hurried home from work or sought to occupy their leisure hours with amusements of one kind or another. Theatre lights were already shining forth, and advertisement neon-signs began to twinkle from vantage points on the many high buildings outlined against the evening sky. There was a feeling of relaxation and gaiety in the air.

It was a motley crowd, with a heterogeneous mingling of rich and poor—virtuous and otherwise—wage-earners and street-walkers, flower-sellers, news-vendors, and idle pleasure-seekers—the infinite variety of humanity to be seen in any of the world's great cities at that hour.

Threading her way skilfully through the busy throng with accustomed ease came an attractive young work-girl, eager to reach her home in a shabby neighbourhood, change into less drab clothes, and issue forth once more in search of such pleasure as might come her way.

She was soon joined by her young workman sweet-heart, who greeted her tenderly ; and after lingering for a few moments to indulge in some shop-gazing and happy converse, the pair were about to continue on their way when there came an unpleasant interruption—that is to say, unpleasant for the young man, though agreeable to the young woman.

The happy couple had for some little time been watched and shadowed by a sophisticated and would-be elegant man of a seemingly higher social status, dressed in fashionable but somewhat flashy evening clothes.

This man was, however, an unscrupulous libertine, who used gay luxurious haunts for his own dissolute and immoral purposes. Attracted by the innocent charm of the pretty work girl, he decided to amuse himself with her for a few hours—for he was at a loose end that evening and hoped she would prove an easy prey. He soon enticed the young girl's attention towards him by his admiring glances ; and then, growing bolder, he made inviting signs to her to leave the side of her workman sweetheart and accept his own escort instead.

The young girl, flattered by the stranger's obvious admiration, and thrilled by the fascinating manners of the smartly-garbed Man-About-Town, foolishly yielded to his enticing invitation ; and presently, she slipped to his side and tripped off gaily with him—leaving her deserted swain amazed and furious at her unexpected conduct. The latter was too bewildered and deeply wounded by her sudden desertion to attempt to follow her ; and after watching her vanish from sight, he moved away with a sad heart and returned to his own home, alone.

* * * * *

In one of the back streets of a mean neighbourhood, a few women and girls stood outside the doors of their shabby homes, gossiping after their hard daily work ; and their children — most of them grubby and unkempt — played about the street in a happy, light-hearted manner.

Presently, the children stopped their games, and their mothers ceased to gossip, too, as the pretty young work-girl—well-known to them all—suddenly appeared in their midst, accompanied by her new admirer, the flashily-garbed *débonnaire* Man-About-Town ; and looks of surprise and gaping wonder, greeted the newcomers. This wonderment increased next moment, when the girl's admiring companion now placed in her hands a neatly-wrapped parcel he had been carrying—obviously a dress-box from a smart shop.

The young girl thanked him very prettily for his gift, and then ran past the now strongly disapproving women into her own tenement home, to get ready for her evening's pleasure—leaving her gay cavalier to wait outside for her return.

The Libertine strolled aside nonchalantly, scarcely heeding the now hostile glances cast upon him from time to time by the women inhabitants of this shabby, but honest, neighbourhood—who seemed to resent the intrusion of such an obvious " toff " into their midst. These women were instinctively aware that his eager interest in their neighbour's pretty daughter boded no good to the latter ; and even the youngsters, sensing the uneasiness of their elders, likewise ceased their play and drew back from the unwelcome stranger.

In a very short time, the young girl returned, completely transformed and looking prettier than ever in the attractive evening clothes presented to her by her new admirer—into whose already passion-filled eyes she gazed gratefully, and almost rapturously, for having thus provided her with such an exquisite fairy-godmother-like outfit. Never before had she been able to wear such wonderful clothes, though, like most other young girls of her class, she had always longed to do so !

Her new acquaintance, too, was gay, his conversation sparkling, and his whole appearance so seductively persuasive that she was only too ready for the evening's pleasure in his company he had promised her. So fresh and lovely did she now appear that even the sex-sated Libertine himself was more than delighted with his charming capture ; and, despite the definitely hostile looks cast upon him by the bystanders, he clasped her eagerly in his arms and even danced a few turns with her in the street.

The transformed young girl was now completely enthralled by the glamorous stranger—so different from the uncultured and often uncouth young men of her own station in life ; and forgetful of the humble but truly loving and steadfast sweetheart she was deserting, she gladly permitted herself to be led away by one who could introduce to her the more dazzling pleasures of the great City—pleasures hitherto unattainable to a poor work-girl.

Perhaps she did not realise—or, at least, care to think of—the heavy price she would eventually have to pay for these transient joys—but the now grim-visaged women, and even the sharp-witted youngsters, she left behind in her humble home street, certainly did ; and they cast mocking glances upon the gay and giddy pair as they danced away and vanished from sight.

*　　*　　*　　*　　*

In a bright and scintillating dance-hall, the Libertine and his charming victim-companion gaily danced the evening hours away ; and no matter how hilarious, or how seductively languorous the music and dancing became, they were always ready to outshine all the other dancers in the room. The young girl, in her first fine ball-dress, was completely intoxicated with the delight of wearing such expensively decorative clothes and with the ecstasy of moving so rhythmically in the firmly clasped arms of so skilful a partner ; and the latter's passion continued to rise as he felt the throbbing heart-beats of the fair young body he held closer and ever closer, knowing with satisfaction that his immediate pleasure was moving swiftly and inevitably to its logical conclusion.

Meanwhile, in much cheaper, if equally bright, dancehalls, filled with dancers of a humbler kind, the unhappy deserted sweetheart of the subtly-enticed but still entranced young girl moved from time to time, seeking his lost beloved one. Gone was his temporary anger because of her desertion of him and of her foolish yielding to the flattering admiration of an amorous stranger ; and he was now eager only to find her again and to entreat her to leave her new and flashy companion and return to his own loving, if less exciting, arms once more.

But where was she in this vortex of a great City's night-time pleasures ? Eagerly he sought her in dance-hall after dance-hall ; but he did not find her.

Already she had passed from his own humble but honest workaday life, and was lost to him within a dazzling but less satisfying world into which he could never enter. She had carelessly chosen the frail transient joy of a single dazzling moment ; and for this she had lightly cast aside the faithful heart that truly loved her.

Suddenly, the unhappy young man realised this tragic fact and knew that his beloved one was indeed lost to him for ever ; and, overwhelmed with sorrow, he stood alone, long after the other dancers had departed, gazing forth into the now gloomy darkness, unseeing and lost to his surroundings.

CHRONICA

In a prosperous Italian town during the fifteenth century, there was a certain amount of unrest. The government of the town was somewhat lax ; the nobles and high officials were often more mindful of their own interests than those of the common people they ruled ; and there were often clashes between factions.

Nevertheless, when the Carnival season came round during the year when this story opens, the people temporarily forgot their differences and plunged wholeheartedly into the revels they loved so well. They sang and danced in the streets, and a grand masquerade was held in which the nobles and high officials took part, to the great admiration and delight of the townsfolk.

The masquerade festivities were led by a handsome young nobleman named Andrea, who was the head of the aristocratic portion of the community ; and in the gorgeous processions and at the balls he was accompanied by his mother, Atlanta, a very gracious fine lady, and his sister Clarissa, who was the most beautiful of all the noble maidens in that district. This family of high degree was an honoured one, and its members were more popular with the people than any of their other equals, because of their high standards of behaviour.

On the other hand, Ferrone, the *condottiere* — a soldier of fortune who was the leader of the town militia —was somewhat of a libertine ; and he found the Carnival an excellent opportunity for further romantic adventures, which, in the present instance, led him into the awkward consequences of a duel. Being an expert duellist, however, the result was in his favour ; nevertheless, there were protests and murmurings among the merry-makers that such an ugly incident should occur during Carnival time, and many black looks were cast upon the hot-tempered *condottiere*.

Another high official who, already unpopular, met with further disapproval during the revels, was Filippo, the Town Clerk—who was a hunchback—because he chose to appear at the masquerade in a fancy costume considered too undignified for one in his position and of his distorted figure. Though the populace laughed at and made fun of him, they were by no means pleased.

There was, therefore, a smouldering undercurrent of discontent among the townsfolk, which, even during the Carnival revels, could be plainly detected by one with an observant eye.

Such a one was Fortunato, a remarkable stranger who now appeared in the town and quickly realised that it was ripe for a change of *régime* and that, in his hands, its inhabitants would be as clay to be moulded according to his own desire.

* * * * *

Fortunato was a man of a strong, compelling personality, brilliant mental attainments, and great determination of character. He was also consumed by an unbounded ambition and a passionate lust for power. It was not long before he had made himself well acquainted with all the three chief leaders in the city— Andrea, the high-born nobleman, Ferrone the *condottiere*, and Filippo, the hunchbacked Town Clerk to whom he now communicated his own ruthless but simplified ideas of government. These consisted of unquestioning obedience by the people to one single ruler, who should dictate and impose his own will upon them—thus avoiding the clash of ideas between a variety of lesser ruling individuals. He pointed out to them that order could thus be more readily secured and maintained by means of a single Dictator than by any other means of government ; and his ideas were eagerly assimilated by these three most important leaders of the community, who were ready enough to carry them out.

But neither the nobles nor the common people were at first willing to consider such a drastic change in their government ; and Andrea, Ferrone, and Filippo set to work to convert them to these new ideas.

To begin with, Andrea brought Fortunato into his own home, where the stranger's vivid personality and strong convictions made a great impression upon the ladies Atlanta and Clarissa, who soon expressed themselves willing to assist in the dissemination of the latter's principles. Clarissa, in particular, was filled with enthusiasm for the new cause ; and her admiration for Fortunato quickly deepened into a passionate love— which was reciprocated by the ambitious stranger, who saw in her a means of more quickly reaching his goal.

Clarissa and her mother indeed proved very helpful to the cause ; for, by means of their social activities, they secured the co-operation of their women friends— and thus the wives and sisters of the nobles and important town officials were able to influence their husbands and brothers and to overcome the doubts and objections of the latter to the establishment of a new *régime* in their midst.

The women's influence and the enthusiastic support of Andrea, Ferrone, and Filippo, together with the strong will and magnetic personality of Fortunato himself, finally brought about the result they desired ; and the stranger who had so suddenly appeared in their midst was now invited to become their sole Ruler and

Dictator, and entire, uncontrolled, and unbounded power was placed in his ruthless hands.

*   *   *   *   *

The rosy future to which the supporters of the new *régime* had looked forward, however, did not materialise. It was true that Fortunato, the new solo ruler, by taking stern measures and establishing a strong disciplinary guard of his own, succeeded in securing perfect order in the city—but it was at the cost of the liberty of the people, who began to suffer many hardships in carrying out the inexorable will of their new Dictator.

Regimentation was enforced, not only in the work and occupations of the people, but in their pleasures also ; and even in such a spontaneous amusement as dancing, freedom of action was not permitted. To their dismay, they found that they were now expected to dance only in a particular approved manner. They found, too, that even the mode of their dress and the materials and colours used in their clothing generally had likewise to conform to certain set regulations. They were confronted with restrictions on every side ; and the lives of all seemed to be cut to a single pattern—consequently, their occupations and pleasures no longer gave them the joy they once did. And restrictions and regimentations quickly developed into oppression and misery. Their former freedom was gone.

Clarissa, though still loving Fortunato passionately and still beloved by him, was, nevertheless, distressed by the severe restrictions and regulations imposed upon the people she had desired to help ; and she soon began to have doubts about the wisdom and benefit of her lover's new *régime*. Even the members of her own aristocratic social circle had to conform to the same restrictions and lack of freedom. Worse than this, she found that her own interviews with her lover were spied upon by the latter's myrmidons; and this, together with the increasing miseries of the people, began to prey upon her mind.

She knew now that a fatal mistake had been made by placing such unlimited power into the hands of a single man—even though that man was the one to whom she had given her heart.

The same doubts and regrets assailed the heart and mind of her brother Andrea. He likewise realised that the people he loved were now suffering misery because of the ruthless iron discipline to which they were compelled to submit under the new *régime*; and he attempted to remonstrate with the powerful ruler. He entreated the latter to relax his stern measures and not to treat the people as slaves or automatons, but as the free human beings they had once been.

But Fortunato, owing to his meteoric success, was now possessed by such a passionate lust for power that he could not bring himself to relax one iota of it, lest his Olympic rule should suffer thereby; and he haughtily refused to consider the humane request of the young nobleman.

Then Andrea, eager to make amends for the fatal mistake he had made, announced that he and his friends would no longer support such an unmerciful tyrant; and, in despair, he left him, sad at heart because of the afflictions he had helped to bring upon his beloved people.

* * * * *

Ferrone the *condottiere* and Filippo the Town Clerk, to whom had been delegated additional authority in military and civic circles respectively, still continued to support the new ruler, despite their knowledge of the dull agony suffered by the repressed people, not caring to defy one whom they had themselves endowed with such illimitable power ; and when they knew that Andrea had withdrawn his support, they determined to spy upon his movements in the interests of their tyrannical overlord.

Andrea had already determined to strike a blow for the liberation of the town from its now hated despotic rule ; and he invited his nobly-born friends to a banquet, at which he entreated them to join him in a revolt.

His friends, having likewise realised the evils of the new *régime*, willingly agrèed to support his enterprise ; and when Andrea impetuously tore off the uniform he now hated, they gladly followed his example.

It happened that Ferrone and Filippo were in hiding nearby, spying upon the movements of their recent colleagues ; and, on observing this last dramatic gesture, the *condottiere* hastened away to bring news of the coming revolt to Fortunato. His departure, however, was observed by Andrea, who suspected him of treachery ; and seeing Filippo about to make off likewise, he called upon his guests to give chase to him— and, in the struggle that ensued, the spying Town Clerk was slain.

Events now quickly hastened to a climax. Clarissa, knowing of the revolt and fearful for her brother's safety, hastened to the abode of Fortunato and pleaded with him to listen to the demands of Andrea and his friends and thus to prevent civil war and discord. To her horror, she found that Ferrone had already arrived before her and that, at his request, Fortunato had given orders for Andrea and his rebel friends to be slain ; and though her lover would now have rescinded the command, because of her tearful pleas, he declared himself unable to do so lest he should thus appear as weak and wavering in his resolve in the presence of his guards and their leader. Having raised up a devouring monster, he was now, in his turn, being devoured by it.

Overwhelmed with grief at her lover's refusal and again distressed by the fact that even in his presence her movements were being spied upon, her mind, already unhinged by the recent miseries endured by all, now completely gave way ; and she was seized by a sudden fit of madness and rushed forth into the street with loud distracted cries.

And now, a strange and remarkable change came over Fortunato. Horrified by the sudden madness of Clarissa—whom he still passionately loved despite the fact that he had compelled her to submit to the stern regulations and restrictions imposed upon all the townsfolk—he now beheld, as in a vision, the evil he had caused by his own lust for power ; and he at last realised that, whereas he had hoped to do good by means of his cult of Absolute Rule, the reverse had been the case.

Now filled with remorse, the once proud Dictator pleaded with his military leader to countermand the order to the soldiers to march against Andrea and the rebels. Ferrone furiously declined to do so ; and, despising his Chief's change of policy, he rejected the latter's authority entirely and challenged him to immediate mortal combat—in the course of which, however, he was himself quickly slain.

Meanwhile, the unfortunate mad Clarissa was still distractedly wandering out in the streets, completely unconscious of what was happening around her, flitting hither and thither like a faded flower blown by the wind. The consequence was that, as the soldiers advanced furiously upon her beloved brother's small force of followers, she was helplessly carried along with them ; and in the overwhelming onrush and excitement that ensued, she was accidentally trodden underfoot and crushed to death.

And now, Fortunato, having arrived upon the scene just as the two forces were about to meet and fall upon one another in a furious clash of arms, made a sudden dramatic but sincere gesture. Eager only to prevent bloodshed and hoping, by the sacrifice of himself, to make redress for the wrong he now felt he had done because of his own overweening and selfish ambition, he rushed forward and flung himself upon the bristling weapons of his own guards, almost instantly falling dead in their midst.

Thus, by the voluntary self-sacrifice of the remorseful and penitent tyrant, the city was saved from the woes under which it had suffered a living death ; and its people were now at liberty to regain a life of freedom and happiness once more.

THE GREEN TABLE*

* *The Ballet from which this story is taken won the first prize of 25,000 francs in a Competition organised by the Archives Internationale de la Danse, Paris, in 1932. It was suggested by the European political situation before and after the Great War of 1914–18; and the topicality of its subject, unhappily, has not waned, but still provides serious thought for one and all.*

TOWARDS the second decade of the twentieth century, war was already in the air, and nations everywhere were wondering how the coming tragedy would affect them—when and where the clash would begin, and how it would end.

In a certain town, a number of clever black-coated gentlemen sat day after day around a long Conference Table covered with green cloth. They represented all shades of political opinion, and but few of them seemed fit to undertake the tremendous responsibilities laid upon them by their various countries. They seldom revealed their true feelings or thoughts, but seemed as though they wore masks on their faces to conceal such feelings and thoughts.

True, some of these gentlemen were diplomats of brilliant intellectual attainments; and they had honestly worked hard to prevent the countries they represented from plunging into the horrors of war. Others had brains of less brilliance; some were arrogant and proud, selfishly refusing to consider any other point of view than their own, being consumed by a lust for power and determined to get their own way at any cost; a few, on the other hand, were willing to make personal sacrifices for the sake of peace.

The latter—who included some of the wiser and more trusted statesmen of their age—were, however, in the minority ; and every day the struggle became fiercer and the storm-clouds piled up blacker and denser.

While the black-coated gentlemen argued and quarrelled around the green Conference Table, the grim figure of Death hovered in the background, waiting for his own Hour to strike—his hour of triumph, when he would hold sway for as many ghastly months or years as Unreason and the Lust for Power should last.

Sometimes, when the squabblings and recriminations grew louder, Death hovered nearer for awhile ; and then he would recede into the shadows once more when, for a brief period, wiser counsels prevailed.

But Death, though sometimes half-hidden, was never absent for long ; and, from the signs of the times and from what he heard in the Conference room, he could safely prophesy that the final result of the proceedings would be in his favour. For this reason, he was already clad in the full panoply of Mars, the dread but splendid God of War — armour, helmet, shield, and weapons — in readiness for the part he believed it was ordained that he should play.

One day, the members of the Conference sat until midnight, and became more uproarious than ever before. Passions rose high, insults were hurled across the table ; threats and imprecations mingled with unheeded calls for toleration, appeasement, justice, and conciliation ; and the sinister form of Death emerged once more and drew nearer and nearer, exultant, and knowing now that his dark shadow was about to be cast upon the world. Such fury and tumult could only have one result—a Declaration of War.

The ruthlessness of those lusting for power was heralded by shots recklessly fired across the Green

Table. The Conference thus ended in disorder, and War was launched upon the world. Then Death set forth, triumphant and inexorable, to spread his dark wings over innumerable battlefields—those unnecessary battlefields that might have remained smiling green meadow-lands and peaceful cornfields, had the gentle voices of Wisdom and Tolerance been heeded.

* * * * *

The God of War had come into his own once more ; and Death, wearing the panoply of Mars, gathered into his mighty sheaves the fair Youth of many countries— thus wasting the Aspirations, Achievements intellectual and physical, and the Joy and Beauty of Life that should have enriched the beginning of a new century. Uniformed figures of thousands upon thousands of young men were to be seen in every city, town, and village—sometimes flushed with excitement and the spirit of Adventure on first setting out for the War ; sometimes wearing the far away indefinable look born of horrible sights and experiences, suffering, and the resigned anticipation of more to come ; and sometimes eager to snatch at every pleasure and physical enjoyment while they might, before being claimed by Death — of whom many of them had already caught a glimpse, and had even heard the ominous rustle of his wings in their own imaginations.

These last were those who besought their sweethearts to satisfy their physical desires before parting from them—or were even found in brothels, in feverish haste to snatch at the ugly shadow of an experience hitherto unknown to them.

Death observed them all, and indulgently bided his time—which he knew would surely come. He also looked on, unseen, at the sad, heart-breaking partings between husbands and wives, sisters and brothers, parents and sons, passionate lovers, and life-long friends.

But, more frequently, Death hovered over the battle-fields and the hospitals ; and he took his full toll of young fighters, and of those not so young. Also, he was not absent from the homes of those they had left behind—many of whom were claimed by him before the survivors began to return. He saw the stricken and the persecuted driven forth from their homes, wandering hither and thither in hopeless misery from their burning towns and villages.

Death also followed in the wake of another figure as sinister as himself—the well-dressed, prosperous, portly form of the Profiteer, who greedily amassed his millions out of the agonies and woes of those who willingly gave their lives for the glory of their countries. At first, the Profiteer was willing enough to work hand-in-hand with Death, who filled his pockets so generously ; but his dread Partner had only contempt for him— and his millions could not save him from the latter's inexorable call when it came.

At last, the terrible conflict ended ; and the sad partings were over, giving place to joyful home-comings and happy reunions for some—though, for others there were no rejoicings, only sad memories. Then, too, there were the halt, the blind, and the maimed to be seen everywhere . . . but what would you, good people? Was it not a Splendid Victory ?

* * * * *

This story ends as it began. Again, a number of clever, black-coated gentlemen, whose faces masked their real feelings and intentions, met around the Green Table ; but this time they fired shots in the air, as a symbol of Peace, so-called.

Then they sat down and began their discussions all over again. How long would it be before these now well-pleased faces were once more distorted by rage ; and how soon would their quiet and seemingly peaceful talks degenerate into high-pitched noisy altercations ?

None could tell ; but the more sober-minded members of that futile Conference, already sensing discord, could hear, in imagination, the wings of Death softly beating the air in the far distance. Could it be, they uneasily wondered, that, one day in the much-too-near future, that same sinister Dark Figure, again clad in the panoply of the dread god, Mars, would slip into the Conference Room once more and hover there in the background, unseen, but inexorably biding his time for his Hour again to strike ?

Words, words, words, fair and foul ! Would they ever drive forth that lurking fateful Figure, and replace him by the glorious True Spirit of Peace ? After all, was not a Change of Heart all that was required ? But COULD this Miracle ever happen ?

PANDORA

HERE is the famous old story of Pandora and her wonderful Magic Box told again as though happening in relation to our modern world.

In the ancient Classical Myth, you will remember, Pandora was a beautiful woman made by Vulcan at the command of Jupiter; and she was sent to earth with instructions to encompass the ruin of Man in revenge for Prometheus having dared to steal fire from heaven and thus benefited humanity against the will of the powerful Ruler of Olympus.

We are told that Venus endowed Pandora with beauty that she might enthral the heart of Man; that Mercury bestowed upon her cunning, that she might deceive him; and each of the gods presented her with various other destructive powers to bring misery upon him. Thus equipped, Mercury conveyed the lovely Pandora to the earth, where Epimetheus, the brother of Prometheus, made her his wife—despite the fact that the latter had warned him never to accept any gifts from the gods. Later on he must have regretted he had not heeded his brother's warning, when his beautiful wife caused so many troubles to fall upon him and all the world.

Pandora had brought with her to earth a Magic Box containing every ill that could harass mankind; and when, out of curiosity, she opened it, all these evil things flew out to afflict the world : Selfishness, Greed, Cruelty Pestilence, War, Hatred, and everything else that makes for misery. But the lovely Spirit of Hope had concealed herself in the bottom of the Magic Box; and when, presently, she emerged, she was able to help and sustain all who were assailed by the ills just released, and thus Mankind was saved from despair.

In this new version of the old Pandora legend, let us imagine the people of our modern world all seeking for something wonderful and beautiful, with which to enrich their lives, or at least to make them bearable—some intangible thing, they know not what, but feel a passionate need for. Let us separate them into Symbolic Groups, and see how they react when, at last, they believe they have found the thing they have been seeking.

To begin with, there is the innocent Youth, still unscathed by the rough, unsympathetic world he has been brought into, simple in his desires, as yet unbiassed in his outlook, and seeking only for the Happiness and Good Things of Life he believes to be his due and that of all other human beings.

Hovering about the Youth is the Mother Group, the Eternal Symbol of Femininity, possessive and eager to guide the children who are born into the world—but dismayed when the Youth stands apart, preferring to seek his own salvation.

Another Group we can describe as the Strong Man— he who would stand for Courage and unwavering, simple forthrightness and the desire for a Fair Deal.

Yet another Group is shown as greedily eager only for Success in Life, the selfish amassing of Riches, but callous to the needs and rights of others ; and this section of modern humanity we will symbolise under the title of the Go-Getter—he who lives to secure his own advantage only.

In addition, a vast Group symbolising the Mass of the People, of every age, type, and character, making up the remainder of the restless modern world, surging everywhere, and seeking that same intangible Something they also believe would satisfy their ceaseless longings—perhaps Something or Some Person to set up on a pedestal and worship ?

Into the midst of these well-defined Groups there appeared one day two dazzling Strangers, both Symbolic and each offering in their separate persons a choice of Gifts to the waiting world. One of these Symbolic Strangers appeared to be the popular choice at first ; and the other was appreciated by one Group only—that of the Youth of the world.

The first visitor to appear in the midst of the restless modern world was a reincarnation of Pandora, a dazzlingly beautiful woman—but one without a Soul, who brought with her Destruction hidden within a glittering jewelled box she held up on high, temptingly.

Pandora was garbed magnificently in royal crimson, purple, and white ; and though she also wore a somewhat sinister headdress of coiled snakes, the people were not alarmed thereby. On the other hand, they were completely enthralled by her regal and astounding beauty ; and the fact that she appeared to have brought gifts for them was another asset in her favour. They did not know what was hidden in the scintillating box she held high up above her head ; but they felt it must be filled with valuable treasures, and they were eager for it to be opened.

All the people surged around this wonderful queenly stranger—all except the Youth, who felt instinctively, he knew not why, that this dazzling visitor, despite her physical beauty and the fact that she was so obviously armed with worldly riches, was not the lovely intangible Something they had been seeking so long. So the Youth turned aside from the crowd of worshippers around Pandora, and continued to wander in the shadows alone, still eager and enthusiastic in his search for Truth.

And presently, that same day, he found what he sought. A second glorious Visitant appeared to him as in a Vision, revealing the exquisitely delicate form of Psyche, Symbol of the Soul or Spiritual part of Man, that Inner Voice of Revelation that speaks to his heart and helps him to soar to a higher plane.

Psyche was robed in pure white, with clear sparkling crystals in her headdress ; and as she smiled upon him with gentle and sympathetic understanding, the Youth felt a satisfying sense of Peace come upon him. He knew that he had found Truth at last in the pure and lovely person of Psyche—the Symbol of the Spiritual Life and of Goodness in Man, whereby he would find true Happiness at last.

The enraptured Youth longed to remain in the presence of Psyche ; but though she glided gracefully about him, he was not permitted to touch her ethereal form—and presently, she vanished from his sight, leaving him, however, with Hope in his heart.

Meanwhile, the still surging crowds were approaching him, with the dazzling Pandora in their midst ; but the now enlightened Youth gazed upon the enticingly attractive stranger almost with horror. Hastening forward, he eagerly described to the throng the exquisite Vision that had just been revealed to him ; and he besought the people to have nothing to do with the soulless Pandora who had enthralled them with her beauty and worldly graces, but to accept the Truth as revealed to him in his Vision of Psyche.

But the people, intoxicated by their own material Visitant, derided the Youth as a foolish Visionary ; and they roughly thrust him aside. Then they laughingly turned once more to the brilliant figure of Pandora, who again held on high her mysterious jewelled box, offering it as a gift for whosoever desired it most and could take it from her.

Soon, the Strong Man and the Go-Getter were both in eager competition for possession of the casket ; and everybody else looked on in excited anticipation as to which competitor would secure it first.

To begin with, it seemed as though the Strong Man would be the winner ; but his honest strength and skill were presently circumvented by the sly underhand actions of the Go-Getter, who thus triumphantly secured the treasured object.

Everybody now crowded around the conquering Go-Getter, eager to see him open the box ; but soon they fell back in horror.

No sooner had the greedy and unscrupulous Go-Getter opened the lid of the casket than out sprang an unending host of hideous monsters, ready to devour all who came in their path. These fearsome monsters represented all the ills and evils that could beset Mankind—War, Pestilence, Disease, Persecution, Violence, Cruelty, Murder, Poverty, Deceit, Avarice, and every other kind of malignant thing. The Leader, or King of these horrible creatures, was a Machine Monster, made of steel, whose body was built up of mechanical tools used in the making of machinery and the engines of War.

Filled with horrified dismay, but hoping to help his doomed fellow creatures, the Strong Man tried his utmost to slay some of the monsters ; but he was quickly overcome and slain by them.

A gruesome scene ensued, as the terrified people fled from the monsters who chased them hither and thither ; but presently, the latter returned into the presence of their soulless mistress, Pandora, whom they now proceeded to crown as their Queen—placing upon her head a grim-looking crown representing a ghastly death's

head surrounded by a rim of sharp glittering spikes.
Then they bowed down before her in homage.

* * * * *

After the loosing of Pandora's horde of hideous evil
monsters upon the earth, Misery reigned supreme.
There were Wars and rumours of Wars everywhere ; and
Pestilence and Poverty followed the devastation and
havoc created thereby. Mothers mourned the loss of
the splendid sons they had reared so tenderly ; and they
were constantly haunted by visions of the ghastly
battlefields upon which their beloved ones had died in
agony.

Nevertheless, these same Parents, and those that
followed them, taking the line of least resistance,
gradually began to accept the new order of life set up
by their soulless, calculating rulers, neglectful of the real
spiritual interests of the younger generation, whom they
thus alienated.

At length, however, a new generation began to grow
up ; and then there appeared on the scene once more
the splendid Youth who had refused to accept the
soulless Pandora and her box of evil gifts, but had
wandered apart and so beheld the fair Vision of Psyche,
the Symbol of Hope and of the Spiritual part of Man.
And with the glorious Youth who wore the Armour of
Truth came a renewal of life and hope for the future.

Even though Pandora and her myrmidons still strove
against the people, her power at last dwindled before the
dauntless figure of the Youth in his innocence and eagerness for the true Joy of Life ; and, in the end, the beautiful but soulless visitant was driven back and found
herself unable to do further harm to those upon whom she
had brought such misery. True, she was not banished
for ever. She was still there in the background ; but,
for the moment, she was rendered powerless so long as

Truth remained triumphant. Though temporarily defeated, she would come back in all her glory later on— for the Choice of Ways is an eternal one and must be met by each succeeding generation and fought out in each human heart.

But, in his present moment of triumph, the happy conquering Youth had no thought of this. He was now again vouchsafed a Vision of lovely Psyche ; and, thus strengthened by Hope and the fair gifts of the Spirit, he then set forth with his companions to help build up the sad and suffering world.

ON STAGE

A BALLET Company was trying out at a rehearsal new aspirants who desired to join its famous ranks.

It might have seemed a dreary enough scene to an outsider—the dark empty auditorium, the bare stage, and the practice-garb of the company's dancers.

It was, however, a wonderful place to all who longed to be received among these already accepted followers of Terpsichore. Then, indeed, it became the gateway to Fairyland itself. What daydreams of beauty were even now being conjured up in the minds of those who waited their turn to be judged worthy or unworthy of admission to the dazzling World of Ballet.

Even the handy-man stage hand indulged in such unlikely dreams as he now leaned upon his broom in a corner, waiting for the rehearsal to end. Though his life seemed to be merely a round of sweeping floors and running errands, he saw so much of beauty in the making and in its final realisation that he was certainly capable of appreciating it. He was even on the way to becoming something of a judge of such matters—despite the fact that he was physically a comical-looking and even Charlie-Chaplin-esque type of person — a comic with more than a touch of pathos about him.

To-day, the handyman was more interested than usual in the trying-out of new candidates for the ballet— or, rather, in one of the competitors who, like himself, seemed to be a lover of beauty, even though, at the moment, she seemed to be incapable of expressing this innate sense of hers to the satisfaction of the exacting ballet-master.

She was a charmingly pretty young girl, but was so shy and obviously scared of the many critical eyes judging her tremulous performance, that she did not seem likely to have much chance of being one of the successful candidates.

She had come with another girl candidate ; and the two were judged one after the other. Her friend was of a much more confident type, and, being entirely free from nervousness, was the better able to do herself justice. Consequently, when her trial performance came to an end, she was judged to be sufficiently advanced to be admitted to the lower ranks of the ballet company, where she would be further trained as a dancer—and her foot was, therefore, on the first rung of the ladder.

But when it came to the shy young girl's turn to exhibit her skill, it was a different matter entirely ; and she was so nervous and unsure in her movements that the ballet-master soon became impatient and declared her to be unsuitable to be accepted into the company.

Nevertheless, the day-dreaming Chaplin-esque handyman considered that the ballet-master had made a mistake. Despite the pretty young girl's nervous, trembling movements, it seemed to this observant man-with-a-broom that there were hidden possibilities of beauty in her dancing. He believed that when her fears had been banished, and her steps were free and steady when alone and unobserved, she was probably a far more interesting dancer than her successful but less poetically understanding companion.

Though merely a stage hand, he felt so confident in this belief that when the resumed rehearsal was over and the company had left the stage with the successful candidates, he sidled up to the shy girl, who now stood aside, weeping because of her failure. He first offered her his sympathy ; and then, in a simple winning way, he explained his own belief in her possibilities and begged her, encouragingly, to try again. The stage was now empty, and there was nobody to observe her ; why not indulge in an exhibition dance, all by herself ?

When he first approached her, the young girl felt that this comical-looking, but semi-pathetic individual was making fun of her ; but when she realised that he was actually serious, she willingly enough accepted his sympathy. Yes ; she *had* been much too afraid of that critical ballet-master to dance as she had hoped and intended to do. Of course, she loved dancing ; and she longed to dance once more upon that wonderful stage.

Well, there it was, her own for the time being ; and, leading her forward, the handy-man left her there to dance alone, while he encouraged her every movement.

Yes ; he had been right. This girl was a born dancer and had a wonderful sense of beauty, as he had believed ; and now that she was able to express herself freely and her fears had entirely vanished, she danced brilliantly. It was a joy to watch her unrestrained movements, as she seemed to float about, lost in a world of her own creating ; and the handy-man was entranced. How he longed to partner that dainty whirling figure ! He felt almost as though he had created her himself and that she was a part of him ; and, in that moment, he loved her. But what had a comical-looking fellow like himself to do with beauty such as this, even if he *had* helped to bring it to birth ?

The handy-man sighed deeply ; but he knew what he must do. Observing that the young girl was still completely wrapped in her dancing dream of enchantment and lost to her surroundings, he slipped away to find the ballet-master whom he quickly brought back to the stage to look once more upon the candidate he had just refused.

As he had hoped, the latter was not only astounded, but entranced. The consequence was that, when the young girl presently ended her dance-dream and came back to the bare boards of the stage, she was greeted by the enthusiastic clapping and welcoming smiles of the delighted ballet-master, who now accepted her eagerly for the company, overjoyed at having discovered a budding star.

He quite forgot that the discovery was not his; but as he proudly led away the now happy young candidate, the lonely Chaplin-esque handy-man philosophically picked up his broom once more. He was a simple, humble fellow, and expected nothing else.

Nevertheless, he had experienced his great moment. That bright particular Star had once danced for him alone, and he had been the first to see and understand its hidden beauty; and it would continue to shine and dance in his heart for ever.

LE BEAU DANUBE
(*The Beautiful Danube*)

VIENNA, on the banks of the beautiful Blue Danube River, was, in 1860, one of the gayest cities in Europe. The Emperor of Austria, Franz Joseph, and his beautiful consort, the Empress Elisabeth, held their brilliant Court there ; and most of the royal and noble folk of Europe were guests at that sparkling Court from time to time. Every day aristocrats bearing honoured names drove in magnificent equipages in the famous Prater, with officers in splendid uniforms riding beside them on horseback and stopping ever and anon to chat and pay compliments to the crinolined ladies within.

In the Park and flower-gardens alongside were to be seen groups of merry children in charge of smart nurse-maids—the latter often stealing a few moments from the strict routine of their duties to engage in mild flirtations with waiting grooms or strolling guardsmen. At times, too, they even ventured to cast saucy and coquettish glances at passing cavaliers of higher degree—which were invariably returned by the latter.

Such was the scene in the Prater one bright sunny day in the early autumn ; and the light-hearted gaiety of the promenading folk was enhanced by the pleasant fact that the day was a general holiday. Consequently, more people than usual were to be seen in the wide Bois and on the grassy and flowery stretches beyond.

Milliners and other girls from the city's smart shops mingled with the merry crowds, eager to catch a glimpse of some famous beauty or to admire the rich raiment of the fashionable and aristocratic young ladies driving by ; but if they envied the latter, they were too full of good humour and of joy in their present few precious hours of freedom to let such a passing mood spoil the fun of their holiday. Their own sweethearts and admirers were there as well ; and when the band struck up a lilting waltz or a gay mazurka tune, they soon forgot about their more fortunate sisters and lost themselves in the frolicsome pleasure of dancing in the park or on the velvet-like grass verges. Liveliness was the order of the day, and a light-hearted spontaneity seemed to envelop all these cheery Viennese holiday folk. The magical sparkle of the lovely nearby river was in their blood ; and it brought joy to their hearts. They had been born with that happy sparkle in their hearts, and as long as the fair river rolled by it would still be their blessed heritage.

Nevertheless, a little cloud of sadness seemed at one time about to descend like a sudden eclipse upon a pair of the happiest lovers out in the Prater on that festive day.

A handsome and dashing young Hussar came winding his way in and out among the lively holiday-makers, eagerly looking for a certain pretty young lady who was his secret sweetheart. Ah ! There she was, now tripping forth, shyly and somewhat apprehensively, from behind yonder bushes. She was apprehensive because this was a clandestine meeting and had been arranged without the knowledge of the young girl's parents, who knew nothing of their daughter's secret romance—which they would certainly have disapproved of.

How lovely she was in her most attractively swaying crinoline gown and devastatingly coquettish rose-trimmed bonnet ! So thought the *débonnaire* young Hussar as he rushed forward to clasp her in his arms with all the joy of a sincere love. True, like other gay officers in the Hussars, he had had other sweethearts ;

but they were now forgotten and this was the real thing at last.

The young girl's heart beat wildly, too ; for, despite lurking fears about this secret romance, she also was tasting true love for the first time. So, when the strains of a lively mazurka were presently heard, she gladly allowed herself to be danced away in the arms of her gallant lover, entirely reckless of the need to avoid publicity.

The young Hussar was equally blind to the imprudence of his act ; and he steered his partner away into the midst of a crowd now gathering around a troupe of strolling players, among whom was a popular Strong Man and an extremely attractive Street Dancer.

The prowess of these strolling players was being blazoned forth in humorous fashion by their " barker " or publicity agent ; and the crowd which had quickly gathered around was already laughing heartily at the latter's comical quips and outrageous praises. The latter, however, seemed justified. The Strong Man was certainly a fine figure, full of brawn and obviously capable of immense deeds of strength. Despite the somewhat vulgar fact that he wore his hair in a greasy rolled lock on the top of his head and carried a cigarette behind his ear, the feline grace of his movements soon made him popular with the bystanders.

The dancing-girl was full of grace, too, and was likewise extremely handsome ; and though she danced with a certain amount of abandon, her performance was excellent and just suited the mood of the holiday crowd, who were delighted with her skilfulness and applauded her enthusiastically.

As her preliminary dance ended, however, there came a dramatic interlude. While the Hussar still stood watching this entertainment, with his arm around the slender waist of his beloved one, the latter, to her consternation, saw her parents and her young sister approaching. Then, before she could attempt to escape, she realised that a far worse catastrophe was about to befall her.

The Street Dancer had suddenly caught sight of the brilliantly uniformed young Hussar ; and recognising in him one of her own former sweethearts, she ran forward to greet him. The young man was transfixed with dismay ; for his connection with the Dancer had been but the " calf-fancy " of his early youth, and his heart was now given wholly to the fair young girl by his side. The latter, however, had understood only too well the implication of the Street Dancer's recognition of, and eager welcome to, the handsome Hussar; and the shock of her consequent sudden disillusionment was so severe that she sank back fainting.

This pathetic little scene had likewise been observed and understood by the now irate parents of the romantic girl ; and, as soon as she recovered somewhat, they led her away, full of indignation that they had found her in such seemingly dubious company.

No sooner had the family party departed than the Street Dancer tried to win back the admiration and affection of her former sweetheart. She danced before him with alluring movements, and tried to entice him to return her caresses and glamorous advances ; but the Hussar was not to be won from his new and true love. When, therefore, the latter, having managed to slip away from her disapproving parents, now returned to the scene, she found that her rival was not so formidable as she had at first feared. Quickly realising that this past romantic episode was indeed dead, she willingly forgave her lover and gladly accepted his tender and contrite embraces once more.

The Street Dancer now accepted her definite defeat with as good a grace as she could muster ; and she retired from the scene with the Strong Man and the other strolling players—probably looking forward to making a new conquest in the near future.

But trouble was yet in store for the reconciled lovers. The still irate parents of the young girl once more appeared before the loving pair ; and again expressing disapproval of their daughter's attachment to a mere officer of Hussars, they flatly refused to give their consent to such a union, despite the passionate entreaties of both parties concerned. The descending cloud became black indeed.

Then it was that the young girl's little sister took up the cudgels on her behalf, and pleaded with the stern parents to relax their veto ; and the latter, unable to resist the sweet unselfish entreaties of their youngest child, at last gave way to her eager request. They now not only gave their consent for the marriage to take place, but even generously bestowed their blessing upon the ecstatic lovers.

Great rejoicings then took place ; and the happy party spent the remainder of the day dancing and making merry with the holiday folk of Vienna. The magical sparkle of the beautiful Blue Danube River had certainly likewise entered the hearts of these joyous newcomers to the festivities in the Prater.

LA BOUTIQUE FANTASQUE

(*The Fantastic Shop*)

NICE, that dazzling Queen-City of the French Riviera, looked quite fairy-like on a certain sunny afternoon in the year 1865. The cloudless sky was as deeply blue as the sparkling Mediterranean below; masses of sweetly-perfumed flowers—mimosa, violets, roses, lilies, camellias, bougainvillea—were to be seen on every side; and the gaily-decorated, paint-box villas and shops looked as though they belonged to a picture book rather than to real everyday life. Even the white yachts and red-sailed boats in the harbour lay still and becalmed, with no soft breezes to stir them; and scarcely a human being was to be seen.

For this was the hour of the afternoon siesta, when all wise folk lay resting within doors, with curtains drawn and shutters fastened. Presently, they would be issuing forth once more, and merry throngs of fashionably-dressed ladies and children, with their attendant cavaliers, would again be seen in the streets and on the *Promenade des Anglais*.

Meanwhile, all was still and like a painted picture in a fairy-tale book; and perhaps there really *was* a touch of magic about. Certainly some very curious incidents presently took place, as though a fairy's wand was, indeed, not so very far away.

* * * * *

As soon as the afternoon siesta was over, there was much activity in one of the most delightful old toy-shops in Nice. The owner of the toy-shop and his young assistant arrived outside the closed gates. They unlocked the latter with a large key and came bustling in, very cheery after their early afternoon rest and quite ready for more good business—which they confidently expected.

The shopkeeper was a rosy-cheeked, chubby, bespectacled little old man, with bushy side-whiskers and white hair ; but though he was somewhat too plump he was full of energy and bustled about as he quickly set his shop in order for the afternoon customers. His assistant was a smartly-dressed, but somewhat comical youth, who seemed to love rushing about and dancing in a fantastic manner as he helped his cheery master. Between them they placed all the chairs in a couple of orderly rows, and carefully dusted the only two dolls that had been left on view in the empty shop.

The dolls were standing on the top of a big box ; and they were dressed very gaily in brightly-coloured peasant costumes. They could move about when wound up ; for their quaint old owner was very clever with his hands, and all the dolls he offered for sale were of the mechanical kind. He liked to be mysterious about them, too, and to cause astonishment to prospective customers. He never exhibited them all at the same time, but kept them in their boxes until the right time came to produce them.

He was wise, however, in taking this precaution ; for, presently, he nearly lost the two peasant dolls he had inadvertently left out that morning on leaving the shop for the siesta hour. A thieving boy crept into the shop as soon as the owner and his assistant had departed for a few moments into an inner room. Making his way stealthily towards the two gaily-dressed dolls, he made an attempt to snatch them from their stand ; but he was quickly discovered by the returning men, who seized their sticks and drove him out.

By this time the street outside was full of life once more, and sounds of pattering footsteps and chattering voices could be plainly heard. No sooner had the flustered shopkeeper and his assistant put down their sticks and tidied themselves after this small but exciting occurrence than their first afternoon customers entered the shop. These were two elderly English ladies, both of them very prim and proper old spinsters, wearing crinoline gowns and poke-bonnets and carrying the absurdly small fringed and tasselled sunshades of that period.

As the obsequious shopkeeper bowed low before them the elderly ladies waved him aside haughtily, but demanded to be shown some of his wares. At a signal from his master, the young assistant carefully wound up the two peasant dolls already on view ; whereupon the latter began to move their arms and legs in a somewhat stiff manner as they slowly turned round and round in a mechanical dance. Then, suddenly, the mechanism ran down, and the two dolls stopped dead, their arms and legs sticking out in comical attitudes.

The two English spinsters were so surprised and delighted that they forgot to be haughty and condescending any longer ; and they had just demanded to be shown some more of these marvellous dolls when a group of new customers entered the shop like a whirlwind.

The newcomers were a rich American business man of the conventional stage type of those days, accompanied by his wife and their two children, a rather rough boy and a tomboy girl. They were all somewhat overdressed, the gentleman in a widely-chequered plus-fours suit, and the lady in an enormous crinoline while the children were likewise much too smartly clad for a holiday afternoon stroll. The latter, however, despite their fine clothes, were extremely boisterous and over-excited ; and they soon had the prim and proper English ladies in a be-flustered state by prancing around them and trying to persuade them to dance in imitation of the dancing dolls. Their indulgent parents, though they called them to order from time to time, did not appear to have much control over them.

In a short while, the visitors were joined by yet another party of prospective customers—this time an equally prosperous Russian merchant and his wife, with their four young daughters. Despite the warm sunny day, these newcomers—who were likewise of the then conventional stage type—evidently deemed it necessary to proclaim their nationality and, consequently, were clad almost as though for a Russian winter sleigh-ride. The father of the family wore a magnificent fur coat and hat, with high fur-trimmed boots to match ; and the mother and daughters likewise displayed far more fur about their walking suits than could have been comfortable.

The two English maiden ladies evidently considered the shop was now more crowded than they liked ; and they presently departed, with somewhat disdainful glances at the warmly-clad newcomers. The American party, too, did not at first altogether approve of the latter ; but they seated themselves and their children sedately on one row of chairs, while the Russian family sat down heavily, but importantly, upon the other row of seats.

The chubby old shopkeeper was delighted to have so many rich-looking customers in his shop ; and rubbing his hands with great satisfaction he ordered his assistant —who had now been joined by a couple of smartly-uniformed porters—to bring forth and exhibit in turn all his most interesting and expensive mechanical dolls and to set them in motion for the delectation of his prospective purchasers.

The two American children again became extremely excited as each new exhibit was produced ; and they jumped off their chairs and skipped around the various dolls, trying to imitate the movements of the latter, despite the annoyed protests and occasional slaps of their parents. The porters and assistant likewise looked daggers at the tiresome children, as though longing to deal more drastically with them. The little Russian girls at first sat quite sedately upon their chairs ; but, after awhile, they likewise became excited and too enthusiastic to keep still any longer.

The first exhibit was a pair of dolls dressed as Tarantella Dancers in gay Italian garb, with strings of brightly-coloured ribbons flying around them ; and, having been wound up by the assistants, they danced with splendid precision all the intricate steps of the Tarantella, as performed by the natives of Italy, shaking their tambourines and twisting and twirling around in the most approved style. As soon as their internal mechanism ran down, however, they came to a sudden standstill then and there ; and the porters were bidden to take them away and to bring forth another exhibit.

The American children again sprang from their chairs and tried to dance the Tarantella themselves—with comical results. Again their parents scolded them and made them sit down quietly once more.

Four dolls took part in the next exhibition ; and all were magnificently dressed to represent Kings and Queens in a pack of Playing-Cards—the Queen of Hearts, the Queen of Clubs, the King of Spades, and the King of Diamonds. Stately curtseys by the Queens and sweeping bows by the Kings began this performance ; and then the quartette broke out into a lively mazurka, which continued until their clockwork apparatus ceased working and caused them to come to a sudden full-stop.

All the customers were delighted with this amazing exhibition, and even the grown-ups swayed about irresistibly in time with the lively mazurka tune. The shopkeeper was equally delighted with the great impression his marvellous mechanical dolls were making upon his wealthy audience ; and he proudly declared that he had even more surprising exhibits yet to produce.

The porters now brought forward a pair of the more conventional type of clockwork dolls which, when wound up, moved jerkily, rather than danced, to the strains of a tinkling musical-box of the kind popular at an earlier period still. One of these dolls was called the Snob and was dressed with all the exaggerated smartness of a Dandy of mid-Victorian days ; and the other appeared as a Melon-Hawker, wheeling a barrow filled with ripe melons. Their performance was a comical one, in which the fashionably-dressed Dandy tried to eat a slice of melon to the accompaniment of many funny capers by himself and the Hawker, which caused much amusement.

All the children shrieked with joy ; and they were even more delighted still when the next exhibit turned out to be a squad of Cossack Soldiers, who marched about and formed-fours with the utmost precision at the commands of their extremely smart officer-in-charge.

When the Cossacks had been marched away, just before their mechanism ran down, a pair of Mechanical French Poodles ran into the middle of the shop. Having been well wound up, these quaint little dancing dogs indulged in such comical antics that the audience became quite hilarious. The American children even rolled over on to the floor in their merriment until hauled back to their seats by their scolding parents, who, by the way, did not altogether approve of some of the more doggy prancings of the toy poodles.

Order having been restored once more, the chubby shopkeeper now proudly announced that, though his last, the next exhibit was quite the best of all. As he spoke, the porters brought on a pair of dolls even more flexible and human-like than any of the preceding mechanical performers. They were dressed as a French youth and girl from the *Quartier Latin* in Paris, the young man in a frivolously tight velvet suit and flashy waistcoat, and the pretty girl-doll very dainty in an extremely short skirt and frilly underwear—the latter saucily exposed in all her movements. On being wound up, this latest couple began to dance the famous *can-can*, the wildest and most abandoned of all the high-kicking dances known to the Gay City.

What a mad frolic this was, and how full of difficult and most ingenious steps and daring poses! The pretty little lady kicked up her slender legs and tossed up her frivolous petticoats in the most audacious manner; and she and her partner skipped about and fell into each other's arms, and sprang high up into the air in most *risqué* attitudes as *can-can* dancers always do. The customers watched their antics with delighted and fascinated eyes until the clockwork apparatus suddenly stopped and the exhibition came to an end amidst thunders of applause.

All the children, American and Russian, now danced about trying their utmost to copy the Can-Can Dancers; and they even mischievously pulled up the frocks of the grown-up ladies to see if the latter were as frilly underneath as was the pert little lady from the *Quartier Latin* in Paris. The American children begged their parents to buy them the dainty little lady doll, while the Russian girls implored their fur-coated father to secure for them the dapper little gentleman doll.

After some bargaining with the delighted shopkeeper, the purchase was finally made by the two wealthy parents ; and the Can-Can Dancers were duly parted and each wrapped up and placed in a separate box. Then, not wishing to carry away the parcels just then, it was arranged that they should be called for next morning ; and the customers departed from the shop, all laughing and chattering together happily.

* * * * *

But the Dolls were not happy. After the chubby shopkeeper and his assistants had likewise taken their departure later in the evening, leaving the shop in darkness, strange things began to happen. Surely, there MUST have been Magic about ! Lights mysteriously appeared from nowhere ; box-lids began to fall off of their own accord ; and out trooped the Mechanical Dolls, all very much alive-O !

What was more, they were extremely annoyed—not to say, furiously angry ! Who had ever heard of such a wickedly callous action as the parting of two happy lovers, who had hoped to spend all their remaining years together ? But this was just exactly what had happened that very afternoon. The rich Russian customer had bought the dapper young man Can-Can Dancer for his ridiculously fur-clad children to take back with them to that shivery country, Russia ; and the rich American customer had bought the dainty little lady Can-Can Dancer for his boisterous youngsters to take to that far-off land, America ! Who had ever heard of such a shocking tragedy ? It was simply not to be borne ! The Can-Can Dancers must be re-united forthwith, at all costs ; and they should *stay* re-united !

In a trice, the dainty little lady Can-Can Dancer was released from her well-packed box by the kind little Melon-Hawker; and no sooner had she rejoined her friends than her lover-partner was likewise unwrapped and released, and rushed to clasp his beloved one in his arms once more.

After much chattering and gesticulation, it was decided that the Can-Can Dancers should depart from the shop at dawn, and that their empty boxes should be parcelled up and tied with string once more, in readiness for the rich purchasers to take away next morning. What a glorious and well-deserved trick to play upon them!

Having decided upon this jolly plan, the dolls spent the remainder of the night dancing and playing games together. They danced much better now than they had done during the afternoon; for they did not need to bother about waiting for someone to wind them up now that they were all alive-O! This was their hour of Magic.

At last, however, their frolics and dances came to an end; and at the first signs of dawn, the Can-Can lovers bade farewell to their kind companions, and left the shop. How? Well, perhaps they found an unlocked window; or, perhaps, the bolted door opened for them of its own accord; or, they *may* have slipped through the letter-box, or even through the key-hole. Who knows? They just disappeared!

When the lovers had gone, their empty boxes were carefully wrapped up and tied with coloured strings, as before, by their friends. Then all the dolls slipped back into their own boxes once more, and silence reigned again in the toy-shop.

* * * * *

Next morning, the chubby shopkeeper and his

young assistant, with the two porters, came bustling into the shop as usual and got their dusting and tidying done as quickly as possible in readiness for the return of the wealthy purchasers of the Can-Can Dancers. They were particularly careful to dust the two parcelled boxes into which they had placed the latter on the previous day ; for what would such important customers say if they were each handed a dusty parcel ? Of course, they must be spotless.

After this, they set out the two dolls dressed as Italian peasants on a long box, as before ; and then they were ready for their customers.

Scarcely had they finished these preliminary tasks than in trooped the American family, accompanied by the Russian family, chattering and full of good spirits ; and all the children pranced excitedly around the shop, clamouring to be given the fine dolls bought for them the day before.

The chubby shopkeeper and his assistant, with many bows and gratified smiles, immediately handed over the two boxes, one to the American children and the other to the Russian children.

On the youthful owners demanding to see their new treasures before leaving, the shopkeeper untied the strings and removed the lids ; and then, to his utter astonishment and dismay, he discovered that the boxes contained nothing but paper ! The Can-Can Dancers had vanished !

All was now confusion and uproar. The irate parents accused the chubby shop-keeper and his assistant of cheating, and began to belabour unmercifully the amazed pair with their sticks ; and all the children joined in the fray likewise, frantically screaming at the tops of their voices and kicking and scratching with all their might. It was in vain that the unfortunate shopkeeper declared that he knew nothing about the strange disappearance of the Can-Can dolls ; nobody believed him, and the uproar became greatei than ever. A slight diversion was created for a few moments by the two porters who, maddened by their present screaming and their former over-boisterous behaviour, suddenly seized the two American children in a fit of exasperation and gave them each a good spanking. This relieved their feelings considerably.

Then, presently, there came another diversion ; and this ended the commotion. All the mechanical dolls suddenly came to life once more, and, springing from their boxes, rushed to the defence of their chubby owner ; and they furiously launched themselves upon the American and Russian customers, young and old, in an attempt to drive them away. The latter, terrified at the sight of such unusual and unexpected partisans and believing that nothing short of Magic could have brought them thither, now rushed, helter-skelter, out of the shop, the door of which was instantly slammed behind them by the now triumphant dolls.

Well, well ! Perhaps the frightened customers were right in what they feared, and Magic HAD been at work in that most Fantastic Toy-Shop !

CHILDREN'S TALES

(*Les Contes Russes*)

A PEDLAR appeared one day in the streets of a Russian town, with dolls of various kinds—which, however, he did not seem so eager to sell as to tell stories about. For the dolls were dressed to represent characters in popular Russian fairy and folk-lore tales ; and as the Pedlar was an excellent story-teller he saw no reason why he should not reveal his undoubted histrionic gifts while offering his wares.

He was a cheery fellow and, as he danced along the streets, he quickly gathered a crowd of peasants and townsfolk about him—most of them young and as lively as himself. They all loved these old tales, which had been told to them so frequently in their childhood ; and they were glad to listen to some of them again as they admired the various character-dolls held up so invitingly for their admiration.

* * * * *

The first doll held up by the Pedlar for the delectation of his audience and possible customers represented Kikimora, the Russian symbol and embodiment of Wickedness. She was exhibited together with her attendant protector, a big White Cat—in its turn the Russian symbol of human Spite and Malice. This was the story the Pedlar related about the pair :

Kikimora, in her infancy, was left in the care of the Cat, and was kept by the latter in a sinister-looking room of a mysterious house, hidden away from the world The nursery-room had but a single window ; and Kikimora was always kept lying in a queerly-decorated wooden cradle by her guardian—who was eager for her to remain a baby as long as possible, lest her power should become greater than his own.

But Kikimora could not be kept from growing, and so developing her powers of evil ; and one day she managed to liberate herself.

It happened that the Cat was not so vigilant that day ; and while he was sleepily dozing beside the fire Kikimora awakened and began to prepare to make her bid for freedom. She stretched herself many times ; and she soon felt that she was growing bigger and stronger with every moment that passed. Her baleful eyes, now revealing her long-suppressed hate and cruelty, flashed like lightning as she peered over the top of her cradle ; and soon, it was only too evident that she was already concocting many evil schemes which she longed to set in motion. She gnashed and ground her terrible teeth constantly, as though becoming more and more impatient to strike with every minute that went by.

At last her great moment came. Just as the dozing Cat began to stir uneasily, sensing something unusual in the air and becoming conscious of impending disaster, the now terrible-looking Kikimora suddenly sprang from her cradle ; and with a blood-curdling yell, already triumphing in her newly-born powers, she fell upon her unready and startled guardian—who was horrified on thus beholding his charge now in the form of a fearsome witch.

A tremendous encounter took place, which ended in a complete victory for the diabolical Kikimora, who soon stretched her one-time faithful protector dead upon the floor, and at last made her eager escape through the window.

With all the verbose eloquence of his tribe, the Pedlar made his spell-bound audience shiver and shake with

horror at this legend of how Wickedness was thus let loose upon the world for the first time.

But only for a moment. Very soon the peasants and youngsters were all dancing and singing around him once more in a lively revel, in which his grotesquely-garbed doll-models of Kikimora and the Cat were both hailed as popular characters—even though such gruesome ones.

* * * * *

The next tale told by the Pedlar had for heroine a beautiful Swan Princess who had been enchanted by a powerful Magician in the form of a terrible three-headed Dragon.

By means of his magic spells, the Dragon kept this Princess constantly in his power ; and he transported her to a splendid palace, from which she could not escape, but where he permitted her to be attended and cared for by her eight sisters.

Every evening at sunset the enchanted Princess was compelled to take on the form of a white swan, and to swim over the waters of a lonely lake or to glide about its borders. Here she had to remain alone until dawn ; and as she moved softly over the waters of the lake or waited upon its banks, she always sadly hoped that some noble knight would miraculously appear and rescue her from the power of the Magician. But no rescuer ever came to the lakeside ; and every night the lovely Swan Princess would droop her snow-white plumy wings in despair, as she sadly waited near the bank for her vigil to end.

At dawn she again took on her natural form ; and her attendant sisters would come to escort her back into their midst once more. Then, at last, her release came— and in a strangely unexpected manner.

One day, in the Dragon's gorgeous palace, the compassionate sisters were dressing the Swan Princess in the rich garments she was still permitted to wear when in her human form ; and, as usual, they moved gracefully about their duties and danced prettily hither and thither, in order to charm away her sadness somewhat.

They were all grouped together in an open courtyard, in which beautiful flowers were growing and a silvery fountain was playing ; and the scene would have been a charmingly idyllic one had it not been spoiled by the presence of the hateful Dragon-Enchanter sprawling near a flight of steps. This fearsome monster, with its three hideous heads, snaky body, and undulating tail, never relaxed its constant guard upon its enchanted captive ; and its glaring eyes and fire-breathing jaws were alarming to behold.

The attendant Princesses, however, tried not to look at the ugly creature, despite the constant fear in their hearts ; and they continued to drape their lovely sister in such a magnificent jewelled robe and royal train that even the unhappy Swan Princess could not help admiring it.

It was just as this charming robing ceremony came to an end that one of the sisters noticed that a splendid Knight in shining armour was riding swiftly towards the palace, mounted upon a fine white horse ; and, next moment, he had dismounted and was in their midst.

To her joy, the Swan Princess saw that this newcomer was none other than Bova Korolevitch, the famous Russian Knight Errant, who lived only to perform noble deeds and to save captive maidens ; and she knew that her rescue was at hand.

And, true enough, the terrible **Dragon who now** rushed upon him had no terrors for this bravest of brave Knights ; and after a brief but fierce encounter he slashed off the three fire-breathing heads that lunged at him and stretched the hideous monster dead at his feet.

Thus was the Enchanter's spell broken ; and the fair Princess fell upon her knees in gratitude and gazed upon her rescuer with love shining from her starry eyes.

But the famous Knight Errant was under a vow to continue to do noble deeds of rescue in many other places ; and, raising the disenchanted Princess to her feet, he sadly bade her farewell and rode away, leaving her to weep in the arms of her kindly sisters.

Once again the Pedlar's tale was received with acclamation by the merry crowd, who again danced about him joyfully ; and they even formed themselves into a procession in which they enacted the burying of the dragon's three fearsome heads.

* * * * *

The third story the Pedlar had to relate dealt with the adventures of a young girl who, having lost her way in a forest, fell into the clutches of a horrible Ogress known as Baba-Yaga. The latter's demon attendants quickly surrounded the youthful victim and brought her into the presence of their wicked mistress, who intended to devour her. The terrified maiden had only one weapon with which to defend herself—her own belief in the power of Good to overcome Evil. She made the Sign of the Cross ; and this instantly destroyed all the evil powers of Baba-Yaga, and banished her and her attendant demons from the scene.

Then, suddenly, the forest became full of lively peasant folk, who danced about the now happy young girl with great joy.

And again, in sympathy with the happy ending of this final story told by the Pedlar, his audience likewise danced around him. Then, strangely enough, there presently appeared in their midst the chief characters in all the three tales to join in the revels.

But how could this happen, you may ask? None can say. Perhaps the Pedlar was a Magician, after all!

GAIETE PARISIENNE

(*Parisian Gaiety*)

On the terrace of Tortoni's Restaurant in Paris a scene of irresponsible gaiety was to be observed one summer afternoon. The Second Empire was at the height of its ephemeral glory ; and the extravagance and frivolity of the Court was reflected in the cafés and open boulevard restaurants, where light-hearted folk met for refreshment and entertainment and to pass the time of day with their friends.

This afternoon, the terrace of Tortoni's presented an even livelier scene than usual. While some of the waiters bustled about arranging the chairs in the large inner room for the dancing and suppers that would take place later on, others attended to the little tables on the terrace of which casual clients and passing promenaders took possession from time to time.

The attendants made no objection when a very pretty young Flower-Girl took up her stand near one end of the terrace ; and when another even more alluring *vendeuse* presently began to set out a fine display of smart and fashionable gloves at the other end they merely smiled upon her. For these daintily-garbed and extremely pretty young girls were regarded as an additional attraction to the place, and so were encouraged to offer their perfumed wares to patrons of the café.

Indeed, so charming were both these youthful *vendeuses* that their fame had travelled far and wide in the Gay City—with the result that newcomers to Tortoni's had often come thither in the first instance to see for themselves whether or not their good looks were as pleasing as reported.

To-day, this was the case with a certain recently-arrived and extremely rich young gentleman from Peru. In so great a hurry was this wealthy Peruvian to make the acquaintance of the attractive young *vendeuses* he had already heard so much about, that he was still carrying the two carpet bags with which he had stepped off the train when he appeared on the terrace of Tortoni's.

He was a handsome, *débonnaire* young man, and it did not take him long to introduce himself, first to the Flower-Girl, and then to the Glove-Seller. So charming were both girls that the wealthy stranger could not make up his mind which he preferred ; and so he contented himself with paying them pretty compliments. Then he danced with both of them in turn to the strains of the café band.

Not so undecided, however, was another newcomer who now made his appearance on the terrace. This was a youthful Baron from Austria, who, having likewise been told of the beauty and charm of the two young girls, had decided he would like to prove for himself whether the reports he had heard were, indeed, the truth.

Unlike the Peruvian, this young nobleman was in no doubt as to which of the girls he preferred ; and being instantly enthralled by the fascinating Glove-Seller, he promptly fell in love with her. Leaving the pretty, but slightly insipid Flower-Girl to the admiring attentions of the first-comer, therefore, he eagerly attached himself to the quite willing Glove-Seller, and soon began a passionate flirtation with her.

Now envious of the young Baron's quick and definitely superior choice, the rich Peruvian was at first inclined to show resentment and jealousy of the new arrival ; but the latter, confident in his own powers of fascination, merely ignored him as a possible rival and devoted himself all the more eagerly to his latest conquest. He invited her to dance with him, and was delighted to find that her graceful movements were as attractive as her personal appearance. When their dance came to an end he led her to a more secluded sheltered corner, where he soon discovered, to his joy, that she already returned his own sudden passion.

The rich Peruvian, perforce, now had to content himself with the little Flower-Girl; and, finding her very pretty and charming, he devoted himself to winning her shy regard.

But quiet love-making was not to be the order of the day at Tortoni's that afternoon. Suddenly the terrace was invaded by a host of gay soldiers off duty, with whom had come for a café treat their own *cantinière* who, tired of serving them herself, had brought them to Tortoni's where they—and, incidentally, herself likewise—could be served by someone else for a change. Her bright idea was quickly granted, and the waiters soon began to buzz around them. A merry party followed; and the *cantinière* found herself in great demand by her military friends as a dancing partner, being passed indiscriminately from one to the other.

While this merry-making was at its height, some far more important and exalted folk arrived upon the terrace, and soon secured the attention of casual guests and obsequious attendants alike.

Among these new arrivals was a Lady Celebrity—a famous Beauty, accustomed to securing the admiration and sole attention of every male present in any social circle in which she found herself. She had just now in her train of admirers a Duke and an extremely smart young Officer, with both of whom she flirted coquettishly; until this moment, she had been much enjoying their exclusive attention.

Now, however, to her chagrin, she found that both her cavaliers had instantly noted the fresher and more delightfully youthful attractions of the Glove-Seller and the Flower-Girl, and were already eager to make the acquaintance of these new charmers.

By various artful manœuvres, the Duke and the smart young Officer managed to attain their object. Nevertheless, they did not meet with the success they had hoped for.

On observing that her attendant cavaliers had left the side of La Lionne, the flirtatious Peruvian deserted the little Flower-Girl and now approached the famous Beauty ; and, being pleased with her more sophisticated charms, he began to thrust his attentions upon her—only to find, however, that she did not desire to receive them. All the latter wanted at that moment was to flirt with her own attendant cavaliers, the Duke and the smart young Officer. She soon succeeded in enticing the Duke back to her side ; and the Peruvian was forced to retire for the time being.

Meanwhile, the smart young Officer, laughing at the Baron's seemingly easy conquest of the fascinating Glove-Seller, approached the latter himself and boldly attempted to snatch a kiss from her under the very nose of her new lover. The Glove-Seller, however, repulsed him indignantly, since she now truly loved the Baron ; and the latter, furious at the stranger's audacity, flung himself angrily upon the cheeky young Officer.

A wild commotion now arose upon the terrace ; and the Baron was about to chastise the kiss-snatcher severely when La Lionne ran forward and imperiously separated the pair.

By making use of all her sophisticated charm and experienced blandishments, the famous Beauty succeeded in bringing the smart young Officer back to his senses once more—and also into her own train of admirers.

Peaceful relations having thus been restored, a grand festival of dancing began on the terrace, in which everyone took part—with the exception of the Baron and the Glove-Seller, who still preferred to wander apart, arm-in-arm, once more wrapped-up in their sweet love-dream.

Among the lively dances that followed was a gay *can-can* by specially expert performers ; the waiters of the café likewise entertained the guests with a humorous dance ; and there were also some stately measures for the more sedate members of the company. Finally, there came a very lively dance, in which all the guests were whirled away in a merry crowd into the gardens beyond.

But the young Baron and his beautiful Glove-Seller still kept aloof from the giddy throng ; and they were last seen that evening disappearing into the darkening shadows of the woodlands, as they wandered forth lovingly into the Realms of Romance.

Then, presently, the Peruvian pleasure-seeker rushed out from the festive scene beyond, still carrying his two carpet bags. He had had enough of Tortoni's restaurant for the time being ; and, jauntily swinging his precious bags, he set forth once more in search of " fresh fields and pastures new."

THE GOOD-HUMOURED LADIES

(*Les Femmes de Bonne-Humeur*)

VENICE, in the eighteenth century, was a very gay city—especially at the time of the Carnival. Then, the fun and frolics of the revellers waxed fast and furious, and mischievous tricks were played upon all ; and if, at times, the fun verged upon licence, well, the light-hearted participants felt that plenty of time for penitence awaited them in the long, sombre Lenten days ahead. For the most part, however, pure bubbling merriment prevailed.

This was especially the case on one such eighteenth century Carnival day, when the traditional festivities— gay masquerades, practical jokes, riotous dancing and feasting—were being held in a small town bordering upon the ancient City of the Doges. Here, a little group of gay and charming young ladies of this lively Venetian town had planned to play a saucy Carnival-time trick upon their long-suffering sweethearts—and, in particular, upon the aristocratic and exquisitely dandified betrothed of a dashing beauty named Constanza.

Wishing to prove the absolute fidelity of this immaculate young nobleman, Count Rinaldo, to whom she had but recently plighted her troth, Constanza enlisted the aid and co-operation of her three girl friends, Felicita, Dorotea, and Pasquina ; and she likewise secured the assistance of her guardian aunt with whom she lived, the Marquise Sylvestra — who, though elderly and decidedly *passée*, was, nevertheless, as giddy as any of the young people.

Between them all, an amusing little plot was devised.

It was decided to send an intriguing-looking perfumed note to the young Count, informing him that he was passionately beloved by a certain lady who would wear a pink rose in her hair that evening at the Carnival festivities ; and he was further invited to seek out this mysterious stranger, since she would be willing to dance with him should he be interested in making her acquaintance. In order to complicate matters, it was arranged that the four ladies taking part in the frolic would each of them wear a pink rose as hair decoration and, donning their masks, would accost him in turn and try to entangle him in a love intrigue. Constanza's pretty and pertly audacious young handmaid, Mariuccia, was handed the perfumed note with instructions to deliver it to the hoped-for victim as soon as he appeared in the square adjoining the elegant abode of Constanza and her guardian-aunt, the Marquise Sylvestra.

The latter giddy old dame was delighted at being admitted into her mischievous niece's little plot ; and she determined to make the most of this, her probably last chance of a pleasant flirtation. She hastily called to her aid, therefore, the expert lady's-maid services of young Mariuccia before the latter set out upon her secret errand. She made the girl help to build upon her wrinkled old face a quite glowing and almost youthful complexion ; to arrange an elegant wig of red-gold curls in the latest high-massed fashion upon her own sparsely-covered pate ; and to lace her tightly into a gorgeous gown, which was just a mass of frilly flounces, bows, and glittering sequins. She was so thrilled at the prospect of the unexpected adventure before her that she did not notice the comical antics of the saucy little Mariuccia, who lost no opportunity of making game of the elderly would-be reveller every time her back was turned.

Blissfully ignorant of the disrespectful conduct of her youthful assistant, the flighty old lady completed her toilet by fastening a pink rose in her elaborate *coiffure* at a coquettish angle and putting a velvet Carnival mask on her rejuvenated face ; and then she rejoined the three young ladies, who had likewise donned masks and tucked pink roses in their hair.

Mariuccia was now despatched to deliver the perfumed note to the young Count Rinaldo, who had just been observed entering the square outside—all the life and movement of which could readily be seen from the large balcony of the Marquise's home.

The square was a handsome one, with several old houses and a campanile as background, and having a fountain and seats in the centre ; and on one side was an open-air café, in which revellers from the early evening festivities had already begun to appear.

Entirely oblivious of his impending victimisation, the exquisite and somewhat languid young Count Rinaldo made his way slowly across the square to the café ; and, dropping gracefully into a chair beside a vacant table, he called to the waiter to bring him some wine. He was gorgeously dressed in the lastest fashion of the day—light satin breeches, embroidered coat and waistcoat, lace ruffles, and elegantly-curled hair ; and for the moment he looked a trifle bored. But not for long.

Scarcely had he given his order to the waiter, than the pretty and pert little waiting-maid, Mariuccia, approached his table with an air of mystery, and handed to him the perfumed note so intriguingly worded by her mischievous young mistress. On reading the note and learning therefrom that he was beloved by a strange lady who would wear a pink rose in her hair at the Carnival Masquerade, the young man was both thrilled and mystified, as had been hoped would be the case ; for, although he dearly loved the beautiful Constanza, he was by no means averse to a little mild flirtation with another charmer at Carnival-time—especially when his fair betrothed was not at his side.

Consequently, no sooner had Mariuccia fluttered away—with many coquettish glances over her shoulders —than Rinaldo rose to his feet and looked eagerly about him ; and lo ! from the other side of the square came four youthful masked ladies of ravishing appearance, each of whom wore a pink rose in her hair. These were Constanza, Felicita, Dorotea, and Pasquina ; and, in turn, they tripped past the young Count, with heads held tantalizingly high in the air, though decidedly saucy gleams flashed from bright eyes as they passed. The masks made an excellent disguise.

Though greatly puzzled on beholding four ladies bedecked with pink roses in their hair instead of one only, Rinaldo felt that among them must surely be the writer of the inviting *billet-doux* he had just received ; and so he decided to accost them all, one after the other—which he proceeded to do. Sweeping off his hat with an elaborate gesture and bowing low before each lady in turn, he announced his name, and even went so far as to express his appreciation of the fair masker's avowed love for him and to accept her partnership at the Masquerade.

But, to his amazement and chagrin, each of the masked ladies passed on her way with a haughty stare, seemingly indignant at his audacity in seeking acquaintanceship with a stranger ; and the disappointed young exquisite returned to his café seat, non-plussed and crestfallen in the extreme.

Soon, however, he was on his feet again ; for, from the same direction, came another and more magnificently dressed lady, who likewise wore the intriguing token of a pink rose in her elaborate *coiffure*. Though this lady's garments were of a heavier and less youthful style than those of the others, she moved with a mincing and decidedly coquettish gait and smiled meaningly as he approached her. For this was the old Marquise Sylvestra, who was somewhat overplaying her part, having no intention of allowing her promised quarry to slip through her fingers.

Delighted at the prospect of securing an admirer so late in her life, even if only for a limited time, the disguised Marquise graciously received the eager greetings and flatteringly amorous advances of the young Count—who was at first completely deceived by her cleverly applied cosmetics, the deep disguising mask she wore, and her seemingly youthful coquettishness. Equally delighted for the moment, he invited his new charmer first to partake of the wine which had now been brought to his table and afterwards to accompany him to the Carnival festivities now beginning.

The masked lady only too willingly accepted his eager invitation, and immediately sat down at the table ; and then it was that the flirtatious Rinaldo received the horrid shock arranged for him by his betrothed.

The Marquise had to raise her mask for a moment, in order to drink the wine offered to her ; but that moment was long enough for her chance partner to realise, to his intense dismay, that his new admirer was quite an elderly dame and not the fair young charmer he had at first glance believed her to be.

Full of disappointment, he now politely tried to avoid having to escort her to the gay and frivolous festivities of the Carnival, making the first excuses that came into his head ; but the eager and triumphant old Marquise laughingly refused to release him, declaring that he had invited her to accompany him to the Carnival, and to the Carnival she would certainly accompany him. So saying, she seized the young Count firmly by the arm, and positively dragged him off to the Carnival festival nearby, very much against his will, but powerless to resist hers.

As soon as the ill-assorted pair had departed from the Square, the lively maid, Mariuccia, brought out a table and set it in a sheltered corner beneath the balcony of the Marquise's house ; and she quickly laid upon it a delectable little supper, having invited her own latest admirer to join her at a festive meal in the absence of her young mistress. This admirer was none other than Leonardo, the spouse of Felicita ; a somewhat irresponsible young husband, who was likewise playing truant on this particular Carnival night.

Leonardo soon arrived, bringing a third party with him, another giddy youth of high degree named Battista, who, though about to be betrothed to Constanza's friend Pasquina, was likewise " shaking a loose leg " that evening. Almost immediately after their arrival, yet another uninvited guest joined the little party. This was the elderly Marquis di Luca, who, though old enough to know better, had also cast his fading, but still appraising and somewhat lecherous eyes upon the distractingly pretty little waiting-maid ; and the flirtatious Mariuccia, willing enough to entertain three admirers instead of one, gave him a welcome reception.

A most hilarious time was enjoyed by all at this unconventional stolen party ; for the vivacious Mariuccia bestowed her charming favours almost equally upon her three admirers—though she mischievously enticed the old nobleman into the performance of frivolous and foolishly amusing antics entirely unbefitting his age and position. As the Carnival music could be heard plainly in the square, she made her three guests dance with her to these lively strains ; and then she herself performed a marvellously pretty solo dance for their delectation.

Then, not content with flirting outrageously with the old aristocrat, she presently persuaded him to dance, in more serious fashion, a stately minuet with her ; but her aged admirer, though he essayed a few courtly steps in a decidedly bibulous manner—having consumed a goodly quantity of the excellent wine set before him by his really charmingly naughty little hostess—was glad enough to stagger back perilously into his seat once more, where he promptly fell fast asleep.

Mariuccia continued to flirt and dance with her other two admirers for a little time longer ; then, seeing her young mistress, accompanied by the latter's lively friends, Felicita and Dorotea, coming into the square, she tripped off gaily—quickly followed by Leonardo, fearful of being discovered playing truant by his wife.

Battista, however, awaited the arrival of the lively ladies ; but on learning from them that his own lady-love Pasquina had been seen in company with one, Faloppa — though he knew the latter preferred Doratea — he became jealous and dashed off to seek his fancied rival.

Constanza having, amidst the Carnival revellers, come across her betrothed, Rinaldo, in unwilling company with her aunt, the coquettish old Marquise Sylvestra, felt decidedly upset because of his seemingly easy conquest by the latter ; and she now almost wished she had never played such a dubious trick upon him. However, her merry lady friends soon set her mind at rest ; and, on being joined by Leonardo and Battista— who soon strolled into the square as though eagerly looking for them—she gladly agreed to their suggestion that they should all now concentrate on making game of the silly old Marquise and the no less silly and almost senile Marquis di Luca.

The latter had already been awakened by the noise around him ; and presently he was accosted by two lady revellers wearing long dark veils. These new-comers were none other than Leonardo and Battista, who had quickly dressed themselves up as gay ladies of the town ; and, between them, they played no end of amusing tricks upon their elderly victim—making comical love to him, plying him with more wine, and inducing him to dance with them until he fell back exhausted into his chair at the supper-table. Then they snatched off their veils and revealed their true identity to his astonished gaze, while all the party laughed hilariously at his discomfiture.

An even more outrageous joke was played upon the frivolous old Marquise Sylvestra. The merry ladies dressed up the café waiter, Niccolo, in the gorgeous garments of a royal Prince ; and when the Marquise presently came heavily frolicking into the square on the reluctant arm of the decidedly unhappy Count Rinaldo, Constanza and her friends pushed forward the disguised waiter and introduced him to the dame as the princely scion of a famous Royal House. The pretended Prince at once began to make love to his new acquaintance, and acted his part as an amorous Royal youth so skilfully that the foolish old Marquise was intensely flattered, as well as being completely deceived as to his true identity ; and, to the hilarious amusement of all, she presently announced that the " Prince " had done her the honour to ask her hand in marriage and that she had accepted his offer.

Then it was that the saucy Mariuccia—who had quickly rejoined the revellers on realising that her own unauthorised supper-party had passed unnoted or was being generously overlooked by her young mistress— at a signal from Constanza, whisked off the mask and gorgeous trappings of the pretended Prince, instantly revealing him as Niccolo, the café waiter.

Furious at the trick that had been played upon her, the Marquise turned first upon the obliging but inoffensive waiter, and soundly boxed the unfortunate young man's ears ; and then she became involved in a rowdy scene with the old Marquis di Luca, who, himself suffering from the outrageous conduct of the young people, now began to lay about him with his gold-headed stick. In the *mêlée* that followed, the wobbling and wavering Marquis accidentally tipped askew the old lady's elaborate wig with his wildly-aimed stick ; and this induced more convulsive laughter among the young people.

But this comical incident also caused happy reunions among the latter ; for while the defeated elderly revellers were now realising the foolishness of their own undignified conduct, Constanza and Rinaldo, Felicita and Leonardo, Pasquina and Battista — the latter no longer jealous — and Dorotea and Faloppa, were all reiterating their loving vows once more, in readiness to join again, presently, in the Carnival festivities — this time in their rightful and legitimate partnerships.

THE THREE-CORNERED HAT

(*Le Tricorne*)

THE ways and customs of the country districts of eighteenth century Spain had advanced very little from those of the later Middle Ages. The peasants were still the simple but passionate folk they had always been. They loved to dance their elaborate national dances on every possible occasion; they engaged in country pursuits with scarcely a thought of life in their crowded towns and famous cities; and though they always helped to swell the enthusiastic audiences at the frequent bull-fights, for the most part they had but little intercourse with the high-and-mighty nobility who ruled—and sometimes mis-ruled—them.

It was seldom that the country folk ever set eyes upon a high official of the town; and when they did they were not too pleased by the latter's overbearing and greedy ways. The " Three-Cornered Hat " class, as they dubbed their ruling officials, were by no means to their liking; and they never lost a chance of playing mischievous tricks upon any pompous person of this order who might unexpectedly appear in their neighbourhood. These lively escapades, too, usually ended very much in their own favour and considerably to the discomfiture of the latter, as will be gathered from this present story.

In a certain country district of Andalusia, situated amidst magnificent mountain scenery, there stood a fine old mill alongside a sparkling stream spanned by a stone bridge leading to the adjoining village.

The miller's whitewashed house stood not far away, a

simple but substantial-looking abode with a vine-covered porch ; for the owner of the mill was fairly prosperous and could afford to live in comfort. A few other sun-baked houses of a similar Spanish peasant type stood at a little distance from the mill, on the white dusty road leading to the nearest town.

One afternoon, while the hot rays of the autumn sun blazed down from the deep, almost indigo, blue sky, the miller stood in the open doorway of his abode, idly playing with a magpie in a wooden cage hanging on the wall beside the door. He was a handsome young man ; and his gay peasant clothes set off his muscular limbs and sunburnt skin to perfection. It was the end of the siesta hour ; and he was just about to pass on towards the mill when his gay young wife came out and lured him into dancing and flirting with her, for awhile, instead.

The miller's wife was an extremely beautiful young woman, dark, vivacious, and full of a light grace in excess even of the usual lissom type of Spanish peasant beauty. She was, too, of a gay and flirtatious nature ; and, though loving her sturdy young husband dearly, she had no objection to catching admiring glances from other roving eyes. This amiable tendency was plainly revealed presently when, after having been kept joyously dancing and flirting longer than was good for his working day, the miller at last reluctantly broke away from her clinging arms and ran hastily to draw water from a well nearby.

At that moment, a gay dandified youth came strolling on to the bridge, where, gazing around, he was greatly struck by the beauty of the miller's wife ; and he remained staring at the latter in astonished admiration. This stranger was most extravagantly dressed in pale-tinted silken befringed and beribboned garments of the latest fashion ; and he wore an elegant three-cornered hat over a brightly-coloured wig—being obviously an " exquisite " from the town.

Taking off his tricorne hat with a graceful flourish, the dandified newcomer began a mimed and silent flirtation with the miller's wife, blowing her kisses and making inviting signs to her with his long graceful fingers—all of which were mischievously imitated and returned by the pretty young woman whilst her husband's back was turned.

But not for long. The miller briskly brought up his bucket of water from the well and set it down upon the ground rather sooner than his coquettish wife expected ; and quickly seeing what was afoot, he fell into a sudden jealous rage and rushed towards the bridge to drive away the impudent intruder. But the giddy young " exquisite " lightly skipped away ; and, before the irate miller could even begin to scold his now repentant wife, a group of seemingly important strangers appeared on the road leading from the town.

First came a couple of tall uniformed footmen bearing a smart sedan-chair, in which was seated a gorgeously-dressed and handsome lady, rouged, powdered, and patched in the mode of the day. This fine and youngish lady was the spoilt, petted wife of the Corregidor, or Governor of the Province, a richly-clothed great lord who himself walked beside his lady.

The Corregidor was by no means a popular official, since he was of a mean, avaricious, and tyrannical disposition. He was very much older than his attractive wife ; and it was all he could do, now, to keep hobbling alongside her sedan-chair—behind which followed a squad of alguazils, or Spanish policemen, forming the great lord's bodyguard.

The hideously striped uniforms of the alguazils gave

them a very sinister look ; and the procession was anything but a pleasing one to the neighbouring peasants who had now joined the miller and his wife, and who, as stated before, had no love for what they called the " Three-Cornered Hat " class.

In addition to his other disagreeable qualities, the old Corregidor, despite his advancing years, was likewise of a lecherous nature ; and no sooner had he set eyes on the miller's lovely wife than he determined to add her to his own innumerable female conquests—mostly unwilling ones.

Consequently, as he now passed by with his pompous little procession, he leered ingratiatingly upon her, and made signs of exaggerated admiration of her beauty ; and when the pretty young woman curtsied with the humble respect due to a great lord, he was pleased, and instantly began to think out a plan whereby he might approach her again later on.

When the Corregidor and his procession had passed on their way, the work of the mill proceeded once more under the expert supervision of the miller. The latter, however, was not too busy to indulge for a few moments in a very mild flirtation with an attractive young peasant girl passing by—as an equally mild reprisal for his wife's own giddy conduct in returning the amorous actions of the smart dandy on the bridge a few minutes ago.

This greatly annoyed the miller's wife ; but her mischievous husband quickly appeased her by enfolding her in a loving embrace. To please her still more, he again held up his afternoon's work a short time longer, in order to join her in some lively dancing—of which she was inordinately fond, as was he himself.

As the miller at last ran off to carry on with his belated jobs his pretty wife happily danced on alone ; and as she was a really excellent dancer she indulged in many elaborate steps and even tried out several new ones with great delight—little dreaming that her graceful performance was being eagerly watched from a discreet hiding-place by the licentious old Corregidor. The latter, having escaped from attendance upon his exacting wife, had soon returned to pursue his plan for the seduction of the village beauty ; and he now gloated over the voluptuous movements of his hoped-for victim, delighted at finding her alone. Very soon he made his presence known and, bowing deeply before her in an exaggeratedly deferential manner, he invited her to accept him as a dancing partner in a minuet.

The miller's wife, shyly flattered by his obvious admiration and appraisal of her dancing, accepted the invitation, and acquitted herself equally well in this stately dance—rather to the surprise of the conceited old lord who, as an expert in the slower dancing measures of the Court, danced with all the ultra-extravagant gestures then in vogue and with the addition of somewhat ridiculous mincing steps of his own.

But the miller's gay wife soon tired of these stately measures, and, in her turn, invited her elderly admirer to join her in a much more lively peasant dance, in which she held aloft a bunch of ripe grapes, hastily plucked from the luxuriant vine growing on her porch.

In this vintage dance the male partner had to approach the tantalising maiden in a series of high dancing jumps and to bite off as many separate grapes as he could. Most of the expert peasant youths in the district would have easily bitten off a goodly number of the luscious grapes during the dancing of quite intricate steps ; but the elderly and very stiff-limbed Corregidor soon found such a feat beyond him—with the result that presently he lost his balance and fell over backwards.

By this time, the miller had again appeared on the scene ; and he hastened to help his wife to put her too ambitious partner on to his feet once more ; but they could neither of them resist laughing heartily at the latter's discomfiture and poking fun at him. This made the Corregidor very angry ; and, as he limped off, he furiously vowed vengeance upon the pair.

His threats, however, had no effect upon the hilarity of the miller and his wife ; and they danced together again in triumphant glee. They were presently joined by a number of their peasant friends dressed in holiday attire, who reminded them that the remainder of the late afternoon and evening was to be spent as a village dancing festival.

Musicians now appeared on the scene, and, to the accompaniment of lively tunes and the merry click-clacking of castanets, a whole series of famous Spanish country dances was performed.

When slight signs of exhaustion began to be shown, the miller brought out wine for the refreshment of all ; and then, as his friends rested awhile, he himself performed for their delectation a truly marvellous solo dance, easily proving himself to be the best dancer of them all.

Terrific applause greeted his really fine performance ; but, as it ended, there came a most unwelcome interruption to these gay proceedings. The same sinister-looking alguazils who had acted as bodyguard to the Corregidor on his first appearance in their midst again arrived upon the scene and, marching up to the panting miller, announced that they had come to arrest him on instructions from the great lord, their master. Refusing to give any reason for this sudden drastic action, or to listen to his indignant protests and to the tearful entreaties of his now distracted wife, the alguazils roughly seized the unfortunate miller and marched him off along the road towards the distant town jail.

Dismayed by this alarming end to their festivities, the villagers sadly returned to their homes; but the miller's wife still remained outside, near the mill, too dazed by what had happened to perform her usual evening duties. She lay on the ground for some considerable time, weeping and rocking herself to and fro in deep distress.

It was now dusk, and silvery rays of moonlight gradually began to light up the scene; and presently, across the bridge, a crouching figure wrapped in a dark cloak came creeping with stealthy steps towards the unhappy young woman.

This was the vicious Corregidor, who, having sent his minions in advance to remove the much too hefty miller from his path, now hoped to carry out his vile schemes for the seduction of the latter's lovely wife by stealing upon her unawares. But a slight stumble betrayed his approach; and, springing to her feet, the miller's wife faced him defiantly.

At first the Corregidor endeavoured to ingratiate himself into her favour by more admiring speeches and a gentle mode of wooing; but the miller's wife broke away from him in distaste and repulsed him with the utmost scorn.

Her disdainful refusal of his advances added fuel to the fire of the dissipated official's sudden passion; and he tried again and again to force his unwelcome attentions upon her. Seizing her round the waist, he began furiously to rain hot kisses upon the scarlet lips that were so temptingly near; but the miller's young wife was strong as well as beautiful, and she managed to slip from his grasp and to rush towards the bridge.

The Corregidor, now inflamed almost to madness,

dashed after her and again succeeded in snatching at her bright skirts ; but in the wild struggle that ensued, he lost his balance and fell into the mill stream.

Though at first she could not help laughing at the undignified splashings and splutterings of her would-be seducer, the miller's wife was also somewhat scared ; and seeing the now bedraggled Corregidor struggling out of the water and seemingly about to pursue her again, she ran towards the village to seek help from her friends, looking round fearfully from time to time lest he should be following her.

But the elderly Don Juan was now at the end of his tether ; and all he could do was to drag himself slowly and stiffly into the miller's still empty house. Here he flung off his dripping hat and coat ; and seeing an old coat of the miller's hanging over a chair he put it on and then lay down on a couch for awhile to recover his lost energy.

He was not left long in peace, however. The sturdy young miller, being a mightily strong fellow, had managed to escape from the alguazils long before reaching the town jail ; and he now came hurrying back jauntily enough to his home. Furious at finding the Corregidor there, and immediately guessing the reason for his presence, he snatched up a stick and belaboured the intruder soundly, heedless of the latter's groans and cries for mercy. Then, leaving his well-beaten victim to recover as best he could, the now satisfied young husband betook himself to the village to look for his wife.

Before leaving, however, he scribbled a taunting message on the wall beside the prostrate intruder. This was to the effect that he was about to seek out the latter's quite attractive and youngish wife, whom he declared to be almost as lovely as his own ; and as the battered Corregidor presently tried to rise and depart he saw and read this impudent message, and fell back again in helpless dismay.

At that moment, the alguazils, in a great state of angry consternation at the loss of their prisoner, came dashing into the miller's house to look for him ; and mistaking the crouching form on the floor for the elusive miller, they set upon him in grim earnest, raining further blows upon him as they roughly dragged him outside.

It took the wretched Corregidor some considerable time to convince his over-zealous underlings of his true identity ; and then the now scared and decidedly sheepish alguazils, fearful of the probably unpleasant consequences to themselves of their rough usage of him, carried off their semi-conscious lord and master with abjectly tender care.

But not before the torn and bedraggled figure of the recently splendidly-garbed official had been recognised by a band of the miller's peasant friends, who at that moment came hurrying on to the scene ; and, consequently, the ignominious departure of the Corregidor was followed by laughing jeers, boos, and cat-calls—a further proof of the opprobrium in which the " Three-Cornered-Hat " class was held by these simple country folk.

With this jolly crowd came the miller and his wife, both full of joy at their happy reunion ; and the whole party kept up another lively festival of dancing until dawn to celebrate the discomfiture of their vicious Governor

ZEPHYR AND FLORA

(*Zéphire et Flore*)

AT a Concert given by the Muses on Mount Olympus a disturbing element crept in, which quickly developed into a plot to separate a happy husband and wife.

The latter charming couple were Flora, the Goddess of Flowers, and Zephyr, the West Wind ; and their perfect happiness was a joy to behold, their constancy being an example to the many less faithful inhabitants of Olympus.

But one of Zephyr's three brothers, Boreas, the North Wind, had conceived an unlawful passion for the lovely Flora ; and, being a big blustering fellow, he hoped to carry her off by force one day and become her lover.

But this proposed abduction was not an easy matter to achieve. In the first place, Flora loved her own delightful husband with all her heart, and cared nothing for the boisterous Boreas ; and secondly, Zephyr himself, knowing of his brother's jealousy, guarded his fair wife well and scarcely ever left her side.

Nevertheless, Boreas bided his time ; and when the Muses held their grand Festival of Song and Dance on Mount Olympus he was filled with deep satisfaction, hoping then to find an opportunity of carrying out his unbrotherly plan, owing to the preoccupation of the guests with the entertainment provided for them.

Even on this occasion, however, many difficulties arose to interfere with his desires. It happened that the Muses themselves admired the handsome Boreas ; and they kept him most unwillingly dancing attendance upon them for some considerable time. He became even more impatient, presently, when, while still pretending to interest himself in his artistic hostesses, he beheld Zephyr and Flora dancing together in an ecstasy of happiness on the flowery lawns below; and his jealousy increasing at this charming sight, he quickly concocted a sly little plot.

He persuaded the friendly and admiring Muses to permit their guests to take part in a delightful new game he had just invented, called " Blind-Man's-Buff "—a game which has come down to our modern world, likewise, as a most intriguing diversion. Receiving their consent, he soon set the game in motion, hoping that it would provide him with the chance he sought of catching the dainty Goddess of Flowers in his arms and rushing off with her while her watchful husband was blindfolded.

His fine plan, however, did not work out as he wished.

When Zephyr was blindfolded for the first time, and sent spinning into the midst of the laughing guests, Boreas looked on with satisfaction, feeling that his longed-for chance would now materialise; but his hopes were quickly dashed. Before he could reach the side of the lovely Flora—who saw him coming, and saucily eluded him—she danced away straight into the arms of the blinded Zephyr himself—who instantly claimed his reward of a kiss.

Full of chagrin at this first failure of his little plan, Boreas roughly set the still blinded Zephyr in motion again, hoping for better luck presently; but, to his even greater chagrin, this time he was himself caught in the eager clutches of his brother, who mistook him for Flora and embraced him with zest—to the merriment of all the other participators in the jolly game and the angry disgust of its inventor.

Boreas now turned aside, sulkily; and, full of envy and anger against his brother, he hid behind a bush and shot an arrow at Zephyr when the latter presently came past his hiding-place. The consequent fall of Zephyr was not at first observed by the other guests, who were occupied elsewhere ; and Boreas hurried away in search of Flora, whom he soon found taking part with the Muses in an elaborate series of dances they had evolved.

When the Muses presently departed, Flora, left alone, danced very charmingly for awhile by herself. Presently, however, she was terrified by the eager approach of Boreas, who snatched her into his arms and began to make passionate love to her.

Flora repulsed him with utter scorn ; but, in the struggle that ensued, she fell from his grasp in a swoon. Now alarmed in his turn at this unexpected result of his love-making, and observing a procession approaching, Boreas hastened away into the background.

The approaching company proved to be a group of mourners bearing in their midst the body of Zephyr, who had died from the wound inflicted by his brother's arrow. The Muses and their guests now held a solemn lament for his untimely end ; and when Flora revived from her swoon she uttered a cry of woe and rushed towards the now limp form of her beloved husband.

But Zephyr was beloved by the Gods ; and so they healed his wound and restored him to life and health almost instantly. Presently, to the joy of all, he rose up, with renewed strength ; and seizing his lovely wife in his arms, he danced about with her once more in an ecstasy of delight.

The Muses were so pleased at this happy reunion of Zephyr and Flora that they bound the ecstatic couple's arms together as a sign that they might nevermore be parted.

Then, after joining in another lively festival dance,

the miraculously restored wedded lovers departed to their own flowery Bower of Delight—and, presently, Boreas was found and duly punished by the Muses for thrusting his unwelcome attentions upon Flora and for his most unfraternal conduct towards his brother.

COPPELIA

(ou La Fille aux Yeux d'Email,
or The Girl with Enamel Eyes)

In a quaint little town of Galicia, towards the end of the eighteenth century, there lived an old Toy-Maker, named Doctor Coppélius, who studied ancient books on Astrology, Alchemy, and even Magic, and who hoped that, some day, he might become a first-class Magician.

Meanwhile, Dr. Coppélius was a remarkably skilful toy-maker ; and, in particular, he made the most wonderfully life-like dolls with clockwork apparatus inside them—with the result that, when he wound them up, they could move their arms and legs and even walk and dance about. He always hoped that people might think they were human beings and that he was, indeed, a true Magician who had endowed them with life.

Finally, he produced a doll which, at a short distance, appeared actually to be a human young lady. He called her Coppélia, and told everybody that she was his daughter. He would place her in a chair on the balcony that opened out from his workshop on the second floor of his house ; and he always placed an open book on her lap as though she were reading. From time to time, as she sat there, he would wind her up ; and then she moved her arms about and even turned her head from side to side to indicate that she was observing the passers-by.

Coppélia appeared to be a very charming young girl of about seventeen years of age. She had a pretty face, with a rosy complexion and cherry-coloured lips ; and her eyes were of a deep shining blue, rather like enamel.

She had well-dressed flaxen hair ; and she always wore a gown cut in the latest fashion of the day. Her little feet were shod in smart velvet shoes ; and she could dance with elegant grace—when wound up. For the most part, however, she was to be seen sitting out on the balcony, with a book on her lap.

So remarkably life-like and charmingly pretty was Coppélia that everybody admired her immensely ; and one young man—a handsome youth named Franz— actually fell desperately in love with her.

This unexpected circumstance caused great jealousy in the heart of a fair maiden named Swanilda, who lived in the house opposite—the reason being that the handsome Franz was the latter's own sweetheart. Before the appearance of Coppélia on the old Toy-Maker's balcony, Franz had had eyes for no other maiden in the town but Swanilda. Now, however, he had eyes for nobody but the truly ravishing Coppélia—greatly to the distress of his loving sweetheart. Not that Swanilda entirely believed that the newcomer was actually a human being ; and, being a sensible girl, she determined to find out the truth about this at the first opportunity.

One day, therefore, when the street was temporarily deserted, Swanilda approached the balcony where the lovely Coppélia, looking smarter than ever, was sitting in a chair above, and, as usual, apparently reading a book. She first of all called out to her a polite greeting ; and, when the pretty maiden above took not the slightest notice of her friendly action, she went further and tried other tactics. She began to dance about and even to perform some quite elaborate steps and curtseys likely to arouse interest in a stranger.

Coppélia, however, still ignored her would-be friendly neighbour, and did not even lift her enamel-like eyes from the book she appeared to be reading; and, presently,

Swanilda returned to her own home, now feeling almost convinced that the newcomer was merely another of the old Doctor's wonderful dolls—though, admittedly, the best he had ever made.

Not thus convinced was young Franz, however, As Swanilda departed into her home her sweetheart entered the street and eagerly ran up to the Toy-Maker's house and stood below the balcony, rapturously gazing at the object of his admiration sitting in the chair above.

Nor was he content with merely gazing ; for the love-sick youth soon began to strike absurd attitudes, clasping his hands over his heart, bowing deeply in adoration, and even throwing kisses to the motionless Coppélia.

As it happened, the old Toy-Maker was watching him secretly from behind the curtains in his workshop ; and, though highly gratified at seeing his marvellous doll thus regarded as a human person, he mischievously decided to play a further deceptive trick upon her ardent admirer. Knowing himself to be unseen by the rapt youth, he slyly stretched out his hand to the back of the doll and wound up her internal mechanism.

The enamoured Franz, therefore, was presently thrown into an ecstasy of joy when the fascinating maiden above began to stand up and to move about, waving her well-shaped arms in greeting, and actually throwing him kisses in return !

But the old Doctor soon tired of his joke and stopped these demonstrations of affection ; and, presently, he came out on to the balcony, and, taking the arm of his supposed daughter, led her indoors with great ceremony.

At this same moment a number of gay young people, many of them the friends of both Franz and Swanilda, came dancing and singing into the street, having finished their day's work and feeling ready for a frolic. Swanilda soon joined them ; and a lively dance now took place.

The dancing was interrupted by the arrival of the Burgomaster, who announced that on the morrow the great Ducal Lord of their district would present a splendid new bell to the town at a Festival, at which the young men and maidens who dwelt therein were expected to take part and to pair off as betrothed couples.

Though Swanilda longed secretly for Franz to choose her as his betrothed bride on the morrow, she also felt annoyed with him because of his strange and foolish fancy for the fair newcomer, Coppélia. However, she could not keep up her appearance of sudden coldness very long ; and soon she was dancing gaily with him once more amidst the happy throng of young folks.

* * * * *

That same evening, as darkness began to fall and the street became deserted once more, old Dr. Coppélius came fussily out from his house to take a walk. He carefully locked the door with a big key, which he then wrapped up in his handkerchief as he strolled along. He was a comical-looking old fellow, with spindly legs that caused him to walk with jerky movements ; and he might easily have been mistaken for a learned Astrologer in his doctor's flowing gown and skull-cap.

But Dr. Coppélius was not to enjoy his walk that evening in peace. Before he had gone far, he fell in with a rowdy party of young revellers, who danced around him in a ring and tried to make him join in their antics. The old fellow was greatly annoyed at this frolicsome interruption to his walk ; but he managed at length to free himself and then continued on his way— blissfully unconscious of the fact that, on mopping his heated brow with his handkerchief after the impromptu dance he had been compelled to take part in so unwillingly, his big house-key had fallen to the ground.

The lost key was presently picked up by Swanilda as she passed by with some of her girl friends. Recognising it as the old Doctor's famous big key, she decided that here was an excellent chance to enter the house, during the absence of its owner and thus to secure a close-up view of the Toy-Maker's mysterious so-called daughter. Her companions being equally eager to take the risk of some magical happenings, she unlocked the door with the big key and all the young folk slipped, quietly and somewhat fearfully, into the darkness beyond.

Then, unknown to Swanilda, Franz, also aware of the Doctor's absence, likewise considered it to be a providential opportunity to enter the house of mystery and to make the personal acquaintance of the ravishing Coppélia ; and he now appeared as the girls vanished from sight. He had brought with him a small ladder ; and he decided to climb on to the balcony and to make his entrance through the window beyond.

It happened, however, that the old Toy-Maker returned at that moment ; and seeing what was afoot, he gamely chased the young would-be intruder out of the street. Then, on his return, puffing and blowing after the chase, he discovered, to his further dismay, that the door of his house was open ; and he rushed inside in frenzied haste.

*   *   *   *   *

Meanwhile, the first intruders, led by the curious Swanilda, were enjoying themselves immensely. Having quickly made their way to the old Doctor's workshop upstairs and set a few candles alight, they were astonished to find a number of life-size dolls lying about in strange limp attitudes. At first, they were somewhat afraid of these ; but curiosity soon overcame their fear, and they then began to admire the rich clothes

322

worn by the models. It was not long before they
discovered the clockwork apparatus that would set
them in motion ; and, presently, all the dolls were
moving jerkily in a succession of comical actions—to the
great amusement of the young people.

Presently, Swanilda noticed a curtained recess ; and,
after many gradual approaches in fear and trembling,
and sudden withdrawals in alarm, she summoned up
all her courage and boldly drew the curtain aside. And
there, within the recess, she found the now motionless
young lady doll, Coppélia, still sitting on a chair in
state and after several more nervous approaches, she
eventually satisfied herself that the latter was, indeed,
merely a very cleverly-constructed life-size mechanical
doll.

At that moment, hearing a movement and peeping
out from the curtain, she saw, to her amazement, that
Franz—who had by this time returned and made a
second and successful attempt to get into the Toy-
Maker's house—was just climbing into the workshop
through the window. Full of mischief, she decided to
play an amusing trick upon him. Slipping back into
the recess and drawing the curtain once more, she dressed
herself in Coppélia's fine frock and, hiding the doll in a
corner, seated herself in the latter's chair. Then she
kept still and bided her time.

Meanwhile, no sooner had the venturesome Franz
dropped in from the window than he was set upon by
the irate Dr. Coppélius, who was lying in wait for him.
The latter, having already driven forth the other young
trespassers, now rushed upon the new intruder and
began to belabour him vigorously with his stick.

The unlucky Franz tried to dodge the blows as best
he could ; and finally he managed to pacify the old
Doctor by declaring that he had conceived a violent

passion for the latter's lovely daughter and desired to marry her, having merely come in to gaze upon her once more.

This statement greatly pleased Coppélius, who was mightily flattered because his marvellous mechanical doll was thus actually mistaken for a living maiden ; and he agreed to consider the young man's offer. Then, suddenly, a crazy idea occurred to him. He decided to try out an experiment he had long been studying in his ancient book on magic, whereby he might transfer a vital spark of life from the love-lorn Franz into his own mechanical doll, Coppélia, and thus change her into a real human being in very truth. He did not know for certain whether the spell would work ; but it was certainly worth while making the attempt.

Consequently, he offered Franz a glass of wine, into which he had dropped, unobserved, a strong drug to make him sleep ; and the young man, exhausted after his belabouring, gladly swallowed this seemingly pleasant drink, and immediately fell into a heavy semi-conscious state. Then the old Doctor, in great excitement, began to mutter *abracadabra*-like words from his ancient book on magic, in the hope of transferring the spirit of the dormant Franz into the body of Coppélia and so to endow her with life.

It was at this moment that Swanilda came out from the curtained recess, clad in the garb of the fair Coppélia, with the idea of giving the latter's maker a real fright. She had already taken the precaution of setting the half-clothed doll in her chair once more before leaving the recess.

At first, on beholding the approaching Coppélia, as he believed, the old Toy-Maker was not in the least scared. On the contrary, he was delighted because he felt that his spell had worked, after all, and that life had, indeed, entered into his wonderful doll from the stupified Franz. His beautiful Coppélia was at last moving and dancing about without any preliminary winding-up, exactly like an actual human being; and he clapped his hands with pride and exultation as she ran about and danced in the most lively and fantastic manner.

Presently, however, to his consternation, his successfully animated doll appeared to be getting out of control; and the old Doctor began to become alarmed. Noting this, the mischievous Swanilda continued her antics more crazily than before. She tore many pages out of the book of Magic; and then she began to break up some of the mechanical dolls lying about the room. In vain their now distracted owner tried to seize the mad doll he imagined he had brought to life; but, every time, she laughingly slipped through his fingers. Thinking to pacify her, he threw a magnificent Spanish shawl over her shoulders—with the result that she immediately broke forth into a seductive Spanish dance with the utmost *abandon*. The same thing occurred when he next presented her with a rich tartan shawl; for this time she danced a wild and almost barbaric Highland dance.

The noise of this giddy commotion at length awakened Franz from his semi-conscious state; and, as the effect of the drugged wine gradually wore off, he began to understand what was happening. When, presently, Swanilda, in one of her fantastic gyrations, dragged back the curtain of the recess and he beheld the semi-robed form of the limp doll seated on the chair within, he realised at last what a stupid fellow he had been ever to have imagined the attractive Coppélia to be a human being; and he humbly entreated the now laughing Swanilda to forgive him for his folly. This she gladly did.

Meanwhile, the now exhausted Dr. Coppélius also beheld the half-clad doll in the recess, and was amazed and furious when he realised that the mischievous creature who had just led him such a dance was, in truth, none other than the pretty maiden from the house opposite, clad in his precious Coppélia's smart frock. Then, when he also realised that his attempted magic had not worked, after all, but was an utter failure, the shock was more than he could stand ; and he fell to the ground in a crumpled heap, overcome with disappointment.

But Franz and Swanilda fell into each other's arms in a transport of laughing joy ; for now the wonderful, but disciedited, Coppélia would never deceive either of them again.

*　　*　　*　　*　　*

Next day, the grand Festival in celebration of the gift of a new bell to the townsfolk took place in the magnificent grounds of the Duke's abode ; and many betrothed couples joined hands and danced happily together. Among them came Franz and Swanilda, the happiest of them all.

Presently, into the midst of the revels came old Dr. Coppélius, very irate because of the damage done to his wonderful mechanical dolls on the previous evening ; but the kindly Duke soon pacified him with a gift of many gold coins, and peace was then restore between him and the young folks.

After this little interruption, the revels continued once more ; and the Festival ended with a magnificent performance of numerous beautiful dances specially arranged for the occasion.

SYLVIA

(*ou La Nymphe de Diana,*
or The Nymph of Diana)

THE action of this story takes place during the
classical period of Ancient Greece. Wandering alone
one moonlit night through a distant forest, a handsome
young shepherd named Amyntas was vouchsafed a
wonderful sight. Although he knew it not, many of the
glades and groves in this particular forest were sacred
to certain gods and goddesses worshipped in those far-off
days ; and mortals seldom entered them. Amyntas,
however, had strayed from his accustomed path and was
eagerly seeking to regain it when, on stopping for a
moment to look about him, he heard a slight rustling
sound not far away from the glade he was about to
enter.

The young shepherd remained silent and still, hidden
from sight by a thick bush, through a thinner patch of
which he could himself peep forth. As he gazed, almost
breathless, a lovely being stepped lightly across the
moonlit glade and almost immediately vanished from
sight. But not before Amyntas had recognised her as
no mortal, her diaphanous short tunic-skirt and the
bow and quiver of arrows she held revealing her to be
one of the huntress nymphs attendant upon Diana, the
chaste Goddess of the Moon and of Hunting.

This chance being was one no mortal should look
upon ; but, in that brief glimpse, Amyntas had fallen
deeply in love with the fair and graceful nymph who
had thus so lightly crossed his path and knew that her
image would never pass from his heart. He did not

then attempt to follow her, lest she should lead him to her stern goddess mistress, who would certainly destroy him for his temerity ; but, continuing on his way, he presently found his old familiar path once more and reached his flocks in safety.

But love now burned in the heart of Amyntas, and he could not keep away from the spot where he had beheld the glorious vision of his beloved one. On another brilliant moonlit night the love-sick shepherd cautiously entered the sacred woodlands once more. Before his arrival a group of immortal folk of the glades —dryads, naiads, fauns, and satyrs, led by the sylvan god Pan himself—had been making merry there. The fauns had chased the Wood and Water nymphs hither and thither, seeking to carry them off as willing captives ; but, sensing the approach of a mortal, they ceased their frolics and hastened away.

So Amyntas found the sacred glade deserted ; and flinging down his cloak and crook, he seated himself on a jutting rock and gave himself up to his happy memories. Then it was that he saw, to his consternation, something he had not noticed when he was last there. A statue of Eros, the God of Love, had been set up on a half-circle of white marble stones ; and it seemed to him that the statue almost glowed with life and that the golden arrow in the bow he held might be shot forth at any moment.

Just as Amyntas was now about to invoke the aid of Eros on his own behalf, he heard the sound of hunting-horns ; and he had scarcely concealed himself behind the statue itself when a company of the huntress-nymphs of Diana came dancing into the glade, led by one more beautiful than any of the others—whom the shepherd instantly recognised as the fair object of his own love-dreams.

This leader of the nymphs, whose name was Sylvia, invited her companions to rest awhile before continuing on their way ; but, before seating herself beside an adjacent stream, she cast a somewhat scornful look at the statue of Eros. As an attendant upon Diana, the chaste Goddess, she had little use for the God of Love. Soon, however, she was destined to fall a victim herself to the wiles of the latter.

One of the nymph-huntresses presently picked up the shepherd's crook and cloak from the ground, where he had so carelessly flung them ; and, full of horror that a mortal should have invaded their sacred grove, Sylvia ordered her companions to search for him.

Amyntas was quickly discovered and dragged before the outraged nymph—who, however, seemed somewhat confused on observing the looks of adoring love cast upon her by the handsome young shepherd.

Another observer hiding nearby likewise noted with anger these looks of love shining in the shepherd's eyes. This hidden observer was Orion, the Black Huntsman-Giant, who roamed the forests and was feared by all the woodland folk because of his strength and ruthless ferocity. Orion had conceived a passion for Sylvia and had long coveted her as his bride ; and, realising that another mortal was about to become his rival, he became furiously jealous and dashed back into the forest to plan how he might destroy this presumptuous youth.

Meanwhile, Sylvia, feeling that the mischievous Eros must be responsible for the young shepherd's love for her, let fly an arrow at the god's statue in her anger ; but Amyntas, horrified by such a sacriligeous action, flung himself forward to stop the arrow—which struck him instead, so that he fell to the ground as though dead.

The beautiful nymph, still angry, was about to fit another arrow to her bow, when the statue of Eros, appearing to come to life for a moment, shot one of his own golden arrows at her instead—which reached her heart, but did not wound her physically.

Instantly Sylvia's hardness melted away, and she felt love in her heart for the first time ; but dawn now appearing, she called to her nymph companions and returned with them to the woodlands.

Orion, the giant Huntsman, now returned to the glade, believing that Sylvia might come again to look upon her lover-victim ; and he began to make a chain of golden links with which to ensnare her.

As he had hoped, Sylvia, heedless of any danger, indeed presently returned to gaze upon the young shepherd she had left as dead, but whom she now truly loved ; but scarcely had she knelt in loving sorrow before his prostrate form, than Orion sprang forth and, soon snaring her in his chain of golden links, carried her off in triumph to his own abode in a cave.

Unknown to him, however, his act of abduction had been observed by another shepherd youth, who had also noticed the seemingly dead Amyntas lying on the ground ; and he ran to bring his peasant companions to the scene.

Among the newcomers was an old man who knew something of the healing art ; and, presently, he was able to revive the unconscious Amyntas, who was immediately eager to find the lovely Sylvia. On now learning of the terrible fate that had befallen his beloved one, he was filled with distress, but boldly declared he would rescue her ; and he now prayed to the God of Love to help him in his quest. Then, to the amazement and awe of the simple peasants, the Statue of Eros faded away, and the living God of Love stood in its place.

As Amyntas knelt humbly before the god, Eros graciously raised him and announced that he would help him to rescue the beautiful Sylvia ; and, with deep gratitude in his heart, Amyntas set forth for the grotto-abode of Orion, the way having been pointed out to him by the gentle god who had thus so opportunely come to his aid. Eros, however, took a nearer path himself, lest the still exhausted shepherd should not arrive in time.

* * * * *

Orion's cave was in a lonely spot, and was a rough and rocky place. Here he had slave attendants, who served their giant master in fear and trembling.

Having deposited his captive nymph on a mossy couch, Orion tried to ingratiate himself into her favour ; but the terrified Sylvia repulsed all his advances with scorn. When he declared his love for her, she fled from him as from a wild beast ; but she soon found that she was unable to escape from the cave since the entrance to it had now been carefully blocked by the slaves, and her captor's strong arms barred her way in every other direction. Keeping her wits about her, however, she next endeavoured to deceive him by appearing as though about to surrender.

Pretending to be exhausted, she asked for food and drink ; and Orion, delighted by her complete change of manner towards him, ordered his slaves to set milk, grapes, and other fruits before her, which the nymph accepted with feigned humility.

Seeing no wine in any of the drinking vessels, she gathered that Orion was unaccustomed to this exhilarating beverage ; and she determined to introduce him to it, hoping thereby to make him sleepy and lethargic. Consequently, she pressed into a drinking vessel the juices from some of the luscious grapes brought for her own refreshment and transformed the resultant liquid into rich wine. She then offered the beverage to the giant Huntsman, who, delighted with her apparently growing interest in him, eagerly drank it. The wine pleased his palate likewise; and, being unaccustomed to it, he quickly succumbed to its heady influence.

At first, however, the new beverage was inclined to make Orion more amorous than before; but Sylvia cleverly managed to keep him at a distance by rising and dancing before him in a glamorous manner. Then, eventually, her captor became so overcome by the wine that he presently fell back upon his couch in a deep slumber. The slaves, having likewise partaken of the wine at her invitation, fell asleep, too; and Sylvia was thus free to make her escape.

She found, however, that the entrance to the cave had been too strongly barred for her to break through; and, full of despair, she called wildly upon the gods to help her.

In answer to her prayers, she suddenly beheld Eros standing beside her; and as the God of Love led her forth into the sunshine once more, he left the cave a wreck behind him.

As in a vision, Eros now revealed to Sylvia the figure of Amyntas still eagerly, but vainly, seeking for her; and the god next devised a plan whereby the lovers should meet again.

* * * * *

Meanwhile, the young shepherd, Amyntas, continued his search for the beautiful nymph who had enthralled him; but, owing to his still somewhat dazed condition, he could not remember the directions given to him by the kindly god, Eros. He just wandered on and on for a long time; and at last he found himself on the outskirts of a wood, close to the sea-shore. He seemed to have arrived at the entrance to another sacred glade, where statues of Bacchus and Silenus had been set up on one side, while a temple of Diana stood nearby ; and a group of young country maidens and fauns were indulging in a wild bacchanalian dance.

As the *bacchanale* came to an end, the weary Amyntas saw that a strange-looking ship had drawn near to the beach ; and from this vessel there presently stepped on shore a personage garbed as a pirate, who was followed by some veiled maidens, whom he declared to be slaves he was desirous of selling.

Amyntas was at first alarmed by this unexpected visitation ; but when, at the bidding of their pirate master, the veiled girls began to dance before him, he was so irresistibly attracted by the exquisite grace of one of them that he begged her to unveil. As she shyly did so, he found, to his delight, that she was none other than his beloved nymph, Sylvia. The seeming pirate was also now revealed as Eros ; and the God of Love was well pleased with his plan for bringing the lovers together. For Sylvia, having been touched by the god's golden arrow, now loved Amyntas as deeply as he loved her ; and both were filled with ecstasy at their reunion.

But dark shadows quickly arose to cloud their happiness. Orion, the Black Huntsman, having managed to escape from his wrecked cave, now appeared on the scene and threatened to destroy the happy lovers, unless the fair nymph was restored to him ; and all was confusion once more. The terrified Sylvia rushed into the Temple of Diana, and frantically called upon her mistress, the chaste Huntress-Goddess, for aid ; and, as the temple doors closed behind her, the fierce Orion began to batter furiously upon them.

Next moment, a sudden storm arose ; and, to the

accompaniment of thunder and lightning, the Temple doors opened, and Diana herself appeared. Drawing her bow, the outraged Goddess shot an arrow straight into the heart of Orion, as retribution for having dared to abduct one of her virgin nymphs.

As the dark Huntsman fell to the ground, dead, the unfortunate Sylvia was next overwhelmed by the wrath of the angry Goddess, who, sternly accusing her of sacrilege in having permitted herself to love a mortal, declared that, in consequence, the disobedient nymph and her lover must die.

Sylvia and Amyntas fell upon their knees and begged again and again that they might be pardoned ; but the avenging Goddess was relentlessly adamant, and drew her bow once more.

But Diana, the fair and the chaste, had reckoned without Eros, from whose love-seeking eyes even the secret romances of the dwellers upon Olympus were not hidden. Springing forward at this tense moment, the God of Love called upon the angry Goddess to hold her hand and to look back upon her own conduct. As he spoke, a vision was beheld by all. Pictured upon the dark storm-clouds, Diana herself was seen bending lovingly over the sleeping form of her own mortal lover, the fair youth Endymion, whose surpassing beauty had so stirred the cold heart of the virgin Goddess that she still kept him slumbering upon Mount Latmus that she might thus caress him without his knowledge and in secret from prying eyes. But not from those of Eros !

The vision faded, and Diana, though now dismayed and agitated, was seen to be no longer angry. How could she condemn one of her attendant nymphs for an offence of which she was herself likewise guilty—that of loving a mortal ?

So Sylvia and Amyntas were graciously forgiven ;

and as the sun shone forth once more, a grand festival of Song and Dance was held in celebration of their happiness.

And, probably, young Master Eros would have laughed up his sleeve, had he possessed such a thing—which, of course, he did not ! Instead, therefore, he showered the Blessings of Love upon all that joyous company.

THREE VIRGINS AND A DEVIL

ONE pleasant summer day three charming young virgins set out together to take a country walk. They had an object in view ; to visit a certain wayside chapel, where they might pray for the betterment of their own souls—which, possibly, needed such helpful supplications, as the following incidents seem plainly to reveal.

Each of these virgins was remarkable for one major fault. The first young woman was a conceited prig, who considered herself to be far more virtuous than any of her friends ; the second was lustful and loved the pleasures and appetites of the flesh more than she should have done ; and the third member of the trio was definitely greedy and grasping.

Except, however, for these particularly outstanding faults, the three young women friends were, seemingly, as virtuous and well-behaved as other young people of their social circle ; and they were all handsome, gay, and pleasing in their manners. They were very well-dressed, and seemed to be blessed with an ample sufficiency of this world's goods. The fact that they were on their way to church appeared to be a sign of their present interest in their own spiritual welfare.

When, at length, the three young women arrived at the little country chapel they sought, however, they did not hasten to enter therein immediately, as one might have thought would be the case. Instead, they began to look about them with much curiosity ; for they had obviously never been in this district before, and they found it strange and even somewhat weirdly sinister. On the opposite side of the road from the chapel there

336

arose a mass of high rocks, in the middle of which was
the wide-open mouth of a cave, whence there shone
forth a rosy glow of light, as though a fire constantly
burned therein.

Though the glowing entrance to the cave was certainly curious, the three young women did not at first
pay much attention to it. On drawing near to the
quaint little countryside chapel, the friends, as before-
mentioned, were in no haste to enter it ; but the prig
virgin soon began to encourage and admonish her
companions to enter before her, evidently considering
that she, herself, was sufficiently well-confessed and
virtuous to wait awhile.

Then she pointed out to her companions the large
open offertory poor-box which stood near the entrance ;
and she suggested unctuously that they should contri-
bute a personal offering to it. This idea, however, was
extremely repugnant to the greedy virgin, who hated
to part with her money. Seeing that this was the case,
the self-righteous maiden calmly snatched off her
friend's smart and expensive hat and indicated that
she should put that most becoming headgear into the
wide-apertured poor-box instead. With the greatest
reluctance, and only because of the stern glances of her
seemingly virtuous companion, the greedy virgin at
length slowly approached the offertory-box and most
disgustedly thrust her charming hat into its depths.

Before any more unwilling sacrifices could be made
or suggested, there came a strange and unexpected
interruption. What appeared to be a decrepit and
extremely poor old pilgrim, wrapped in a dingy habit
and wearing a palmer's wide-brimmed hat, issued forth
from the rosily-glowing cave-mouth ; and, hobbling
along painfully with the aid of a crooked, gnarled stick,
he approached the trio and begged for alms. When, at

first, being alarmed, they refused, he brandished his knobby stick ominously ; and, as he did so, his habit slipped aside slightly, revealing the sinister fact that his limbs ended in cloven hooves.

Observing this, the prig virgin prudently, and somewhat hurriedly, collected money from her reluctant friends' purses, and handed the alms to the stranger. The latter now openly cast aside his pilgrim's disguise and revealed himself in his true scarlet colours as a gay devil who had just emerged from the lower regions by way of the rosily-glowing cave-mouth—which obviously led thereto.

The three virgins quickly recovered from their first alarm at the transformation of the most unpleasant old pilgrim into a lively devil dressed smartly in scarlet ; and the latter immediately proceeded to entertain them. Producing a fiddle, he began to play gay dance tunes upon it, skipping about merrily as he did so ; and, within a few moments, he had all the three young women likewise dancing around and with him, keeping time with their twinkling feet and tossing up their decorously long skirts with what could only be described as unbridled *abandon*.

It soon became evident, however, that a mere dancing revel was not the true object of the scarlet-garbed stranger's sudden appearance, but that he had more serious business afoot—namely, to entice these seemingly virtuous, chapel-visiting young women to follow him to the well-heated regions he had himself just come from, via the rosily-glowing cave-mouth. Nor was it long before the now giddily dancing trio grasped this ominous fact ; but for some considerable time longer they resisted his purpose and tried to struggle against it.

Their efforts, however, gradually became feebler ; and the enticements of the stranger then grew stronger and stronger. The three friends found it a delightful pastime to dance to the gay music played for their benefit; and though this cheeky fellow took many liberties with them, they liked his jolly good-humour and found it difficult to resist his quite fascinating blandishments.

The wily red devil now began to tackle the three maidens singly. He approached the greedy virgin first, and slyly presented her with a handful of rich glittering jewels, which she gloated over with the deepest joy Never before had she received such a valuable gift. Her cupidity knew no bounds; and when she realised that many more such dazzling gems awaited her from the same source if she took the rosy path indicated she was no longer reluctant to do so. Escorted by her eagerly expectant partner, she danced away with him to the cave entrance—where the triumphant devil gave her a sudden mischievous push, so that she tumbled headlong into its wide-open glowing mouth.

Well-pleased with his first conquest, the jovial stranger next tackled the lustful young woman, with whom he proceeded to make use of every fascinating charm he possessed; and he found her an even easier prey to his seductive persuasiveness than her greedy friend. After flirting outrageously with her for a short time, he set her desires aflame to such an extent that all her pretended scruples vanished as she danced passionately away with him to the open mouth of the cave— where she likewise received a contemptuously vicious push that toppled her, neck and crop, into the rosy-tinted abyss.

There now remained only the prig virgin to deal with; and she proved to be the toughest customer of all. Her excessive conceit and self-righteousness caused her to resist the coaxing blandishments now presented to her and to find satisfaction in struggling against them. At first, nothing the stranger could say or do would induce her to follow the example of her weaker companions ; and she felt even better pleased with herself than ever when she decided to flout his eager advances by running up the steps of the little chapel and beating upon its door as though about to seek sanctuary within its portals.

Not that she intended just then to vanish from the sight of her pursuer—she was, as a matter of fact, secretly enjoying his pursuit of her—but because, like the conceited prig she was, she desired to impress him with her apparent saintliness. She hoped, of course, that he would follow her even to the door of sanctuary ; but here she was mistaken.

The red devil, like all his diabolic brethren, was traditionally unable to tread on holy ground ; and he now fell back a few yards and crouched down in a huddled heap, as though sulky because of his temporary defeat. But, so far from sulking, he was actually hatching a clever little plot. He now seemed to fall into a fit of furious tantrums, like those of a naughty child ; and he began to roll over and over, and to kick the ground with his cloven feet, to beat his chest with his fists, and to exhibit every sign of uncontrollable rage.

This trick had the desired effect. The priggish virgin, flattered beyond measure at being the seeming cause of such a wild fit of tantrums—and by no means desirous of being left in splendid isolation at the chapel door—now ran down the steps and began to soothe and comfort the huddled scarlet figure on the ground, hoping that her act of consolation would presently result in a renewal of the recent pleasant interlude.

It did. The wily devil let her soothe and fondle him

for awhile ; and then he suddenly sprang up with restored vigour and seizing his intended victim in an iron grasp, danced madly around with her once more.

Then, before his now willing partner had time to change her mind, he dashed towards the open cave mouth and plunged into the midst of its rosy glow, exultantly dragging his third prize with him.

L'APRES-MIDI D'UN FAUNE

(*A Faun's Afternoon*)

ONE glorious afternoon in Arcadia, a happy care-free Faun was disporting himself on a sunny hill-slope over-looking a valley where flowed a sparkling streamlet leading to a shallow pool.

The Faun was alone ; and, for a little while, he enjoyed the solitude and desired no other company than his own. He had a pipe with him ; and as he reclined on the flower-spangled grass, he amused himself by playing a number of gay little tunes—at times rising and dancing to them, indulging in light and airy leaps and bounds, twisting and turning his lithe body and even cutting comical capers.

Then, he became tired of his own company and, flinging himself once more on the grass, he began to feel just a little bored and to long for someone else to join him in his sylvan haunt.

Presently, to his joy, his wish was granted. Hearing the welcome sounds of silvery laughter coming from the lower part of the hillside, he raised himself slightly and peered downwards. What he saw filled him with delight.

A bevy of dainty nymphs came dancing along the path beside the streamlet, obviously intending to bathe in the shallow pool beyond.

At first the mischievous Faun thought it might be amusing, unseen from his niche above, to watch the nymphs disporting themselves in the pool ; then he decided that it would be much more fun to play with them, and invite them to dance and frolic with him on the hill-side. So, rising to his feet, he bounded eagerly down the slope towards the merry newcomers ; but the nymphs at first ran away from him in fear. They did not altogether like the strangeness of his hairy body, his goat-like feet, or the little horns above his brow — even though these latter curious ornaments were half-hidden among the most fascinatingly tight little curls they had ever seen. Surely it would be wise to give such an extraordinary creature a wide berth ?

But curiosity soon got the better of caution ; and, one by one, the nymphs returned—first, coyly to peep at the intriguing stranger they had disturbed, and then to come, hesitatingly, into the open.

The Faun was more than pleased with the charming looks of the nymphs ; and gladly he ran to meet them, eager to make love to them. But his actions were so daring, and his unrestrained movements and antics so rough, that the nymphs were more alarmed than before ; and, this time, all but one of them ran away, pell-mell, and made no attempt to return.

It happened that the nymph who presently came back, still full of curiosity about the lively stranger, was the prettiest and daintiest of them all ; and the Faun was so delighted to see her again that he pursued her with a more gentle and ingratiating manner. The nymph now began to think that he might be a pleasant play-mate for her, after all ; and she was pleased with his admiration and even allowed him to dance with her a short time.

Her beauty and close proximity, however, quickly inflamed the naturally amorous nature of the Faun ; and his dancing movements and close embraces became so passionate that the lovely nymph was soon terrified and struggled wildly to escape from his grasp, wishing she had followed the more prudent example of her companions. Making use of all her strength, she managed, at last, to disentangle herself from the eager clasp of her captor—in her haste letting fall a light scarf she wore as she fled swiftly from his sight. Fear seemed to lend wings to her feet like those of the god Mercury ; and the disappointed Faun was again left alone and disconsolate.

Even now, however, the foolish nymph did not like the idea of leaving her pretty scarf behind ; and, presently, she tip-toed back to a small hillock, from behind which she peeped out to see where she had dropped it. Observing that the Faun had already discovered it and was now holding it in his hands and fondling it tenderly, she decided that discretion was the better part of valour and reluctantly fled back to her companions ; and this time she did not return.

At first the Faun was very sad at the loss of his lovely captive ; but, after awhile, as he lay once more alone on the sunny hillside, he recovered his good spirits, and comforted himself by caressing the scarf he had secured as a trophy and reminder of a very pleasant afternoon's interlude.

LE SACRE DU PRINTEMPS

(*The Rite of Spring*)

THE springtime in Ancient Russia was the season when certain curious and even terrible religious rites were practised by the primitive tribes that dwelt therein.

The members of one of these wild tribes were worshippers of the Earth and the Sun ; and they believed that it was their bounden duty to offer up a human sacrifice to the all-important Goddess of Spring as soon as the snows had melted and the sun had begun to warm the earth. Like many other primitive tribes they practised this gruesome custom to ensure that the crops they were about to sow would bear fruit abundantly and that their food for the year would thus be provided.

It was also necessary, they were assured by their elders, for a human sacrifice to be made in order that the women of their tribe should continue to be fruitful likewise, so that their numbers might increase and that the tribe would thus be strong enough to overcome attacks from other wandering tribes of the hills and plains.

Here is a picture of what happened on one of these solemn but sinister occasions.

On the moonlit night before the selected day for the annual Springtime Sacrificial Festival, the young men of the tribe assembled together in a wild and hilly country district to take part in the elaborate ritual dances always held as a prelude to the main Rite of Spring to be enacted at sunrise on the following morning.

These young men were the warriors of the tribe—fine, handsome youths, full of the zest of life, who should have leapt and danced lustily in the joy of their strength and virility. Instead, however, their natural exuberance was suppressed and kept under stern control by their two strange leaders, whom they deeply revered and feared to disobey.

The chief of these leaders was an ancient woman of the tribe, so old that none could remember her birth, but who was believed already to have lived for three hundred years. The other leader was a Seer or Wise Man, also very old ; and he was one who could prophesy, and was well versed in the ancient lore of the tribe. In the background stood the elders of the tribe who, despite their hoary locks, were youthful compared with the patriarchal leaders whose instructions they still obeyed as children.

Under the command of these aged but still impressively authoritative leaders, the young men performed many strange ritual dances ; and their movements were heavy and even clumsy, since they seemed to be under an obligation to keep their bodies bent towards the ground, as though worshipping the god who ruled the latter. This they did to the accompaniment of wild, harsh barbaric music and the monotonous stamping of their own feet ; and they presented a weird appearance in the moonlight. Their limbs were wrapped around with strips of coloured cloth, while a roughly-designed straight tunic-like upper garment completed their somewhat ungraceful attire; and the latter, together with their uncouth earth-worshipping movements, made their monotonous performance more grotesque than graceful.

Later on, however, when these main ritual dances had ended, the male performers were joined by the young women of the tribe ; and then their movements lightened somewhat. The young women wore similar garments to those of the youths, though their straight and rather shapeless tunics were longer ; and their long hair hung around them loosely in neatly plaited braids.

The ritual dances now took on a more definitely lively aspect, as the youths and maidens moved together rhythmically ; but they still performed the pattern of these tribal dances under the strict direction of the Seer, or Wise Man, who moved among them from time to time.

Presently, these ceremonial dances ceased, and the Elders of the tribe came forward to bless the dancers and the earth they trod upon, entreating the latter to become fruitful and to bring forth rich crops for the benefit of all ; and with this solemn ceremony, the preliminary Rite of Spring came to an end.

*   *   *   *   *

Early next morning, at sunrise, all the members of the tribe assembled once more in a wide open space near the crest of a high hill, which provided a natural altar for the tremendous ceremony about to take place—the sacrifice of a Chosen Maiden to the Goddess of Spring.

Again the Ancient Leaders, the Old Woman and the Wise Man, led and directed the proceedings ; and after the men of the tribe had retired into the background somewhat, the young women advanced—for this was their Day of Honour, and they were now commanded to dance in front of the company. From among their ranks, the Chosen Maiden—she who was to sacrifice herself for the benefit of all—would presently step forward ; but, until that moment, they were all regarded as equals and danced as such. They danced together with zeal the stiff formal measure which was the traditional dance for this great Festival of Spring ; and as they moved through the various set figures, they did not at first know to whom among their numbers had been given the high honour of offering herself as a willing sacrifice to the Goddess of Spring.

For some little time the ritual dance of the young women continued ; and then, suddenly, one of their number, an exquisitely beautiful maiden, stepped forward from their ranks and began to dance alone. This, then, was the Chosen Maiden, whose bounden duty it was, as well as her fanatical pleasure, to dance at an ever-increasing speed until she dropped dead from exhaustion—a willing human sacrifice and propitiation to the powerful Goddess.

Gradually, the other young women drew back slowly leaving a wide open space for this last performance of their highly honoured and specially gifted companion.

At first the lovely Chosen Maiden danced rhythmically and slowly, as though in a dream ; but gradually she worked herself up to faster and ever faster movements, whirling herself round and round and hither and thither into a perfect frenzy of ecstatic joy in her own incredible performance.

Did any young man in the background step forward a pace to gaze with agonising despair upon the madly gyrating figure in the centre of the ritual ground-space ? Did he make a sign of resigned and sorrowful farewell as she whirled past him ? And was he her lover, who had hoped to dwell in happiness with her until the end of his days ?

Perhaps—but, if so, the rapt Chosen Maiden, now leaping and whirling in an ecstacy of religious fervour, saw him not. Lost to her surroundings, and sustained by her sacrificial zeal, she continued to dance on and on in a mad delirium, ever increasing her speed until she seemed scarcely to touch the ground with her twinkling feet.

But this orgy of ritual dancing came to an end at last. The exhausted human frame could endure no more. Suddenly, the gyrating figure stood still for a moment, swayed slightly once or twice, and then fell to the ground, dead.

The lovely Chosen Maiden had made her sacrifice ; and the Rite of Spring was over.

AUTUMN LEAVES*

* *This simple story provided one of the favourite Ballets of Anna Pavlova.*

THIS is a picture of a late Autumn day in an exquisite woodland glade in the midst of a Park.

The trees were all gleaming with gold and rich russet tints ; and at the edge of a flower-bed on a bank a single lovely deep yellow and amber Chrysanthemum still remained blooming as a glowing reminder of Autumn's earlier glory.

How bravely and proudly the richly coloured blossom on its slender stem waved in the rising wind, as though eager to stand up to the coming onslaught as long as it had the strength to do so. How long would that be ? Alas, not long. The rising wind grew boisterous and rough, and began to come in ever-increasingly fierce gusts ; and, at last, in one of the sudden squalls, the graceful Chrysanthemum, unable to stand up any longer, was uprooted and cast to the ground. There it lay for a while, fading, and tossed hither and thither by the mischievous breezes.

It happened, soon afterwards, that a young Poet was taking a stroll through the Park, stopping every now and again to watch the fallen autumn leaves being blown and whirled about the grassy glades, and endeavouring to find inspiration for a poem from his surroundings. Suddenly, he beheld the uprooted Chrysanthemum ; and, full of pity for the lovely flower, he picked it up and tenderly caressed its now tumbled petals.

But the wind was still in a wild and frolicsome mood ;

and presently it returned with greater force than before and triumphantly caught up the Chrysanthemum from his hand and tossed it to the ground once more.

Again the Poet picked up the beautiful blossom ; and, this time, he carried it very carefully to a nearby fountain, where, after reviving it somewhat with water, he placed it on a mossy stone beside him as he seated himself on the outer stonework and began to write his poem.

To his dismay, however, the rude and boisterous wind yet again tossed up the now fading flower, and sent the latter whirling among a shower of fallen leaves which it was sweeping before it in a golden cloud as it rushed along. The unlucky Chrysanthemum was already too far gone to survive such an unequal contest ; and, after being whirled hither and thither in company with the madly dancing autumn leaves, it again fell to the ground, softly fluttered its bruised petals as though drawing its last breath, and rose no more.

Finding himself powerless again to revive the beautiful blossom, the Poet caressed it once more ; and then he stood gazing upon it with deep pity.

Just then, however, the pretty lady to whom he was betrothed, came along the glade to join him in his stroll ; and the sight of her so revived his drooping spirits that he took her by the arm and led her away through the Park.

Then, presently, the mischievous wind dropped once more ; and a shower of gold, red, and russet leaves softly fluttered to the ground and made a dazzling carpet-background to throw into relief the still exquisite beauty of the fallen Chrysanthemum.

LA BAYADERE

(*The Dancing-Girl*)

THIS is a romantic story of Ancient India.

A certain splendid young warrior, named Solor, after spending some weeks on a dangerous but very successful hunting trip, decided to send a trophy-gift to his royal master, the Rajah Dugmanta, as an act of loyalty. This gift took the form of the most magnificent tiger he had slain during the course of his recent hunting adventures —the largest and finest he had ever seen.

Having despatched his attendants to the Royal Palace with this valuable trophy of his prowess, Solor sought relaxation and rest.   He made his way with a light step and a joyous heart to a certain temple, where he hoped to meet a beautiful bayadère, or dancing-girl, named Nikia, whom he dearly loved and hoped, eventually, to secure as his bride.

On arriving outside the temple, he was met by one, Magdaveya, a fakir who was disposed to be friendly towards the lovers, who told him that Nikia was just then engaged in conversation with the Chief Brahmin attached to this place of worship.

Magdaveya's announcement was not very welcome news to Solor, who knew that this particular priest had conceived an unlawful passion for Nikia, and that the latter had been embarrassed thereby.

The beautiful Nikia was, indeed, enduring a painful interview with the Chief Brahmin, who, though suspecting that her affections were already engaged elsewhere, was, nevertheless, eager to become her lover himself. But Nikia was filled with horror at the thought of such an illicit connection, since Brahmin priests were not permitted to marry ; besides, she truly loved the brave warrior Solor, and hoped to wed with him. Therefore, she indignantly repudiated the suggestions of the amorous Priest ; and though the latter, maddened by his passion for her, pleaded his cause again and again, she refused to listen to him.

It was at this moment that the old fakir entered to inform her that the famous warrior, Solor, waited outside and desired to see her ; and, now filled with joy, she hastened away with much relief.

The Brahmin priest, having noted her look of sudden happiness at the mention of Solor's name, now knew definitely where her affections were engaged ; and he was overwhelmed with jealous envy and vowed to be avenged upon the lovers at the first opportunity.

Meanwhile, Nikia and Solor had met outside the temple, and were enraptured as they greeted one another. Although Nikia, as a bayadère, was bound to serve as a special dancing-girl in the temple and also to take part in the palace revels when bidden to do so, Solor passionately besought her to give up her office as chief dancer very soon and to go away with him instead and become his bride.

This was not an easy object to attain, and the consent of the Temple Authorities and of the Rajah would be necessary before the lovers could gain their hearts' desire ; but Nikia loved Solor dearly, and was willing to sacrifice her dazzling future for his sake. Nevertheless, she wished to be sure of him ; and she would give her consent only on condition that her lover would plight his troth to her by a solemn vow sworn in the presence of the Holy Fire that burned in the temple. This Solor was willing to do ; and after further sweet love-making, the happy pair wandered away to make their vows

before the Holy Fire—little dreaming that their conversation had been overheard by the jealous Brahmin
priest, who had followed Nikia and remained hidden
nearby for this purpose and who now renewed his own
vows of vengeance against both.

*   *   *   *   *

The great Rajah Dugmanta had been much gratified
upon receiving the magnificent tiger sent to him by his
favourite warrior, Solor ; and, determining to reward
him very handsomely, he sent to command his immediate
presence.

When Solor, now rested and suitably attired, appeared
before his royal lord, he found him surrounded by the
utmost splendour. Richly-garbed courtiers and guards
stood on either side of the throne ; and the Rajah
himself wore the most gorgeous robes of all, while his
jewelled turban sparkled like the rays of the sun.

Among the women slave attendants stood Gamsatti,
the beautiful daughter of the Rajah ; and as the
Princess's dark eyes fell upon the handsome warrior—
of whose deeds of prowess she had already heard—she
instantly fell in love with him. She was, therefore,
overjoyed when her royal father rose and, placing her
hand in that of Solor, announced to the latter that the
reward for his valour in slaying the magnificent tiger just
received should be the hand of the lovely Princess
Gamsatti.

But this announcement, so pleasing to the Rajah's
daughter, was certainly embarrassing to the young
warrior, because of his vows to Nikia. Nevertheless,
he knew that it would be dangerous, if not fatal, for him
to refuse this great honour that was being offered to him
—what was more, as he lifted his eyes and gazed upon
the smilingly happy face and eager eyes of Gamsatti, he
was suddenly enthralled by her exquisite beauty. For

the moment, he forgot about his vows to Nikia, while
even his former love for the latter faded into the background ; and he now eagerly accepted the unexpected
prize awarded to him. The Rajah was then graciously
pleased to announce the betrothal ; and, in honour of
the occasion, a grand Fire Festival was commanded to be
held.

At this splendid function, the Temple bayaderes and
the palace dancing-girls had to perform some wonderful
and most intricate dances ; and among the principal
dancers who took part and led the procession of Fire-
worshippers was Nikia, the chief Temple dancer, and
Aiya, the Princess's favourite slave maiden. Nikia
had not yet learned of her lover's defection ; but she was
soon to do so in the course of the Festival dance.

The jealous Brahmin priest was likewise attending the
Festival, not only by the right of his office, but as the
Rajah's own guest of honour—for the priest had much
power in the land. Despite the honour about to be
conferred upon his rival in love, he still determined to
avenge himself upon the latter—and also upon the lovely
bayadere who had so scornfully rejected his own illicit
offer of love.

At a convenient moment, therefore, he approached
the Rajah and informed him in a low voice that Solor
and Nikia were lovers ; and then he related to him the
secret love interview he had witnessed between the
pair outside the Temple.

This whispered conversation was overheard by the
Princess Gamsatti, who stood nearby ; and, full of
jealous anger, she caused Nikia to be withdrawn from
the ceremonial dance and to be brought to her side. She
then triumphantly announced to the dancing-girl her
own betrothal to Solor, the Warrior.

At first the bewildered and thunderstruck bayadere

refused to believe that Solor had broken his vows to her, made before the Holy Fire, or that he could no longer love her ; but when at last she realised that it was, indeed, the truth, she was heart-broken. Nevertheless, when the Princess next tried to bribe her into promising never to see Solor again, she refused to give him up, since she hoped that he would yet return to her.

A violent quarrel now arose between the rival maidens; and Nikia, losing control over herself, drew a dagger and would have slain Gamsatti, had not the latter's slave, Aiya—who had also left the dancing procession at a signal from her royal mistress—held her back and snatched the weapon from her.

Then, as Nikia was now forced to return to the dance, Aiya comforted her mistress by promising to find some means of removing the much-too-fascinating bayadère from the royal maiden's path. Nor was it long before an opportunity presented itself.

Later on, at the wedding of Gamsatti and Solor— which went forward without delay—more splendid revels than ever held before took place ; and again the bayadères of the Temple and the dancing-girls of the Palace were the chief entertainers of the brilliant company gathered together at the invitation of the Rajah.

Among the wedding festival dancers was the lovely Nikia, who had been commanded by the Rajah to lead the others as being the most graceful exponent of them all. During her own special performance Nikia was presented with an elegant basket of flowers by the slave girl, Aiya ; and with this charmingly decorative adjunct to her equipment held delicately in her arms, she continued to dance a few more steps.

But Death was in the basket. Embedded among the sweetly-perfumed flowers, a small poisonous snake had been carefully concealed by the cunning Aiya, eager to aid her royal mistress, as promised ; and, presently, Nikia received a severe bite from the emerging reptile, and dropped the basket with a cry of pain. It was soon seen that the unfortunate dancing-girl's poisoned wound was a fatal one and that her last minutes were numbered. But the Brahmin priest was versed in such matters ; and, again eager to secure Nikia as his own inamorata now that Solor was the accepted bridegroom of the Princess, he rushed forward to the still dancing victim, announcing to her that he carried an antidote which would save her life and which he would administer to her instantly if, in return, she would promise to bestow her favours upon him.

Nikia, however, turned from him with loathing, and continued to dance. Soon after, feeling her strength waning, she turned to Solor, prophesying that disaster and death would befall him because he had broken his Holy Fire vows to her ; and then, after performing a few more faltering steps, she fell to the ground, dead.

* * * * *

For some considerable time Solor the warrior was inconsolable because of the death of Nikia ; for now, overcome with grief and remorse, all his former love for her had returned in superabundance—the transient glamour cast upon him by the Princess Gamsatti having quickly faded.

Life seemed to hold no further interest for him ; and nobody could arouse him from his apathy and black despair. Even when Magdaveya, the kindly fakir, sought to distract him for a while by bringing into his presence a group of very skilful snake-charmers, he scarcely looked at the strange antics of the writhing reptiles.

Next, the fakir tried to work a spell upon him that should bring him back to his normal state once more ; but that also was unavailing, and the warrior—his soul wounded almost to death by the remorseful sorrow that assailed him—bade his well-meaning friend and the snake-charmers depart and leave him alone with his grief.

Left alone, Solor continued to smoke opium, as the only solace left to him ; and presently he fell into a deep slumber induced by the narcotic. Then, at last, he found oblivion from his grief by means of a wonderful dream, in which, after floating among the clouds and the stars for awhile, he felt himself wafted to the Land of Shades. Here, he seemed to wander about as though lost, but ever seeking for the Shade of his beloved bayadere. Then, at length, among a group of other dead bayaderes, he did, indeed, find his own adored Nikia, and, after imploring and receiving her forgiveness, renewed his vows of love to her. Peace then came upon his remorseful soul ; a Peace which he knew would not leave him again, even in death.

* * * * *

When Solor awakened from his comforting dream, he grieved no more, believing that, in due time, he would again meet his own true love and never be parted from her.

The happy time he looked for came speedily ; and the prophesy of Nikia was truthfully fulfilled. No sooner had Solor returned to the great reception hall of the Royal Palace and seated himself beside his Princess bride, Gamsatti, than a terrific and awe-inspiring storm arose ; and a great ball of fire struck the building and utterly destroyed it, together with all within it.

THE SLEEPING PRINCESS

(La Belle au Bois Dormant)

(A Ballet Version of the famous story of " The Sleeping Beauty ")

A CERTAIN King Florestan was giving a splendid party in his magnificent palace to celebrate the christening of his infant daughter, the Princess Aurora.   Everybody of importance in the land, and from all the neighbouring countries, had been invited to attend.

The guests were received by the Grand Chamberlain in the vast marble hall of the palace, which was decorated with festoons of flowers and hung with rich brocade draperies.   At the top of a small flight of steps stood a golden cradle, in which lay the royal baby ;   and on either side were attendants and soldiers on guard.

The Grand Chamberlain, or Master of the Ceremonies, was trying to keep an eye on everybody, while at the same time checking over a long list of names from a scroll he held in his hand to make sure that all the invited guests were duly arriving.   He had arranged special places for all the visitors, and, if any guests happened to stray away a few steps, he bustled after them fussily and waved them back into position at once.

When all but the most important guests had arrived, a fanfare of trumpets sounded and King Florestan and his Queen entered the hall, both wearing jewelled crowns and the most gorgeous royal robes and attended by high Officers of State, lords, ladies, and pages.   The guests bowed low before them ; and the royal pair bowed graciously in return before seating themselves upon their gilded thrones.

This was the signal for the entry of the most important guests of all—a group of dazzling fairies, who had been specially invited to attend the christening-party that they might bestow wonderful fairy gifts upon the baby Princess.

They came fluttering in airily, each important fairy guest accompanied by her own cavalier and a number of attendant fairies. Among these dainty guests were the Fairy of the Woodland Glades, the Fairy of the Crystal Fountains, the Breadcrumb Fairy, the Fairy of the Camellias, the Fairy of the Enchanted Garden, the Fairy of the Golden Vine, the Fairy of the Song-Birds, the fairy of the Lilacs ; and many others. The delightful fairy gifts they bestowed upon the royal child included Beauty, Kindness, Wit, Grace, Sweetness Wisdom, Gentleness—in fact, every quality likely to cause her to grow up happy and beloved.

The most powerful of all these fairy guests was the Lilac Fairy ; and she was also the loveliest of them all. Hers was to be the last of the fairy gifts bestowed. Just as she was about to step forward and wave her magic wand over the infant Princess, as all the others had already done, however, there came an unexpected and most alarming interruption.

Even as the King and Queen were congratulating themselves upon the many marvellous fairy gifts that had already been bestowed upon their precious daughter, a sudden black cloud seemed to darken the hall. Then there came a vivid flash of lightning, followed by the crashing of thunder, and a strange and terrible person appeared in a chariot drawn by gigantic rats and bats.

This was the Wicked Fairy, Carabosse ; and she was in a mighty rage because she had not been invited to the christening-party. The fussy Master of Ceremonies had, most carelessly, omitted to include her in his long list when sending out the fairies' invitations !

But, invitation or no invitation, she had now come to the party ; and, at once, she began to make herself extremely disagreeable. As the King and Queen and all their guests shrank back in alarm upon the unexpected appearance in their midst of the terrible Carabosse, the latter furiously stamped about the marble hall, pouring out her wrath upon everybody because no invitation had been sent to her. And every time she stamped and shouted and raised her arms in a threatening attitude, her attendant rats and bats followed her around and likewise stamped, or flapped their wings, or squeaked, and used threatening gestures.

Then the angry Carabosse ran up the short flight of steps leading to the royal cradle and, raising her wand on high, screeched out : " I will bestow a Fairy Gift upon the baby Princess ! When she reaches the age of sixteen years, she shall prick her finger with a spindle and DIE ! "

As the old Witch returned to the centre of the hall, the King and Queen, and all their guests, filled with horror on hearing this fearful prophecy, fell upon their knees and entreated the vengeful fairy to have mercy upon the innocent Princess ; but Carabosse laughed them all to scorn. And she chuckled all the more when the King suddenly turned upon the wretched Chamberlain and began to threaten him with dire punishment for having made such a fatal omission.

When the triumphant Carabosse was again about to mount the steps, as though to do bodily harm to the royal child, then and there, she found her way suddenly blocked by the Lilac Fairy ; and, knowing that the latter had powers equal to her own, she cowered back in frustrated fury. Then, mounting her chariot once more, and attended by her fierce rats and bats, she departed as suddenly as she had arrived, in a cloud of darkness and amidst thunder and lightning.

All was now confusion and dismay. The Queen and her ladies sobbed aloud and wrung their hands helplessly ; and the King and his lords again roundly scolded and belaboured the unfortunate old Chamberlain for having brought such disaster upon them all by his carelessness.

However, the good and lovely Lilac Fairy now stepped forward and declared that, not having yet bestowed her own gift upon the royal child, she could at least modify the doom pronounced by the wicked Carabosse—even though she could not actually prevent the first part of the prophecy from taking place. She then announced that the spindle wound should not be a fatal one, but that, instead of dying from its effects, the Princess should fall into a deep slumber, together with the whole Court. Thus she would remain sleeping quietly and safely for one hundred years ; after which, a handsome young Prince would arrive upon the scene and awaken her with a loving kiss, which would break the spell.

Having thus spoken these comforting words, the Lilac Fairy then waved her wand in blessing over the infant Princess and over the grateful King and Queen and their Court ; and happiness reigned once more.

* * * * *

The Princess Aurora grew up into the most beautiful, the most highly-gifted, and the best-beloved royal maiden in the world ; and, on her sixteenth birthday, four splendid young Princes arrived at the Court as suitors for her hand in marriage.

Again, great festivities were held in celebration of the Princess's birthday ; and on this occasion a grand entertainment of dancing took place in the bright flowery gardens of the Palace. The first performers were a joyous group of village youths and maidens, who trooped in to exhibit their skill in a special birthday dance, each carrying a hooped garland of flowers and tripping lightly to the lilting strains of an exquisite waltz tune.

As soon as the lovely Princess Aurora appeared on the scene, she herself danced most gracefully before the guests ; and, after the four suitor Princes had been presented to her, she danced with each one of them in turn.

The young Princes were full of admiration for her beauty and grace ; and each of them offered her a rose as a love-token. The Princess Aurora, however, did not seem eager to accept any one of them as her future bridegroom ; and, to the disappointment of the royal suitors, she somewhat teasingly gave their roses to her mother, the Queen. Then she danced again, still more enthrallingly ; and the festivities continued with ever-increasing gaiety.

Presently, however, a black-coated old dame, who had been lurking in the background, drew near to the Princess and humbly begged her to accept a small birthday gift she had brought ; and Aurora, always kind to old people, graciously took it with smiling thanks. When unwrapped, the parcel was found to contain a spindle—for the strange cloaked old dame was none other than the Wicked Fairy, Carabosse !

The Princess had never seen such a curious object before—for all the spindles in the land had been destroyed by command of the King, who had thus vainly hoped to prevent the Witch's evil spell from ever falling upon his beloved daughter ; and, unconscious of her danger, she began to play a lively game with it, tossing it into the air and catching it again as she gaily danced about. The King and Queen, and all their Courtiers, however, were horrified, knowing only too well what a fatal gift this was ; and they entreated the royal maiden to throw it away—especially when they presently recognised the black-cloaked stranger as the vengeful Carabosse.

But the laughing Princess, heedless of the warning cries of those around her, gaily continued to play with her new and most original gift. Presently, however, she did, indeed, cast it from her—for the sharp spindle had pricked her finger, and the wound was a painful one. For a short time longer, she continued to dance about ; but, at last, she fell to the ground, as though dead.

Everybody was filled with dire dismay and grief, knowing the significance of what had happened ; and though, at a command from the King, swords were drawn and an angry dash made towards the now exultant old Witch, the latter immediately vanished in a sudden thunder-cloud, cackling more triumphantly than ever and delighted that her long-prophesied evil spell had seemingly worked so satisfactorily.

But her hoped-for victim was not dead, after all. Even as the Wicked Carabosse vanished and the light returned, the lovely Lilac Fairy appeared upon the scene and issued her commands. Slowly and sadly, the unconscious Princess was carried into the Palace and laid upon a golden couch ; and the King and Queen and their whole Court followed and likewise took up various positions, grouping themselves around her.

The Lilac Fairy now waved her magic wand over the entire gorgeous company, and all fell instantly into a deep slumber—the Princess no longer appearing as one dead, but likewise breathing softly in the sweet healthful sleep of youth.

After this, the Lilac Fairy laid a spell upon the Palace and its surroundings. Tall trees in a dense forest closed around it, and trailing creepers sprang up everywhere ; and over all there fell a cloud-like curtain of spiders' webs and long cobwebs, which increased as time went by.

There, in this secluded and almost impenetrable spot, in perfect safety and hidden from sight, lay the beautiful Princess Aurora, thus doomed to sleep with her royal parents and their Court for many many years to come, her strange story gradually becoming a scarcely-believed legend and her whereabouts an unsolved mystery.

* * * * *

One day, about a hundred years later, a handsome young Prince, named Florimund, was hunting with a gay party of friends on the outskirts of the dense forest that surrounded the hidden palace of the Enchanted Sleeping Princess and her Court.

Despite the exuberant spirits of the lively Courtiers who accompanied him, the young Prince himself was by no means gay. All day he had experienced a curious feeling of expectancy, as though something unusually strange was about to happen to him—what, he did not know. Time almost seemed to be standing still. He felt far too restless and preoccupied to take much interest in the grand hunt that had been arranged for his amusement; nor was he greatly entertained when various groups of his splendid retinue presently performed several elegant minuets and other stately dances in a woodland glade for his further delectation. Indeed, he was merely bored, because his present dreamy mood did not respond to such an elaborate performance. These doubtless very graceful dances performed by duchesses, marchionesses, and their lords did not arouse his usual admiration to-day. One of the nobly-born huntresses, a certain charming young countess, had rather hoped that the prince would admire her good looks and like her company sufficiently well to remain by her side all day ; but Florimund presently bowed politely to her and wandered away alone.

Gallison, the Prince's tutor—a rather comical old fellow—and his favourite Courtier, likewise tried to arouse Florimund from his strange apathy ; but they, too, had to retire when their royal master impatiently bade them continue the hunt without him and leave him alone for awhile.

Prince Florimund, thus left with his own thoughts for company, wandered about for awhile, still very restless and curiously conscious of something unusual about to happen to him. He had never before been in this strange forest, which now became denser and more mysterious as he wandered along. Nevertheless, though gradually cutting himself off from his gay companions with every yard he went, he had no desire to retrace his steps—on the contrary, he felt himself more and more irresistibly drawn forward with every step he took, as though invisible hands were urging him on apace.

Gone now was his early morning apathy, and an exciting eagerness had taken its place. Each additional yard he covered gave him a thrill ; and every opening vista seemed fraught with the portent of coming adventure. Then, presently, the air seemed full of music and the sound of silvery voices. Surely, these must be fairy sounds ? This was an adventure, indeed !

Suddenly, he noticed a sparkling stream among the trees ; and, floating in a frail pearly boat drawn by gorgeous butterflies, he beheld an exquisite fairy form, clad in filmy lilac draperies, a crown of stars upon her head, and carrying a shining wand in her hand.

It was the Lilac Fairy ; and as the young Prince bent low before her in awed admiration, she related to him the wonderful story of the lovely Princess Aurora who, after one hundred years spent in an enchanted sleep, now awaited her awakening by the kiss of a royal prince.

As Florimund listened to her with joyful eagerness,

the Lilac Fairy waved her wand and showed him in a vision the beautiful Sleeping Princess herself, lying peacefully upon her couch, breathing softly, and still young and lovely as when the enchantment had first fallen upon her so many years ago.

Even as he gazed upon this wonderful Dream-Land Princess, spell-bound by her beauty, the vision gradually faded away—but not before Florimund had fallen deeply in love with her. He now eagerly implored the Lilac Fairy to lead him to this exquisite maiden immediately, declaring that he could not bear to live another moment without her. His new friend replied by inviting him to step into the pearly boat beside her—which he gladly did ; and the pair then floated down the stream for a long way, drawn gently by the fluttering butterflies. Presently, however, they left the boat and found themselves in an unbelievably dense forest, through which the young Prince began, painfully, to thread his way.

Then the Lilac Fairy, full of mischief now that their goal was almost reached, led the royal youth a pretty dance, teasingly pointing out the way down endless forest paths, suddenly beckoning him to follow her, next moment vanishing and as suddenly reappearing once more in an entirely different direction. But Florimund was now so eager to meet the beautiful Sleeping Princess that he would have followed his fairy guide for many more long hours. The Lilac Fairy, however, realising what an ardent lover he had already become, did not keep up her teasing tactics too long ; and presently, they drew near to the Enchanted Palace.

The young Prince became more and more amazed on observing the twining masses of creepers and the curtains of spiders' webs that surrounded the long overgrown gardens ; but by eagerly following the beckoning fairy hither and thither, he managed to thread his way through the tangled paths—and so, at last, he reached the Palace entrance. Without even casting a glance upon the still sleeping and snoring guards, he rushed inside to the great hall, where the King and Queen and all their Court lay still wrapped in the deep slumber of Enchantment. In the middle of the hall was a golden couch ; and upon this lay the beautiful Princess Aurora sleeping as peacefully as a little child.

Overwhelmed by the exquisite picture she made, Prince Florimund dropped upon his knees beside the couch and softly kissed the sleeping maiden upon her lips — and at the kiss of Love the magic spell was broken and the awakened Aurora and her Prince fell into each other's arms in an ecstasy of joy.

At the same moment, all the other sleepers awakened likewise ; and the King and Queen gladly consented to the marriage of their beautiful daughter with her royal rescuer.

* * * * *

The Marriage of Princess Aurora and Prince Florimund was celebrated with the greatest magnificence ; and at the splendid ball that was held afterwards not only the Lilac Fairy and her fairy companions, but many famous personages from the Land of Fairy-Tales came to dance and to join in the revels. Among these last-named interesting guests were Red-Riding-Hood and the Wolf, Bluebeard and Fatima with Sister Anne, Harlequin and Columbine, Puss-in-Boots and the White Cat, Goldilocks and her Prince, Beauty and the Beast, Florestan and his two sisters ; and many others. Besides these fairy-tale folk, there were also wonderful dancers from Russia, China, and other countries ; and a specially entrancing pair of Blue-Birds were greatly admired.

In fact, each new pair or group of performers seemed to dance better than the previous pair or group ; and the exquisite dancing of the Royal Bride and Bridegroom was the most brilliant performance of all.

And if the time-honoured statement is now made that Princess Aurora and her beloved Prince Florimund lived happily ever after, surely none but a curmudgeon could doubt it !

SWAN LAKE

(*Le Lac Des Cygnes*)

THIS famous story has as its setting the days of romantic young Princes and Enchanted Princesses, when Wicked Magicians were at the height of their sinister power, and when the course of true love, consequently, did not always run smoothly.

The action begins on a late afternoon in the autumn. A handsome young Prince, named Siegfried, was celebrating his coming-of-age birthday and was making merry with his friends in the vicinity of his Castle home, beyond which lay a mysterious and very wild forest. The trees gleamed with crimson and amber autumn tints as the last rays of the almost setting sun fell upon them.

A number of peasant youths and maidens had been invited to join in these festivities, and their bright but simple clothes provided a pleasant contrast to the rich silks and satins of the courtiers' costumes. The young people felt happy and gay ; and they danced and played lively games until the sun began to set. The revels were in charge of the Court Jester, who never ceased making jokes and cutting capers.

Nevertheless, the Jester was not actually as care-free as he appeared to be. Every now and again he would stop in the midst of his amusing antics and look uneasy and almost sad, as though he felt a cloud might presently darken the bright scene—that, perhaps, some trouble might even befall his beloved young Prince.

Wolfgang, the elderly tutor of Siegfried, too, did not seem altogether easy in his mind, as though he had been dragged thither somewhat against his will. This was probably the case, since it was his duty to instruct the young Prince and to see that he studied affairs of State rather than amused himself too frequently. However, having joined the party, he saw no reason why he should not enjoy the good fare provided. Consequently, he permitted himself to drink rather more wine than was good for him—with the result that he became not only quarrelsome, but extremely undignified in his behaviour. He insisted on dancing with one of the village maidens ; and when the latter mischievously caused him to flop to the ground heavily and unexpectedly, he was heartily laughed at by the Prince and the rest of the company.

This absurd incident revived the tutor's feeling of uneasiness—especially as, at that moment, his royal charge's rather severe mother now approached the party, followed by her own dignified ladies and attendants.

The Princess-Mother was far from pleased when she found her son in the company of peasant folk. Even when she realised that his courtiers were likewise dancing with the peasants she was still somewhat disapproving and was at first inclined to upbraid her son for thus wasting his royal time instead of studying with his tutor. However, the young Prince was so charmingly polite to her that she soon smiled upon him once more.

Nevertheless, before returning to the Castle, she reminded Siegfried that at the State Ball to be held next evening in honour of his coming-of-age, a number of royal maidens were to be present, from among whom he would be expected to choose one as his prospective bride.

Siegfried found this reminder extremely distasteful to him. He was a young man of a romantic nature and had never yet seen a maiden he felt he could love. Nevertheless, he knew that his mother's wish was also that of his royal advisers, and that, as Heir to the Throne, he must bow to her will.

Consequently, when the Princess-Mother and her ladies had returned to the Castle, Siegfried determined to make the most of his last few hours of freedom ; and he called upon his young friends to continue their dancing and to make this last youthful revel a mad and happy one.

And still the lively Jester, though he now indulged in more fantastic capers than before, felt his strange foreboding of coming tragedy. The first little cloud had already appeared to darken the bright skies of his beloved Prince's happiness ; and he could not help feeling that some disaster was not far away—but what, he knew not.

In some mysterious way, the Jester's strange foreboding was likewise now sensed by the young Prince Siegfried who, as the setting sun grew crimson in the west and long dark shadows began to steal into the glade, wandered a little apart from his companions almost with an air of sadness.

As the sun finally disappeared and the dusky twilight began to fall, a flock of wild swans was seen passing overhead ; and immediately the royal youth decided that a swan-hunting party would make a pleasant finish for the last few hours of his birthday. This was agreed upon ; and the present revel came to an end.

Later on, towards midnight, armed with crossbows, the hunting-party, headed by Siegfried and his favourite companion, Benno, made their way to a distant clearing in the forest, where they halted beside a large and mysterious-looking lake. Very soon, thinking there might be swans in the neighbourhood, Benno and the other huntsmen dashed off into the bushes to look for them.

But the young Prince remained alone beside the lake, still wrapped in his own quiet thoughts and strange forebodings ; and, presently, as soft midnight chimes were heard from a small chapel nearby, he beheld a marvellous sight.

A procession of graceful white Swans came gliding softly and silently over the lake from the other side and landed on a grassy bank quite close to the spot where the young Prince stood. Then, to Siegfried's amazement, as each swan came off the water, it took on the form of a lovely maiden clad in foamy, plume-like garments of snowy whiteness.

The most beautiful of all the Swan Maidens wore a crown upon her head ; and, as she moved shyly towards Siegfried, she announced herself as Odette, the Queen of the Swans, and entreated him not to permit his huntsmen to shoot at her or her companions.

The young Prince gladly gave his promise, and announced his own name and rank. He had never before beheld such a beautiful maiden as Odette, nor one so innocent and charming ; and he had already fallen deeply in love with her.

Then Odette revealed to him that a wicked Magician named von Rothbart—who dwelt in a tower on the lakeside—had laid a spell upon her and her companions whereby they were compelled to take on the form of swans which swam on the lake throughout the day, or took short flights round about it. At midnight, however, they became maidens once more until dawn, when they again returned to the lake as swans. This terrible spell could only be broken if Odette herself should meet and love a noble young man whose love for her should prove to be as great as her own for him, and who would promise to wed with her and to love her for evermore.

When this sad story came to an end Siegfried immediately declared his own love for the beautiful Swan Queen ; and as Odette had likewise conceived an equally deep passion for the young Prince they plighted their troth then and there. Afterwards, they danced together in an ecstasy of joy.

But, in quick succession, there came two alarming interruptions to this sweet idyllic love-making. Von Rothbart, the wicked Magician, wearing a fantastic and exaggerated head-dress in the form of an enormous owl, suddenly appeared and attacked the Prince, who, however, after a fierce struggle, succeeded in driving him off.

As the Owl Magician vanished from sight the Prince's huntsmen friends, led by Benno, returned and tried to shoot at the Swan Maidens with their crossbows, imagining them still to be actual swans ; but Siegfried rushed forward instantly and forebade them to do so while Odette, their Queen, hastened to stand in front of them in a protective attitude.

Then, seeing that they were now safe from harm, the Swan Maidens began to dance joyously on the banks of the lake ; and, presently, they were joined by a group of four young Cygnets, who danced a charmingly intricate dance by themselves. But Odette, their Queen, slipped away from their midst and strolled aside with her lover, Siegfried, for a few more happy moments.

The young Prince now invited beautiful Odette to attend the State Ball at the Royal Castle next evening, at midnight, when she took on her maiden form ; and he promised to choose her as his royal bride from among all the other princesses and noble young maidens who were to be present. Odette only too willingly agreed to do so.

Then, when the first rosy signs of early dawn began to appear, Odette and her Swan Maidens all became real swans once more and floated away gracefully over the lake ; and Siegfried and his huntsmen returned to the Prince's abode.

* * * * *

At the Royal Castle next evening, a brilliantly festive scene took place. The Castle was a blaze of light, and all the courtiers and guests wore magnificent costumes and dazzling jewels. Royal and noble visitors from many different countries were present ; and all gave exhibitions of their own national dances. A gorgeously-dressed masquerade was likewise held ; and everybody seemed happy and gay.

All but the young Prince Siegfried, who could think only of his lovely Odette, Queen of the Swans, who could not appear upon the scene until after midnight had struck. The Court Jester was likewise indifferent to the gay scene around him ; for he still felt a sense of sadness and an uneasy foreboding of coming tragedy.

When, later on, at a signal from the Princess-Mother, a group of six royal maidens appeared, from amongst whom Siegfried was expected to choose his prospective bride, there was great excitement in the ballroom. Most of these high-born maidens were beautiful and full of grace ; and when they entered, one by one, and curtseyed before the Princess-Mother and her son, they were greatly admired and there was much speculation among the courtiers as to which of them would be selected as their future Princess.

But Siegfried, though he duly danced with each of the royal maidens, showed but little interest in them. In his mind's eye, he could still see no one but his lovely white Swan Maiden.

Then there came the sound of a new arrival. Suddenly, there was a fanfare of trumpets and a mysterious man entered, sinister-looking but gorgeously dressed, leading by the hand the most beautiful young maiden that any of the company had ever beheld. These newcomers were announced as " The Knight of the Black Swan and his daughter Odile."

So royal-looking were the strangers that everybody was impressed ; and the Princess-Mother beamed with pleasure when her son, the young Prince, ran forward eagerly to greet the exquisite maiden and to entreat her to dance with him.

The reason for Siegfried's eagerness was that this lovely new arrival had the features and graceful form of his beloved Odette, and he believed her actually to be the Queen of the Swans herself, but now clad in shimmering and glittering garments. He danced again and again with her ; and, presently, he announced to his approving mother and to the company at large that this was the fair and nobly-born maiden he chose as his bride and whom he would love for evermore.

But, alas ! Prince Siegfried was being cruelly deceived. These mysterious strangers were none other than the evil Magician, von Rothbart, and his own equally deceitful daughter, Odile, whom he had transformed by means of his magic in such a manner that she appeared in the eyes of the love-lorn Siegfried to be, indeed, the beautiful Swan Maiden, Odette, in her human form. The masquerading Odile, eager enough to become the young Prince's bride, had played her part so cleverly that the deceived Siegfried had promised publicly to wed with her and to love her for evermore—and thus he had already broken his vow to sweet Odette, who must now remain under the Magician's spell.

Even as Siegfried was so willingly and lovingly dancing with the false Odile, some of the guests, to their surprise, observed that a plumy white Swan had appeared outside one of the windows, against which it was beating its soft wings as though in deep distress. This was the

now despairing Swan Maiden, Odette, waiting for her
transformation at midnight and unable to enter the room
until then.   But the young Prince did not see the snowy
bird outside the window, because his masquerading
partner was laughing up into his love-lit eyes and was
cunningly keeping him from looking in that direction by
means of her coquettish actions.

Then came the tragic climax ; and the Jester now knew
that his recent strange forebodings of coming disaster
were, indeed, true ones.

Immediately after the young Prince had announced
to the company that he had chosen Odile to be his bride
—sincerely imagining her to be Odette—and that he
would love her for evermore, there came a terrific
crashing of thunder and all the lights were instantly
extinguished.   In the darkness, however, and above the
noise and confusion that followed, the eldritch cackling
laughter of the Magician and his deceitful daughter could
be heard as they vanished from the scene.   Terrified
shrieks rent the air ; and the alarmed and disappointed
Princess-Mother fell to the floor in a fainting condition.

The unhappy Siegfried now realised, too late, that a
wicked trick had been played upon him; and when,
presently, he beheld outside the window the distressed
Swan still beating its wings despairingly in a vain
endeavour to enter, he instantly recognised it as the real
Odette whom he had, so unwittingly, forsworn.

Frantic with an equal despair, but eager to explain
the cruel deception that had victimised him, the unhappy
young Prince rushed outside—only to find that the
distressed Swan had already vanished.

* * * * *

The broken-hearted Queen of the Swans, already
transformed, quickly made her way to the lake-side,
where her attendant swan maidens awaited her; and

they all wept together mournfully when she told them the sad story of how her lover, the Prince, had broken his vow to her by swearing to love the false Odile for ever — and how they were thus all doomed to remain under the Magician's evil spell.

Even as she spoke, however, the distracted Siegfried hastened to her side, eagerly explaining the wicked trick that had been played upon him and entreating her to pardon him for having thus allowed himself to be deceived; and the beautiful Odette forgave him willingly, for she still loved him dearly. She pointed out, however, that even her forgiveness would avail them nothing since she was now doomed to die.

At that moment, von Rothbart again appeared before them, once more in the guise of a fantastic Owl; and, by means of his magic arts, he caused the deep waters of the lake to rise up in a mighty flood, so that the attendant Swan Maidens fled hither and thither, fearing they would be drowned. Siegfried furiously attacked his evil enemy; and again, after a desperate encounter, he succeeded in driving him off.

As the royal youth once more returned to the spot where he had left his beloved one, he was in time only to behold Odette vanishing beneath the troubled waters of the lake, into which she had cast herself in the belief that her doom was at hand; and, full of grief and despair, the young Prince likewise plunged into the depths to die with her.

Thus was the wicked Enchanter's spell broken at last by this supreme sacrifice; and the waters of the lake became calm once more as the flood abated.

As dawn now began to break, the Swan Maidens found, to their joy, that they were no longer transformed into swans, but were free to retain their human forms for the remainder of their lives.

Then, as they rejoiced together at the lake-side, they beheld, rising from its depths, their former beautiful Queen, Odette, and her devoted lover, Siegfried, re-united as spirit forms and floating away together towards another realm where happiness would be theirs for evermore.

*　　*　　*　　*　　*

Several other varying terminations have been given to this charming story. In one version, it is stated that when Siegfried rushes distracted from the ballroom into the Castle grounds beyond, he discovers that Odette, still in her Swan form, has been fatally wounded by an arrow shot from the crossbow of one of his huntsmen. He kneels beside her, tenderly trying to comfort her ; but she dies in his arms. Full of grief because he would never again see his beloved one in her human form, and caring no longer to live without her, he draws his dagger and stabs himself.

In another version, Siegfried is said to carry his doomed Odette to the highest point above the flood—in the original Petipa version this is a nearby hill—and then to announce his willingness to die with her ; and this sacrifice likewise breaks the spell and sets free the Swan Maidens.

In yet another version, the lovers, re-united after their sacrifice for love, float away together across the lake in a golden boat drawn by Swans. In both these last two versions, the Wicked Magician is killed and his evil power is destroyed for ever.

The end of the Magician in one of these varying finales shows him as being hoist with his own petard, as it were. He is himself caught up in the vortex of the flood waters he has raised in the lake, and is thus drowned as he disappears into the depths below—a truly just retribution. In most present-day versions of this ballet the Court Jester is omitted, but he appears still in the Russian Soviet Ballet presentations.

LE DEJEUNER SUR L'HERBE
(*Luncheon on the Grass*)

ONE lovely summer day, soon after midday, a party of gay young people came trooping into a park to bask in the bright sunshine and to enjoy a simple luncheon on the grass. They chose a pleasant sheltered spot at the back of an old ruined castle; and the girls and their attendant cavaliers set out a delightful *al fresco* meal.

First, they spread a clean white cloth on the grass upon which they laid fresh fruits and other light foods; and they even added bouquets of flowers as decoration. Some of the young people flung themselves to the ground and began to help themselves eagerly to the good things at once; and the air was soon filled with laughter at the merry quips and jokes that passed between them.

One of the prettiest of the girls at this gay picnic was a coquette; and before she joined the feasters on the grass she preferred to enjoy a little flirtation first with one young man and then with another. Several times she allowed herself to be chased and captured; but before the coveted reward of a kiss could be secured she would make her escape and slip away to join another admirer, upon whom she would likewise practise her little coquetries—greatly to the amusement of the other young folk. Finally, however, one of the boldest cavaliers seized her firmly by the waist, and she was then persuaded to sit down on the grass beside him and to enjoy the titbits he plied her with.

Only one member of the party did not seem to be in the mood to enjoy the lively company around her. This was a pale, gentle young girl, who seemed of a very different type from the others. She was quiet and dreamy, and seemed to be wrapped up in her own hidden thoughts—romantic thoughts of adventure and love. The gay young men present at the picnic, with their quips and sallies, did not appeal to her more sensitive nature ; and when they tried to draw her into their lively circle, she declined their advances and drew back. Having partaken of a little fruit, she sauntered away and seated herself upon the low-lying branch of a tree, where she was half-hidden among the cool green leaves ; and here she remained alone to dream her sweet dreams and to conjure up images of the romantic hero who would, she hoped, some day invade her young life. He would be very different from these giddy young men at the picnic—who had already almost forgotten her existence, she knew.

The latter were far more interested in competing for the smiles and favours of the pretty coquette, who enticed them instantly to her side with merely a saucy glance ; and the other girls at the party were thus left to clear the cloth and to tidy the picnic baskets before they, too, joined in the various games and competitions.

It was the youths who did best in the competitions who were most in favour with the flirtatious belle. To please her, they leapt high into the air, cut amusing capers, ran races, and performed intricate dances ; and at the end of these sportive competitions she crowned the best among them with flowers.

Then the pretty coquette herself indulged in an elaborate dance to show off her own charming graces ; and her performance was rapturously applauded by her many admirers. Not to be outdone, however, the other girls likewise danced, each with her own special cavalier ; and the merriment continued until sundown.

All this time, the young girl who sat apart continued

to dream her sweet day-dreams, forgetful of, and forgotten by, her companions. Then, she suddenly sat up,
aroused by the sound of a stranger's approaching footsteps. A handsome young vagabond, interesting-looking,
pale, with brown curls and warm red lips, emerged from
a glade nearby, and advanced towards the picnic folk;
and the half-hidden day-dreamer sat up and gazed with
a beating heart upon him, feeling—curiously enough, and
not knowing why—that he was a kindred spirit.

The newcomer, however, was not well-received by
the young men of the party, who resented his intrusion
into their midst ; and they were inclined to chase him
away. But the solitary young girl couched on the low
tree-branch had already felt the charm of the stranger so
strongly that she was now fully awakened to what he
might mean to her. She advanced towards him, therefore, attracted mysteriously by something in his pale
countenance that made her recognise in him the romantic
hero of her dreams, with whom she might share adventure. He it was, she believed, whom she could love,
and to whom she could make her vows.

But the young men of the picnic-party, jealous of
the stranger's romantic looks, still would not permit
him to remain ; and they now roughly drove him off—
but not before he had noted the eager longing in the
eyes of the day-dreaming young girl, who now sadly
slipped back into the shadows.

The dusk of early evening had already fallen ; and
the young picnic folk, already weary, began to depart,
couple by couple—the coquette, still gay and flirtatious,
being, however, escorted by more than her share of
admirers eager to take her home.

All the company had completely forgotten the solitary
and dreamy young girl who had preferred to spend her
afternoon alone ; and she now stepped forth from the

shadows, weeping softly because her recent litt'e
romance had ended almost at the moment of its birth.
But had it ?

She turned quickly, almost in alarm, at the sound of
approaching footsteps ; and her heart leaped with joy
as she beheld the graceful form of the vagabond youth
issuing forth once more from the now misty glade.   The
hero of her dreams had returned !

The youthful stranger instantly observed the trembling young girl and came eagerly towards her, knowing
that he, also, had found romance.   He took her silently
into his embrace, to which she willingly yielded herself ;
and then, hand-in-hand, they joyfully walked away
together towards the Road of Adventure.

LA FIANCEE DU DIABLE.

(*The Devil's Fiancée*)

DURING the early days of the eighteenth century a very romantic young traveller and his devoted valet-attendant happened to be making a journey through a wild and lonely country district of France, far away from any town or village ; and, one dark evening they found themselves overtaken by a violent thunderstorm—one of the worst they had ever experienced.

Having completely lost their way, and being already benighted, the wayfarers felt considerably relieved on stumbling on to a winding path that led up to a *château* of somewhat forbidding aspect. As lights showed in some of the upstairs windows, the traveller and his servant decided to knock at the door and crave permission to shelter from the storm.

There was no answer to their repeated knockings ; but as the door was unlatched they stepped inside. After passing through the entrance hall, they found themselves in what appeared to be a large and handsome reception-room—which, however, was empty and wore an air of neglect, though a dim light shone therein.

A large and ornate gilded doorway at the far end of the room seemed to lead to the main part of the mansion ; and smaller doors were also to be seen at the sides.

An eerie atmosphere pervaded the place ; and the young traveller and his valet shivered slightly as they moved about, somewhat fearfully, but with intense curiosity. They both felt that this was the kind of old *château* that might easily be haunted—or, at least, be the abode of evil spirits. It was not long before they discovered that their surmise was a correct one. Meanwhile, they were glad to have found shelter from the storm.

Presently, they heard the sound of approaching footsteps ; and, not feeling too sure of their welcome, they retired to the ante-room, to await a favourable time to reveal their presence.

From one side door there now entered a group of household servants. First came maids carrying brooms and dusters, who proceeded to sweep and to dust away the cobwebs in feverish haste ; and they even made attempts here and there to scrub the floor and to polish the furniture. They were followed by footmen, who hastily arranged the chairs against the walls.

All this frantic activity seemed to indicate that some immediate festivity was about to be held unexpectedly ; and from the chattering and actions of the maids, the hidden intruders gathered that the daughter of the house was about to be wedded, and that her bridegroom-elect was expected to arrive at midnight to take her away— but at the mention of the said bridegroom shivers of fear ran through the busy menials. Nevertheless, when their hurried tasks were finished, they indulged in a stolen dance, until driven away by the butler, or major-domo.

The young traveller and his servant watched these proceedings with surprised interest ; but they felt there was something sinister afoot—and the valet heartily wished they had never entered the *château*. Next moment, however, his young master felt glad that they had done so.

No sooner had the household servants departed, than the bride-elect appeared on the scene, with her attendant bridesmaids ; and she was so beautiful in her bridal attire, and, withal, so sad and thoughtful, that the traveller's heart went out to her at once as he eagerly watched her every movement.

The bridesmaids were gay enough, and they tried to cheer their friend as they helped to put the finishing touches to her toilet. They held up mirrors that she might admire her simple headdress; and they entreated her to smile and to dance about with them.

But the lovely young bride still looked unhappy; and she seemed to have been betrothed against her will and to have no desire for her almost instantly expected bridegroom to appear on the scene

Presently, she sent her bridesmaids away, wishing to remain alone for a few moments with her sad thoughts; and then it was that the young traveller made his presence known. At first the sad bride was startled and alarmed by the sudden appearance of the stranger; but as he reassured her and explained the reason for his presence, she lost her fears and seemed glad to have him beside her. Indeed, she quickly returned his already passionate interest in her with a like sympathetic interest; and as they now gazed into one another's eyes, a deep mutual love sprang up in their hearts, and they felt so great a joy in each other's presence that they were quickly lost to all else.

They were soon brought back to the present, however, by the return of the bridesmaids, who, shocked by the intrusion of a male stranger and of the obvious attraction for him of the bride-elect, endeavoured to separate the pair. Nevertheless, they likewise were pleased with the gallant looks of the handsome young stranger; and quickly realising the love that had so suddenly sprung up between the pair they accepted the situation, difficult though it was. Therefore, when their friend entreated them to leave her once more, that she might enjoy another brief moment alone with the stranger before parting from him for ever, they immediately did so—though somewhat reluctantly, knowing that the unwanted bridegroom was already due to appear on the scene.

Again lost to the world for that short magic spell, the now enraptured pair experienced a joy such as they had never imagined could ever be theirs ; and then the bride tore herself away hastily and fled to rejoin her maidens in readiness to lead the bridal procession. The valet, who had hovered in the background until this moment, likewise now rejoined his master—wishing more than ever that the latter had never entered this mysterious *chateau* and feeling that the now love-sick young man was being rushed towards a vortex of trouble. Nor was he mistaken.

Suddenly, as the hour of midnight struck, there came the noise of a clamorous arrival, accompanied by the prolonged crashing of renewed thunder-claps ; and, amidst vivid flashes of lightning, the splendid gilded doors at the far end of the room were flung wide open, as the bridegroom and his magnificent attendant retinue entered.

The intruders stared in amazement and awe at this dazzling but sinister assembly. Flashes of lightning continued from time to time to play about the tall, impressive, and graceful figure of the bridegroom, who was clad in elegant garments of such a vivid scarlet that it hurt mortal eyes to gaze upon ; and he wore a voluminous flowing cloak, likewise of scarlet, and a scarlet plume in his black hair. His eyes seemed to flash like fire or living coals ; and his features, handsome though they were, were of the Satanic kind—as well they might be, for this sinister bridegroom was none other than the Devil himself.

The latter's vast retinue was likewise of a demoniacal

kind—the male attendants being garbed in black and revealing small horns on their heads while the females were gorgeously dressed in all the colours of the rainbow.

This fearsome bridal party rushed into the now brilliantly-lighted hall with exaggerated hilarity ; and, instantly, they were all engaged in an orgy of wild dancing. Their diabolic leader, however, quickly had them under control ; and as the pale drooping bride, with her maidens, and accompanied by her parents, entered, he went forward to greet her, taking her by the hand and insisting that she should dance a measure with him.

The unhappy bride, though horrified as she beheld her affianced lord, could not refuse so powerful a command ; and soon she was being whirled hither and thither in a maze of wild and sensuous movements—which, nevertheless, exercised a kind of magic spell over her, so that, against her will, she almost seemed more reconciled to her fate for the moment.

But when, as the wild dance ended, her sinister bridegroom bent to kiss her, she shrank back in fear ; and, at that moment, unable to restrain himself longer, the traveller rushed forward with a drawn sword in his hand, challenging her scarlet-garbed partner to mortal combat. But he was soon overcome.

With a sardonic smile, the sinister bridegroom struck the sword from his hand ; then, as his victim shrank back, horrorstruck and powerless, he snatched a fiddle and began to play it, bidding the over-bold young man to dance until he dropped dead from exhaustion.

The unfortunate traveller at first tried to resist this terrible command ; but the diabolic fiddler had laid a spell upon him, and he was compelled to obey. He began to dance, therefore, at first slowly and somewhat clumsily, but gradually increasing in speed and grace until he more than matched the finest dancer he had ever beheld.

It was in vain that the now distracted bride tried to stop this fatal dance : every time she flung herself between the pair she was politely, but firmly, thrust aside by her satanic bridegroom—who was himself now wildly dancing as he fiddled, and who, from time to time, seized her likewise and forced her to join in and make a trio.

A wilder orgy than ever now followed, as all the other members of the company likewise took part, making a whirling delirious rhythm that grew madder and ever madder as the moments passed by.

At one time the bride found herself dancing with her beloved stranger-lover ; and, for a brief moment, the unhappy pair felt rapture once more. Then she was snatched away again by her sinister *fiancé*.

The latter, however, still had the orgy well under control ; and gradually he drew aside his own madly gyrating myrmidons to form an audience once more ; and when the bride and her maidens had likewise sunk back to rest, unable to dance any more, he concentrated upon his now gasping victim, compelling the latter to dance faster and faster to the accompaniment of the diabolic fiddle he played.

But, at last, the climax came—unexpectedly so far as concerned the Prince of Darkness, who thus lost his hoped-for victim, after all.

Just as the tortured traveller began to stumble and totter on the verge of collapse, his faithful valet—who had been watching the dreadful scene in fascinated horror—seeing his beloved master falling to the ground, suddenly rushed frantically to one of the windows and flung it wide open and the light of early dawn and **the** inrush of fresh air put an end to these diabolical sorceries.

Instantly, the brilliant lights were extinguished ; and, to the accompaniment of thunder and lightning, the sinister Bridegroom and his entire retinue of horned demons vanished, taking the sad little Bride and her maidens with them.

The vast hall was empty now—save for the form of the valet bending anxiously over his collapsed master and waiting hopefully for him to recover consciousness once more.

LES FORAINS
(*The Travelling Players*)

LATE one evening, a troupe of travelling players
came moving slowly through the woods towards the
suburbs of a small town in France. They brought all
the various parts of their travelling theatre with them ;
and their properties could not have been many, since
they carried them all on a single handcart. What was
more, one or two members of the company travelled
on the handcart, too. For some were tired already and
needed to rest before giving their performance that
same evening. The others helped to push the handcart,
or walked beside it.

For a short distance, one of the men players carried
in his arms a young girl acrobat ; and when they
arrived at their destination in the suburb he set her
down with loving care. For everybody in that little
company depended on everybody else ; and the good
of all was the care of all. The young girl instantly
got up and began to stretch her limbs and to make them
supple once more.

Having arrived at the spot where they were to play,
all was immediately hustle and bustle. Weariness was
forgotten, and enthusiasm for their chosen life was
quite apparent. They were players, and it was their
job to play their little parts to the best of their powers ;
and, as soon as they arrived, some of them began to
rehearse at once. They were a party of circus players,
and needed to keep themselves in a fit condition ; and
they could not afford to neglect their constant exercises.

The young girl acrobat and some dancers practised
their steps, and did a few turns at the splits ; and a

clown tried out his comic antics and acrobatic tricks once more. The men of the party set to work at once to put up the stage ; and, since they were experts at the job, it was soon in readiness for the performance.

A few villagers strolled up to look on in the background while these necessary preparations were being made ; and gradually an audience gathered in front, and the jingling sound of small money being collected was heard.

When finally set up, the little theatre looked bright and cheery ; and when the curtains were finally drawn aside, a good and well-practised little entertainment was given to the rural spectators by these enthusiastic travelling players. The young girl acrobat was in fine form—her rest in the man's arms on the way had done her good ; and she gave an excellent performance. The clever girl dancers were likewise in good form ; and, when dressed up in their tarlatan and spangles, they certainly did not seem to be the same weary travellers who had been trudging along the road a few hours before.

The clown and other male performers might never have had to wheel their stage properties on a handcart from the last village, so lively and full of fun did they appear to be. The conjuror-magician performed all his usual tricks so slickly as to completely mystify his simple, but admiring audience ; and the Siamese Twins went through their own special little act to the open-mouthed wonderment of the spectators.

A Sleeping Beauty act was contrived with a charming effect that delighted all who beheld it ; and the result was surprising indeed, considering the slenderness of the little company's resources and the many difficulties they had to contend with.

In one of the acts, a couple of white pigeons had to be released ; and there was a sigh of relief from the company when these pet birds were safely enclosed in their cage once more. They all loved these pigeons, and regarded them as being among their most valuable properties.

It was easy for an observer to see that the young girl acrobat and the young man who had carried her for the last part of the journey were lovers ; and at odd times during the performance they were able to snatch a few kisses and enjoy ecstasy for a moment or two. But they quickly returned to earth once more—and to their work as players, which they loved so well.

At last the performance came to an end, and the audience departed ; and then the travelling players had to take down their little theatre and to pack their properties on to the single handcart once more. How tired they all were, and how glad they would have been to rest ; but they must travel on to the next village without delay and rest on their way as best they could.

Wearily, they set to work ; and at last the handcart was packed, and they began to move along once more. And then came a shock for them all. They were almost out of sight of their recent activities when one of the company suddenly remembered that the cage containing the two precious white pigeons had been left behind !

Full of distress, the young girl acrobat slipped off the handcart where she had been set by her anxious lover, and ran back to the spot where the pet birds had been left. There they were, still cooing softly on their perches ; and, picking up the cage, she hurried back to rejoin the waiting party. Tired though she was, she felt happy as she tripped back with her feathered pets ; for it would have been a real tragedy had the beloved white pigeons been lost.

And so, the Travelling Players passed on their way.

GIFT OF THE MAGI

A CHEAP furnished flat in New York in the first decade of the present century ; Christmas-Eve, and a pretty young wife in tears on the shabby sofa. And why ? Because she had not the wherewithal to purchase a really worth-while gift for her well-beloved and hard-working husband !

After saving and scrimping for months on end, all she could now produce was $1.87 cents ; and what could one get with that worthy of her splendid Jim ? Just nothing. So the charming and generous-minded Della continued to weep.

But not for long. Suddenly she sprang to her feet, all smiles once more, her eyes now bright and shining with the great idea that had come to her " out of the blue." Rushing to the narrow shoddy pier-glass on the wall, she shook down her masses of rich waving brown hair. It fell well below her knees. People were willing to buy wonderful hair like hers, and to give good prices for it, too.

But Della's lovely hair was one of the two great treasures prized above all others by this young pair of happily-married lovers—the other was Jim's fine gold watch, which had belonged to his father and his grandfather. Should Della's glorious hair be shorn, they would have but one treasure left. But, surely, the Christmas gift she would buy would provide a new treasure to take its place ?

Not another moment longer would she hesitate. On with her old coat and her old hat ; and out into the street she ran.

*   *   *   *   *

Snow-flakes were softly falling ; but the shop windows were brilliantly lighted and full of dazzling gifts.

But, first, to business. Della ran eagerly up the staircase that led to a Hairdressing Salon ; and when she came out into the street once more, her big and rather flopping hat looked very strange above her bobbed head. But she had $20 now in her purse, keeping company with her slowly-accumulated $1.87 cents ; and she was full of joy as she hastened from store to store in search of her precious gift.

Della knew exactly what she wanted—a plain but exquisitely-made platinum fob-chain, as good to look at as Jim's fine old gold watch. At last she found it, and came out of a smart jeweller's shop minus $21, and with 87 cents only left in her purse.

Full of joy, she hastened back to the furnished flat—which, though shabby, she had made into a real temporary home for herself and Jim ; and she set about preparing the evening meal.

Certainly, she had received a horrid shock on first beholding her shorn head in the mirror ; but, after attending to it with her curling-tongs, it looked rather better. " And it will soon grow again ! " she thought, hopefully.

Nevertheless, she was scared stiff when, presently, Jim ran up the stairs and into the apartment—and there stood staring at her with a strange look in his eyes, which she could not understand in the least—not anger, or dismay, or even astonishment !

She begged him not to look at her like that, but to admire the gift she had bought for him.

But Jim had her in his arms first ; and Della knew that he loved her just the same, hair or no hair. Then the young man proudly brought forth from his pocket a small parcel, and bade her open it—his Christmas gift to her. This was a lovely set of side and back combs of real tortoiseshell, with jewelled rims—expensive combs which she had longed to possess for many weeks past, but which were now no longer suitable for her cropped head !

And when she produced the exquisite platinum fob-chain and eagerly called upon her beloved one to bring forth his fine old gold watch to be attached to it, he could not do so. He had sold the watch to buy the jewelled combs as a Christmas present for her !

But they both smiled the sweet smile of true love as they mutually decided that their precious gifts must just wait awhile before they could be used ; and then they settled down happily to their evening meal.

* * * * *

Do you think these two young people were foolish, or wise ? Surely, they were wise—the Magi were the Inventors of the charming custom of giving Christmas presents ; and, you will remember that the Magi have always been known as the Three Wise Men of the East. Then, it follows that such loving, generous souls as those of Della and Jim are the wisest of all who give and receive gifts. They gave all they had. They ARE the Magi !

THE DESCENT OF HEBE

HEBE was the lovely Goddess of Youth and the Handmaiden of the Gods on Olympus. She was one of the daughters of Jupiter and Juno ; and it was because she was so dexterous and so gracefully quick in her movements that she had been chosen to serve the gods and, in particular, to be their cup-bearer. It was also a part of her duties to care for the brilliantly-coloured peacocks which always attended Juno, the Queen of Olympus, wherever the latter went ; and her royal mother's splendid chariot was likewise in her charge.

But it was mainly as their cup-bearer that Hebe enjoyed serving the radiant gods ; and it gave her a thrill every time she filled their goblets with the sparkling nectar they loved to drink ; and the grace of her movements as she poured forth the life-giving liquid became famous all over Olympus.

It was, therefore, a terrible shock to the fair Goddess of Youth when, one day, while serving the gods with nectar during a festival she slipped and spilled a few drops of the precious shining liquid. Such a surprising and unfortunate occurrence had never happened to her before ; and Hebe, covered with confusion, hurried away and hid herself, hoping that this one and only clumsy action in her service had not been observed by the Great and Shining Ones.

But, alas, it had ; and poor Hebe's hiding-place was soon discovered by Mercury, the wing-footed Messenger of the Gods, who presently appeared before her with a stern message from her royal master and father. As a punishment for having spilled a few drops of nectar, Jupiter condemned her to be banished to the Earth for a spell ; and Mercury now bade the weeping handmaiden to follow him to a certain place where her dreaded journey was to begin.

When the two Servers of the Gods arrived at the starting-point, Night, closely enveloped in her cloak of darkness, was already waiting in her chariot ; and her black prancing steeds were impatiently champing at their bits, eager to set forth upon their journey to Earth with the delinquent handmaiden.

But when Hebe now realised more profoundly what was about to befall her, and remembered the precious joys she was leaving behind, she drew back in horror and refused to step into the waiting chariot ; and she passionately entreated Mercury to take her back to bright Olympus—which, however, he refused to do.

Then Night, feeling sympathy with the weeping maiden, tried to comfort her ; and she conjured up for her a wonderful vision of an earthly scene. In this vision, Hebe beheld a handsome young man of splendid stature and superb strength engaged in various sports and actions—leaping, dancing, and performing many deeds of prowess. It was a living picture of the young Hercules, already the most famous and athletic hero on Earth ; and his physical beauty and graceful strength so greatly impressed fair Hebe that she instantly fell in love with him and longed to be in his presence.

No longer reluctant to take her compulsory journey, she sprang eagerly and lightly into the waiting chariot, and entreated Night to set forth to Earth at once— which the Dark Charioteer, well-pleased with her strategy, was willing enough to do.

Throughout the journey darkness reigned ; but when, at last, the Earth was reached, daylight was breaking ;

and as Hebe stepped forth from the chariot, Night threw off her gloomy cloak and vanished from sight.

Slowly, the Chariot of Apollo, the glorious Sun God, began to cross the heavens ; and with the rising of the sun, Hebe found the Earth a much pleasanter place than she had expected.

Presently, to her joy, Hercules, the splendid young man she had beheld in the vision shown her by Night, appeared upon the scene ; and, perceiving the beautiful strange maiden, he approached her with an equal joy. Quickly returning her obvious love for him, Hercules proceeded to woo her eagerly ; and their sweet romance deepened with every hour that passed.

So far from finding her enforced exile to Earth irksome, Hebe was now filled with intense happiness ; for when Hercules was not making love to her he entertained her with his gay leaping dances and revealed to her the amazing power of his mighty strength. Hebe, too, would enrapture her earthly lover with her own graceful movements ; and then they would dance joyously together. Sometimes, other youths and maidens would join them in a merry revel ; but when they had departed the happy lovers would wander off, hand in hand, to roam in the woodland glades.

At last, however, this joyous interlude—far from being a time of punishment—came to an end ; and Hebe was ordered to return to Olympus once more. Her fault had been graciously pardoned ; and the gods were now eagerly waiting for her to serve them as before. Consequently, the Chariot of Night again arrived on Earth to take the exile home.

Hebe was reluctant to go, because she had found happiness on Earth ; but she had no choice in the matter and was compelled to obey the will of the mighty Jupiter.

All the celestial inhabitants of Olympus were glad to receive back their beloved and beautiful handmaiden ; and Hebe again felt the thrill of pouring forth the sparkling nectar into the golden goblets of the gods. Then, later on, her joy was completed ; for her earthly hero-lover, Hercules, was translated to Olympus and made immortal, and she was permitted to become his bride and to dwell with him for evermore.

GALA PERFORMANCE

AT a certain Theatre Royal, towards the turn of the century, a grand Ballet Gala performance was to be given before a fashionable and critical audience. For, many weeks before it took place, the greatest interest and excitement had prevailed inside and outside the theatre ; for the crowning event of the performance was to be the joint appearance of three equally world-renowned star ballerinas on the stage at one and the same time. They were to dance a wonderful *pas de trois* in a ballet specially composed for them.

To behold three famous ballerinas dancing together " at one fell swoop " would certainly provide a thrill of delight for the audience ; but, meanwhile, it was providing a thrill of quite another type for the unfortunate Conductor of the Theatre Royal orchestra and the still more unfortunate Ballet Master—both of whom were nearly driven to distraction at the final rehearsal and were sick with worry and apprehension before the curtain went up on the actual performance.

The three star ballerinas hailed respectively from Moscow, Milan, and Paris ; and they were all three highly temperamental, each being accustomed to receiving and accepting the ballet world's attention, admiration, and applause for herself alone. This being so, how were they to be satisfied with a third share only at the forthcoming Gala performance ? Nobody felt inclined to say ; the optimists who had arranged the performance least of all. The only thing the latter could do was to hope for the best.

The famous trio did not appear on the scene until the

final rehearsal before the curtain went up. The *cory-phées* were already busily practising their *ensembles*, entrances and exits; and as they danced hither and thither on the tips of their toes, they whispered excitedly together, wondering what the famous ballerinas would look like and what marvellous new steps and effects they would introduce.

Excitement was at its height when the first of the visiting stars appeared from the wings, closely followed by a weary-looking dresser and attended by the bowing and admiring ballet-master. This lovely lady, full of grace and pride in herself was known as " *La Reine de la Danse* "; and she came from Moscow. Though she presently performed a few pirouettes, and listened with haughty condescension to the obsequious ballet-master's humbly-tendered instructions, she was far more interested in her own immediate appearance and decorative garb. Her pirouettes were mainly given that she might herself thus observe the effect of her exquisite ballet-dress from all points; and every now and again she would stop to storm at the long-suffering dresser, who seemed cowed by this critical mistress.

Nevertheless, though the ballerina from Moscow did not deign to rehearse in any proper manner, the ballet-master's worst moments were yet to come with the arrival of the other two star dancers who now appeared from the opposite wings, one after the other. One of these was the ballerina from Milan, " *La Déesse de la Danse* "; and the other was the ballerina from Paris, " *La Fille de Terpsichore.*" Both were escorted by their male partners.

These two ladies were likewise beautiful and full of grace, each with a style peculiar to her own nationality; and it was easy to see that each would desire to have her own way and the premier position in the performance that was to follow—as was already the case with the first arrival.

All three ballerinas now glared at one another, each eager to pick holes in the other two and to point out such imaginary defects to the anxious ballet-master—who was soon reduced to a state verging on hysterics in his hopeless endeavour to persuade these brilliant but most distracting stars to shine just exactly as he desired them to do.

When the glittering ladies were not glaring with furious jealousy at one another, they were flirting lightly with their admiring partners, or scolding the unhappy dresser because of some omission or faulty work in their garb or *coiffure*—all to the ill-concealed amusement of the giggling *coryphées*. Even when the Conductor was appealed to on various points by his worried colleague, he also could do little with such lovely but temperamental ladies—except to be intensely flattered when they obviously desired to flirt with him.

And so, this most unrehearsal-like rehearsal went on, until it was time to clear the stage just before the performance began ; and all the exhausted ballet-master and Conductor could hope for was that " everything would be all right on the night ! "

And, strange to say, it was—more or less.

When the curtain rose upon the actual Gala performance a magical change took place. The various movements of the ballet went forward smoothly in the order intended by their creator, all the dancing *coryphées* giving of their best, forgetful of their rehearsal giddiness and thinking only of their admirers in front.

Thunderous applause greeted the appearance of the three famous ballerinas from Moscow, Milan, and Paris, who, mindful of their world-wide reputations, performed their *soli* and *ensembles* with all the exquisite grace and perfect finish expected of such shining stars. What was more, they smiled continuously upon one another when they met in the dance, as though with a sisterly love deep and sincere ; and though their sweet smiles changed suddenly to the spitfire baleful glances of "Kilkenny Cats" as they vanished into the wings, the delighted audience was none the wiser. If the ballet-master had to separate these snarling felines in ballet skirts, he evidently did so dexterously ; for next moment they would appear before the footlights, hand in hand, smiling sweetly upon each other and the audience, in answer to the latter's enthusiastic applause.

Again and again, this happened ; and then things became a little out of hand. Each ballerina seemed positively determined that the last "curtain" should be hers alone. They broke away from each other, and each perversely tried to keep the stage for herself and her last deep curtsey. No sooner had the dancer from Moscow sunk to the ground in a cloud of spangled tulle, than the dancer from Milan sank in another cloud of tulle in advance of her ; and then the dancer from Paris curtsied a little nearer to the footlights than either of the others.

This sort of thing went on for quite a long time, the excitement and applause of the audience becoming more and more intense as it was realised that a competition was actually taking place. More and more thunderous applause encouraged every advance made by the competitors. Then, just as the last adventurous ballerina was about to curtsey almost upon the foot lights, the curtain was hastily rung down.

The Gala Performance had come to an end—to the great relief of the harassed ballet-master and his equally worried colleague, the Conductor of the Orchestra.

LILAC GARDEN
(*Le Jardin aux Lilas*)

LET us picture for a moment an exquisite garden, in which lilac trees in full bloom spread a shaded purple, lavender, and mauve beauty everywhere, and filled the air with an intoxicating sweet but heavy perfume. It was a perfect evening in early summer-time, and the loveliness of its blossoming gave the garden an air of enchantment. One expected, almost at any moment, to see Titania come tripping forth from one of its many violet-tinted avenues, followed by her attendant sprites, to dance in a fairy ring.

Instead, however, there presently appeared in one of its more open spaces, a bevy of Edwardian young people, wearing gay evening attire, who laughingly began to dance in and out among the heavily-laden lilac bushes. They were guests at a farewell party being given that evening by one of their company—a beautiful young woman named Caroline, who was about to be married. Later that same evening she would leave her guests and depart with her betrothed to the latter's abode, there to become his bride.

Though the lively guests were happy and gay, Caroline herself was not ; for this was to be a marriage of convenience, and her heart was already given to another. She was willing to abide by the contract which had been arranged for her, since it was a matter of necessity ; but she felt that she would be more resigned to her loveless fate if she could enjoy one last tender kiss and passionate embrace from her own true lover, who would always be first in her affections.

How desperately she longed for this last joyous interview—and how difficult it was to achieve ! Her whole object in giving this farewell party was her eager desire that she might thus realise this longing of her heart ; and she had invited her young guests to dance in the shadowy lilac garden, hoping that, by this means, she and her beloved one might meet there, unobserved, in one of the heavily-perfumed paths.

Presently, to her joy, as she was dancing sedately with her betrothed, she saw her lover approaching from another lilac-clustered alley ; but her joy was instantly overshadowed by fear of the discovery of her secret, so that she signalled frantically to him to retreat— which he most reluctantly did.

Caroline was obliged to dance away with her betrothed, and to join her other guests in their revels ; but, presently, she managed to escape for awhile to the same spot, hoping for the happy meeting she longed for. However, she found there, instead, one of the women guests, who also appeared to be lurking among the lilac bushes obviously awaiting a clandestine meeting.

Unknown to Caroline, this elegantly-garbed guest had for some time past been the mistress of her own *ancé* ; and she had availed herself of an invitation to the party in order to meet her lover—but not for the last time, she hoped, since it was her intention to persuade him to agree to continue their present irregular relations even after his marriage.

Disappointed that the newcomer was not the one she was expecting, she scarcely heeded the greeting of her hostess—of whom she was intensely jealous—but moved away quickly to seek the bridegroom-elect elsewhere.

Almost immediately after she had departed, Caroline's own beloved one came forward with eagerly outstretched arms ; and for a brief spell happiness held them enthralled.

But Caroline's fears for the discovery of her secret again beset her ; and she kept slipping from her lover's grasp to watch fearfully for the approach of her *fiancé*. Finally, the sad-hearted pair wandered off to a less-frequented part of the garden ; and scarcely had they vanished from sight than the bridegroom-elect and his former mistress appeared at the trysting-spot, tripping in together as dancing partners.

However, though this sophisticated pair danced correctly and elegantly for the deception of any possible onlookers, they were, nevertheless, arguing fiercely. The young woman whom he had formerly adored as his mistress no longer seemed so desirable to the already more decorous middle-aged man about to be married, who now hoped to put his irregular past behind him ; but his partner still desired their old relationship to continue, and she entreated him passionately and even angrily to agree to her request. So unguarded did she become in her beseeching attitudes and distracted tones that her harassed companion kept stopping their dance to glance about him anxiously, fearing lest the now more desirable Caroline should unexpectedly appear upon the scene—for he wished, above all things, to keep this unorthodox love episode of his past unknown to his bride-to-be.

Annoyed by her persistence, he angrily compelled his clinging partner to dance away with him, hoping thus to release himself from her embarrassing importunity among the thronging guests in another part of the garden.

For a little while, Caroline and her lover managed to elude her *fiancé* and his clinging mistress ; but, at last, they could no longer do so.

The hour came when the affianced pair had to depart to the bridegroom's home ; and the two opposing couples now met for a few brief moments face to face, and even danced together, almost unseeingly, in a group of four as the final chords of the distant dance music crashed forth the signal for the farewell party in the lilac garden to end.

By this time, however, Caroline was so deeply engrossed in the woe of parting from the man she truly loved that she completely failed to notice anything strange in the behaviour of her *fiancé*. All she realised was that, in her own distracted eagerness to keep secret the true state of her affections by behaving normally while dancing with her beloved one, she had not yet been able to snatch from him that last passionate kiss she longed for ; and now it was too late !

At the same moment as she realised this sad fact, her *fiancé* roughly thrust aside his still importunate mistress and seized the hand of Caroline, which he tucked firmly beneath his arm, as he led her away triumphantly through the throng of handkerchief-waving guests. He, in his turn, was likewise so engrossed by his endeavours to free himself from the clinging arms of his former mistress and to make a dignified departure with his bride, that he did not observe the latter's last despairing gestures of farewell to the man she still truly loved.

Thus, neither Caroline nor her *fiancé* learned each other's secret during those last few passionate interludes ; but they left behind them two very sad hearts in that exquisite Lilac Garden, with its shaded purple and lavender beauty and its heavily-perfumed air.

PILLAR OF FIRE

In a small town, at the beginning of the present century, three sisters lived together in somewhat difficult and inharmonious circumstances.

Though but three in number, this small family was a divided one, the eldest and the youngest sister forming a close alliance, from which the unfortunate middle sister, Hagar, found herself excluded.

It may have seemed to some observers that there was a natural reason for this division. The eldest sister was considerably older than either of the others ; and, as head of the little family, she would consider it her duty to devote herself more particularly to the interests of the little sister rather than to those of the middle one —whom she would probably regard as being old enough to take care of herself. Had she, on the other hand, been inclined to share her affection and care for the younger girl with the second sister, a much happier household might have been the result.

As it was, however, Hagar found herself " the odd man out " ; and, being of an extremely passionate and romantic nature and needing someone on whom to lavish the overwhelming riches of a loving heart, she was, consequently, the more eager to seek love from the opposite sex. She was an attractive young woman ; and, though lacking the extraordinary beauty and early youthful charm of the youngest sister, she hoped for a lover to bring her romance and happiness at last— the happiness she craved for and so long denied to her in her family life.

With the—to her—formidable spectacle of the elderly

and crotchety spinster sister—strait-laced, narrow-minded, censorious, and no longer possessed of charm—constantly before her eyes, Hagar dreaded the prospect of ever becoming like her ; and she equally dreaded the quickly approaching time when her little sister, now of early teen-age, would blossom forth into full beauty and thus prove a serious rival. Already the latter showed signs of realising the power of her dawning beauty, evinced by an increasingly assured gaiety and self-confidence in her own roguish kittenish ways—characteristics, curiously enough, encouraged by the guardian elder sister, who, though strait-laced herself, seemed inclined to condone the opposite behaviour in her pretty young charge whom she had persistently indulged from an early age. The elder sister also felt some jealousy of Hagar's still highly probable chances of matrimonial happiness—which she herself had missed and was no longer likely to secure ; and, consequently, she had no objection to thrusting a more youthful rival in her marriageable sister's path.

But Hagar, despite these frustrating influences in her home life, presently found the happiness she longed for ; and meeting the one and only man at last, she poured out upon him all the wealth of a passionate love—which he, likewise, returned in full measure.

For some considerable time afterwards, therefore, the long-thwarted Hagar was intensely happy, and looked forward to the continuance of a joy that would increase with the years ; and then, an incident occurred which dimmed all the dazzling light that shone so gloriously around her, so that it seemed as though a dense black cloud had enveloped her entire world.

* * * * *

One day, it happened that the three sisters were sitting together on the steps outside their house—or, rather, the eldest and the youngest sat chatting together in their usual confidential manner, while Hagar sat apart, knowing herself to be excluded from their secret confidences and brooding over the fact. Despite the recent happiness her lover had brought her, she still longed for the sympathy of her sisters, and would gladly have shared her joy with them ; but they still regarded her as one apart. Both, too, were jealous of her unexpected happiness—the elder because she herself would never know such joy, and the younger because she resented the fresh beauty that Love had brought to one older than herself and because her own quickly budding and more undoubted charm had not yet secured her the admiration her pleasure-loving nature demanded. She almost longed to cut her sister out ; and, presently, she was filled with excitement as a curious chance of doing so seemed about to occur.

Seeing Hagar's lover approaching towards her own side of the steps, she suddenly became bright and kittenish in her manner and began to indulge in playful antics with her guardian sister, her bright eyes sparkling with roguish gaiety, so that her beauty seemed more brilliant than ever before. For the first time, the approaching young man appeared to realise the astounding attractions of this teen-age girl ; and, dazzled by her fresh beauty and delighted with her pretty kittenish ways, he moved towards her with a smile, almost as one in a dream.

The young girl was more than pleased with the admiration she had so unexpectedly inspired in her sister's lover ; and she continued to entrance him with her dainty, almost unconscious, flirtatiousness—not so much, probably, from a sense of triumph as from the natural playfulness one would expect from a kitten eager for notice and loving a game.

The elder sister was equally pleased with the success of her youthful charge, and rather encouraged her in this, her first flirtation—regardless of the fact that it was with one already promised to another. Nevertheless, her natural sense of prudery shortly returned ; and she gently took the young girl by the arm and led her into the house, though with a graciously indulgent smile upon the still dazzled young man.

The kittenish young girl likewise cast many encouraging parting glances upon her unexpected admirer—now shy, now coquettish, but all of the eager, half-questioning, half-inviting kind. Then she withdrew her hand from his involuntary grasp slowly and reluctantly, and bestowed many more alluring backward glances upon him as she finally vanished within the house—leaving the young man silent and motionless, as though still lost in an exquisite dream of beauty.

Meanwhile, the whole of this charming little scene had been observed by the astonished and almost stunned Hagar, whose passionately loving heart was thus stabbed through and through as she watched, with fascinated intensity, the growing admiration in the eyes of her lover as he gazed upon the fresh damask-rose beauty and dazzling charms of her suddenly-blooming young sister.

Could it be that he had forgotten her own existence already on beholding the loveliness and attractive gaiety of a mere child ? But was the latter a mere child now ? Had she not in that same moment miraculously opened as a flower-bud does and revealed her former veiled glories to the devouring gaze of one who adored beauty ? And Hagar, with despair in her heart, realised that this revelation of exquisite beauty had filled the gazer upon it with an awed delight.

Seeing her lover thus rapt and lost to his surroundings

and even to her own presence, the unhappy young woman—now filled with an agonised disillusionment and an overwhelming grief, believing him already to have transferred his avowed love for herself to her young sister—staggered aside in an abandonment of woe.

It was at this psychological moment that she was caught on the rebound by another admirer, a somewhat unscrupulous young libertine who had long desired to possess her. Having arrived upon the scene at the same time as Hagar's lover, he also had observed all that had passed between the latter and the beautiful but kittenish young girl.

Now eager to take advantage of Hagar's disappointment, despair, and possible resentment, this chance opportunist led her aside and pleaded his own suit so successfully that the stricken young woman recklessly agreed to give herself to him. Impetuously believing her lover to be false to her and seeing him now wandering away still apparently wrapped in the sudden ecstasy that had so strangely seized him and, consequently, thinking herself no longer wanted, she did not care what happened to her ; and, eager only to escape from the immediate scene of her disillusionment, she allowed herself thus to be led away by one she could never love, giving herself up to his desires as though still in the midst of some horrible nightmare.

* * * * *

When Hagar eventually returned to her home, she was more wretched than ever before. All the gossiping neighbours shunned her and even pointed fingers of scorn at her—encouraged in their censorious attitude by her elder sister who, always stern and unsympathetic towards her, did nothing to mitigate her present unhappiness.

As a further example of petty self-righteousness, the

older woman even tried to prevent the unhappy Hagar from so much as touching her young sister, as though fearing contamination for the latter—whom she ostentatiously drew aside whenever the trio happened to meet or pass one another.

For some time, the unfortunate, passion-tossed Hagar seemed to be on the verge of a mental collapse ; and then, almost as suddenly as it had descended, the black cloud of misery that had enwrapped her was lifted, and the bright sunshine of joy broke through upon her once more.

* * * * *

Meanwhile, Hagar's lover had quickly awakened from the sudden ecstatic state that had rendered him unconscious of his surroundings on the occasion of his fateful meeting with his *fiancée's* fair young sister.

It was true that he had, for the moment, been enthralled by the latter's exquisite budding beauty and youthful gay playfulness—but this was merely the fascination of an artist for beauty for its own sake, and of human delight in the sight of irresponsible kittenish joy in life. His heart and passions had never been touched thereby for a moment—for all his love was already truly given to Hagar. Even though he had temporarily forgotten the latter's presence for the moment when gazing upon the charming picture of her beautiful young sister, he had still remained her lover, and hers alone. The young girl was merely an exquisite picture that had delighted his artistic senses only ; but Hagar was still the real human being he loved.

When, however, his contemplation of this fair picture was over and he awakened from the almost trance-like effect it had had upon him, he found Hagar herself had vanished ; and it was a long time before he saw her again. Then, later on, when he learned that, in her despair, she had recklessly given herself to another man —whom he knew she could not love—he was grief-stricken that such a terrible fate should have befallen his beloved one and that he, in his own temporary aberration, should have led her into so tragic a misconception of his actions.

But he did not despair of a happy issue from this woeful state of affairs ; and, for this purpose, he diligently sought for his lost love. When, at last, one day, having learnt that she had returned to the neighbourhood, he came face to face with Hagar outside her own home, alone and deserted by all, he hastened towards her eagerly, with open arms, explaining her misconception of his attitude to her young sister and passionately declaring once more his own deep, unchanged love for her.

And when Hagar realised from her lover's attitude how impetuously mistaken she had been and knew that he still loved her, she forgot all her past woes ; and the now happy lovers fell into each other's arms with rapture and thankfulness that their black cloud of misery and misunderstanding had vanished for ever and that the light of true joy illumined their hearts once more.

ROMEO AND JULIET

DURING the fourteenth century, in the City of Verona, a bitter private feud had existed for many years between the two noble families of Capulet and Montague ; and to such an extent was this carried that even in the streets open brawls frequently occurred when partisans of the rival houses met.

One evening a masked ball was being held at the palatial home of Lord Capulet ; and though of course uninvited, a young and romantic member of the Montague family, named Romeo, decided to attend these revels out of sheer bravado. Disguised in the garb of a pilgrim, therefore, and duly masked, he went thither, accompanied by his friends, Mercutio and Benvolio, likewise disguised and masked.

As the young men made their way to the ball, Mercutio—who was a charming youth, gay and nimble-witted—entertained his friends by describing to them his poetic ideas of Queen Mab's visitations to them in their dreams ; and he even made them linger on the way by enacting some of his charming fantasies for them. At length, however, they arrived at their destination, where, owing to their disguise, they were admitted without question into the house of the family foe ; and, for awhile, nobody knew that a hated Montague was taking part in the revels.

Very soon, Romeo noticed a beautiful young girl among the guests, with whom he almost instantly fell in love. He spoke her praises aloud to his friends ; and his voice was recognised by a kinsman of the Capulets, a fiery-tempered youth named Tybalt, who immediately challenged him. Peace, however, was quickly restored by Lord Capulet, who revered the laws of hospitality and would not permit even an enemy to be harmed in his own house.

Romeo now learned that the lovely maiden he already adored was none other than the daughter of Lord Capulet, and that her name was Juliet ; and he presently secured an opportunity of being presented to her, and found her as sweet and gentle as she was beautiful.

Though dismayed that he had thus fallen in love with the daughter of his family's enemy, Romeo determined to see Juliet again ; and after leaving the masquerade with his friends, he returned alone, after the festivities had ended, and made his way into the orchard garden that surrounded the Capulet mansion, where he wandered awhile, absorbed in the new joy that now filled his heart so completely.

To his delight, Juliet herself presently appeared on a balcony that led from her sleeping chamber. She, also, was rejoicing in the strange sweet love which had likewise so suddenly filled her whole being at the ardent gaze of the handsome young man garbed as a pilgrim, who had conversed with her at the ball ; and she wished to breathe forth her happy thoughts into the moonlit night. Even though she had already learned, to her equal dismay, that the noble youth who had so quickly won her heart was the son of her family's foe and that she ought to hate rather than love him, she knew that her feelings for him would never change. Realising the difficulties in the way of her happiness, however, she murmured aloud softly :

" O Romeo, Romeo ! wherefore art thou Romeo ?
   Deny thy father and refuse thy name ;
   Or if thou wilt not, be but sworn my love,

And I'll no longer be a Capulet.
'Tis but thy name that is my enemy :
Thou art thyself, though not a Montague.
What's Montague ? it is not hand, nor foot,
Nor arm, nor face, nor any other part
Belonging to a man. O, be some other name.
What's in a name ? that which we call a rose
By any other name would smell as sweet ;
So Romeo would, were he not Romeo called,
Retain that dear perfection which he owes,
Without that title.—Romeo, doff thy name ;
And for thy name, which is no part of thee,
Take all myself ! "

On hearing these words, which proved to him that Juliet returned his love, Romeo now made his presence known to her. Next moment, he had scaled the balcony and had clasped her in his arms.

Although Juliet had been promised by her parents to a young man of noble family, named Paris, she gladly listened to Romeo's passionate declaration of love, and vowed she would wed none other than he. Then, in answer to the impatient calls of her old nurse from within the chamber, she reluctantly tore herself away from his embrace and retired to rest.

Next day, Romeo visited a good old monk named Friar Laurence in his cell in a neighbouring monastery, and begged that he would arrange a secret marriage that same day between himself and Juliet ; and the kindly Friar agreed to do so, hoping that such a union might end the feud between the two families. Then a message was sent secretly to Juliet, who visited the monastery cell later that day ; and there the good Friar married her to Romeo, and gave the happy pair his own and the Church's blessing.

When, after a last loving embrace, Juliet had returned

to her own home, Romeo made his way to a certain street where he had arranged to meet his friends Mercutio and Benvolio. Here he found, to his dismay, that they were hotly engaged in another encounter with the fiery-tempered young Capulet, Tybalt, who still resented their intrusion of the evening before. Before he could intervene, Mercutio fell, mortally wounded ; and, full of grief and indignation at this untimely end of his beloved friend, Romeo drew his own sword and, furiously attacking Tybalt, dealt him a death blow likewise.

News of this encounter and its fatal results quickly spread ; and on the arrival of the Duke of Verona, who had been summoned by the watch, sentence of immediate banishment was pronounced upon Romeo.

Now full of despair, but compelled to depart from Verona, Romeo determined to see his beloved Juliet once more before leaving the city. When darkness fell, therefore, he repaired once more to the Capulet garden, and there he was joined by the now weeping Juliet who had already heard the terrible news. The lovers could spend together only a short time ; and then, with a last passionate embrace, Romeo was obliged to depart. He made his way to Mantua, where, by means of friends and messengers, he could receive news of his secret fair young bride, from whom such a cruel fate had parted him.

Juliet now found herself in ever-increasing difficulties. Her parents determined that her marriage to her betrothed, Paris, should no longer be delayed ; and the nuptials were announced to take place in a few days' time.

It was in vain that the distracted Juliet, fearing to reveal her secret marriage to Romeo, the enemy of her family, pleaded her extreme youth, her indifference to

Paris, and the family mourning for their kinsman, Tybalt ; her parents were adamant in their command that she should be wedded to Paris on the appointed day, and preparations for the marriage went forward.

Then it was that the unhappy Juliet bethought herself of the kindly old monk, Friar Laurence ; and she paid another secret visit to his cell. Eager to assist the lovers, the old monk gave Juliet a phial containing a potion which he bade her to swallow on her bridal day, since it would cause her to fall into a deep trance-like slumber—with the result that her friends, thinking her then to be dead, would place her on a bier in the family vault. Here, on awakening, after a lapse of forty-eight hours, she should be rescued by Romeo and secretly conveyed by him to Mantua, where they would dwell together in happiness. The good old Friar promised to send messengers to Romeo with news of their plan, bidding him to come secretly to the vault on the night arranged and rescue her ; and Juliet thankfully took the phial and returned to her home, where she now agreed to her parents' plans.

When the day of her marriage to Paris arrived, she secretly drank the potion she had received from Friar Laurence ; and then she moved serenely among the assembled wedding guests. Presently, however, the drug took effect, and lovely Juliet, in her dazzling bridal robes, fell to the ground as though dead. Full of consternation, the guests departed ; and the grief-stricken parents, believing their beloved daughter to be indeed dead, caused her to be placed on a bier and carried away to the family vault to await burial.

Friar Laurence, after waiting to hear how his plot had succeeded, now sent a messenger to Mantua to give the news to Romeo and to bid him come at once to the Capulet vault to rescue his fair bride on her awakening.

But the messenger arrived too late. Romeo had already received an earlier message from another friend giving him the terrible news current in Verona that Juliet had died suddenly on her bridal day ; and he was filled with the utmost grief and despair. He resolved, however, to look once more upon the beautiful features of his beloved one ; and, defying his sentence of banishment, he rode off at a frantic speed to Verona, arriving there at midnight of the second day since Juliet had been reported dead.

Securing a torch and making his way to the Capulet vault, he was disturbed on finding another visitor there before him. Not at first recognising this intruder as Count Paris—who had likewise come to mourn at the side of his lost bride—Romeo drew his sword and rushed madly upon him. After a short but furious encounter, Paris was slain ; then, taking up the torch to look upon his fallen antagonist, Romeo felt great remorse as he now recognised the features of Paris and remembered that this noble youth had also loved the dead maiden.

After this, he knelt, overcome with grief and despair, beside the bier of Juliet, and gazed for the last time upon her lovely features. Then, resolved to live no longer without her, he drew forth a phial of poison he had already secured from an apothecary during his journey, and quickly swallowed its contents ; and, next moment, he fell dead beside his beloved one.

A few minutes later, Juliet awakened from the deep trance-slumber simulating death induced by the drug given her by Friar Laurence ; and, slowly raising herself, she gazed fearfully upon her gruesome surroundings. Then, on beholding the dead body of her beloved Romeo lying beside her, the empty phial of poison still clasped in his hand, she was horror-struck ; and she clasped his limp form in her arms. Full of despair, she kissed his lips again and again, hoping thus to imbibe some of the poison he had swallowed—for she had no desire to live on without him.

Meanwhile, the commotion within the tomb, occasioned by the encounter between Romeo and Paris, had been heard by the watch, who had hastened to bring both Capulets and Montagues to the spot ; and, presently hearing the sound of alarmed voices and approaching hurrying footsteps, Juliet became distracted and desperate. Finding the remains of poison on her beloved one's lips to be unavailing, she snatched at the dagger he wore and plunged it into her heart, falling dead beside the body of Romeo as the kinsfolk of them both now hastened into the vault.

* * * * *

Horror-struck at the tragic sight that met their eyes, the bereaved parents were filled with woe ; and over the dead bodies of their children, both Capulets and Montagues now joined hands in remorseful humility and solemnly renounced their selfish family feud for ever.

BAR AUX FOLIES-BERGERE
(*Bar at the Folies-Bergère*)

THE bar of *The Folies-Bergère* in Paris, during the early months of the fateful year 1870, was one of the liveliest bohemian resorts in that still Gay City. Actors, actresses, and artists of all kinds frequented it; and its *clientèle* was celebrated everywhere for an irresponsible lightheartedness.

One day, however, before these bohemian folk began to pour in towards evening, the barmaid in charge found herself alone behind the counter, with nobody to serve. For a short time, she seemed lost in her own thoughts; and these were none too happy, to judge from her serious expression and the occasional sighs she gave vent to. She was in love with the smart and handsome waiter who shared her duties; but she had little hope of her love being returned, with so many charming and lively lady clients engaging his attention so frequently. To be sure, she was a good-looking young woman herself; but the competition was too great. What chance had she amidst so much elegant feminine glamour?

With another deep sigh, the love-sick barmaid quickly pulled herself together and set to work to put her counter into first-rate order, in readiness for the early evening inrush she knew she might expect. Again she dusted her already immaculately shining glasses and bottles, and polished up the gleaming metal handles and lids of the various fitments upon her up-to-date counter.

She next glanced in the mirror to see if her appearance was as spick and span as usual. As she did so a couple of her regular customers, a rather disreputable bohemian pair known to her as Gustave and Adolphe, sauntered in—lurched would perhaps have been a better description of their gait, since they seemed already to have partaken of as much strong drink as was good for them, a fact the experienced barmaid could plainly see even from the corner of her eye.

Nevertheless, when they flopped into a couple of chairs at one of the small tables that were set around the sides of the room and ordered further drinks, she willingly enough served them.

Then, as she turned back towards the bar once more, her heart gave a sudden bound, as Valentin, the gay and *débonnaire* waiter, came briskly through the doorway, complete with tray of glittering glasses and a spotless folded napkin over his arm. What a handsome fellow he was ; how lively and fascinating his manner ; and how deeply she loved him ! Would he have time to have a word with her ?

But the dashing waiter, despite his charm for every member of the opposite sex he came in contact with, also had a keen eye for business ; and having almost immediately been followed by a lady customer, he proceeded to take her order without delay, since she was an important client.

Not only important, but extremely pretty, was Grille d'Egout, a member of the smart *can-can* troupe now performing at the adjoining theatre. So Valentin soon returned with this charming customer's drink ; and, as he placed the glass beside her, he mischievously stole a quick kiss from her—knowing well enough that she would not resent it, since all the pretty girls who came into the bar adored the lively waiter.

Grille was soon joined by a couple of her *can-can* colleagues ; and then the sound of chatter and laughter was heard—even the misty-eyed, foggy-brained bohemians, Gustave and Adolphe, now roused themselves and began to exchange *risqué* stories.

Seeing everybody thus happy, Valentin the waiter invited the barmaid to come forth from behind the counter to dance a few steps with him—which she gladly did, even though she knew herself to be merely a stop-gap and was aware that her now seemingly eager, but much too volatile, admirer would soon be bestowing his always welcome attentions elsewhere. Still, he was hers for the moment, and it was a joy to be in his arms once more and to be whirled around by him a few turns—for he was an exquisite dancer.

But this deliriously happy moment came to an end all too soon ; and the arrival of fresh customers quickly recalled the dancing couple to their duties—Valentin light-hearted and all smiling briskness once more ; and the barmaid likewise smiling, but with an aching heart.

Among the newcomers was an extremely lively elderly gentleman, obviously out for a spree ; and he was followed by La Goulue, the lovely Star of the Theatre and the Toast of the *Quartier Latin*. This lady was glamorous indeed, with brilliant black eyes, scarlet lips, and a seductively dazzling smile ; and she was dressed in the height of the fashion of her period, with voluminous frilly skirts of the richest materials and colourings.

The gay old gentleman, so obviously out for a frivolous frolic, was delighted on beholding such a galaxy of feminine beauty around him ; and he called for a generous supply of champagne for everybody. This was quickly forthcoming, so that the merry sound of popping corks was now added to the sound of unrestrained laughter and the buzz of conversation. The *can-can* girls quickly obliged him by sitting on his knee, tweaking his hirsute adornments, and every now and again whirling him about in their hilarious dances.

When, however, the lively girls tried to inveigle him into dancing the *can-can* with them, their elderly beau declined the honour and breathlessly dropped into a chair, leaving the entire dancing space available for their own performance—which was enthusiastically applauded by all the company. Never had any of them seen the *can-can* danced with such spirit—nor such saucy revelations of high-tossed frilly underwear and silken-stockinged dainty limbs.

The gay old gentleman was delighted and eagerly plied the pretty dancers with more champagne to revive them as they breathlessly flopped about him at the end of their performance.

It was soon evident that the waiter, Valentin, always over-susceptible to feminine charm, was completely enthralled by the brilliant, voluptuous beauty of La Goulue, the famous Star of the *Folies-Bergère*: and again the heart of the loving but unloved barmaid sank within her, as she watched the eager ministrations of the seemingly bewitched young man. As he served the lovely actress, he bent over her tenderly; and soon, he abandoned all pretence of attending to her wants as a waiter and indulged openly in a violent flirtation with her—to which she as eagerly responded.

When, presently, at the request of the company in general, the brilliant Star generously rose and performed a wonderful solo dance, the enraptured Valentin gazed upon her every movement with passionate delight; and when she presently invited him to join her as a dancing partner, his enjoyment was so obvious that the heart of the barmaid yet once again felt a stab of acute pain. She continued to perform her duties at the bar, however, with brisk deftness and a smiling face; but she could not prevent a brief glance of sadness and a half-gesture of entreaty to remain when, presently, the dance having ended, the entranced waiter left the room arm-in-arm with his seductive partner. But he did not even see her action, never lifting his passion-filled eyes for one moment from the lovely La Goulue ; and the barmaid turned again to her duties with an aching heart.

The Star and her infatuated escort were soon followed by the *can-can* dancers and their elderly admirer, together with the other customers who had drifted in from time to time, attracted by the lively sounds of revelry ; and, presently, the room became empty once more, save for the tired barmaid and the two bohemian *habitués*, Adolphe and Gustave. The latter disreputable pair now sprawled in a huddled heap at the table where they had sat all through the evening ; and an odd snore or two revealed the fact that they had fallen asleep.

The barmaid, occupied with her own sad thoughts scarcely heeded them as she now set about the task of clearing up and tidying her bar once more.

Presently, however, an old charwoman came in with a bucket of water and a cloth, and proceeded to swab the tables. Seeing the two dozing customers still at their table, she went up to them and sprinkled them liberally with water—in the matter-of-fact manner of one who had performed a similar service many times before.

This timely baptism of water awakened the two bohemians, who at once rose slowly and shook themselves as though equally well accustomed to receiving such a service ; and having each meticulously produced and placed a visiting-card on the table, they lurched away arm-in-arm, with unsteady steps.

By this time, the weary barmaid had finished her last job ; but having set her bar in perfect order, she did not depart immediately. Instead, she remained for awhile resting her elbows upon the counter, wrapped in her own sad thoughts and wondering whether she would ever get used to the aching void in her heart.

CHECKMATE

LOVE and Death once met to play a game of chess, with the mortal lives of human beings as pieces in the game. They sat on opposite sides of a table in a shadowy secret place, with the chessboard between them—Love, fair and beautiful; and Death, dark and sinister. Both were dressed as warriors in battle array.

The fateful game was over quickly. Love made the first move ; then sat back to await, with bated breath, the reply of his dread opponent.

It came, all too soon—sure, pitiless, and inexorable. The cold bony fingers of Death closed deliberately over the piece he knew would give him the victory, and moved it slowly into position ; then he, too, sat back and waited.

For a few agonised moments, Love pored over the problem so cleverly set, hopefully seeking a way out—then sprang up with a cry of despair. There *was* no way out ; it was Checkmate ! The dark and sinister warrior had won.

* * * * *

Here is the story of the game played by the two immortal warriors, Love and Death. with their human Pieces.

Upon a chequered floor came all the Pieces to take part in the chess-game encounter between the Reds and the Blacks. The gay little Pawns were the first to come tripping into position. They were light-hearted, as usual, for they felt no responsibility for these war activities that had so suddenly blown up in their midst. They left all the serious business of war to their officers and betters—the high and mighty Knights, the Castles, the Bishops, and the Royal Personages who ruled over them.

They were glad to be merely Pawns in the Game; so they skipped lightly and gaily into the positions allotted to them—and if the Red Pawns and the Black Pawns made faces at one another, well, that was only natural, since they were on opposite sides.

When the two Red Knights had taken up their positions next, they were followed by the two Black Knights. The latter were haughty and arrogant; and it was easy to see that they belonged to the aggressors in the coming conflict.

The same behaviour was to be noted in the case of the Black Queen, who next entered with a regal air. She was beautiful, but proud, and her movements quickly betrayed the fact that she was also unscrupulous and would use every means in her power, fair or foul—even her own beauty—to bring about the downfall of her enemies.

Almost immediately, the Black Queen began to make use of the latter feminine weapons. It was plain from the start that one of the Red Knights was obviously enthralled by her exquisite beauty and had conceived a sudden passion for her; and, quickly observing this pleasant fact, she sought to undermine his loyalty by engaging in a flirtation with him. She smiled graciously upon him, and carelessly let fall a red rose at his feet as she passed him by. The Red Knight, delighted by her apparent favour, snatched up the rose and pressed it passionately to his lips as she moved away, accompanied by her own Black Knight.

This sentimental interlude was quickly ended by the arrival of the Red Royalties. The Red Pawns came forward with their standard and set it up behind the throne now draped in readiness for its royal occupants. The Red Bishops and two Castles next took up their positions ; and the Red Knight and his companion Knight stood together before the throne upon the entrance of their King and Queen.

The Red King and Queen were both rather 'weak characters, and showed little capability of being able to deal with their present dangerous position. It was quite obvious that they had no desire for the coming contest and were totally unprepared for it. The Red King was old and tottering ; and his Queen, though braver and less nervous than her royal mate, was likewise not of a strong personality.

The battle-ground having been set, the contest began. The Black Queen, with some of her company, led the attack herself with fierce determination ; and she soon succeeded in weakening the defence line of the Reds.

This greatly scared the Red King ; but, though he moved forward both his Bishops to help his quickly-wavering line, his position went from bad to worse. A greater disaster still occurred presently when the Red Queen, weak though she was, bravely went to the aid of her already almost defeated lord, and begged that mercy might be shown to the tottering old King. But the Black Queen scornfully refused to listen to her plea, and, instead, handed her over as a captive to one of the Black Knights.

Then it was that the Red Knight who loved the Black Queen realised that the latter meant to be ruthless and would even slay the unhappy weak Red Monarch ; and his chivalry rising above his own private passion, he now boldly challenged his beloved one to mortal single combat.

The Black Queen accepted his challenge ; and a fearful duel began. The Black Queen was a daring and skilful fighter ; but she soon realised that the Red Knight was even more skilful still and knew that she must resort to cunning in order to maintain the success she had already gained. Just as the Red Knight was about to strike the fatal blow that would have stretched her dead at his feet, she suddenly smiled so sweetly and alluringly upon him that all his former passion for her returned with double force.

Although the Red King and his anxious companions loudly cried upon him in distressed tones to slay the royal enemy now at his mercy, the Red Knight could not bring himself to strike the fatal blow at one so beautiful and well-beloved—and one whom he now believed must surely return his love since she smiled thus sweetly upon him.

Despite the now frenzied cries from the Red King and his followers, the love-sick Red Knight gently lowered his sword to the ground, expecting his beloved opponent to do the same.

But the Black Queen had not love, but hatred, in her heart ; and having thus gained by her false trick the few moments she required, she instantly drew a dagger and drove it into the heart of the Red Knight, who fell dead to the ground.

A newcomer appeared upon the scene. This was the sinister figure of Death, who followed in triumph the body of the unfortunate Red Knight as it was borne away by his defeated followers.

The early end of the wretched Red King now seemed imminent ; but the Black Queen, with the triumphant sadistic cruelty of a cat with a mouse, chased him hither and thither, calling upon her warriors to block his paths of escape at every point or turn. The glory of her victory would certainly have been the greater had she now shown magnanimity. Instead, she continued to reveal only a desire to torture a defeated fellow sovereign.

The exhausted old Red King, driven from pillar to post by his relentless and gloating enemy, at length found himself flung back upon his own throne once more, alone and helpless. Here, however, he enjoyed for one exalted moment a brief return of the strength of youth and of the truly regal spirit he had almost forgotten he once possessed. Struggling painfully to his feet again, he brandished his sword for the last time and boldly defied his enemies as they were about to fall upon him. Then, he wavered and tottered, and finally fell to the ground, dead.

Thus, the ruthless Black Queen was baulked of her prey ; and the struggle ended in Checkmate.

THE HAUNTED BALLROOM

A MERRY party had taken possession of the sombre but splendid old family mansion-home of the Master of Tregennis. The guests were all young and lively ; for they had come mainly at the invitation of young Tregennis, the Master's son and heir, who was still little more than a youth.

The gay young guests all greatly admired the beautiful old house ; and they were intrigued by its old-world atmosphere—so different from the modern homes they had themselves come from. They were even still more intrigued on learning that one of the largest rooms in the house was kept locked-up and never occupied ; and there was a real thrill when the rumour went round that this mysterious unused room was haunted.

Nothing would satisfy some of these light-hearted, careless young people than that they should be allowed to enter this so-called haunted ballroom ; and late one evening three ladies of the party persuaded their youthful host to lead them thither. It was in vain that young Tregennis declared his father had forbidden him to enter the room ; the eager ladies were so insistent that at last he agreed to their demand—though somewhat reluctantly. Waiting until his father was otherwise occupied, he secured the key, led the way to the old ballroom, and unlocked the door.

On entering the room, the young intruders saw, by means of a dim light shining into it through the open door, that it was entirely bare and empty, and that thick dusty ropes of cobwebs hung like fringes from the enormous old-fashioned lustred chandelier in the centre of the ceiling. Except for some dim and dusty old family portraits hanging on the walls, there was nothing else to be seen in the room—which had obviously not been opened for a great many years and long before these sensation-craving young people were born.

The ghostly atmosphere and deep silence of the cobweb-draped room caused young Tregennis to shiver, as though apprehensive of impending eerie happenings in connection with his family ; and he tried to induce his friends to leave the room now that their curiosity was satisfied, being anxious to lock it up again. But the lively young ladies would not hear of this ; and, laughing mischievously at his obvious uneasiness, they began to dance about, stirring up the dust with their long evening gowns as they flirted their fans in a frivolous manner as though coquetting with invisible partners.

Just as their young host was becoming really distressed in his anxiety to get them safely out of the room, his father appeared in the doorway and gazed upon the intruders with much disapproval and annoyance. Dismissing his now trembling son with a dignified gesture, the Master of Tregennis gathered the young ladies together and informed them that the old ballroom had a most sinister history. The heirs to the family estates, for several successive generations past, had lost their lives by supernatural means in that same room —hence his reason for keeping it locked and unvisited.

The frivolous young ladies, on hearing this tragic story, were now glad enough to take their departure ; and, as they slipped quietly out of the room, they shivered slightly and cast fearful glances behind them.

The Master of Tregennis stood for a few moments, alone, in the haunted ballroom, gazing into its cobwebby depths with troubled eyes, wondering whether, indeed, he might not meet his own doom therein ; then, with a philosophic shrug of his shoulders, he also departed.

* * * * *

A little later that same night, a strange transformation scene took place in the haunted ballroom. The dim, portrait-lined walls seemed to become almost transparent, so that the star-spangled sky beyond could be plainly seen ; and a pale ghostly light began to fill every part of the room. A spectral masked male figure, wearing the evening clothes of a past generation and carrying a musical conductor's baton, suddenly appeared and began to conduct an invisible orchestra. A host of ghostly dancers quickly filled the room and went through the intricate measures of weird and orgy-like dances to the strains of the wild music which now filled the air.

Just as this unearthly revel was at its height, the Master of Tregennis—wearing a dark cloak flung hastily over his shoulders—once again appeared in the doorway, having been awakened suddenly from an uneasy slumber and drawn irresistibly to the haunted ballroom.

He was instantly hailed by the strange masked conductor who told him that this spectral company awaited his leadership as host ; and, flinging off his cloak, the Master plunged into their midst, as though compelled by some unseen power. At first, he sprang with high leaps into the air and whirled himself around the room in a mad solo dance ; and then he began to dance with the other ghostly figures—most of whom he recognised as the originals of the portraits of his own ancestors of bygone days.

But not all the dancers belonged to past generations. Three of the female dancers reminded him of the three young ladies brought thither by his son earlier in the evening ; and they danced an alluring dance before him with fluttering fans. One of these ghostly fan-dancers presently began to dance alone; and the Master of Tregennis was so attracted by her unusual beauty that he seized her in his arms and rapturously whirled her round and round the room. At first the music they danced to was a voluptuous waltz measure; but soon it changed into wilder and ever wilder rhythms, and the pace grew fast and furious.

The Master of Tregennis danced on and on, as though under a spell; and so enthralled was he by the beauty and irresistible charm of his phantom partner, that he did not notice she was actually holding him in a death grip from which he could not escape. Nor did he notice the triumphant glances of the other whirling figures about him. Compelled by the irresistible occult forces around him, he continued to dance on, faster and ever faster, until his human frame could endure the strain no longer; and, at last, he staggered and fell to the ground, dead.

Then, all the spectral dancers and the sinister conductor suddenly vanished; the semi-transparent star-spangled walls returned to an opaque and dusty appearance once more; the ghostly light faded away; and the haunted ballroom was left, dark, silent, and empty, save for the body of its new victim—yet another Master of Tregennis.

*   *   *   *   *

The sinister sound of ghostly chimes coming from the haunted ballroom awakened the sleeping household, the members of which, rushing thither in alarm, were filled with horror on entering and beholding its lifeless occupant. The three young lady guests, in particular, shuddered regretfully, and even self-accusingly, as they looked upon this seemingly gruesome sequel to their light-hearted evening frolic; and they cast glances of remorseful sympathy upon their youthful and sadly-stricken host, as though humbly craving his pardon. Then they turned away and followed the retainers who were reverently bearing away the dead body of the Master ; and the youth was left alone.

But young Tregennis heeded them not, nor even noticed their quiet departure. Lost to the world around him, he remained staring blindly into the darkness of that fateful room ; for he realised that he was himself now the Master of Tregennis and that, sooner or later, the doom of his ancestors likewise awaited him in the Haunted Ballroom.

JOB

JOB, a rich and powerful Shepherd-Chief, sat one evening towards sunset with his wife in the shadow of a mighty tree, not far from his comfortable dwelling-place. There were mountains to be seen in the distance, whereon his flocks of sheep were grazing contentedly; and nearer at hand were the spreading pastures, where his vast herds of cattle fed in equal contentment. Nearby, also, fields of waving corn were to be seen.

Job was a very wealthy chief, and his worldly possessions were great; he was likewise a good and God-fearing man and had always led an upright life, doing many good deeds and eschewing evil. Everyone spoke well of him.

So, perhaps, it was not wonderful that Job should feel happy and well-pleased with himself, as he sat with his wife that evening, while the sun went down in a blaze of glory behind the mountains. He felt happier and even more prosperous still when he was presently joined by his seven stalwart sons and his three fair daughters; and, when the young people began to indulge in an evening revel of dance and song, his heart swelled with pride in his fine family and in the luxury and comfort with which he had been able to surround them.

At length, he arose and, stretching out his arms towards the rose-coloured skies, uttered his evening praises and thanks to God; and his wife and children joined him in his prayers. Nevertheless, Job could not prevent some self-righteousness from mingling with his thanksgiving; nor could he help feeling a certain amount of self-pride in his own worldly achievements, and in the many good deeds he had done.

As the light faded and darkness crept on apace, Job and his family folded their cloaks around them and settled down to sleep.

But, strange to say, their slumbers were not so peaceful as usual ; and Job, the good-living, prosperous Chief, was troubled with disturbing dreams of coming evil for the first time in his life.

* * * * *

That same night, Job was granted a vision of his own Spiritual Self, up in the heavens, seated on a plain throne in the midst of the Children of God, who danced before him. A flight of steps seemed to lead down to the earth ; and at the bottom of these steps there was seen to be the handsome, but sinister, figure of Satan, the Spirit of Evil, the Angel of Darkness ; and soon it became evident that the latter was jealous of the far-famed goodness of Job. He declared cynically that the Godhead was being deceived and that Job was only good because all had gone well and easily with him during his life ; and he demanded that the righteous and prosperous Chief should be tested by ill-fortune falling upon him—when the good man would probably turn from his Heavenly Master and curse Him. The testing of Job having been agreed upon, the vision faded from the sleeper's troubled consciousness.

But the heavenly scene remained, and Satan was left triumphant in the fact that he was about to bring evil and misery upon one who had never before suffered trial and tribulation. Then, filled with evil joy, and accompanied by thunder-claps and lightning-flashes, he set forth eagerly to carry out the dreadful plans he had conceived in the blackness of his heart.

* * * * *

Next day, the sons and daughters of Job were holding high revels at some distance from their comfortable home. The sun was shining brightly, and they were happier than usual as they danced, and sang, and feasted with their friends ; and they had no thought of evil.

But Evil was about to fall upon thcm unawares. Satan, the Dark Angel, descended upon the earth ; and, at his command, a band of murderous robbers fell upon the revelling sons and daughters of Job and slew them all.

* * * * *

Again, Job sat with his wife near his home, still disturbed by his ill dreams of the past night.

Suddenly, three messengers appeared before him, bringing the terrible tidings, not only of the loss of his beloved children, but also of the destruction of his flocks and herds, and of all his worldly goods " at one fell swoop."

At first, the stricken Chief was so full of grief at the loss of his beloved children and of dismay at the destruction of his means of wealth, that he could find no words to say ; and it was not until three of his former friends appeared before him in the guise of Comforters that he was aroused from his apathy.

When he had been prosperous, these fair-weather friends had been full of his praises ; but now that evil had fallen upon him, it was a different story. Though they pretended to have come to him as Comforters, they now hypocritically declared that such dire misfortunes were not likely to have befallen him had he been the righteous man they had formerly believed him to be ; and they soon began to rebuke him severely, and to blame him for having done evil things that had displeased God.

This unjust and hypocritical condemnation of him by his former fawning friends caused the now unfortunate Job to cry out, not only against their smug injustice, but also against the injustice of God for permitting such woes to come upon one who had always endeavoured to live a good and useful life ; and he drove away his false Comforters in righteous anger.

When the latter had gone, he invoked a further Vision of the Godhead ; but this time, being still filled with anger and rebellion, he was shown instead a vision of Satan, surrounded by evil followers and gazing down upon his grim handiwork in triumph ; and he fell back in horrified dismay.

*   *   *   *   *

Presently, however, a real Comforter came to the unhappy Job. This was Elihu, Son of the Morning, a beautiful and truly virtuous being, whose fair countenance shone with the radiance of one who knew, served, and loved God.

Elihu pointed out to Job that true virtue lay in the thoughts of the heart as well as in the doing of good deeds ; and though he gently reproved him for his injustice to God and for doubting the Divine Wisdom in allowing misfortune to fall upon him, he did not accuse him of having done evil deeds. He explained that calamities were often sent to try the patience of those they fell upon, to strengthen their characters, and to make them feel sympathy with other unfortunate folk ; and Job then began to realise that he had done wrong in railing against the Divine Will. He also realised that before these terrible misfortunes had overwhelmed him, he had nursed too much pride in his heart because of his successful life and numerous good deeds, and that he had been lacking in true humility.

Therefore, the stricken Chief now sincerely repented of his spiritual misdeeds, and humbly begged God to pardon him. His prayers were heard ; and he was granted yet another Heavenly Vision, in which he now beheld the Godhead enthroned in glory and surrounded by Angels and the happily dancing Children of God.

Even as he gazed upon this glorious vision, he beheld Satan, the cause and instigator of the evils that had befallen him, come forward and triumphantly announce his victory over the famous Shepherd Chief.

But having already accepted the humble repentance of Job, the Godhead now poured forth Divine Wrath upon the Tempter ; and, scorning the latter's mocking pretence of homage, He stretched forth His arm and, amidst flashes of lightning, the Dark Angel staggered back and rolled to the bottom of the glittering staircase once more.

* * * * *

And now, joy returned to the repentant and humbled Job. All his flocks and herds, his waving cornfields, and his worldly goods were restored to him ; and, greatest joy of all, his beloved sons and daughters were likewise given back to him and his devoted wife.

Great rejoicings were now held by this happily reunited family ; and in the midst of their joy, they offered up homage and thanksgivings to the Divine Godhead, Who, in His wisdom, had seen fit to part them asunder and to bring them together again in an even stronger bond of Love.

And special thanksgivings came from the once over-proud and wealthy Shepherd-Chief himself, who had passed through the gloomy Darkness of Misfortune, and had emerged, purified and with humility in his heart, into the Light of true Spiritual Happiness.

ORPHEUS AND EURYDICE

WHEN Orpheus, the most famous Musician of Ancient Classical Greece, learned that his beloved wife, the beautiful nymph, Eurydice, had died from the bite of a poisonous snake he was filled with despair. Even the exquisite music he made upon his lyre could not comfort him—Music so enthrallingly magical that not only did it make wild beasts become as tame as lambs, but even caused the forest trees to uproot themselves and leap into the air, and the ancient rocks to dance! When Orpheus struck his lyre the wildest tempests were calmed and the tossing waves of the ocean ran smoothly once more ; and evil thoughts in the hearts of men were transformed to thoughts of loving-kindness instead.

But Orpheus could not make music that would bring back joy to his own torn heart ; and as he stood at the tomb of his lovely Eurydice he laid his lyre on the stone steps that led therein, and bowed his head sadly as he called frantically upon his beloved one to return to him.

So full of woe was he that he scarcely noted the elaborate rites that were being performed at the burial service, or who the mourners were who placed white flowers upon the tomb ; nor did he notice the black-veiled figure standing at the top of the steps—who was none other than the God of Love himself.

His grief was so deep that all the light of the world was darkened for him ; but when the ceremony was over and the mourners had departed he began to rail in anger against the gods for having robbed him of his heart's treasure. Then his anger changed to entreaty, and he implored them to restore the life they had taken ; and he declared himself willing even to journey to the Under-World and to brave all the dangers that might meet him there, if only he could bring back to earth his beloved one.

Then, as he bowed his head in silent woe once more, the black-robed figure who had remained at the top of the steps, flung off his veilings and revealed the dazzling form of the God of Love—who now came forward and announced that the gods had taken pity upon him and had granted his plea.

As Orpheus looked up with hopeful joy, the God of Love added that he might journey to the Under-World, if he were brave enough to charm with his music the terrible three Furies who guarded the entrance ; but the gods commanded that when Eurydice was brought forth to him, he must not look upon her beloved features until they had both returned to earth. Should he fail to obey this command, his beloved one would be snatched back instantly to the Land of Shades, there to dwell for evermore.

Though he shuddered with horror at the thought of this last cruel and almost impossible condition, Orpheus had no fear of the dangers he might encounter ; and, snatching up his lyre, he set forth at once upon his terrible journey to the Under-World.

Many were the difficulties and perils he had to encounter before he reached the entrance to Hades ; and then came his most terrifying experience of all. Mounting guard at the gloomy cavern-like approaches to Tartarus, amidst rolling black thunder-clouds and vivid flashes of lightning, he beheld the fearsome Furies, the three Goddesses of Vengeance, who appeared as fierce blood-thirsty winged females with serpents entwined in their hair ; and these horrible creatures threatened him with menacing arms and refused to allow him to pass through the portals they guarded. It was in vain that Orpheus pleaded with them to have pity upon him and to let him go on his way to seek his beloved one. The Furies merely gloated over his bleeding heart, and still barred his way.

Then, though despairing of moving such heartless monsters, Orpheus took up his lyre and, plucking the strings, began to sing one of his own beautiful songs ; and so exquisite was his music that he charmed even these vengeful and implacable Furies. They listened enthralled, all their menacing threats gradually dying away ; and when his song came to an end, they ceased to bar his way and let him pass on into Tartarus.

Orpheus continued to sing to his lyre as he proceeded on his journey through these gloomy and terrifying regions ; and many lost and tormented souls listened to him with delight and forgot their woes as he passed them by.

At last Orpheus issued forth from the darkness of this dreadful place, and passed on to the borders of the Elysian Fields, where a soft but dazzling light pervaded the scene. Here, lovely flowers were to be seen on every side ; and celestial beings moved everywhere with joyous grace. All was happiness and peace in this exquisite abode of Departed Spirits.

As Orpheus stood there, entranced, the God of Love drew near once more, bringing Eurydice with him ; and as the hand of his beloved one was placed in his, the Maker of Sweet Music was now filled with deep happiness. But he remembered the cruel condition imposed upon him by the gods when granting his request ; and he kept his eyes averted as he began the return journey, bringing his beloved wife with him, thankful that she was thus being given back to him.

Eurydice, though overjoyed at being restored to her adored husband, was puzzled and distressed by his attitude towards her ; and she could not understand why he refused to look upon her or to embrace her as had been his wont. She even began to wonder whether he still loved her ; and she entreated him to smile upon her once more.

But Orpheus, though longing passionately to gaze upon her and to twine his loving arms around her lovely body, knew that he must not do so ; and, with an agonized heart, he continued to lead her on upwards towards the earth, with his eyes ever averted.

* * * * *

Meanwhile, a group of merry peasants and joyful children were awaiting the return of the happy lovers—for the splendid and dangerous journey of Orpheus was known to all his friends ; and, to while away the time, this welcoming company danced and played lively games.

Presently, they beheld Orpheus emerging, followed by the lovely Eurydice. The latter, however, was feeling sad, because her beloved one still refused to look upon her. Then, as they gazed, Eurydice became more importunate in her pleading for some show of affection from her seemingly indifferent husband ; and again Orpheus disregarded her entreaties, knowing that a few more steps only would bring their dreadful journey to an end.

But, alas ! Those few steps were too many ; and the last distressed pleadings of Eurydice were more than he could bear. Unable to restrain himself further, he turned to clasp her in a joyful embrace, and thus gazed upon the features he loved so well—and, by so doing, he disobeyed the instructions of the gods.

Instantly, Eurydice sank to the ground, lifeless once more ; and in that same moment, the three terrible Furies appeared and triumphantly mounted guard over her dead body.

Knowing that his beloved one was now lost to him for ever, Orpheus was overcome with woe ; and he staggered away, filled with despair, from the presence of his now sorrowful friends.

PROMENADE

THIS is a very short story about the simple doings and casual contacts of a few charming people on a bright sunny afternoon—all of which took place in a quiet woodland district not far from a town in Brittany, round about the time when Napoleon was First Consul in France.

In an open glade an elderly butterfly-hunter lay on his back on the grass eagerly conning a book about butterflies preparatory to giving chase to any such beautiful insects as he might presently observe in the woodlands around him.

He was quite alone at the moment, and seemed wrapped in his studies and lost to the world around ; but his butterfly-net lying beside him was, nevertheless, conveniently placed for instant action, if necessary.

Unaware of the old Lepidopterist's presence, a prim school mistress presently shepherded her little class of young lady pupils into this quiet glade. Seating herself carefully upon a wooden seat nearby and spreading out her skirts neatly, she gave permission to her charges to dance and play, while she watched their charming gambols with an indulgent smile.

The young ladies slung their poke-bonnets over their bare arms by the ribbon strings that bound them, as they danced about merrily, with their long muslin frocks blowing most unprimly in the breeze ; and they practised many of the intricate steps taught them by their dancing-master, and gave quite a pretty performance— which might have delighted anyone but a solemn old Lepidopterist.

Suddenly, however, a rare butterfly happened to come fluttering flirtatiously over the very head of the recumbent figure on the grass; and instantly the latter was on his feet, full of eager expectation. Seizing his butterfly-net, he rushed madly in pursuit—to the great amusement of the young ladies, who laughed merrily as they watched his comical antics until he vanished into the woods beyond. Their watchful governess, however, was filled with consternation at this most unexpected interruption by a member of the opposite sex—even though an elderly one; and she hurriedly gathered her young charges into their usual formal " crocodile " once more and led them away to seek an even quieter spot.

No sooner had the school-girls departed than the old Butterfly-hunter returned, somewhat hot and flustered; and he settled down to continue the conning of his book. Again he became so engrossed in its fascinating pages that he did not even notice the entrance into the glade of a handsome young officer in the smart uniform of an infantry regiment; nor did he observe the latter accost a trio of pretty young ladies—of a somewhat older age than that of the school-girls—as they emerged from another woodland path.

These newly-arrived young ladies were dressed in the extreme of the latest fashion of the day, and had chosen the brightest of colours; and they were undoubtedly out to fascinate any susceptible male they might encounter during their afternoon stroll. Since the dashing young officer was entirely to their liking, they gladly responded to his audacious greeting; and they were willing enough to accept his escort and even to dance with him when he presently made this pleasant suggestion to them. The young officer—also out for a gay, unconventional afternoon's amusement—danced

with this trio of sophisticated young ladies with the
utmost zest ; and their sylvan revel was scarcely heeded
by the deeply engrossed Lepidopterist, who ran in and
out amongst them from time to time, with his net at
a dangerous angle, whenever he caught sight of another
butterfly.

But the flirtatious officer soon whirled his three pretty
ladies a little further afield ; and the elderly student
again had the glade to himself.

Not for long, however. An assignation had been
made for a *tête-a-tête* meeting in that same spot by a
pair of devoted lovers—an aristocratic young man and
yet another pretty young girl—who had but a very short
time to spend together. They were very much in love
and their romantic meeting seemed obviously to be a
stolen one. All too quickly the time went by ; and with
a last passionate embrace, the lovers had to part and go
sadly, and separately, on their way.

Their arrival and departure had hardly been noted
by the absent-minded butterfly-hunter, still absorbed
in chasing his winged quarry. Nor did he pay heed
to a very young girl, who now entered the glade, alone,
and endeavoured to express her still immature feelings
and shy longings by means of a strange dance she began
to perform on thinking herself unobserved. Then,
catching sight of the Lepidopterist, this timid young
girl took her departure almost in a panic.

The butterfly-hunter, however, found the next invasion of his quiet glade more to his liking. A buxom
peasant wench now appeared on the scene, accompanied
by two admirers—the one young and lively and the
other quite elderly and somewhat dull. It was soon
plain that the peasant girl preferred her youthful swain ;
and it was not long ere this lively pair danced away
together, full of bucolic high spirits.

Seeing that the elderly deserted swain looked decidedly disconsolate, the butterfly-hunter approached him and was delighted on learning that he also was something of a lepidopterist. Consequently, he decided to make use of him at once—namely, as a means of transport. His new friend being as much interested as himself in seeking butterfly specimens a little further afield, therefore, he nimbly jumped on to his back ; and, thus mounted pick-a-back, he induced his astonished human steed to amble along at a somewhat unsteady pace, whilst he himself swooped about eagerly with his butterfly-net.

No sooner had this ludicrous pair passed out of sight than a real invasion of the glade took place by a number of gay Breton peasant lads and lasses, who had decided that this spot was an ideal one for the special dance-revels they intended to hold that same afternoon. Full of joy, they now came tripping, hand-in-hand, into the glade to perform every country dance they knew ; and soon the woodland depths re-echoed to the sounds of happy laughter and singing, the clapping of hands, clicking of heels, and stamping of feet, as the lively young people went through the many evolutions of their famous folk-dances.

The sound of these jolly revels soon drew back to the glade those who had passed through it earlier in the afternoon ; and, attracted by the gaiety of the peasants, it was not long before they all joined them in their revel. The young school-girls, heedless of the prim governess's scandalised protests, broke up their hated " crocodile " and quickly lost themselves in the whirling maze of dancers ; and their example was followed presently by the flirtatious young officer and his three pretty ladies. Then came the romantic lovers—who had managed to snatch another few stolen moments together—the

timid young girl, and the peasant sweethearts ; and all
were drawn willingly into the dancing vortex. Even
the butterfly-hunter could not resist sharing in the
exuberance of such a joyful throng ; and, brandishing
his net, he sprang straight into their midst from the
back of his human steed ; and the latter, thankful to
be rid of his much-too-energetic Old-Man-of-the-Sea,
soon followed suit.

And there we will leave them—marvelling, as we do
so, that such a gay kaleidoscopic scene should have
evolved so spontaneously from a summer afternoon's
promenade in a quiet woodland glade.

THE PROSPECT BEFORE US

ON the stage of the King's Theatre, London, one day in 1789, a ballet rehearsal was in progress. The ballet was in charge of the famous choreographer, Monsieur Noverre, who was exhibiting no great enthusiasm. As a matter of fact, he and his wife, Madame Noverre, were more interested just then in discussing their contract, which did not by any means satisfy them. However, they became more alert presently, on the entrance of the manager, Mr. Taylor, with a party of patrons, who had expressed a desire to see a rehearsal.

Another visitor, uninvited, hovered in the background; this being Mr. O'Reilly, the manager of the rival theatre, the Pantheon. The latter gentleman looked somewhat dissipated, and was also feeling gloomy since things were not going well with him. He was, consequently, envious of the much more lively manager of the King's, where business was brisk and where all the best artists had been engaged to perform. Among these were the famous dancers, Monsieur Vestris and Monsieur Didelot, who were ably supported by the company's own fine, if somewhat temperamental *première danseuse*, Mademoiselle Théodore ; and Mr. O'Reilly longed to secure these and several other good performers also at the King's for his own theatre.

The manager of the Pantheon, therefore, did not feel too happy as he watched the rehearsal of the Company and Principals of the rival theatre, now being specially rendered for the benefit of the latter's patrons and their visitors. Even when Mademoiselle Théodore showed temper with her partner, he sighed ; for he would willingly have put up with her tantrums if only she would sign a contract with him.

However, when the patrons and invited visitors had departed and the cheery Mr. Taylor genially offered his fellow manager a complimentary box for the season and likewise invited him to join him in a drink, he began to feel in somewhat better spirits ; indeed, after a few more glasses of his rival's excellent wine he became quite hilarious before finally taking his departure.

* * * * *

Very soon after having received his patrons at the above-mentioned rehearsal, Mr. Taylor's good fortune suddenly deserted him ; for the King's Theatre was burned to the ground. The fire broke out during a crowded performance ; and wild scenes took place. Mr. Taylor ran hither and thither in a frenzied state because he was unable to prevent the total destruction of his beloved theatre ; and despite the fact that every possible effort was made to save it, nothing could be done in the matter and the building and its precious contents became a mass of smoking ruins.

Now full of despair, the once cheery Mr. Taylor found himself compelled to look on at the now growing success of the formerly depressed Mr. O'Reilly, manager of the Pantheon Theatre, who immediately benefited by his misfortune.

O'Reilly quickly realised that he, at least, possessed a good and whole theatre, whereas his former rival now had only burnt-out ruins to contemplate ; and, pulling himself together, he began to make hay while the sun shone. He gathered together funds by organising noisy street shows to advertise his once ill-patronised house ; and with no King's Theatre to outshine him he began to see prospects of filling the Pantheon at last.

Mr. Taylor's famous dancers, Vestris, Didelot, and

Théodore, together with many other members of his once fine Company, thrown out of work because of the fire, were now only too glad to offer their services to Mr. O'Reilly, who gleefully gave them tempting terms ; and, in a very short time, rehearsals were in progress at the Pantheon for a brilliant season there.

On the opening night, now magnanimous in his turn, Mr. O'Reilly placed a box at the disposal of Mr. Taylor ; and the latter could not help but feel chagrin as he thus looked on at the performance of his own former bright stars in the ballet firmament—a most successful performance now filling the pocket of the fickle and uncertain O'Reilly. The spectacle nevertheless acted as a spur to his own renewed activities. He had already approached his former patrons and had found them willing to support him in his efforts and plans for the rebuilding of the old King's Theatre ; and presently, to his joy, his plans for its restoration were duly carried out.

Like the phœnix of old, the new King's Theatre arose upon the burnt-out ashes of the destroyed building ; and within a year or so, Mr. Taylor had all in readiness— save his former dancers. The latter were eager enough to join him once more—for Mr. O'Reilly's short spell of prosperity had not lasted, and he was already again faced with failure and bankruptcy. He was, consequently, as eager to part with his expensive artists as he had a short time ago been to secure them. But difficulties arose regarding the transference of the Pantheon's patent to the new King's theatre ; and the financially involved O'Reilly and his disappointed dancers could not avail themselves of the bright prospects of the newly-restored King's Theatre, but had to resign themselves to the coming crash at the Pantheon.

* * * * *

And, now, a most extraordinary thing happened. As luck would have it, history actually repeated itself, inasmuch as, following the example of the King's, the Pantheon Theatre likewise caught fire one day and was burned to the ground.

But whereas Mr. Taylor had been full of despair at the loss of the King's, Mr. O'Reilly, on the contrary, felt nothing but joy when he beheld the Pantheon blazing away merrily. He felt he no longer needed to think about his business and financial worries, nor about keeping on the employment of his much too expensive artists ; for this lucky fire settled the matter for him, and his dancers, being out of work once more, were now free to go back to their former manager.

This they very gladly did ; and Mr. Taylor received them with open arms. Rehearsals began at once for a new ballet to be arranged by Monsieur Noverre ; and when it became known that success was now certain for the coming season, all the members of the Company were delighted and renewed their efforts with zest.

The joyful news was brought them by Mr. Taylor himself, who appeared on the stage at one of the rehearsals with some of his patrons, as he had been so fond of doing in the past.

On this occasion, too, as once before, Mr. O'Reilly, the unsuccessful manager of the now burnt-out Pantheon, likewise appeared on the scene. This time, however, he was by no means gloomy ; instead, he was drunkenly hilarious, having been toasting, not wisely but too well, the lucky stroke of fortune that had solved his business cares and financial worries so miraculously for him.

Consequently, he proceeded to behave in a wildly boisterous and unseemly manner, chasing the pretty ballet-girls about the stage and creating such an uproarious disturbance generally that the rehearsal had to be abandoned; and the patrons and visitors left in disgust.

Thus, the two managers once more found themselves together and alone on the stage of the King's theatre. Although, by this time, the blindly intoxicated O'Reilly had fallen helpless to the ground, Mr. Taylor again decided to treat him in a kindly manner. Having dragged him to his feet and set him precariously in a chair, he brought out wine and glasses. To his dismay, however, O'Reilly instantly seized the bottle and poured the wine over his own head, as a sort of libation to the God of Chance for having come to his aid in the matter of the Pantheon fire; and then he staggered away, still hugging the empty bottle.

Again Mr. Taylor was left to his own thoughts—which were by no means complimentary to Mr. O'Reilly.

———

The burning of the old King's Theatre and the Panthéon Theatre in the late 18th century, within a year of each other, actually occurred. Monsieur Noverre and Monsieur Didelot were both famous dancers, choreographers, and ballet-masters of that period; and Monsieur Vestris and Mademoiselle Théodore were likewise world-renowned dancers of the time.

The title of the ballet is taken from Thomas Rowlandson's well-known picture of that name, in which Didelot and Théodore are shown dancing together. The décor and atmosphere of some of the scenes also seem to be suggested by this artist's work.

TIIE RAKE'S PROGRESS

THIS is a story of London's High and Low Society in the 18th century.

A certain prepossessing young man had recently become heir to a comfortably substantial fortune, the possession of which quickly went to his head—with the result that he spent it all in an amazingly short time and ended his brief meteor-like career as a fashionable " exquisite " in dire poverty, misery, and death. So, we will call him " The Rake," and the story of his speedy ruin and downfall " The Rake's Progress."

* * * * *

Late one morning the Rake rose from his bed, wrapped himself in a gorgeous dressing-gown and, with many yawns, submitted himself to the obsequious ministrations of tailors, jockeys, fencing and dancing masters, and a number of more than doubtful rogues and hangers-on, all eager to " pluck " this newly-hatched " pigeon." Unused to riches, or to the ways—and vices—of the fashionable high-society life of his period, the wealthy young man was only too glad to avail himself of the advice and services of anyone who appeared capable of initiating him into such ways and vices.

After an early life of dull and dreary poverty, it was certainly very exciting, and even thrilling, to have more money than he could seemingly spend ; and, since he was of a pleasure-loving nature, there appeared to be no limit to the gaieties in which he might now indulge. Nor did the fact of having had no experience in such matters daunt him in the least ; for he was only too quickly surrounded by those well-versed in the art of spending other people's money.

On this particular morning, therefore, on entering his luxuriously-furnished reception room—a fine house, complete with servants, having been one of his first purchases—he found many persons waiting for his favours.

An obsequious little tailor came running up to him with a tape-mesaure over one arm and a half-finished, full-skirted brocade coat of the latest cut over the other. The Rake willingly enough submitted himself to the ministrations of the smiling tailor—for, although he had already an extravagantly-filled wardrobe of gaily-coloured fashionable clothes, he still felt pride in every new garment made for him. Dealers in jewellery likewise found him a ready customer ; for he loved the scintillating glimpses of watches, fobs, chains, rings, studs, and cravat-pins flashing from his now elegant person.

Presently, having finished with the tailor and other vendors of personal finery, and dismissed a Hornblower— who was trying to teach him something of the art of music—he was accosted by a seedy-looking touting jockey, who readily enough persuaded him to employ his services in a forthcoming race.

Having got rid of the jockey, the Rake finished dressing for the day, and next put himself in the hands of a smart little dancing-master whom he had hired to teach him the latest dances now being performed in high fashionable circles. Though an apt enough pupil, the Rake was soon somewhat bored and preferred to watch the dancing-master himself perform an intricate solo dance for his entertainment.

As a matter of fact it seemed pretty obvious from the first that this newly-enriched young man had not a real liking for high society—his true tastes seemed to tend more to the free and easy vulgarity of the under-world. This latter fact was evidenced presently when his dancing-lesson was interrupted by the arrival of a pretty, pale young working-girl, accompanied by an irate but calculating mother, who demanded com-pensation for her daughter's dishonour and betrayal at the hands of the too-wealthy youth.

Already the young man had made himself well-acquainted with, and experienced in, the licentious habits of his new, thoughtless companions ; and although this innocent girl who had become his victim did not belong to the more riotous circles he usually frequented, she was, nevertheless, of humble origin. What was more, she truly loved him and harboured no resentment in her heart against him, nor had any personal desire for monetary reparation.

Not so, however, her mercenary parent. The latter stormed and made an ugly scene ; and, to end it, the young libertine flung her a bag full of guineas. The avaricious mother's clamour subsided at once ; and, well-pleased with the result of her visit, she led away her weeping daughter. The latter, nevertheless, cast a longing look upon her brilliantly-dressed and gay lover—who seemed almost like a fairy prince to her simple mind.

* * * * *

The Rake continued giddily and recklessly with his mad career of spending ; and, gradually, his vast fortune was frittered away and he fell into debt. At first he scarcely realised this unpleasant fact ; and so long as he could avoid meeting his creditors face to face, or being served with a writ, he carelessly proceeded upon his primrose path to ruin.

Most evenings he was to be found with his vicious, pleasure-loving companions in a certain house of ill-fame, surrounded by prostitutes and a noisy rabble of licentious youths, all sponging on him for the remainder of his almost diminished fortune and ever encouraging him to further excesses. Here, scenes of the utmost license took place, and quarrels were frequent.

On one such occasion, finding the rowdy scene more than he could stand, the Rake came stumbling and staggering out into the street, half-drunk, but quite capable, presently, of receiving a most disagreeable shock. Out from a dark entry came a couple of hefty, blustering uniformed men, obviously bailiffs ; and, behind them came the timid little tailor ready to present to his one-time wealthy client a long bill for clothes supplied and still unpaid for.

This unwelcome trio had been lying in wait for several hours in order to apprehend the spendthrift debtor as he emerged from the brothel, knowing well enough that he would be unsteady and dazed, and, consequently, the easier to drag off to the debtors' prison—but they had reckoned without the devotion of one who was still his faithful friend coming to his aid. This was none other than the simple working-girl, who, having learned of this trap to ensnare her still well-beloved seducer, had lain in wait likewise, clutching a small bag containing her own hard-earned savings.

She now ran forward eagerly and entreated the tailor to accept this money in payment, or part-payment, of her lover's debt. To her relief, her offer was grudgingly accepted, and the tailor and bailiffs withdrew ; but when the devoted young girl turned to speak to her former " fairy prince," she found that the ungrateful youth had likewise vanished into the darkness.

* * * * *

The foolish and vicious young Rake seemed totally unable or unwilling to stop his mad Progress to Ruin;

The gambling craze now seized him firmly in its strong grasp ; and he spent night after night in various gambling dens, always vainly hoping to win back at least a portion of his lost fortune, and always finding himself deeper in the mire.

His still faithful and devoted girl friend could not again prevent him at last from being apprehended and clapped into a debtors' prison, where he languished for many months. Even here, however, the young girl would wait outside on a stool, day after day, working feverishly at her sewing or embroidery in order to earn money to help him during his incarceration and when he came out into the world once more ; but the day of his release never came. Instead, his self-inflicted misfortunes caused the Rake's mind to become unhinged ; and, finally, he was flung into a mad-house —the infamous Bedlam of the 18th century.

What a terrible scene here met the frenzied eyes of the now completely insane young man ! Men with many manias were to be seen on every side. Here was one who imagined himself to be the Pope, or some other high ecclesiastical dignitary, standing upright in a bare strongly-barred cell, wearing long clerical robes, a mitred head-piece, and carrying a long Cross, and spending the whole day muttering chants until he fell to the ground exhausted. In another barred cell was a lunatic who believed himself to be a mighty King of Mediæval times, wearing a crown and carrying a sceptre. A distracted card-player, who dealt himself endless hands of cards ; a pretended sailor, furling and unfurling invisible sails ; a sinister-looking man with a rope, everlastingly enacting the gruesome details of the Hangman's office ; all these were likewise to be seen.

No wonder the Rake gradually became madder still. Weak, half-naked, suffering cruelly in body and mind, he would claw wildly but weakly at the walls and barred door; or he would fall, breathless and exhausted, to the ground, face downwards, in abject misery. Next moment, he would spring to his feet in a raving frenzy and dance madly with an almost superhuman energy.

During one of these frenzied attacks, the sad-faced girl he had betrayed came in to visit him ; for she still loved the wretched lunatic and hoped to be of some slight comfort to him until his last moments came. When he presently sank to the ground once more, she sat down beside him ; and, lifting his head into her lap, she fondled it tenderly.

As she did so, a party of fashionable visitors, engaged in morbid sight-seeing, came into the room, and gazed around curiously at the terrible scenes ; but though some of them may have known the Rake in his prosperous days and even shared in his rowdy pleasures, they completely ignored him now and passed out again somewhat hurriedly.

But the sad young girl remained ; and when, presently, her lover was seized with the paroxysms of death, she soothed him gently until he drew his last weak sighs in her arms.

Thus ends the story of a recklessly wasted life and of a devoted and selfless love.

ALPHABETICAL INDEX

Ballet in 1 Act.

Book : Sobeka (Boris Kochno).

Music : Handel (selected and arranged by Sir Thomas Beecham, Bart.).

Choreography : 1st Production : George Bálanchine.
2nd Production : Ninette de Valois.

3. Vic-Wells Production in entirety, Sadler's Wells Theatre, London, 1939, Petipa choreography reproduced b y Nicolai Sergueeff; Scenery and Costumes by Nadia Bénois.

4. Sadler's Wells Revival in entirety, at Covent Garden, London, Feb. 20th, 1946; production by Nicolai Sergueeff after Petipa. (Two new dances added by Frederick Ashton.) Scenery and Costumes by Oliver Messel. (Margot Fonteyn as *Princess Aurora*, and Robert Helpmann as *Carabosse* and *Prince Florimund*)

NOTE : Several other Ballet Companies have produced from time to time Act 3 only, under the title of *Aurora's Wedding* and *Grand Pas d'Action*.

SPECTRE OF THE ROSE, THE (*Le Spectre de la Rose*) .. 141
Ballet in 1 Act.
Book : J. L. Vaudoyer (from Poem by Gautier).
Music : Weber.
Choreography : Michael Fokine.
Scenery and Costumes : Léon Bakst.
First Produced : Théâtre de Monte Carlo, 1911.
Covent Garden, London 1911 (Diaghilev Production).

SWAN LAKE (*Le Lac des Cygnes*) 370
Ballet in 4 Acts.
Book : V. P. Begitchev and Geltser.
Music : Tchaikovsky.
Choreography : 1. Reisinger ; 2. Marius Petipa and L. I. Ivanov ; 3. C. Korovin, with A. Golovin ; 4. Michael Fokine.
Scenery and Costumes : Various artists. (See below).
First Produced : 1. Moscow, 1877. (Choreographer, Reisinger)

2. Maryinsky Theatre, St. Petersburg, Feb. 17th-29th, 1894 (Act 2 only). Jan. 15th-27th, 1895 (in entirety, with Choreography by Petipa and Ivanov).

3. Moscow, 1901. (Act 2, C. Korovin)
   (Act 3, A. Golovin)
4. First London Production, Hippo-
   drome, 1910. (Imperial Russian
   Ballet)
5. First Diaghilev Production,
   Covent Garden, London, 1911.
   (Choreographer, Fokine) with Kar-
   savina, Nijinsky and Bolm.
6. Last Diaghilev Season, Covent
   Garden, London, 1929. (Spessiva
   as *Odette-Odille*)
7. Camargo Society, Savoy Theatre,
   London, 1932.
8. Revival by Sadler's Wells Com-
   pany at Sadler's Wells Theatre,
   London, 1934. (Petipa and Ivanov
   Choreography) with Scenery and
   Costumes by Hugh Stevenson.
   (Markova as *Odette-Odille*)
9. Ballet Rambert, (Nijinska Choreo-
   graphy), with Markova as *Odette-
   Odille*. (Extracts only) 1931.
   Ballet Rambert Revival (Act 2),
   24th July, 1937, at the Casino de
   la Jetée, Nice. (Maude Lloyd as
   Odette. Later, *Odette* danced by
   Prudence Hyman, Nina Golovina,
   Sally Gilmour and Belinda Wright.
   Décor for present production by
   Harry Cordwill.)
10. Ballet Theatre Revival, New
    York, 1940. Choreography by
    Anton Dolin (after Petipa, and
    re-staged by Anton Dolin) ;
    Scenery and Costumes by Lee
    Simónson and Ballard. (Markova
    as *Odette-Odille*)
11. Revival by Sadler's Wells Ballet,
    at the New Theatre, London,
    Sept. 7th, 1943, produced by
    Nicolai Sergueeff (Petipa and
    Ivanov choreography) with
    Scenery and Costumes by Leslie
    Hurry. (Margot Fonteyn as
    Odette-Odille)